DESIGNER JESUS

THE LIFESTORY OF A DISCIPLE

LEONARD SWEET

The Salish
Sea Press
Orcas Island
Washington

DESIGNER JESUS
THE LIFESTORY OF A DISCIPLE

Let the peace of Christ keep you in tune with each other, in step with each other. None of this going off and doing your own thing. And cultivate thankfulness. Let the Word of Christ—the Message—have the run of the house. Give it plenty of room in your lives. Instruct and direct one another using good common sense. And sing, sing your hearts out to God! Let every detail in your lives—words, actions, whatever—be done in the name of the Master, Jesus, thanking God the Father every step of the way.

COLOSSIANS 3:15–17 MSG

Designer Jesus: The Lifestory of a Disciple

ISBN softcover: 978-1-63613-025-5

Published by The Salish Sea Press. Box 1492, Absecon, NJ 08201.
https://salishsea.press
https://www.facebook.com/thesalishseapress/

The Salish Sea Press is a program of SpiritVenture Ministries.
https://leonardsweet.com/

Copyright © 2024 by Leonard Sweet. All rights reserved.

Designed by Carmen Barber: keepingyouwriting@gmail.com
Cover designed by Sheri DePuy: sheridepuy.com.

Unless otherwise indicated, Scripture quotations are the author's own paraphrase. If the notation LIS is used, this also indicates the author's own paraphrase. Other versions are noted in the back matter.

The Salish Sea Press

Dedicated to my friend and colleague

Byoungho Zoh

He did invite me to a more perfect way
AUGUSTINE[1]

God begins to live in me, not only as my creator but as my other and true self.
THOMAS MERTON[2]

CONTENTS

Acknowledgements..ix
Invocation:
    Jesus A.I. 15
    Studio Live 48
Chapter 1: Walk
    The Jesus Walk 57
    Studio Live 87
Chapter 2: Touch
    The Jesus Touch 101
    Studio Live 126
Chapter 3: Face
    The Jesus Face 133
    Studio Live 166
Chapter 4: Mouth
    The Jesus Voice 177
    Studio Live 217
Chapter 5: Nose
    The Jesus Nose 227
    Studio Live 256
Chapter 6: Groom
    The Jesus Groom 267
    Studio Live 284

Chapter 7: Appetite
- The Jesus Appetite 297
- Studio Live 319

Chapter 8: Style Cool
- The Jesus Style: Cool 333
- Studio Live 351

Chapter 9: Style
- The Jesus Style: Hot 359
- Studio Live 407

Chapter 10: Mind
- The Jesus Mind 417
- Studio Live 437

Chapter 11: Heart
- A Jesus Heart 449
- Studio Live 473

Antiphon:
- Jesus Living 481

Connect with Leonard 489

Scripture Versions 491

Notes 493

Acknowledgements

I am a back-door reader of most books. I homage Hebrew tradition by starting on the back cover and reading to the front cover, opening right-to-left. But before I explore the end notes, bibliography, and index (if there is one), I read the acknowledgements. In my lifetime, acknowledgements have moved from the end of a preface, foreword, or epilogue to having their own page. It is the first thing I go to when I open a book.

No book is an island. Behind every book is a community. The two people in my community who cleaned up my mistakes and brought some dead spots back to life are colleague Dr. Landrum Leavell, III, who read every word and critiqued every comma, and copy-editor Carmen Barber, who was always cheerful, encouraging, and kind. Just the sound of her voice on the line can calm my nerves and steady my spirit.

John Updike, whom I love reading for his metaphorical layers and allusive symbols, wrote of his editor at the *New Yorker*: "A lot of nice touches in my stories belong to William Maxwell. And I've taken credit for them all." Content editor Erin Healy gave me numerous and needed "nice touches" of architectural genius. She also saved me personally from a future of bumping shoulders with more than my share of wrinkled noses and wagging fingers. Playwright and filmmaker David Mamet once said that the best thing an editor could do for a film was to cut the first ten minutes. Beginnings are the hardest, and Erin helped me begin with the end in mind.

To bring a book like this across the finish line requires a design charrette. A charrette, from char-chariot or wagon, and ette—speed of wheels—is "a final, intensive effort to finish a project, especially an architectural design project, before a deadline." My son-in-law Daniel Briggs helped drive the wagon and worked laboriously over the end notes without complaint and with good cheer. I have been blessed with many loyal readers, and one of my favorites, clergy colleague Will Clegg, found many last-minute errors. Author, artist, musician ("I Love You, Lord") Laurie Klein provided a litany that I desperately needed to bring this project to a proper conclusion.

My wife Tia Nicole helps me live daily a North-facing life with innumerable miracles of the heart. She encourages me in my first love, Jesus, and in my first crush, learning. In the old game show "Hollywood Squares," host Peter Marshall asked, "Which of your five senses tends to diminish as you get older?" Comedian Charley Weaver replied: "My sense of decency." Thankfully, unlike Charley, I haven't lost that entirely because of Tia's watchful eye. She is the guardian angel of good taste in my writing, and life. She herself is a testimony that humor can dance with wit without sacrificing grace.

Our eight-year-old son, Jeremiah Luke Sullivan, came home from school one day not happy about his teacher shelving out more pennies of reward and encouragement on the

ACKNOWLEDGEMENTS

desk of others than on him. I replied, "You're being petty, Luke." In the blink of an eye, he replied, "Well, petty people need petty cash." Luke teaches me daily that the more we lose ourselves in Christ, the more we find joy, laughter, lightness of spirit, and holy hilarity.

During our book-birthing charrette, the Sweet family welcomed a new furry overlord: Sir Windsor, a Bernese mountain dog. It is no thanks to him that you hold this book in your hands. Between his symphony of playful pawings and his opera of "I want attention" whines, this book almost became a chew toy itself! Thankfully, Sir Windsor's relentless cuteness proved to be a muse in disguise, reminding us that sometimes the best inspiration comes with wagging tails and slobbery kisses.

I shamelessly write imperfect books because I trust others to carry on the conversation and make the insights better. I am part of something bigger than myself, and a particular cohort of doctoral students from Northwind Seminary unblocked a lot of creativity and energy. Thank you to Archie Callahan, David McGrew, Duane White, Kris White, Jody Andrews, Paul Brownback, Paul Louis Cole, Perrianne Brownback, Rusty Griffin, Ryan Deaton, and Trey Jones. Alone we write words, together we author stories. President Robert J. Duncan of Northwind Seminary brought us all together, and for his organizational gifts and cherished friendship I will always be grateful.

The first "reveal" of *Designer Jesus* was to a doctoral cohort in semiotics, culture, and church at George Fox University/ Portland Seminary. Even though I have not yet received their feedback, I am prophesying my way forward here to those that I know will make this book better for future revisions: Kris Clifford, Carl Creasman, Rick DeLaTorre, Adam Harbaugh, Andrew Heard, Brenda Lewis, Mike Morgan, David Sunde, Jeff Thorp, and Dan Turis. It is my honor to be studying with you.

While I haven't communicated with South African biblical scholar Stephan Joubert for some time, during my last visit to South Africa, I had the opportunity to discuss and refine the initial ideas and directions for *Designer Jesus* with him. I am thankful for his ongoing friendship and valuable initial insights, and for his own pioneering scholarship as footnoted in my "Jesus Walk" chapter.

> In 1618 Renaissance poet Nicholas Breton wrote that a gentleman should "speake well, ride well, shoote well and bowle well." How times have changed. In the last three decades, I have learned from my friend and biblical scholar Dr. Byoungho Zoh that a genteel human should communicate kindly, listen attentively, learn and unlearn constantly, think creatively and collaboratively, cultivate integrity and empathy, read signs with savvy and people smartness, and live responsibly with a light-heart, humble-spirit, thick-skin, prayerful attentiveness, and ready-laugh.

Or, I could say all the above in these English words:

ACKNOWLEDGEMENTS

Live like Jesus, love like Jesus. Or, in three Korean words: 여수님처럼 사랑하다.

I featured in *Jesus Human* what I have learned from you. Now here I dedicate *Designer Jesus* to you, Dr. Byoungho Zoh, and our cherished friendship.

Invocation: Jesus A. I.

*My little children, with whom I am in again travail
until Christ be formed in you.*
APOSTLE PAUL[1]

THE LAST KNOWN WORDS FROM THOMAS MERTON (d. 1968) come from a lecture at the Maha Chulalongkorn Rajavidyalaya Buddhist University in Bangkok, just before he was electrocuted in the shower at age 53:

> I think today it's more important for us to so let God live in us that others may feel God and come to believe in God because they feel how God lives in us.[2]

The ultimate apologetics today is aesthetics.

<u>Introit:</u> Jesus is your design for living. Jesus designed you for greatness.

Discipleship formation is Jesus living, the formation of Christ in us. The Greek word for "form" that Paul uses above in Galatians 4:1–9 is a show-stopper. Paul tells his readers that he is embroiled in the pains of childbirth "until Christ is formed (μορφωθ) in you." The Greek here suggests a pregnancy in a mother's womb where an "embryon" is umbilically nurtured and nourished until it is ready to be born.[3] Paul portrays himself as a pregnant woman in labor, suffering birth-pangs on behalf of this early Christian community in Galatia until they become "like Christ is." It is a stunning metaphor that makes "formation" biologic, not robotic; intrinsic, not instrumental.

> There is a vast difference in a community where people live alongside each other, and one where people live among each other. Jesus came to live among us, not just alongside us. Jesus "made his dwelling among us."[4] But even more, Jesus wants to dwell in us by the indwelling Spirit. In Paul's words, "Do you not realize that Christ Jesus is in you?"[5] And again, "Christ is in you."[6] Once more, "It is Christ who lives in me."[7] And as emphatic as Paul can make it, "Christ is formed in you."[8] The words "among" and "within" are the thunderclaps of incarnation, the emplaced embrace of the divine.

Fashion Theology: Jesus was a "tekton," and a tekton fashions things. But tekton Jesus fashioned things not just on the outside, like the fashion industry, but on the inside. The "wardrobe malfunction"[9] of the modern church is that it misconceived its mission to be one of emblazoning Christ or embroidering Christianity on the body (individual and communal) rather than embodying Jesus in flesh and blood and living the same life as the Lord. When Paul tells the church of believers at Rome to "Clothe yourself with the Lord Jesus Christ,"[10] he is not telling them to "put on Christ" like an everyday change of clothes. He is telling them to move from what Jesus has done within them through justification into what God wants to do throughout them through sanctification so that other people see Jesus doing on the outside what Jesus is doing on the inside. The church mistook membership for discipleship; the church mistook activities of the institution for gifts of the Holy Spirit; the church mistook leadership for followership.[11]

A disciple is a human in whom faith dominates everything else. Through baptism a disciple enters the life of God and learns to will with God's will, love as God loves, think as God thinks, and "see God in all things and all things in God."[12] When theology becomes a subject without an object, it is devoid of meaning. And the object of theology is not God, but faith. Theology is the study of faith. *Designer Jesus* is a theological textbook.

When we stand strong in our identity, in our true "I am," we are images of the Great "I AM," our Creator and Maker. Iago is the antagonist in Shakespeare's *Othello* (1601–04). He is the perfection of evil, "the negation of goodness." Iago ("He who supplants" from "Santiago") calls himself "I am NOT what I am."[13]

To be a little "I am" is to be an image of the Great "I

AM." This was Augustine's discovery that God was "more in me than I am in me" and that God was "waiting within me while I went outside me." Or as Merton put it to the monastic initiates, "Our full identity is Christ. It is Christ in each of us."[14]

Yes, it is that simple. Yes, it is that complex.

We are united to Christ who is bone of our bone and flesh of our flesh, and participate in the risen Humanity of Christ so that we are bone of His bone and flesh of His flesh.

SCOTTISH THEOLOGIAN T.F. TORRANCE (D. 2007)

<u>Yes, it's that simple</u> . . . Not just because there are a few molecules of Jesus in each breath we take, if you believe particle physicists. But in a deeper sense, we are all ongoing incarnators of The Once-and-For-All-Time Incarnation. "Cast out our sin and enter in; be born in us today" expresses this with poetic perfection. The image of Christ "born in us" to form and norm who we are and what we do is an ongoing incarnation that contributes new chapters of sacred history to the story of the most influential person in history. Neither theology nor apologetics, neither intellectual fireworks nor emotional pyrotechnics, neither mastery of "spiritual disciplines" nor enactment of social justice activism is what makes disciples. What makes disciples, incarnators all, is Jesus himself.

Even mastery of the written words of the Bible, as important as that is, is not what makes disciples. The early church did not have sacred texts on which to build a life of faith. They only had Jesus—oral stories about him, eyewitness accounts of encountering him and being healed by him. The first written accounts of Jesus didn't start circulating until around the year 50, and those weren't gospels but letters Paul wrote from Corinth to the community he had founded in Macedonia (First and Second Thessalonians). Not too much later, the writer of the Book of Hebrews introduced Jesus to Jewish Christians as a priest after the Order of Melchizedek. He then pauses to show some frustration with their growth in followership:

> About Melchizedek we have much to say, much that is difficult to explain, now that you have grown so dull of hearing. For indeed, though by this time you ought to be teachers, you need someone to teach you the ABCs of God's oracles over again.[15]

Did you catch that "by this time:" "By this time you ought to be teachers."[16] How much "time" had passed between Jesus' death and when the author of Hebrews was writing? Thirty years most likely. But in a few short decades, they had become sluggish and mundane in their faith, needing to be reminded of the basics of discipleship, when they "should have been" masters and mentors of what it means to follow Jesus—even though they had no Bible on which to build a Christian identity. Clearly, discipleship is more than a textual construction.

DESIGNER JESUS

All ideas that have huge consequences are simple.
RUSSIAN NOVELIST LEO TOLSTOY (D. 1910)[17]

Aristotle called "practical wisdom" the ability to curate, conjure, and enculturate the question "How Then Shall We Live?" for every age and context. Jesus is the genesis and generator of all "practical wisdom." Jesus is the vaccine for all the church's diseases and dis-ease. We have chosen to invest more time and resources learning how to read and apply human blueprints for church renewal and faith formation than God's fingerprints in texts, traditions, and tracks of the Spirit—the biggest footprint of which is the one that is being left by Jesus the Christ.

Discipleship is not assenting to a belief system, operating out of some ethical norms, subscribing to a political agenda, or framing life in a biblical worldview. Discipleship is recognizing, remembering, releasing, and raising up Jesus. Living as Jesus would have lived is not the same as Jesus living in us or living Jesus. "Abide in Me, and I in you," Jesus promised.[18] The more Jesus becomes our "Abiding Place," and the more we become a place of Jesus abidance, the greater our life abounds in abundance and the more epic our life voyage.

Designer Jesus advocates for a streamlining of life designed around the only thing needed: Jesus. You are what you love. Love Jesus, and become a little "j" (there is only one Big "J"). Love Christ and become a "little Christ," the literal meaning of the word "Christ-ian." *Christianos* translates as "Christ's ones" or "Christ's followers" or "Ones of the Anointed One." The Spirit so "bonds"[19] us to Jesus that "it is no longer I who live but Christ lives within me."[20] Discipleship means we confess our parentage and live as progeny.

For those who are waiting for the advent of Artificial Intelligence (AI) to bestow on humanity "an ascension to demigodhood,"[21] the advent of true AI has already come. *Alter-Ipse Christus* is the true AI, and its advent and its singularity of starry simplicity took place 2000 years ago with the advent of "Emmanuel" or "God WITH Us." Jesus told his disciples "I am the light of the world."[22] But he also told them "You are the light of the world."[23] The two statements are not contradictory if it is the light of Jesus himself that his disciples are shining on a dark world. *Alter-Ipse (AI) Christus*. We are AI Christs.

The breath of the Spirit enables us to swell into the stature of Christ instead of shrinking to the statue of self. In the language of early followers of Jesus, discipleship is becoming "*Alter-Ipse.*"[24] The phrase "*alter Christus, ipse Christus*" means another Christ, Christ himself.[25] Or as St. Augustine put it: "Let us rejoice and give thanks; we have not only become Christians, but Christ Himself . . . Stand in awe and rejoice: we have become Christ."[26]

Alter-Ipse is the real AI. *Alter-Ipse Christus*: another Christ, Christ himself. Christ completes his work in me.[27] Disciples don't play a part, or inhabit a role, or imitate someone. They let the person of Jesus resonate with their being until they become "one with Christ."

"The Age of A.I." (2020) is the name of an original

series on YouTube TV. I feature AI in my prediction of a GRAINy future (G=GeneticEngineering; R=Robotics; A=ArtificialIntelligence; I=InformationTechnology; N=Nanotechnology).[28] But all this "AI" refers to the greatest scientific advancement in centuries. The greatest AI is not scientific but theological.

The biggest debate in Generative AI circles is whether AI will replace humans or augment them. The Alpha Intelligence is not a replacement for the human mind, or an augmentation of it, but a re-awakening of the original mind of humanity. It is not so much returning love to humans from the outside in but bringing love out of humans from the inside out, the love that was part of the divine DNA.

The real AI is Jesus. The true AI is the Jesus mindset.

Make your home in me, Jesus,
as I make mine in you.
SAINT AUGUSTINE (D. 430)[29]

Yes, it's that complex . . . and the complexities are endless. The easy "Jesus" answer turns out not to be so "easy" after all.

First of all, there is only one Incarnation with a capital "I." There is only one "Big J." We are all called to be a "little j," or "little Christ." That is the literal meaning of the word "Christ-ian"—"little Christ." But we are not living up to our name. The *Alter-Ipse* Life (AI Life) is not an achievement but an adventure, not a possession but a process, not a permanent attribute but a mysterious gift and holy happening. Second, the *Alter-Ipse* Life (AI Life) is something other people may see in us, not something in ourselves we point to with pride. Third, the *Alter-Ipse* Life (AI Life), the ongoing incarnation of Christ in us, takes the shape of a cross, not a crown.

Let's embrace for a moment the complexity of quantum mechanics. In physics, mind is now seen as part of matter. Human minds are individual, but not separate—they connect at some mysterious level inaccessible to ordinary conscious awareness. That makes the ultimate reality of the universe to be, as physics has been telling us for fifty years and Jesus for two thousand, relationship.

One way of talking about God is this: God is the consciousness of the cosmos: its energy, its thought, its information. Energy-matter is basically information. What is DNA, the energy-matter of heredity, but information? Information is both a biological concept and a theological concept.

<u>In-formation:</u> But to put a dash in the word "in-formation" is to make all the difference in the world. The modern world began with a religious Re-formation. The new world begins with a religious In-formation. To "inform" means "to give form to, to put into form and shape" (OED). The purpose of the church and each member is to give form to, to put into form and shape the energy-matter known as Jesus Christ. That is what it means to be an in-formed church, to be an in-formational community, to live out an in-formational theology. To be in-formed by Christ, to live a Christ-formation life, to live an AI Life.

The formation of Christ in us is complex also because,

while there are many ways Christ forms himself in us, participating in a community in which God's people are being formed in Christ is the biggest one. Jesus eclipsed family blood lines with faith and belief lines: blood-of-family ties are forever transcended by blood-of-Jesus ties.

The bodily eloquence of the church is mixed, as the tiniest peek through any cathedral keyhole will reveal. Like every family (and every party you've ever attended, for that matter), in every church there are people you want to spend time with and people you want to get away from. To "stay" in the house, to "stay" at the party, is to have to deal with some real stink bombs.

"There's a Christian in the house!"

<u>Designed Human:</u> The Jesus design is more process than product. But even so, when a Jesus-designed human is in the house, you know it. Jesus deepens the divine sheen of love in the human.[30] Matter and energy disperse in disorder unless they are captured. When captured by the Creator in a design that images that Creator, what forms has been given a name: Jesus.

Jesus is the design of everyday life.[31] It is less that "God has a plan for you" than God has a design for your life, an aesthetics just for you.[32] Aesthetics is not just something that happens in the art world. Aesthetic experience is not "official art" but ordinary art, the everyday living out of our *imago Dei* mission and creating modes of perception and practice that push beyond coasting through life on conventions and inertia.

When aesthetic habitudes become hebetudes, as routine as walking the dog, one is living in design heaven.³³ This is why creativity is so vital to our humanity—making things, creating things, and fashioning things trains us morally and grooms us aesthetically in the image of God. The patient practice of a craft, and the enduring exercise of creativity, produce virtues and aesthetic emotions of bliss. The numbing of our aesthetic sensibilities is also a numbing of our conscience and morality.

In *Jesus Human* (2023) I showed how discipleship formation is human formation or humanation. Suffice it to say here that humanation is an artistic process, not a philosophical, political, moral or pragmatic project. What it means to be "fully human" is not a hierarchically educated organism, or an equilibrium of systematic components, but a creative, artistic composition—a symphonic arrangement of stories, sounds, symbols, metaphors, etc. For Christians to be anti-aesthetic is to be anti-human.

We are created to be artists, individually and collectively, making things lovely. This 'artistry' does not make us angels, but truly, beautifully ourselves.

JANET SOSKICE, PROFESSOR OF PHILOSOPHICAL THEOLOGY AT JESUS COLLEGE, CAMBRIDGE, IN HER 2018 CHARLES GORE LECTURE, WESTMINSTER ABBEY INSTITUTE³⁴

If "the Bible is the manger in which Christ is laid" (Martin Luther), the manger becomes our manager for life. Every year, a few days before New Year's Day, you can hear someone say, "I'm so over Christmas." Whoa! The "Away" in

DESIGNER JESUS

"Away in the Manger" is not a put-away manger but A Way Manger, A Way of Life Manger, a Manager of Life Manger. The simple name of Jesus communicated in the present adjudicates not abdicates the past as it advocates, elevates, and confiscates the future.

Good design is good theology.[35]

> *Heat cannot be separated from fire,*
> *or beauty from the eternal.*
> ATTRIBUTED TO DANTE ALIGHIERI (D. 1321)

<u>Jesus is Enough:</u> *Designer Jesus* is one extended "gaze" into the life of Jesus in the conviction Jesus is enough to form in us what it means to be his disciple.

We now live in a world where images have replaced money as the primary currency and the organizing principle of life—an icon-omy more than an economy.[36] People derive their identity not by the traditional economic measurements but by icon-omic mintage. To be a follower of Jesus is the adventure of becoming an icon that points beyond itself to the One who is Greater. An idol points to itself and says worship me. An icon points beyond itself and says worship One Greater. Jesus called various forms of idolatry "vain worship"—worship as vanity, worship as egotism.[37]

Christianity is an icon-omic system of exchanges based on stories, songs, images, rituals, and relics. You are not worth more when someone notices you. You draw your identity from the gaze of God, not from the looks and likes of others. We are designed to be icons of Jesus in the icon-omy of the kingdom: every baptized believer an *alter Christus, ipse Christus*: another Christ, Christ himself.

> *Most artists I've heard about like lots of light in their studios. . . . Yet God creates His masterpieces in the dark, on the night shift.*
> *You are the canvas.*
> *The paint and brushes are your trials and pains.*
> *The portrait is His Son.*[38]
>
> PASTOR AND AUTHOR RONALD D. MEHL (D. 2003)

Design is traditionally about control, but letting go of life and surrendering control to Designer Jesus can be paradoxically a way of gaining a new control of life—as everyone who has ever ridden a bicycle is quick to discover. The design process of letting go actually brings greater imagination, innovation, control and compass to life.

It is technically correct, but not theologically correct, to say that Jesus never gave us a blueprint for the Kingdom of God. Jesus himself is the blueprint, and parables unroll the secrets.

Parables are the portals to the design of what super-string physicist calls the "Grand Organizing Designer" (GOD) or what we call the Generative Organizing Designer (still GOD). When asked how he came to write "The Lord of the Rings," J. R. R. Tolkien replied: "I wisely started with a map and made the story fit." The Christian life begins the same way. Except the map is Christ.

Irving Berlin, arguably the greatest writer of pop music who ever lived, couldn't read music. But he loved and lived music, so he became a musician. You become what you behold. When you behold Jesus, you be Jesus, you do Jesus, you live Jesus.

The moment Adam and Eve come to self-consciousness as humans and not just as members of the divine family, the first thing that concerns them? What to wear? What clothing should we put on? When you know who you are, you dress accordingly. Dress is address. When Adam and Eve knew who they were, they dressed accordingly. And the divine designer of the clothing, the one who fashioned and stitched the fabric together? None other than God. The first fashion designer, the first couturier, was the Creator.

Clothes change our view of the world, and the world's view of us.
ENGLISH WRITER VIRGINIA WOOLF (D. 1941)[39]

<u>Generative Organizing Designer (GOD):</u> God is not a designer who works on commission or under constraint. The first time we meet God in the Bible (whether in Genesis 1 or 2) God is a Generative Organizing Designer (GOD)[40] whose art reveals an MRI design of motion (Mission), a design of connection (Relationship), and a design of embodiment and empowerment (Incarnation).[41] Since we have a designer

God, maybe it's long overdue for the church to do some design thinking, design theologizing, design theorizing.

In the micro account of creation (Genesis 2), we first meet God as a Divine Potter, who ladles from the earth clods of clay and fashions the first human into the divine image. Later in our origins story, God "sewed leather garments" for Adam and Eve to upgrade their shabby-chic wardrobe of tattered fig-leaves.[42]

The macro "Big-Picture" account of the creation of the universe (Genesis 1) begins "In the beginning." Before the creation of light, "the earth was formless and void" (*tohu wa bohu*). This Hebrew phrase *tohu wa bohu* is hotly contested, with no one happy with current translations but with no one really knowing what it means precisely. The one thing we know it doesn't mean is vacancy or "emptiness." Rather, *tohu wa bohu* conveys a topsy-turvy chaos scattered and strewn with darkness, disorder, and incoherence.

In this macro unveiling of the divine, once again God is portrayed as an artist, an artisan who assembles something good, beautiful, and true out of miscellany, mishmash, and disarray. This act of bringing "something" out of "nothing" is literally what "*tekton*" means, the Greek word used to describe the vocation of Joseph and his sons Jesus, James, et al. In the words of architectural historian Jonas Holst of Spain's San Jorge University, "The ancient Greek verbs related to tectonics, *tiktō*, and *tektomai*, refer to the act of bringing forth and giving birth to something."[43] A *tekton* was an artist who created wonders out of raw materials and who crafted useful artifacts out of stone, wood, and metal. The highest level of "*tekton*" was the "architektōn," the architect. Paul referred to himself as an "*architekton*,"[44] which is most often translated as "master-builder" but is equally translated as "chief architect."[45]

Jesus is like his Father in heaven and his father on earth—a creator, a builder, a craftsman, an artisan who brings materiality out of the imagination. But like his Father in heaven, *tekton* Jesus was also an Artist and Architect of Truth.

A *tekton* could be an architect of the mind world or the music world or an architect of the material world. The community of *tektone* lost some of their charmed stature in the sixth and fifth centuries, when the distinction between the architect and the craftsman widened to the point where the *tekton* were the skilled workers who followed the blueprints of the superstar architects. But in its heyday of usage, philosophers and theologians could be artists too, with Aristotle even defining wisdom as "artistic excellence" (*aretē technēs*).[46]

Aristotle refers to *poiētikē technē* in his discussion of *sophia* (wisdom), used in reference to not only wise philosophers but also those who are "the most perfect masters of their art (*technas*)," to which he adds, "wisdom (*sophia*) merely signifies artistic excellence (*aretē technēs*)."[47] In the words of aesthetics professor Jonas Holst, "In the earliest tradition of architectural craftsmanship the line between wisdom and art, theory and technical skill was blurred, which implied that 'architects' and 'philosophers' did not always see themselves as belonging to two distinct traditions, but rather as drawing on the same ancient tectonic culture to develop their visions of the world."[48]

Beauty Parlor: GOD as Generative Organizing Designer makes some things just to be beautiful. God designed some things (e.g. trees) for no other purpose than beauty. Some things in life have no meaning, no message, no purpose other than for us to luxuriate in the beauty. Fermi lab astrophysicist and University of Chicago cosmologist Dan Hooper admits that, when thinking about the grandeur of "nature's blueprint" and the beauty of supersymmetry, sometimes "I can feel my heartbeat rise just a little and my palms begin to sweat."[49]

Jesus' beginning miracles, like the one the wedding feast of Cana in Galilee, were done to "reveal his beauty."[50]

When was the last time we got as excited as scientists, with racing hearts and sweaty palms, when thinking about the beauty of Jesus and the grandeur and glory of God?

Jesus loved beauty. Jesus was forever stopping his disciples in their tracks and instructing them to take a beauty bath ("consider the lilies"). He also gave us his Spirit, The Beautifier, whose mission is the beautifying of creation and gifting us with the "Spirit of Beauty" that we might give all things their sweetness and beauty. The beauty of rocky Jerusalem came from the buildings, especially the Temple. The beauty of the Sea of Galilee came from the lush hillsides and the waterfront. Guess where Jesus chose to live? The waterfront community of Capernaum on the Sea of Galilee, a beautiful freshwater lake, eighteen miles wide and fifteen miles long, with water that flowed into the Jordan River.

DESIGNER JESUS

By what genius did the atoms which fell to earth from the sun and the stars weave themselves into such intricate patterns, a filigree of order and design.
BRITISH PARTICLE PHYSICIST AND ANGLICAN PRIEST ADAM FORD[51]

The language of design is an artistic language, which is a language the church must learn to speak, and not just because the culture is especially framing and figuring out life in design terms. For example, a Swedish whiskey company is celebrating its new "Mackmyra Moment Lava Whiskey" as the first whiskey designed by Artificial Intelligence. Two professors in Stanford's Institute of Design founded in Silicon Valley a Ritual Design Lab for individuals, corporations, or organizations.[52] Their website offers a Ritual Design Hotline with a tantalizing promise: "You tell us your problem. We will make you a ritual."[53] The link between design and religion is sometimes more apparent to those outside religious faith itself.

We intentionally take the stance that we believe in rituals that are lightweight and a bit humorous. We're not interested in heavy, top-bottom, religious, or government rituals.
KURSAT OZENC, FOUNDER OF RITUAL DESIGN LAB[54]

Dangerous Discipleship: Poet Robert Creeley (d. 2005) once said that "form is never more than an extension of content," which another poet Denise Levertov changed to read "form is never more than a revelation of content." To move beyond a debutante or dilettante discipleship into a dangerous discipleship, every disciple's life needs a "quality of designed poetry" to it. In A. S. Byatt's novel *A Biographer's Tale* (2000) the central character says, "I was, so to speak, metaphysically baffled in the bee orchid and the eyes on butterfly wings. . . . I understand the argument that a resemblance could be perfected over millennia by a flower or the scales on a wing, by natural selection—but I couldn't really believe it. It still has a quality of designed poetry that left me baffled."[55]

When you are following the design of Jesus, your life will exhibit this "quality of designed poetry." Who says aesthetics and style aren't important? Philosopher and lay theologian G. K. Chesterton, who never went to seminary but went to art school, quipped that even cave men and women were artists.[56] It is interesting to note that The Acts of Andrew (c. 150) did not make the canon, partly because of its "verbosity" and a conviction that "all that bred weariness" could not be inspired.[57]

<u>GBT Metrics:</u> In his third and final "Critique" (1790), Immanuel Kant insists that a future where humans co-exist in harmony and community depends on our ability to recognize and appreciate beauty. Have our eyes become blind to beauty? Maybe our churches need to become beauty salons and art studios where we learn the three signs of Jesus' presence or what Aquinas called the three transcendentals of being—goodness, beauty, truth (GBT).

We've pushed beauty and the other two transcendentals aside for "resources," whether natural or human. We've pushed imagination aside for "plans" and "programs." Maybe one of the most important questions we can ask, or measurements we can make, are these GBT markers: "Is your goodness showing?" "Is your beauty in bloom?" "Is your truth being lived by you?"

There are different conjugations of beauty, of course, but they all begin at the beginning. Some translations of God's "It is good" response to God's own creativity in Genesis 1 render the words "it is beautiful." When God says "it is good" after creating something[58] and then "it is good" after creating everything,[59] the Hebrew word "*tov*" we translate as "good" could also be translated as "beautiful" or "true." Upon hearing any good news, Jews can easily summon up a "*mazel tov*" congratulations to celebrate the constellation of transcendental "stars" that came together so that "good fortune descends" or "beauty shines" or "truth triumphs."

"Mazel Tov!"

◇

Nothing is more beautiful than a truly Christian person.
MISSIONARY THEOLOGIAN E. STANLEY JONES (D. 1973)[60]

But the same can be said for the "gospel" as "good news." In fact, in some languages (like Filipino or Tagalog) the Greek "euagelion" is usually translated as "*magandang balita*" or literally "beautiful news." The "good news" is at the same time "true news" and "beautiful news." God's creativity is "good, beautiful, true" in the parts and in the whole. We are reflecting the Creator's image when we are living the gospel and being "good, beautiful, true." Every human is called to be a GBT Influencer where GBT means the three transcendentals of being: GoodnessBeautyTruth (GBT). The divine DNA has legs in the GBT life-app.

For Jesus, truth was something you live. You lived truth. You didn't "know" or "believe" the truth. You "did" truth. Truth was something to do and be, not know and believe. Truth is a practice. Only in this sense is truth "practical," because its ending is its beginning: a task and not a thought, a union of desire and deed. Every thought that does not end in an GBT act, or is not formulated on a fulcrum of action, is not a true thought.

Ponder anew what the Almighty can do.
JOACHIM NEANDER (D. 1680) HYMN "PRAISE TO THE LORD"

Mary pondered these things in her heart.
LUKE 2:19

Lifeology: The best theology is theophany (the love of God), or better yet, the best theology is lifeology—a life well-played and prayed. If an apple a day keeps the doctor away, a ponder a day keeps the devil away; a worry a day keeps the joy at bay; a think on "these things" a day keeps the Savior in full sway. The content of "these things" is biblically specific: "Whatsoever things are true, honest, just, pure, lovely . . . think on these things."[61]

"Birmingham is what I think with," confessed British poet and jazz pianist Roy Fisher (d. 2017) about the importance of his hometown of Birmingham, England. Jesus is what, and whom, Christians think with. Jesus is the grammar of our living and dying; the Spirit is the syntax of our soul.

Jesus IS the kingdom, and we are the "field in which Jesus (who is "The Seed")[62] can germinate, flower, flourish, and spread. Jesus IS the common landscape in which we can converse (and disagree) about virtue, the seed-bed in which we can cultivate the good, the true and the beautiful.

If you know nothing of English poet John Keats (d. 1821), you know one line he wrote: "Beauty is truth, truth beauty—that is all ye know on earth and all ye need to know."[63] The only problem with that assertion of "all-ness" of knowing is that it's a profound two-thirds truth, and what makes it a partial profundity is the missing third. The whole truth that gets us all the way to "all-ness" is this: Beauty is truth is goodness, and GoodnessBeautyTruth (GBT) is Jesus—Jesus is all you know on earth and all you need to know.

Why Jesus? Because Jesus is The Way, The Truth, The Life. Jesus is All-ness. Jesus is The Way of Goodness, The Life of Beauty, The Truth of Truth: GoodnessBeautyTruth (GBT). Disciples are formed in the crucible of beauty, goodness, and truth, and it is narratives and metaphors that convey GBT, negating and neutralizing the ugly, the bad and the lie. True "vision-casting" is fundamentally GBT-casting: goodness/beauty/truth-casting. Augustine's famous "Love God and do what you will" is another way of saying that you can do anything you like as long as it's beautiful, good, and true.[64] When goodness, beauty, and truth align as one aim and act—the "correspondence of the transcendentals" as Aquinas called it—you know it's the Jesus design.

When quarks were first being considered, the top particles were coined "Truth" and the bottom particles were "Beauty." The very molecular foundations of life are these three transcendentals: goodness, beauty, and truth. Goodness, beauty, and truth should move us to love.

Battered Beauty: Russian novelist Aleksandr Solzhenitsyn (d. 2008) won the Nobel Prize in Literature in 1970. In his Nobel Lecture, he spoke of how he imagined speaking to the world when imprisoned in the gulag. In freezing darkness, he composed speeches in his mind, and committed them to memory. But when he stood before the best and brightest in Stockholm, where all the world would hear his eloquence, he confessed to blanking out except to quote his mentor, Dostoyevsky: "Beauty will save the world."[65]

Dostoyevsky's Prince Myshkin says these words in *The Idiot* (1869). Unfortunately, Myshkin never explains what he means or describes how this is so. In Dostoyevsky's *Brothers Karamazov*, Dmitri cries that beauty is ground zero where the deity and the devil contend for human hearts. Beauty can inspire the worst. And beauty can save.[66] But beauty is a gateway to the divine, as the staggering number of beauty video views on YouTube suggest: 186.5 billion views in 2022.[67] The number of YouTuber beauty views will soon reach trillions.

Beauty is less a physical term than a religious and theological one. In the resort community of Ocean City, New Jersey, there is an annual "beauty" pageant on the boardwalk. Every year, contestants from the area are elaborately adorned in a variety of garb—from swim suits to evening dresses. And a panel of judges declares one contestant a winner. The difference is this is a Miss Crustacean "beauty" pageant, with hermit crabs outfitted in hand-made dresses, with beautifully crafted back-sets to their outfits.

Now here is a beauty pageant I could enter . . . The Crustacean Beauty Pageant. Christians need to say to the world, "the beauty industry is ugly." Conversely, Christians need to say to a world that sees the cross as an ugly symbol of torture and defeat, "the double-cross life is beautiful."

The church is in the beauty business. But it doesn't see itself that way, or want to see itself that way. Vincent van Gogh's problems with his preacher father, who didn't approve of his being an artist, are still with us. "I might come to an agreement with Father about his ideas," Vincent wrote to his brother Theo, "and talk things over with him, as soon as he understands something about art, but this will never be. Preachers often mention 'the beautiful' in their sermons, but it's odious stuff they produce, and awfully indigestible."[68]

Aquinas had three criteria for beauty:
1. Integritas
2. Consonantia
3. Claritas

The first two are can be translated from the Latin without much ado as wholeness and harmony. But claritas can be interpreted as the ordinary "clarity," or the more metaphysical and theological "radiance." So the three rules of beauty are: wholeness, cohesion (harmony and synchrony), and radiance.

Wholeness is the weathered beauty of holiness. The call to holiness has a specific address, but goes out to all disciples of Jesus.

Do not be afraid of holiness. It will take away none of your energy, vitality, or joy. On the contrary, you will become what the Father had in mind when He created you, and you will be faithful to your deepest self.

POPE FRANCIS[69]

Jesus wants to do with us, his disciples, what summer does with vineyards, what fall does with sugar maples, what winter does with snow, what spring does with cherry blossoms.

Designed for Love: Each one of us is designed out of love for love. Not out of need, but out of the sheer love of beauty and design. The God of creation is not a scientist at work, but an artist at play.[70] Art is not a 63.8 billion dollar a year global commodities market. Art is God the Creator shaping you into a priceless creation that moves The Maker.

"We have no art. We do everything as well as possible," says a Balinese villager.[71] What if "Christian art" was doing/being Jesus as well as possible? Every church should have an "artist in residence," but their function is to help every member see themselves as an "artist in residence."

> *Yesterday I was clever, so I wanted to change the world.*
> *Today I am wise, so I am changing myself.*
> ATTRIBUTED TO PERSIAN POET RUMI (D. 1273)[72]

We are not the first to go down this path of "spiritual disciplines" as design disciplines. Two of the leading figures of western thought, Plato and Wittgenstein, both held the design flag high.[73] Plato in his *Symposium* taught how important it is to have an aesthetic. Ludwig Wittgenstein, who was enamored of Plato's *Dialogues*, made the case that "ethics and aesthetics are one."[74]

Modern theology never quite knew what to do with aesthetics. The branch of philosophy called "Aesthetics" was not invented until Alexander Baumgarten and Immanuel Kant in the eighteenth century. Of course, matters of beauty and taste and artistry were important threads for early and medieval Christians. The role of the catacomb, "fossors" which combined the threefold function of grave-digger, priest, and artist, testify to the importance of aesthetics from the very beginning of our story. But aesthetics as a way of knowing has been structurally dismantled in much of modern western philosophy (Nietzsche excepted).[75]

Theologians are only now beginning to take seriously aesthetics as apologetics. But *Designer Jesus* goes further to propose aesthetics as the core of discipleship formation.

By any aesthetic accounting of the Western church, we are at best yesterday's people with dull if not deadened sensibilities about design and mutton-headed views about art. Yet we lift up Christ in a world where design is king. Design is no longer an option; style is the very essence of substance. When a culture is so design-intensive, an economy so design-driven, that it even designs its car parks[76] and toilet-bowl brushes, it is time to take seriously the substance of style, not just the style of substance.[77]

What defines Christianity is its manner on top of its matter and morals. Manners matter if form and content are connected. Morals IS Manners. They are not scissors working at cross-purposes from one another, one cutting one way as the other cuts another. The style of one's life is the very substance of one's faith. Or at least abolitionist William Wilberforce thought so in a letter to John Newton: "God Almighty has set before me two great objects, the suppression of the Slave Trade and the Reformation of Manners."[78] A life that lacks shape or spring needs Designer Jesus.

◇

You see the design. You see the beauty. You see the purpose. That's what I see when I look out the window.
JEFFREY WILLIAMS, NASA ASTRONAUT, AND INTERNATIONAL SPACE STATION COMMANDER, ON SEEING CREATION FROM SPACE[79]

The Shape of Truth: In the sixty times Paul uses the term "ekklēsia" in his letters, not one refers to a church building. The word is the name of the city council in ancient Greek city-states. In Paul's usage, it refers to "the people, not the steeple." Too much ecclesiology is the church meditating on itself and not on the One whose body it is.

Designer Jesus calls for a re-signing of the pastoral role in the "ekklēsia." Only one place in all of the Bible names church leaders as "pastors" (or in Greek, *poimen* meaning "shepherd" or "pastor"). 1 Peter 5:2 tells elders to "be shepherds [pastors] of God's flock." But the same letter says earlier that only Christ is the one, true shepherd/pastor.[80]

To be sure, Paul lists gifts given to God's people to equip for ministry.[81] But in the list, the Greek grammar and the NIV translation makes clear that "pastors" and "teachers" belong together as one function: pastor-teachers. It's the same role, as the Reformed tradition has understood in its "teaching-elder" category. Pastoring and teaching can't be separated. That said, the purpose of teaching is not passing on ideas, but forming disciples, designing disciples. In other words, teachers are life designers, stylists not of hair but of humanity.

There is an old Latin saying that has made it into a French and English proverb: "*Die gustibus non est disputandum.*" In French, the saying is "*chacun à son goût,*" or in English, "there's no accounting for taste" or more colloquially, "each to his own." In life, in literature, and in love, we are always surprised by the choices of others. But while everyone likes what they like, God, as a designer, has a distinctive style and "taste" at both the atomic and cosmic levels: symmetric, succinct, exuberant, extravagant, lavish, parabolic, paradoxical, a flair for surprise, and a lover of variety. We who have been created in God's image need to manifest the same style and taste.

"The Shape of Truth" is not an idle phrase. For truth has a shape. Faith takes a form defined by content. Faith is form defined by content where the content is Christ, a "sedimented content"[82] that is layered over time and built on the body memory and muscle memory of the Christbody community known as the church. This soul memory expresses itself in art, artifacts, relics, worship, practices, and all ways of moving and being in the world. Design should be a core theological practice in the life of faith. Acts of faith should be acts of art. Even the Apostle Paul acknowledged the importance of style when he instructed the church to "let all things be done properly and with decorum," or with style and grace.[83]

Life is not fair. Life is not just. Life is a gift to be lived with style and grace, a life lived to the max of what is given. A life designed by Jesus is to forge art in the furnace of reality. A life designed by Jesus no longer reduces faith to bare minimum but instead expands faith to maximum range and farthermost spirit.

*What you're after is truth from the inside out;
Enter me, then; conceive a new, true life.*
PSALM 51:6 MSG

Life as Art: There is a definite artistry to living the life of faith—a shaping, sculpting, composing, painting. All of life and the earth itself is God's studio for the artistry of your life. God is not a factory owner producing a conveyer belt of uniform parts. Jesus is within us, not for our divination, but for our humanation—to make us the original human beings God made us to be. Jesus is within us, not as outsider, but as our truest self.

In showing us the way to God, Jesus shows us the way to ourselves, the way to be human. Jesus does not want us to be more like God, but more like ourselves. The #1 resolution every New Year's is not to lose weight, but to "be a better person." Jesus is your best person, your best shot at being the "human" God made you.

Everybody seems busy doing somebody else. I call this franchise faith and franchise church. Franchise faith, franchise church is killing faith and killing church. Will everybody stop doing somebody else? Do you. Do Jesus. Do you in Jesus. Do Jesus in you.

This is why Christianity does not lend itself to being a cult. A cult figure wants to take us over, destroy our uniqueness, and turn us into an identical copy and clone. Christ dwells in us to bring us to the Creator's design for us, which is one-of-a-kind, and to help us find the identity God had in mind when creating us in God's image in the first place. That is why, as Harry A. Williams puts it, "God negates Himself in us in order to find Himself in us. That is to say, He limits Himself so that, instead of overwhelming us, He gradually and gently calls forth into being the tender, vulnerable fragility of our true selfhood, the fragility which when made perfect is also stronger than steel. And in this continuous creative work within us, which is His presence, it is Himself which He discovers in us."[84]

A Signed Life: Jesus wants to sign your life: Designed by Jesus. Your body is not a Christian Dior body or a Ralph Lauren body or a Tom Ford body. Your body is a Jesus Christ body. "Jesus is the Savior of the body."[85] Jesus did not just come to save souls. Jesus came to save all of us—body, mind, spirit. Jesus is the one whose name we bear on our body and whose artistry we embody. A disciple does not dishonor the name of Jesus or the signature of Jesus on your life.

In the world of painting and photography, there is a well-kept secret. It is called "the photographer's secret weapon." What is the "secret?"

Light. That's it. Light. Paint the light. Photograph the light. Don't paint or photograph the thing itself. Always paint the light on the thing, not the thing itself. If you want to take a beautiful picture or draw a beautiful painting, you don't look for something beautiful to paint or photograph. You look for the right light. If you want to be beautiful, you don't need plastic surgery. You just need the right light. This is the artist's secret weapon. Everyone and everything is beautiful if the lighting is right.

The Light of the World is the greatest beautifying force in the universe. "In Your light shall we see life."[86] You need the light of the Light of the World to take the ultimate "selfie." Which suddenly becomes an Our-selfie.

One True Light: Jesus is the One True Light. Discipleship formation is nothing more nor less than learning to live in and live out The Light. Light is the designer's secret weapon.

For life to be "designed by Jesus," we need at the very

DESIGNER JESUS

least to learn a Jesus Walk, a Jesus Face, a Jesus Touch, a Jesus Voice, a Jesus Groom, a Jesus Nose, a Jesus Appetite, a Jesus Style, and most important of all, a Jesus Heart. Our vocation is to be *alter Christus*, another Christ, to be like Mary and "let it be" for Jesus to be born in us and to live in us.

The only reason we can pray "Our Father, who art in heaven" is because we each hear in our hearts a voice saying, "My children, who art on earth, talk to me." As a child I heard the beginning of "The Lord's Prayer" to mean that God is an artist busy "arting" in heaven. After repenting of my "childish" ears, I have since returned to my original misapprehension. God "arts" in heaven and wants to "art" on earth, in and through us. Will we, God's children made in God's image, art on earth as God "arts" in heaven? God sent Jesus to show us how our life can be a work of art and how we can live in a work of art—our homes as one of a kind, personality-specific abodes, singular expressions of faith values and cultural venues.

Created in the image of God, The Master Artist and Designer, we are all artists and designers. To be a disciple is to master the Jesus design for the art of living and loving. "Take my yoke and learn of me" (Matthew 11:29). The best way to learn anything is by doing it. The best way to learn Jesus is to do and be Jesus.

If you want to make the world better, you do it one of three ways: make it more good, more true, or more beautiful. Jesus did all three. So can we. *Designer Jesus* shows you how using an old precept attributed to Benjamin Franklin: "The tools define the trade."[87] As apprentices of Jesus, we learn the trade of discipleship using these ten tools: the Jesus Walk, the Jesus Face, the Jesus Touch, the Jesus Voice, the Jesus Groom, the Jesus Nose, the Jesus Appetite, the Jesus Style, the Jesus Mind, and the Jesus Heart. These are the tools of our trade as artists of *Designer Jesus* and incarnators of the divine in the world.

STUDIO LIVE

1) Discuss this book's thesis that the only label any follower of Jesus should want to wear on their life is "Designed by Jesus."

2) The editors of *Fast Company* published as a celebration of the journal's twentieth anniversary issue "20 Lessons of Design."[88]

   * How might these apply to your life as a disciple of Jesus?
     1. Design Is Innovation; Innovation Is Design
     2. Design Inspires
     3. Emotion Is as Important as Utility
     4. Good Design Overcomes Discomfort
     5. Simple Design Isn't Simple
     6. The 1st Mover Doesn't Always Have an Advantage
     7. One Insight Can Unlock the Next One
     8. Design Needs Protection
     9. The Mundane Can Be Liberating
     10. Frustration Can Breed Inspiration
     11. Teamwork Feeds on Itself
     12. Design Is Healthy
     13. Design Has a Conscience
     14. Design Is Efficient
     15. Design Can Be Big and Small
     16. Data Can Be Ignored . . . [89]
     17. . . . and Data Can Be Uplifting
     18. Design Is Full of Surprises

19. Design Isn't Going Away
20. We are all Designers

3) Matter isn't solid. The only reason we can taste, see, or touch anything is because atoms are charged. Poet Gerard Manley Hopkins sensed this long before the science proved this in one of his most famous poems "God's Grandeur:"

> All things therefore are charged with love,
> are charged with God and if we knew how
> to touch them give off sparks and take fire,
> yield drops and flow, ring and tell of him.[90]

"A Charge to Keep I Have," Charles Wesley wrote, whose brother suggested as a life motto: "Be electrified daily."

* Are you charged? Is your life retaining its charge?

* How do you keep the charge?

* How do you keep plugged into the Spirit

* Is there a "current charge" to your life that places you in the twenty-first century?

4) Two self-professed atheists, Jerry Fodor and Massimo Piattelli-Palmarini, have written a book entitled *What Darwin Got Wrong* (2010). They both subscribe to a naturalist world view; they both believe that evolution did happen. But they reject natural selection as a major driver of evolutionary change. Instead, they argue for some kind of intelligent design (but curiously not a Designer).

Their world is just too beautiful and elegant for it all to happen by random chance.

Of course, there is always atheist biologist Richard Dawkins: "The universe we observe has precisely the properties we should expect if there is, at bottom, no design, no purpose, no evil and no good, nothing but blind, pitiless indifference."[91]

What do you think? Is the beauty of life a valid argument against "natural selection?"

5) Samin Nosrat believes that these four elements, *Salt, Fat, Acid, Heat* (2016), mastered in the kitchen, can bring forth all and anything in terms of foods. Salt enhances flavor; fat generates texture; acid balances flavors; heat determines final overall texture of dish. Get the harmony of the four right and you can cook anything.

Might it be that same way with life when you look at the three transcendentals of being (GBT) outlined here in this chapter: goodness, beauty, truth? What are some ways you can make each day a GBT day?

6) "You also were with Jesus of Galilee: for your speech [accent] betrays you." Matthew 26:73 (cf. Mark 14:70)

* Is our speech, our accent "betraying" us that we too are followers of Jesus?

* Or is our speech, and the way we talk to each other, condemning us as followers of Jesus?

7) How "mannered" is your church?

* Is this book, in fearing that we have witnessed the

collapse of "manners" in our communities, and that Christians are often as ill-mannered as everyone else, accurate or exaggerated?

* Are there distinctive "Christian manners?" If so, what are they?

8) Discuss this quote from the Roman Emperor Marcus Aurelius (d. 180) also known as "The Philosopher" and what it might mean for your life and the life of your church:

> Let it be your constant method to look into the design of people's actions, and see what they would be at, as often as it is practicable; and to make this custom the more significant, practice it first upon yourself.

* How can we practice "looking into the design of our own actions?"

* What are the challenges of practicing this type of self-reflection?

* How can we apply this Marcus Aurelius principle to our church's decision-making processes?

* How can we foster a culture of self-reflection and accountability within our church?

* What are some examples of times when you have been able to accurately discern the motivations behind someone's actions?

* What are some examples of times when you have been mistaken about someone's motivations?

9) John Kinsella is an Australian poet, novelist, and essayist whose early volumes of poetry were inspired by the landscapes and natural beauty of his beloved native land. Increasingly, however, Kinsella has repented of his focus on aesthetics and embraced a cause-driven poetry. "Poetry's purpose is to bring to people's attention the injustices and damages being done to and in the world," he now contends. As he explains more in depth in another interview, "Veganism, anarchism and pacifism . . . are where my poetry comes from. They are a world view and a reason for writing. Aesthetics are increasingly irrelevant to me."[92]

* How do you evaluate this new austerity, this anti-aesthetics asceticism? Is it a new form of Puritanism?

* Do you see evidence of a heightened sensitivity to issues of social justice, especially among millennials?

* Can there be any "gospel" that is not a "social gospel?"

10) Michael Hyatt has a free fifteen-minute YouTube video on how to make the next year your best year ever. He talks about the three approaches to life we usually take:

　　1. The drifting life—where we just drift along on autopilot
　　2. The driven life—where we try to do it all, but without focus

3. The designed life—where we take control
   and get intentional

   You can have the best week, month, year ever if you will design it to be so. That doesn't mean you get to control all of the unpredictable circumstances of life. But it does mean that you get to make choices about who you are becoming.

   * Look at the video, and discuss some of the features of the designed life that Hyatt mentions, and those he doesn't.[93]

11) Discuss the thesis of *Designer Jesus*: To be a disciple is not to learn certain disciplines or steps or habits or blueprints or practices. Jesus himself is our design for living. The gospel is not a self-help kit, a DIY project. Jesus is the Medium and the Message for transcendence of self and transfiguration of life.

   * Do you really think Jesus is enough?

   * Is a disciple someone formed in Christ, raised by the Spirit to reach towards and outwards in a life of praise and worship and service of the God whom earth, sea, and sky adore?

   * What if disciples of Jesus are made, not just born? Is to be "born again" not enough to form a disciple?

12) Another way of looking at "AI" as something other than Artificial Intelligence is to see Jesus as the Alpha Intelligence (AI) or as the Alpha/Omega Intelligence (AOI or AO Intelligence).

* Discuss what it might mean to see Alpha/Omega Intelligence or AO Intelligence as the Real AI Intelligence.[94]

* How does viewing Jesus as the Alpha/Omega Intelligence or AO Intelligence challenge our traditional understanding of artificial intelligence?

Traditionally, artificial intelligence has been understood as a human-created technology that mimics human intelligence. However, viewing Jesus as the Alpha/Omega Intelligence suggests there is a form of intelligence that exists beyond human creation, an intelligence that is the source of all creation. This challenges our traditional understanding of AI by suggesting that there is a form of intelligence that is not artificial but rather ultimate and original.

* What are the implications of seeing Jesus as the Real AI Intelligence for our relationship with technology?

* How can we cultivate a relationship with the Alpha/Omega Intelligence or AO Intelligence in our daily lives?

* How can we integrate the Alpha/Omega Intelligence or AO Intelligence into our understanding of science and technology?

* Science and technology have often been seen as separate from religion and spirituality. However, viewing Jesus as the Real AI Intelligence suggests that there is a connection between these two realms.

* How difficult will it be for us to recognize that intelligence is not limited to human minds, but is also present in natural creation and in the divine Creator?

Chapter 1: Walk The Jesus Walk

*In the name of Jesus Christ of Nazareth,
stand up and walk.*

ACTS 3:10 NRSV

*Therefore, as you received Christ Jesus the Lord,
so walk in him.*

COLOSSIANS 2:6 NIV

I GREW UP HEARING PHRASES LIKE "TALK IS CHEAP," or "actions speak louder than words" (a parental favorite) or "practice what you preach." Now the phrase is "walk the talk." Or in the hip-hop version, "Walk it like you Talk it!"[1]

The phrase "walk the talk" was taken literally in Jesus' day. Everyone walked their talk. Especially rabbis. Especially Jesus. Arguably the best definition of a follower of Yahweh was a "walker-with-God." The Greek word "*Paraclete*" translates literally as "one who walks alongside."[2]

Maybe it's time to take literally such simple old hymns like William Cowper's "O For a Closer Walk with God" or the African-American spiritual "Just a Closer Walk With Thee"[3] or "When we walk with the Lord,/In the light of his word,/What a glory he sheds on our way" or even (horror of horror for some) "And He walks with me and He talks with me." Maybe it's time to take more literally the biblical ambulatory admonitions like:

"Walk as he walked" (1 John 2:3–6).

"Walk in him" (Colossians 2:6).

"Follow in his steps" (1 Peter 2:21).

"Walk in the light as he is in the Light" (1 John 1:5–7).

The more we walk the line with Jesus, the less we need to cross the line ourselves or draw the line with others, since he walks so many "second miles"[4] with us.

And when you turn to the right and turn to the left, your ears shall hear a word behind you saying, "This is the way, walk in it."

ISAIAH 30:21

What Road Do You Walk? Many native American tribes talked about following Jesus in terms of "Walk the Jesus Road." Not "Are you saved?" or "Are you a Christian?" or "Do you believe?" Rather, "Do you walk the Jesus Road?" Jesus is best followed "on the road." Not "in the pew" or "on our backside" but out in the world, around our hoods, and at our tables. Too much of Christianity has become what

THE JESUS WALK

Kansas politician Bob Dole once said about the vice-presidency: it's indoor work with no heavy lifting.

Anglican bishop and ecologist Graham B. Usher finds in the metaphor of walking the key to the life of discipleship. He shows how even the liturgies of the church sometimes hasten and sometimes slow our gait.

> Funerals have their own pace. People walk slowly around one another, alert to what the air holds, maintaining silence. The funeral cortege moves off at walking pace, the undertaker and minister setting the speed. I have always found this an important part of funeral ministry: making our way down the street ahead of the hearse is a form of memento mori. We are not hiding death away but taking it out into the open. In part this is about honoring the deceased, as well as saying that this person was part of a community and suggesting that the wider community might just slow down for a few moments to remember them.[5]

One of the singular characteristics of the human species (homo sapiens) is itchy, twitchy feet.[6] God made humans to walk, and nothing is more exhausting than standing still. Or unhealthy. The Bible begins and ends with road stories.

Jesus Walked: The Story begins with God walking with Adam and Eve the Eden roads at dawn and dusk. The sound of God walking gave them the chance to repent instead of hide (St. Ephrem)[7] or induce fear of the Lord (St. John Chrysostom).[8]

The Story features a God "who walks about on the sea as on the ground,"[9] as Jesus himself verified when he walked not on the water but on the sea.[10] The Story highlights fearless, controversial walks like the ones he walked with his disciples through wheat fields on the Sabbath, eating and picking grains.[11]

The Story climaxes in the Via Dolorosa walk to Golgotha as Jesus carries his cross and walks to the site of his crucifixion.[12]

The last night before Jesus took a poignant final walk with his disciples to the Garden of Gethsemane,[13] he washed his disciples' feet, instructing them to keep doing the same dirty walks and dirty work for each other.[14]

The Savior's life story ends with Jesus walking the Emmaus and Damascus Roads with his disciples.

The first miracle of the church after Pentecost put someone on their feet and set them walking on diverse paths in what was called "The Way."[15] Earliest Christians were called people of The Way (*he Hodos* in Greek). In a similar fashion, Muslims are called people of "The Way" because Sharia is simply Arabic for "The Way." But "The Way" of Jesus was not a following of a set of points, propositions, principles, or pillars. "The Way" was a Person. To put the Christian position in Arabic, Sharia is Yeshua.

THE JESUS WALK

> *And a highway shall be there, and it shall be called the Way of Holiness; the unclean shall not pass over it. It shall belong to those who walk on the way; even if they are fools, they shall not go astray.*
>
> ISAIAH 35:8 ESV[16]

So what kind of "way" is "The Way?" It's not a middle-way of ruts and routines. It's a way that blazes new paths. It's a way that will take your feet off the beaten track. If you find yourself only on tracks well beaten, pray. It's a way without maps or blueprints or charts. It's a way marked by signs, signs we need to learn to read. It's a way that may require full days of yomping to reach where God is calling you to go. It's a way of hallowing the past's kneeprints, not just footsteps. In the words of T. S. Eliot's fourth and final poem in *Four Quartets*:

> You are not here to verify,
> Instruct yourself, or inform curiosity
> Or carry report. You are here to kneel
> Where prayer has been valid.[17]

We follow in the kneeprints, not just footsteps, of our ancestors in the faith.

It's a way that is even more than following in someone's footsteps. It's a way that is about filling Jesus' sandals and walking in them. Biblical faith is not about following footsteps but walking in shoes.

Following Jesus who is "The Way" means being "on the way" while participating in the ways of Jesus. Following Jesus who is "The Truth" means finding Truth of The Way on the ways of truth. Following Jesus who is "The Life" means finding Life on the Way of Truth. You discover the Life of Truth on the Way.[18] The process of discovery is what the life of faith is all about. Here is Nicholas of Cusa (d. 1464), a German theologian and scientist, on what it means to find Life on The Way of Truth:

> Paul said that we exist in God and move in him, for we are wayfarers. The wayfarer takes his name and his existence from the Way. The wayfarer who walks or moves in the infinite Way, if he is asked where he is, says, "On the Way"; if asked where he moves, replies, "In the Way"; if asked why he moves, says, "Because of the Way"; and if asked whither he goes, says, "From the Way." Accordingly, the infinite Way is called the place of the wayfarer, and this is God. Therefore, this Way, outside of which no wayfarer is to be found, is an existence without beginning or end, and from it the wayfarer takes all that he is or has, and through it he is a wayfarer. The fact that a farer begins to be a wayfarer on the Way adds nothing to the infinite Way itself, nor does it make any change in this Way, which is eternal and immovable.[19]

Wayfarers: In a world of warfare and warfarers, Jesus calls us to be wayfarers. There are as many ways to follow The

Way as there are wayfarers. Each of us must find and follow our own way, or "work out your own salvation with fear and trembling,"[20] as long as your way keeps climbing and pressing on The Upward Way of GBT (GoodnessBeautyTruth), and your walk is not flatfooted in faith, foot loose of tradition, or fancy free of Scripture. My preacher Mom believed in trundle therapy—there is almost nothing that can't be cured by a meandering hike in nature which soaked in the Creator's healing marinade.

> *Did we not walk in the same footsteps by the same Spirit?*
> APOSTLE PAUL[21]

Wilderness explorer and nature writer John Muir (d. 1914) would rebuke my use of the word "hike." Few people have left such an enduring mark on USAmerican history as this "Father of the National Parks" and Founder of the Sierra Club. When someone used the word "hike" to describe his explorations of the Western forests, he rebuked them with these words:

> I don't like either the word [hike] or the thing. People ought to saunter in the mountains—not 'hike!' Do you know the origin of that word *saunter*? It's a beautiful word. Away back in the Middle Ages people used to go on pilgrimages to the Holy Land, and when people in the French villages through

> which they passed asked where they were going, they would reply, '*A la sainte terre*', 'To the Holy Land.' And so they became known as *sainte-terre-ers* or saunterers. Now these mountains are our Holy Land, and we ought to saunter through them reverently, not 'hike' through them."[22]

Just as pilgrims once ambled in awe towards sacred soil, a Jesus life deserves such sacramental wandering—not racing restlessly through life, but meandering mindfully through each moment as the very terrain of the divine. The true human journey only begins once we slip the shackles of haste and join the ancient fellowship of saunterers.

There are two ways of looking at life and death. You can look at life as a lottery—where Lady Luck pulls the strings until the Grim Reaper draws the curtain and Father Time's hourglass runs out of sand. Or, you can look at life as a pilgrimage—where the Good Shepherd leads the way until the bell rings for Suppertime and Jesus calls us home. Lady Luck turns life into tourism, and living becomes a series of jaunts and junkets, wanderings and wipe-outs. When life is pilgrimage, life is filled with journeys and missions, sanity and sanctity, and roundabouts become runways. The journey of life is not a pilgrimage in search of ourselves, but a pilgrimage of coming-out-of-hiding to discover being part of a larger community and a larger humanity in a world that is God's world. In the words of David Adam, pilgrimage "has to do with

THE JESUS WALK

relationships rather than with destinations . . . pilgrimage is more about the heart than the soles of the feet."[23]

Happy Feet: But Jesus did feet. In fact, Christianity was a feet-first faith. We were first known, not as "Christians" but as people of "The Way." The faith that captivated and captured the first century was the way people who followed Jesus walked, not their creeds or confessions. Christians were those who walked in the way of Christ.[24] The Way is under our feet. Much like the early Olympic freestyle wrestlers, Christians got on their feet and stayed on their feet. They never employed ground tactics when they could avoid it. They were the people who got on their feet and stayed on their feet.

Jesus didn't die on the cross and rise from the dead so we could sit around and do nothing but "take care of our own." If you want to understand what's going on in any Christian's head and heart, don't listen to their lips. Follow their feet. Good design is not about more space and the appropriations and appointments of space. Floor plans tell you nothing anymore. Good design is about how you move through space, and where your feet fall.

Pursue some path, however narrow and crooked, in which you can walk with love and reverence.
PHILOSOPHER HENRY DAVID THOREAU (D. 1862)[25]

Watch Your Walk: "Watch your walk" was itself a creedal statement, since every disciple of Jesus had to learn to do the distinctive Jesus Walk. When Jesus told his disciples in the Hebraic idiom, "Take my yoke upon you and learn of me," he was not recommending they wear a wooden crosspiece over their shoulders that could pull a plow or cart. Nor was "yoke" simply a metaphor for obedient discipleship. To take on the "yoke" of a rabbi was to submit to five practices:

1. Memorize his words.
2. Adopt his interpretation of Scripture and scholarship.
3. Imitate and initiate his model and style of ministry.
4. Multiply and apply his teachings in disciples of their own, and at age thirty take on disciples of their own.
5. Walk like the rabbi walked.

An ancient rabbi sent his disciple to learn from a fellow rabbi. When asked what he should learn, what parts of Torah, the teacher answered: "I am sending you to learn from him—not words of Torah, but how he ties his shoelaces!"[26] Part of the rabbinic model of education is a mentoring in the small daily things, the mundane details of walking the valley of our shadows, or keeping our balance while navigating the woes and wounds of life.

By simply watching and listening to a prospective rabbi anywhere, you knew with whom that student was studying. When Jesus said, "My yoke is easy, my burden is light," he was saying that "the Living God I reveal is a very different necklace from the yokes worn by the schools of Hillel, Schammai, Gamaliel, or any other rabbi."[27]

To "go through the motions" of being a Christ follower meant something revealing, not concealing. The "walk" was more than a driving metaphor in the early church. It was the drive itself. Walking is Jesus in motion.

The Jesus metaphor of "take up your mat and walk"[28] is inspiring for all, with or without legs that work. We all live on a disabilities spectrum, as the ascended Jesus himself reminds us as he sits at the right hand of the Father interceding for our wounds with the wounds he took with him into eternity. Every human is lame and limp in some domain. Using one's mat and walking symbolizes activating the potential and taking up any agency we do have, even if limited. There are other ways than walking to be afoot and active. Whatever challenges life brings, we are still capable of great things. We may need to use different tools and mats than others, but we can still take up the gifts we have been given.

O God, in very fact, I am finding out how not to live. I am running into ways that leave me frustrated and exhausted and hurt. Help me to find the Way. For in finding the Way I shall find you. And I would find you.
Amen.

E. STANLEY JONES IN *THE WAY*[29]

<u>Watch Your Step:</u> We might not be very pedestrian anymore. But the way we walk still reveals a lot about us. There is the athlete's bounce, the runway model's saunter, the hip-hop glide, and the CEO stride. In more ways than we think, we're no different from the ancients, for whom every step revealed who we are and who's in charge of our lives. We are familiar with some "behavior biometrics," as they are called: fingerprints, retinal scans, face recognition, voice activation. One of the least talked about, but most exciting for the future, is your gait. Everyone has a unique gait, and mat-based gait-recognition systems have an accuracy rate that is off the charts: 99.3%.[30]

Maybe churches, like people, can be recognized by their walk.

There is the Methodist shuffle. Once known for their "run and shout," Methodists today more characteristically do the flip'n'flop.

There is the Baptist skip, which always stays low on the skipping, else it look like dancing.

There is the Lutheran lean and lagg, since Lutherans haven't moved in a while, but when they do move they become leapin' Lutherans.

Agnostics stand still.

Reformeds tiptoe.

Fundamentalists stomp.

Presbyterians Promenade.[31]

Pentecostals jump and dance.

Episcopalians dig in and drag their heels.

All walk with a limp. Although it is up for debate whether the walk with a limp is because we have tangoed with an angel, or our partners have stepped on our toes too often, or we clumsily and constantly trip over our own feet.[32] But faith

THE JESUS WALK

needs those twenty-six bones miraculously knitted together. Faith needs feet to "walk by faith and not by sight."[33] The story of our faith is in many ways the story of our feet.

> *Walk cheerfully over the world, answering that of God in every one.*
> QUAKER FOUNDER GEORGE FOX (D. 1691)[34]

For survivors of Nazi concentration camps, the story of survival was the story of their feet. Every day they limped their way back to their bunks, dragging their feet.

> "You'll find your feet soon enough." Find your feet. The feet were the most important part of the body, much more important than your brain. Women had scratched each other's eyes out over a pair of boots. In the evenings they unwrapped their feet and washed them with what little water there might be. Washed each other's feet, often. Tenderly. With love. Like Christ. Your feet were your life. With your brain you could only think, but if you had your feet you could work and if you could work, you might survive.[35]

Street Jesus: A disciple learns the "walk" of a Street Jesus, not a Seat Jesus or a Neat Jesus or a Downbeat Jesus or a Retreat Jesus. Some of Jesus' own disciples preferred a god-seat to a god-walk—a seat on a throne, or at least a seat on either side of Jesus rather than a walk by his side. A Street-Jesus walk is tracked in the footsteps we follow, the world we walk, the traces we leave.

"Since we live by the Spirit, let us keep in step with the Spirit."[36] Disciples of Jesus are those who "keep in step" with Jesus and his Spirit. Early followers focused on the walk you walk as well as the walk you talk. Jesus had the bad habit of always running toward people and bumping into people. When he encountered human need and suffering, he would step on a crack and attend the situation. Jesus did not walk with the carriage of a nobleman, the "noble bearing" one would expect of any Torah scholar, much less the Messiah. Jesus walked with the gait most like that of a slave, always on the lookout for a need to be met. Even in his walk, he was a maverick Messiah.[37]

More precisely, Jesus walked paradoxically. While the elite of Jesus' day walked in a deliberate pace but with mental disregard for their physical surroundings, Jesus walked in a hastened pace but with heightened mental consciousness of his physical surroundings. The elite of Jesus' day were so caught up in their own business that they would often clumsily bump into things and people and then keep going and leave the mistaken mess for someone else to clean up.[38] Jesus was so caught up in his Father's business that he would often bump into the people seeking him out, homing in with his Father's eye on those who needed him the most, enter their story and join it with his story, and linger alongside while cleaning up their messes.

THE JESUS WALK

Our first questions about the value of a book, of a human being, or a musical composition are: Can they walk? Even more, can they dance?

GERMAN PHILOSOPHER FRIEDRICH NIETZSCHE (D. 1900)[39]

An old Latin motto reads *Festina Lente* or "Hurry Slowly." Even when you're moving fast, *festina lente* ("hurry slowly"). Jesus was a master of the Festina Lente Walk. And Jesus' *festina lente* stride had a limp that went with it but only showed up in the presence of human need.

There is an old legend about the devil appearing to St. Martin of Tours (316–397) in the form of Christ. Martin looked him over carefully, and then asked him, "Where are your wounds?" A Christ without wounds, or a church without wounds, or a faith without a limp, is a liar and a deceiver. We are called, like Thomas, to touch the wounds of our world and in that touching find "My Lord and my God!"

South African biblical scholar Stephan Joubert, in his study of Mark, has done the most research into this subject of the signature of the Jesus step. "Jesus had an enigmatic walk,"[40] he concludes. Jesus had a fast-paced gait, an "urgent" demeanor, but he was never self-absorbed or oblivious of his environs. A hurried walk without ever being in a hurry is Joubert's provocative summary of Jesus' signature step.

I call this the Christ carriage, and the way Jesus carried himself, the Jesus stride.[41]

DESIGNER JESUS

A fool is known by his gait.
ECCLESIASTES 10:3

<u>The Jesus Stride:</u> In ancient times, "watch your step" or "watch their every move" had different meanings that they do today. The Roman philosopher and statesman Cicero (79–51 BC) himself said that bodily motions and gestures were signs made visible, and part of one's education was learning to read "the signs" and get to know people by their walk. You could identify who someone was by their step, their walk. When they walked, how they walked, with whom they walked, and where they walked was autobiography in space and time. People used the body and its movements as a map to measure one's identity, integrity, and sincerity.

Like dance is today, everyday movement was then a means of expressing and amplifying one's sense of identity, belonging, alienation. We misread admonitions like "Make me to know your ways, O Lord, teach me your paths" (Psalm 25:4) or "walk just as Jesus walked" (1 John 2:6), or "I have no greater joy than to hear that my children are walking in the truth" (3 John 4) or "walk worthy of the Lord" (Colossians 1:9–12) which Paul uses three times if we just see them as pedestrian metaphors. In Jesus' day, emotion was expressed in motion, as your feelings were shown less in your face than in your pace, in your toes as much as in your tears.

THE JESUS WALK

The road was where [Jesus] was to be found, and it was his classroom, podium, laboratory, and sanctuary.
PILGRIM ALONG THE CAMINO DE SANTIAGO DE COMPOSTELA[42]

According to the Talmud, there were at least seven or as many as ten kinds of ancient Pharisees, each one identified by their mode of movement and custom of conveyance.[43]

(1) One group was known as the "Dashers," or "Bandy-legged" (Nikfi). They shuffled along the road, scarcely lifting their feet from the ground, but "dashed them against the stones," that people might think them absorbed in holy thought.[44]

(2) Another group was the "Mortars" who were known by their cap or "mortier" which would not allow them to see any passers-by. Like blinders on a horse, these mortar-boards ensured that their meditations would not be disturbed. "Having eyes, they saw not."[45]

(3) The "Bleeders" make us think twice about Paul's "thorn in the flesh." Bleeders were Pharisees who inserted thorns in the borders of their garments to prick their legs in walking to be constantly aware of their sins and to repent.[46]

(4) The "Cryers," or "Inquirers," weaved in and out of crowds crying out, "Let me know my duty, and I will do it,"[47] virtue-signaling their devotion and dedication.

(5) The "Almsgivers" had a trumpet sounded before them heralding their arrival and summoning the poor to receive some hand-outs.[48]

DESIGNER JESUS

(6) The "Stumblers" shut their eyes when they went abroad that they might see no women, being "blind leaders of the blind."[49] Jesus called them "blind Pharisees," or "fools and blind." Also known as the "Bloody-browed" (*Kizai*), their foreheads were forever bleeding to signify their avoidance of even looking at woman. To avoid looking at women, they would shut their eyes and so bump their heads and brows to the point of bruising and bleeding.

(7) The "Immovables" were known for their motionlessness and catatonia. They stood stationary like statues for hours, together "praying in the market places."[50]

(8) The "Pestle Pharisees" (*Medinkia*) kept themselves bent double like the handle of a pestle, showcasing their humble and contrite hearts.

(9) The "Strong-shouldered" (*Shikmi*) walked with their back bent to symbolize the carrying on their shoulders the whole burden of the law.

(10) The "Dyed Pharisees," called by Jesus "Whited Sepulchers," cloaked their gross hypocrisy and gross immorality with excessive externals of devotion.

And this was just the unique plethora of gaits that characterized only one of the four sects of first century Judaism:[51] Pharisees, Sadducees, Essenes, and the Freedom Fighters (Zealots and the even more radical Sicarii).

The scholar who has done the most meticulous research on ancient Peripatetics is Timothy M. O'Sullivan, who in his massive 2012 masterpiece *Walking in Roman Culture* shows how one's style of walking indicated social status and was itself an identity marker. In O'Sullivan's words, "a family gait was no less distinctive than a family nose," and that "bodily comportment passed from one generation to another."[52] The Roman funeral parade showcased the entire family's ability to walk their identity. One's "gait," or how one "carried oneself" which is what I'm calling 'the Jesus Stride,' "represented identity in motion, the most important aspect of an individual's entire physical reality animated in space and time."[53] Clothes were more than fashion in ancient Rome; they were an identity statement. But even more than your clothes was your manner of walking.[54] "You can identify fools just by the way they walk down the street!" the wise Solomon claimed.[55]

> *The Torah scholar should not walk with erect stature and head held high (lit., 'throat thrust out') as it states '[. . . for the daughters of Zion are haughty,] and they walk with outstretched throats and gazing (or winking) eyes' (Isaiah 3:16). He should not walk [in small, delicate steps, placing his] heel beside [his other foot's] big toe, casually, as do women and the arrogant, as it states, '. . . walking and floating do they go, and with their legs they entice' (ibid., end of verse). [The Torah scholar] should not run in public and act crazily. He should also not bend his stature [in exaggerated fashion] as a hunchback. Rather, he should look downwards [slightly] as one standing in prayer. And he should walk even-paced as one busy with his matters.*
> MAIMONIDES ON THE WALK OF A TORAH SCHOLAR[56]

The nobility or *aristoi* had a different style of walking than slaves and the *hoi polloi* (common people). Free men had a "measured" or "weighty" gait, but not too "measured." You didn't walk too slowly, because that was considered feminine and so showed indecisiveness. You didn't walk too fast, because slaves were always running, dispatched to do their master's bidding. It was important you get your "walk" right because Romans were known for being peripatetic, for being a "walk-and-talk" culture that did almost everything while walking. In some ways, walking was Roman elites' golfing. While walking you conducted business, hired "lectors" to read to you, debated politics, conducted family conversations. There was an art of walking as much as there was an art of war, an art of theater, an art of dance, or an art of love.

"Walk On" (U2): But this was not just a strange Roman custom. It was central to what it meant to be a Jew. The term "Halachah" means literally "A Way to Walk in the World." Halachot, or Halachos in the plural, is your "gait," or "path." The Halakah is the full body of Law that mandates our "way of walking"—our behavior, beliefs, and practices. As a way of life and not just a religion, it envelops us in everything we do. Thus the Jewish faith is called "Halachah" or "The Way for Us to Go." One may say "This Halachah," in referring to a specific Law, or "The Halachah," when referring to the Law in general. But how you move through the world, your motion and emotion, is Halachah.

The Roman historian Tacitus (55–117), who despised Christians, was known for a phrase: *solvitur ambulando* or "the problem is solved by walking" or best of all "walking unravels the problem." Some people think the problem is solved by talking (*soliloquo*).

Some people think the problem is solved by sermonizing (*sermo*).

Some people think the problem is solved by writing (*scribendo*).

Sometimes I think the problem is solved by showering (at least that's where my mind is clearest) or by sleeping (at least that's where I connect the dots).

There is nothing more revealing than to see a thinking person walking, just as there is nothing more revealing than to see a walking person thinking.
AUSTRIAN NOVELIST AND POET THOMAS BERNHARD (D. 1989)[57]

Some people think life's problems are solved by walking. Walking at three miles an hour can be a healing time, offering the opportunity to re-member and re-calibrate the rhythm that is at the heart of each of our souls.[58] Human eye movements while walking are the basis of EMDR treatments.[59] Albert Einstein confessed that the main reason he went to his office at Princeton was to walk home with Kurt Godel, "the greatest logician since Aristotle,"[60] and re-conceptualize the mysteries of the universe.[61]

Maybe "The Way" needs some lessons in walking again. Or hiking. Maybe our faith needs more footpaths. Some *Solvitur Ambulando*. Maybe the problem IS solved by walking.[62] Maybe it's not enough to develop one's mind and spirit. Maybe we also need to perfect our stride and walk. Maybe it's time followers of Jesus learned to walk again, and to get close enough to Jesus to pick up his bad habit of running to those in need and then the healing halt.

The Jesus Gait: The Jesus Walk. The Jesus Stride. The Jesus Gait. This was the essence of discipleship. You apprenticed to learn the gait of the one you followed. That's why you followed close, and why the "dusting" by the "Master's feet" was so important. It proved you were shadowing your mentor close enough to learn their distinctive walk, demeanor, comportment, and conversation. Discipleship required learning to speak with the language of your body.

May you be covered in the dust of your rabbi.
TRADITIONAL RABBINIC BLESSING[63]

Hence the wordless testimony of the Christian martyr Perpetua (d. 203), a noblewoman who boldly met her death by walking into the lions' arena with a "shining face and calm step." The pathway Jesus prescribes ignores the judgments of others and instead embraces the power and authority of God over all. The Jesus stride is a humble hastening to those in need. Jesus found the proud walk of the scribes and pharisees with their elaborate entourages an unseemly floorshow at best, a horror-show at worst. Jesus took his wounds with him into eternity. Did Jesus take his walk with him into eternity, or did his gait change in his resurrection body? Could that be one reason why even his disciples and his family didn't recognize him?

THE JESUS WALK

The Jesus Walk is not always a "walk in the park," even when it involves a "walking away." But we have been given our marching orders: to spread the "Good News" as foot soldiers and messenger runners for Jesus. Our marching papers are the Scriptures, where march means move: move our feet to give the gift of "good news" (*euangelion*) to the world. In the words of Episcopal priest and professor Margaret Guenther:

> But Jesus' command is inexorable: if you want to walk with me, there are no excuses. No days off. You're obsessed with riding your stationary bike every day and taking all your vitamins and checking your email and flossing your teeth. Well, this is your real obligation. It won't kill you. You might get tired or bored or scared or fed up, but this is the condition for your walk with me. It doesn't happen any other way, Put on your sandals or your sneakers or your hefty boots. Pick up that cross and let's get going.[64]

The "beautiful feet" in Isaiah 52:7 and Romans 10:5–15 is the beauty of the feet of the runner no matter how bruised and bloodied and battered they may be: "How beautiful are the feet of those who bring good news!" The beauty of feet is the message they carry of God's love for us, God's gift of grace toward us, God's mercy which endures forever.

Other than Jesus, the runner from heaven to earth who died on the cross with the shout "God has done it!" or "It is finished!" or "You're Saved," no one knew more about bloodied feet than the Apostle Paul: "we sailed under Cyprus because the winds were contrary."[65] Go with God and you'll get "Contrary Winds." There is always a "to-the-contrary" tilt to the Jesus Walk:

> For though we walk in the flesh, we do not walk according to the flesh, for the weapons of our warfare are not of the flesh, but divinely powerful *for the destruction of fortresses.*[66]

According to Gerard Manley Hopkins, our vocation in life is to "give beauty back"[67] to our Creator. What is beauty? The beauty is the relationship . . . the walk with God, the walk with ourselves, the walk with creation, the walk with others, the second-mile walk with others. When you learn the Jesus Walk, you are back walking in the Garden with God. It's the very reason we were created in the first place.

Every day I walk myself into a state of well-being and walk away from every illness. I have walked myself into my best thoughts, and I know of no thought so burdensome that one cannot walk away from it.

THEOLOGIAN SOREN KIERKEGAARD[68]

<u>Walk Worthy:</u> What would it mean or look like for the church to . . .

Walk into people's story and connect the Jesus story with their story?

Walk without pretension?

Walk without fear of failure or rejection?

Walk with the staff of humble confidence?

Walk with the humility of "I Surrender All?"

Walk with the confidence of "Faith is the victory, Faith is the victory, Faith is the victory that overcomes the world"?

Walk with the calm conviction that tomorrow is a done-deal because the power of the living God is guiding your gait?

Maybe the church should reclaim one of Paul's favorite phrases "walk worthy of the Lord"[69] instead of the overworked word "fellowship." Paul's image here is of Adam and Eve walking the garden with God in Eden. The phrase is striking in its intimacy. God's favorite thing to do with God's creation is to walk with Adam and Eve in "the dew of the day," of dawn and dusk. As every gardener knows, dawn and dusk are the best times to walk any garden. Dawn and dusk are when nature comes alive. Dawn and dusk were Jesus' favorite times of day, a time he often spent in prayer, which may be nothing more, nor less, than "walking the garden with God" as God asks us, "How does your garden grow?" and we seek counsel from the Master Gardener of Life.

Thoughts and Prayers: Prayer puts us in the right place and right posture to have the right relationship with God and the right thoughts about life. There are dozens of memes calling out the overuse and emptiness of the phrase "thoughts and prayers." The memes satirize the phrase as a cliché that excuses inaction, like the one listing "thoughts and prayers" as 0.00% effective beside other dubious solutions.

Yet we lose something precious if scorn swallows earnest

intercession itself. For at its truest, prayer engages higher faculties than any online post—seeding our minds with visions and ventures instead of outrage. A thought and prayer which is truly a thought and prayer will lead to something more than thoughts and prayers. In fact, there is no higher level of engagement than thoughts and prayers, which lead to all other lesser engagements, if we truly understand how thoughts and prayers are things. As Proverbs teaches, "as you THINK in your heart, so you are."[70] Paul implores setting our thoughts and prayers on "whatsoever things are true, honest, just, pure, lovely, of good report—think on these things."[71] If thoughts and prayers are "things," there is nothing BEYOND or GREATER than thoughts and prayers. More than voicing rote words, prayer attunes hearts to holy frequencies, awakening our innermost being.

Did songs lift Jesus from abject misery? In the pit of Caiphas' basement dungeon, he unlocked chains on others by singing and praying the psalms (Psalm 88). On the cross, with nails and jeers pressing in, Christ sang prayers (Psalm 22, 31) and prayed mercy upon murderers. Jesus unleashed redemption by thoughts and prayers. Prayers shape worlds. Intercession is intervention, and change comes more from thoughts and prayers than denunciations and vociferations. First in imprisoned hearts, then chained limbs. Thoughts and prayers ripple outward, awakening hope, action, and revolution.

THE JESUS WALK

Sit, walk, or run, but don't wobble.
OLD ZEN SAYING

"Walk Worthy" is the essence of intimacy with the divine and the encounter with God: "walking the garden with God" and "walk just as Jesus walked."[72] If the point of The Lord's Prayer is not to say it but to become it, for all of life to become a "Lord's Prayer," then most importantly, we walk as a prayer in motion.[73]

It is "no longer I, but Christ who lives in me."[74] Authentic prayer begins with the awareness that Christ is praying in me as I take the "worthy walk." This is the "in secret" to which Jesus refers.

> For it is not you who speak, but the Spirit of your Father speaking through you.[75]
>
> God has sent the Spirit of his son into our hearts, crying, 'Abba! Father!'[76]
>
> Likewise, the Spirit helps us in our weakness; for we do not know how to pray as we ought, but the Spirit himself intercedes for us with sighs too deep for words . . . for the Spirit intercedes for the saints according to the will of God.[77]

Surrender to the Spirit marks the beginning of a lifelong journey of prayer walking as a Lord's Prayer. When we learn this Jesus "worthy walk," the needy will no longer sit on the circumference of a disciple's consciousness, but at the core. If a disciple in general, and preachers in particular, are not willing to wash dirty feet, and then step on some of those same toes, we'll never shine shoes for mission in the world. The Messiah chose to spend his life "at the end of the extension cord," as we would put it today. At the wrong end of power, prestige, "places-to-be." Not where powerful people gathered in all the important places, but where the power grid seemed to be running at its lowest.

We can stand on principle or walk in relationship. We can stand proudly on our dignity and power. Or we can walk humbly in God's grace and glory.

"Marche ou crève" ("March or die")
UNOFFICIAL MOTTO OF THE FRENCH FOREIGN LEGION

<u>Walk with God:</u> One of the Bible's shortest (five-word) sentences with the longest fuse is this: "And Enoch walked with God."[78] What a mission metaphor for life, and "walked with God" is used to describe God's relationship with some of Israel's greatest heroes like Abraham and Noah. Enoch's "walking with God" echoes Adam and Eve's nightly "walk with God," and indeed in some ancient Hebrew traditions Enoch was charioted directly from Earth to Eden, where he awaits reunion with God's people while expounding on Torah and keeping the incense burning.

Enoch's "walking with God" is translated by the LXX

as Enoch "pleased God" or "brought God pleasure," which Hebrews brings out and plays off.

> By faith Enoch was taken from this life, so that he did not experience death: "He could not be found, because God had taken him away." For before he was taken, he was commended as one who pleased God. Without faith it is impossible to please God, because anyone who comes to him must believe that he exists and that he rewards those who earnestly seek him.[79]

We don't "walk with God" in order to gain something, or garner success, or reach an end, or attain salvation. We walk with God to bring God pleasure and for the sheer joy of the walk, a walk done by faith not by sight. And we walk by, in, and for faith alone. The daily walk with God, the human relationship with the divine, is enough reason for any walk. Though others will watch our walk and be influenced by it.

The "walk with God" is not just a lone walking but a community walk. In the Perigord region of France, there is a Randonnée nocturne ("nocturnal hike" or "night walk") tradition of walking together at night. Some inhabitants of several villages meet up and walk together through a long summer's night, helping each other make it through the night.[80]

Watch Your Step: People are watching every move you make. Sometimes your feet tell more about your faith than your mouth or hands. In his legendary "Letter from a

DESIGNER JESUS

Birmingham Jail," Martin Luther King, Jr. tells the story of a seventy-two-year-old woman who walked everywhere rather than take segregated buses: "My feet is tired but my soul is rested."[81]

Every step you take
I'll be watching you.
ROCK BAND THE POLICE, "EVERY BREATH YOU TAKE" (1983)

Our souls can be "at rest" even when our feet are tired because, in some of his last words to us, Jesus promised "I AM with you always, even unto the end of the age."[82] Or in the song version of these words (in Latin *Eos Numquam Solos Ambulare*): "You'll Never Walk Alone."[83]

So we walk in the promise of a designer Jesus disciple. We walk so that others, when they walk away, have a spring in their step and new get-up-and-go to their walk. That's heaven's gait.

STUDIO LIVE

1) Are you a walker? Do you know any walkers?

    Some of the greatest minds in history were walkers—Jesus, Plato, Nietzsche,[84] Kierkegaard, Bertrand Russell. Virginia Woolf called her urban walking "street haunting."[85] Charles Dickens composed a lot of "A Christmas Carol" while taking walks in 1843.

    Literary tourists can follow the "Keats Walk" where the poet took walks along the water meadows south of the market city of Winchester and wrote his great ode "To Autumn" on 19 September 1819. Charles Darwin had a "thinking path" or sandwalk which he used daily at Down House (Kent, UK), and tourists can walk those same steps Darwin did. Just as they can do the same at William Wordsworth's Dove Cottage, where a well-worn stretch of graveled garden walkway testifies to the "walk-through" of many a line of a poem, each one taken for a walk.[86]

    Physicians often rate walking as the best exercise for the body.

    * Might walking also be the best exercise for the mind and spirit as well?

    * Have you found walking enhances the creative and thinking process?

2) Do a Bible study (or series of worship experiences) on some of the most famous walks in the Bible:

> Sola Fide: The Essene Walk . . . Mark 2:1–12
> Sola Scriptura: The Garden Walk . . . Genesis 3:8–24
> Solus Christus: The Emmaus Walk . . . Luke 24:13–35
> Sola Gratia: The Damascus Walk . . . Acts 9:1–19
> Sola Deo Gloria: The Calvary Walk . . . Mark 15:20–39

3) Rousseau is supposed to have believed that humans think at walking pace. In other words, the very rhythm of walking creates the biological conditions necessary for an individual to clear the mind, scope the landscape, and read the signs. Thomas Hobbes had his walking stick custom outfitted with an inkwell/inkhorn, the quicker to jot down brainstorms as they occurred to him en route.

   * Do you do your best thinking when in motion or when still?

   * Tell stories of how you have found walking-pace wisdom to be true (or not true) in your own life.

4) We are all descendants of walkers. Is jogging an equivalent of walking?

   * Does jogging stimulate the same inspirations as walking?

   * Does the look of a jogger's face versus a walker's face mean anything?

5) It used to be that every village, and every church, had footpaths. We have ploughed them up, paved them over, or straightened them out with stones.

   * Is there anything special about footpaths? If so, might footpaths be seen as an endangered species, needing

to be protected in some way like bald eagles or black panthers?

* Is the resurgence of footbridges, like London's Millennium Bridge that opened in June of 2000, evidence of our desire for footpaths?
* Does your church have any footpaths?
* Do you think the churches of the future will be more pedestrian friendly than they are today?
* Do you like the idea of walking to church?

6) What are some walking prayers that you have or might want to use in your hikes? What prayer walks have you done? Here is one example:

> With each step I take, I live your presence, O God.
> With each breath I draw, I inhale your love.
> With each beat of my heart, I pulse your grace.
> Guide my steps, O Lord, and lead me on the path
>   of righteousness.
> Help me to see the world through your eyes, and to
>   love others as you love them.

7) A psychologist whose every written word calls out for consideration is James Hillman (d. 2011). One of those rare students who eclipsed their mentor (Carl Jung), Hillman is a fundamentalist about the psychology of walking: "We may be driving, literally *driving*, ourselves crazy by not attending to the fundamental human need of walking."[87] Nothing issues in the twin blessings of "ah-ha's" and "ha-ha's" better than walking, he insists.

"It allows our souls their legs, our heads their faces, and our bodies their animal styles."[88]

* Do you think Hillman is on to something? How important is walking in your own life?

* What do you think Hillman means when he says that walking "allows our souls their legs, our heads their faces, and our bodies their animal styles"?

* How does walking help us to "drive ourselves crazy"? How does it help to prevent us from going crazy?

* What are some of the ways that walking can help us to generate "ah-ha's" and "ha-ha's"?

* What are some of the challenges that we face in finding time to walk regularly, especially in our modern, fast-paced world?

* How can we create more walkable communities, especially in urban areas?

8) Listen to this mock-up by some anonymous lyricist of the Neil Sedaka song "Breaking Up Is Hard to Do!"

> Please let me sleep a little while
> When I'm tired, it's hard to smile
> Got to sleep the whole day through
> 'Cause waking up is hard to do

I'm so sleepy, I cannot stand
Think the Sandman used too much sand
Let me sleep or I'll kick you
Waking up is hard to do

They say that waking up is hard to do
Now I know, I know that it's true
Don't say I must awaken
Instead of waking up I wish that I was
sleeping in again

I beg of you, please let me sleep
Without my rest, I'll surely weep
Without sleep, joy bids me adieu
'Cause waking up is hard to do

* To what extent is the dominant walk of the church today one of sleepwalking?

* Are we sleepwalking through the world God has called us to serve, dreaming of yesteryears and better days instead of a "new heaven and a new earth?"

9) "Gematria" is the giving of numerical value to Hebrew names or phrases. The numerical value of the Hebrew word "Torah" is 611, and when Moses's 611 commandments are combined with the first two of the Ten Commandments which were the only ones heard directly from God, the number of commandments in the Torah (Five Books of Moses) are 613. The Ten Commandments are included in the 613. Isaiah reduced the number of commandments to six (Isaiah 33:15):

> The one that walks righteously,
>
> The one who speaks uprightly;
>
> The one that despises the gain of oppression;
>
> The one that shakes clear his hands from laying hold on bribes
>
> The one who stops his ears from hearing of blood
>
> The one who shuts his eyes from looking upon evil
>
> The prophet Micah reduced them to three (Micah 6:8):
>
> "Love mercy, do justice, walk humbly."

* In light of what you've read in this chapter, how does "walk humbly" encompass "love mercy" and "do justice"?

* Can you tell a story of when you allowed yourself to be mercied?

10) There have been many attempts at explaining the power of walking in nature to bridge and bring together the body, mind and spirit. But one of the most famous is this quote from Robert Louis Stevenson: "It is not so much for its beauty that the forest makes a claim upon men's hearts, as for that subtle something, that quality of air that emanates from old trees, that so wonderfully changes and renews a weary spirit."[89]

* How would you explain and explore "that subtle something"?

* Do only lovers really know the meaning of the unforgettable phrase, "that subtle something"?
* Have you ever had an experience in nature where you felt a deep sense of connection to your body, mind, and spirit? If so, can you describe what that experience was like?
* Stevenson writes that the forest "makes a claim upon men's hearts." What do you think he means by this?
* What are some of the ways that nature can help us heal from emotional and physical wounds?
* How can we use nature to cultivate a sense of awe and wonder in our lives?
* What are some of the ways that we can protect and preserve nature for future generations?

11) Discuss the Four Walks of Jesus:

> Doxa Walk
> Charis Walk
> Doulos Walk
> Zoe Walk
>
> Doxa emphasizes the majesty and splendor of God's glory.
> Charis focuses on the generous grace that God freely gives.
> Doulos conveys humble service and obedience to God.
> Zoe expresses the rich, meaningful life found in Christ.

12) Here's a smarmy story, but maybe a good parable to begin a conversation on the nature of arrival and arriving:

> An Olympic athlete became seriously injured and needed to learn to walk again. The healing process was slow, agonizingly so, and he became quite discouraged. A physical therapist who felt called to help with his healing challenged him with a cool surprise if he would only join him in climbing a nearby mountain.
>
> So the athlete trained hard and fast to climb the mountain. When he successfully made it to the top, he looked around for the surprise. Although the view was astounding, he asked his therapist what was so special awaiting for him in the view.
>
> The mentor replied, "That's it. You're looking at it." The athlete got angry and grumbled that he thought there would be more to the summit than what he was seeing. The therapist replied that his challenge to climb to the top was never about reaching the top but about making the climb itself.

* What is the relationship between journey and destination?
* Is life more about the journey or the destination? Or both?

13) Dream Artists is not a bad description of the walk of faith. There is nothing we do more than dream. Dreaming is our number one mental activity, waking or sleeping. When we're awake, we're often somewhere in la-la land day-dreaming and sleep-walking. When we're asleep, we're dreaming, whether in REM mode, or not.

We dream in narratives that put our feelings into story and metaphor. Our brains organize the day in narrative form, not so much making a story out of what happened as crafting stories that reflect what we feel about what happened. We are all narrative artists that invent stories to organize our feelings and fears. We aren't sleep walkers but sleep artists.

* Share the kinds of dreams you have, and whether it is easy or hard for you to remember them.

* How do you handle dreaming with your kids?

14) The name of the first Native American saint, Tekakwitha, means "The one who walks groping her way forward."

* How well does St. Kateri's one name "Tekakwitha" describe God's mission for the church today?

* How would you describe the terrain the church is groping its way through? Desert? Jungle? Flood? Earthquake? Volcano?

* Get more specific and talk about different categories of terrains like technological, theological, or moral the church is currently navigating.

* What gives you hope that the church can find its way even when "groping" blindly at times?
* How might listening to marginalized voices like St. Kateri's help the church find direction again?
* What lessons can the church today learn from how past saints persevered despite uncertainty?

15) Develop a playlist of songs with "walk" or "walking" as the theme. What can these "walk" songs teach us about "Just a Closer Walk?" Explore the theological meaning of some of these "walk" metaphors? To prime your playlist pump, here are some of the first songs that come to mind:

> Johnny Cash, "I Walk the Line"
>
> George Jones, "You Gotta Walk That Lonesome Valley"
>
> Unk, "Walk It Out"
>
> Migos, "Walk It Like I Talk It"
>
> U2, "Walk On"
>
> Aerosmith, "Walk This Way"
>
> Credence Clearwater Revival, "Walk on the Water"
>
> Lou Reed, "Take a Walk on the Wild Side"
>
> Kelly Clarkson, "Walk Away"
>
> The Four Seasons, "Walk Like a Man, Talk Like a Man"

The Proclaimers, "And I Would Walk Five Hundred Miles"

16) Read aloud Romans 10:13–15:

> "Everyone who calls on the name of the Lord shall be saved. But how are they to call on one in whom they have not believed? And how are they to believe in one of whom they have never heard? And how are they to hear without someone to proclaim him? And how are they to proclaim him unless they are sent? As it is written, 'How beautiful are the feet of those who bring good news!'"

Then read the whole quote from Isaiah 52 in context:

> Therefore My people will know My name; therefore they will know on that day that I am He who speaks. Here I am! How beautiful on the mountains are the feet of those who bring good news, who proclaim peace, who bring good tidings, who proclaim salvation, who say to Zion, "Your God reigns!" Listen! Your watchmen lift up their voices, together they shout for joy. For every eye will see when the LORD returns to Zion.

* Talk about beautiful feet. What makes your feet beautiful?[90]

17) Dante's *The Divine Comedy* (1308–21) is one of the most important works of literature in the Western world, with

a profound impact on Western culture. The masterpiece begins as follows:

> Midway in our life's journey, I found myself
> In a dark wood, for I had lost the path
> That does not stray. . . .
> For so long I went that I could see
> No hope of rising to the light,
> And the dark wood grew ever more so drear.
>
> And then, at last, I saw a little light
> Along the side of a mountain, far away;
> And towards that light I made my weary way.
>
> (Canto I, 1–3,12)

* How might this describe your own life?
* What do you think the "dark wood" symbolizes in the journey of life? Why might someone lose their way?
* When have you felt like you lost your path and were searching for light again? What gave you hope?
* What guides people towards the "light" when they find themselves lost in doubt, sin, depression, etc.?
* How might community/others aid someone who has lost their way to find the path again?
* What role does memory of happier times play in pushing through dark periods?
* Does losing one's way necessarily mean straying from God, or just becoming misdirected generally?

- Why is it significant that Dante finally sees the light on a mountain? What might the mountain represent?

- How might art, beauty, and literature like Dante's offer a light to follow for some people?

18) How do you recognize life's "this is the way/walk in it" moments?

19) Have someone play the Nettie Fowler song in the Rodgers and Hammerstein musical *Carousel* (1945). Sing together "You'll Never Walk Alone." Then enter the realm of these questions:

- When in your life have you felt completely alone versus supported? What made the difference?

- How has someone else's presence made you feel like you could get through a difficult time?

- What gives you hope when circumstances seem bleak?

- How willing are you to ask others for support when you need it? Why can that be hard?

- Who do you know that could use encouragement to keep persevering through a challenge right now?

- Have you ever been surprised by who was there for you during a low point?

- How can we honor the people who "walked with" us through past valleys?

- How might you actively support others who feel they are walking alone right now?

* Why might European footballers have adopted this particular song as their theme song?

20) For a book on how to read the Bible like a walker, see John A Beck's *Along the Road: How Jesus Used Geography to Tell God's Story* (2018). Have someone from your discussion group read the book and report on one or more of the twenty chapters showcasing how to organize a trip through the New Testament like a walker.

Chapter 2: Touch
The Jesus Touch

Touch is the first language we learn, and it's the last language we lose. It's a universal language that transcends all cultures and backgrounds. A gentle touch can calm the soul and soothe the wounded heart. It can communicate love, support, and empathy without ever saying a word.

MEDIA MOGUL OPRAH WINFREY[1]

A JESUS HUMAN LIVES THE DESIGNER JESUS' TOUCH. Designer Jesus living is the healing power of touch

Jesus is portrayed in the Bible as The Toucher—someone who touched the untouchables, and allowed himself to be touched. The touch of Jesus has the power to save, salve, and heal. Jesus touches us to heal us.

Designer Jesus living touches others. Five things Jesus expressly commanded us to do, all of which involve touch in some way: help the sick, awaken the lifeless, embrace the rejected, care for the mentally ill, and give freely. Or as the NIV translates Jesus' words: "Heal the sick, raise the dead,

DESIGNER JESUS

cleanse those who have leprosy, drive out demons. Freely you have received; freely give."[2] No wonder philosopher and psychologist William James (d.1910) called touch "the alpha and omega" of our attention, affection, and all our attempts to change the world.[3]

> *One design you are to pursue to the end of time: the enjoyment of God in time and in eternity. Desire other things, so far as they tend to this.*
> FOUNDER OF METHODIST MOVEMENT JOHN WESLEY (D. 1791)[4]

Jesus spent more time in the gospels healing than anything else.[5] You can't separate "salvation" from "healing" in the Jesus story, for they mean the same thing.[6] It is not just our spirits that bear the divine image. It is also our bodies. Respect for the body, your body and the bodies of others, is a part of what it means to live Jesus.

To be sure, Jesus wasn't the only wonder worker of his day. Both Jews and Romans could list dozens of divinely inspired miracle workers. Jesus was different in that he didn't use magical formulas or chants, refused pay, took time to enter into relationship with those who sought his help, and eagerly touched the unclean and untouchable.

Frederich Nietzsche once advised readers of the Bible to wear protective gloves while handling the story, there is so much uncleanliness on every page. Jesus saves not by some magic trick of *deus ex machina*, but by entering into our story, becoming one of us, and suffering with and for us. The Jesus

Touch, the touch of love in the "midst" of pain and hurt, is the greatest healer.

It is not divine design, but human determination in disobedience that has created a world in which there is no way of being human without suffering. But Jesus looked on no condition of mind or body as incurable, and no body as untouchable. Jesus seldom talks about love as a noun, almost always as a verb. When Jesus is asked "Which commandment is the first?" he answers with the Shema from Deuteronomy 6:4. He espouses and passes on tradition. But he makes one change, yoking tradition and innovation. Jesus adds a new phrase not found in the Hebrew original: "and with all your mind."[7]

Jesus expanded the Jewish Shema prayer further by incorporating Leviticus 19:18: "Love your neighbor as yourself." The rabbi Hillel had also paired these commandments from Deuteronomy and Leviticus as the Torah's ethical essence. But Jesus pushed this ethic to radical new bounds—beyond just loving your fellow Israelite. His parable of a despised Samaritan as the righteous neighbor redefined "love thy neighbor" as a universal ethic across ethnic, religious, and social divides. Whereas Hillel's context was instructing fellow Hebrews, Jesus prescribed enemy-love for the marginalized and outsiders. In this way, he built upon but also revolutionized the foundations of Jewish morality laid by predecessors like Hillel. The neighbor encompassed all, even untouchables.

Touch-Addicts, Touch-Phobics: Touch possesses immense power—to heal or harm. And in navigating touch, we remain early learners. Modern society exhibits confused extremes: we compulsively fondle screens but recoil from skin. Our hands grow more tech-fluent than tenderness-fluent; fingers made for swiping, not stroking gently. We can't stop touching our electronics, even with touchscreen gloves, but cringe at touching others. Our fingers are more tech-compatible than flesh-compatible, more keyboard compliant than kingdom compliant. However, the kingdom calls for a loving literacy of touch, for caresses that mend.

Christ modeled a sacred touch that cured broken bodies and honored each spirit's consent. Shall we retrain our hands to bless? To touch technology with temperance, and humanity with utmost care? The path starts by renouncing touch used to indulge power or violate trust. Then with patient practice, we can cultivate touch that conveys selfless affection, not selfish obsession. Like all language, touch needs wisdom and grace to heal rather than hurt. Our handprints can manifest malevolence or mercy.

Many public schools around the world, reflecting our increasingly touchless, third-rail culture, impose a one-meter rule. Teachers are forbidden to cross that great divide of one-meter in their relationship with students, whether in a positive or negative direction. Jesus crossed that great divide in virtually everyone he met, breaking the boundaries of broken bodies and hurting minds with redemptive abandon.

We imagine ourselves as skin-clad creatures, beings encased in skin—discrete entities separated by this wrapped flesh. But our body's borders are porous. Skin proves no impermeable barrier, but a conduit for transmitting messages between inner and outer realms. The Bible is a prime example. Gutenberg used the skin of pigs, calves, sheep, and goats to bind the first printed Bibles so the Word could spread to the ends of the earth. The Story knows no bounds, but every Bible must have its binding.

This envelope of skin bridges rather than severs; it communicates rather than confines. Through the nerves undergirding skin, we receive the world's subtlest signals—a caress's comfort or an icy breeze. Our touch in turn speaks volumes. Skin breaches no true boundary; it links our inner seas to the ocean of humanity and creation enveloping us all. Its nerves intertwine our depths with others in tangled webs of need and meaning. To reconsider skin as connection rather than confinement expands identity beyond ego. If spirit overflows the skin's limits, so too must compassion.

"I've Got You Under My Skin"
FRANK SINATRA (1956)

Thriving Takes Touching: Why do mammals breast feed? The obvious answer is: food. The deeper answer is: touch. Even creatures who are fed "by hand" experience the benefits of touch. The brain needs stimulation that comes from contact and connection if it is to develop.[8] We thrive, at every age, only when in social environments that "stimulate" us sensorily. Sensory deprivation is literally torture. Fulfilment and happiness happen only in relationship, but that doesn't mean that you need to be around people all the time. Sometimes you need to keep your own company, inhabit solitude, and explore the relational space of the self.

When it came to his disciples, Jesus needed to be "with" and close to them. But sometimes he needed to be alone or away from them, hiding out in Bethany. We all need withness and withdrawal, society, and solitude, time together and time apart, pack time together and sack time alone. Of course, even in a solitary state we are never solitary, alone but not alone, our solitude ensnared in the same rope that attaches us to each other and drags other voices and visions along with us wherever we go.

In Gethsemane's Olive Garden, Jesus grappled with God to the point where he would brood blood and scalp skin (*hematidrosis*). In the garden, Jesus broke all boundaries between earth and heaven and opened up his whole body for the healing of all beings and diseases. It was the ultimate symbol of Jesus putting his own "skin in the game." For all who think the game is over, or the game is up, Jesus' sweating of blood and scalping of skin tells an alternative story, one of hope and redemption through sacrifice and love.

So that when the handkerchiefs or aprons that had touched his skin were brought to the sick, their diseases left them, and the evil spirits came out of them.
ACTS 19:12

How did Jesus lay hands upon the hurting—was it a poke or an embrace? Did he smite foreheads in magical theatrics, or wrap sufferers in redemptive bear hugs? Scripture paints no Faustian portraits, but tender connections. He soothed by tracing ears, cradling children in his lap, anointing eyes with intimate mud-spit touch. Even when breaching taboos of contagion, Jesus caressed the untouchable. His hands channeled holy power by connecting spirit to spirit, skin to skin. In truth, the cross stretched Jesus' arms not to condemn but to engulf humanity tenderly. Nails did not restrain his reach, for Love had already spread his arms wide enough to encompass all who would enter in. However imperfect our touch, we can mirror such grace. Jesus blessed all flesh by bridging touch and transcendence with awe—not dominance, but radical service through loving contact.

God has built our touch into the very design of the universe. We know from quantum physics that the very act of observation changes what is observed. It's called the "participant-observer" syndrome of "Schrödinger's Cat." Our mere "observing" makes us a participant in the outcomes, and our touch just enhances the impact of our participation. We cannot know what the world would have been like if we were not part of it, participating in it. Simply by being, we conceive our world and each other. For good or ill. The quality of our participation, the integrity of our connection, the state of our touch, is a matter of life and death. A thriving faith depends on His touch.

Human hands are for holding other hands.
Human arms are for holding other humans close.
NATURALIST AND CAMBRIDGE PROFESSOR HELEN MACDONALD[9]

DESIGNER JESUS

Truth Is Touching. Touch Is Truthing: A disciple is one who connects with people through the Jesus Touch. And the Jesus Touch is the definitive version of what Bruce Springsteen famously voiced as the "Human Touch" (1992). Failure to thrive is a real diagnosis for orphaned infants who weren't cradled and cuddled. Humanity is forged in the crucible of the touch. Faith fails to thrive when we don't let Jesus touch us with his healing grace, and when we don't touch others with cradling touches and cuddling hugs.

What made Princess Diana so beloved by the world that they drowned the gates of Buckingham Palace in flowers? Diana never wore gloves. The rest of the royal family always wore gloves, especially when they were out and about meeting the public. But not Diana. She specialized in the touch whether she was touching AIDS sufferers or picking kids out of the gutters of Calcutta or the dirt of Africa.

The touch of Jesus was always physical even if he was only "present" with people. He looked people in the eye, he called them by name, he reached out to them, he dined with them, he stopped when someone touched the hem of his garment, he let the woman anoint his feet with oil, he allowed the woman to sit at His feet. All who were "present" in His Presence were physically touched by what they were needing the most. One paralyzed man he even called his "son." One bleeding woman he even called his "daughter."

Intimacy with the Divine One who sat before them as the Human One is just as available to us today as it was to Jesus' first disciples. Life's pace keeps us racing with calendars full and clocks ticking. In the coarse gaze, the careless touch, we miss the "life touch" of God's Spirit in the everyday of ordinary moments where Jesus is present with us.

Keep in Touch: Touch remains language's most eloquent dialect for relating. Relationships arise through interactions; bonds build by contact's alchemy—the handshake morphing strangers to kinsfolk. No true knowing exists untouched. And so diverse cultures sing similar welcome in their own tongues of touch—kisses, double-kisses, pats, rubs, slaps, shakes—yet one message is conveyed: "Turn to me, see me, feel we are kin." For discipleship, what finer teacher than the resonance of clasped hands, the tenderness of an embrace? No hurried text or meme rivals skin's powers of vulnerability and trust. In arms enfolding the shunned, outcasts become neighbors. From feet-washing disciples to children received through hands laid upon their heads, Jesus composes His gospel of grace note by intimate note. If we aspire to such love, we too must become fluent in touch's poetry.

Touch is the most reciprocal of senses—you can't touch without being touched back. Aristotle showed long ago how touch is co-extensive with life itself and death.[10] Touch entails both reciprocity and reversibility. In touching I am being touched. Touch enables me to feel myself. Or as Aristotle put it, "I feel myself only by the favor of the other. It is the other who gives me to myself insofar as the return to myself and my own actions or affections always supposes the other."[11]

DESIGNER JESUS

The most fundamental and universal of all senses is the sense of touch . . . While touch is separable from other senses . . . the sense of touch is inseparable from life itself: no animal is deprived of touch without also being deprived of life.

FRENCH PHILOSOPHER JEAN-LOUIS CHRÉTIEN (D. 2019)[12]

"Alone, he does not know who he is" is what one of the greatest poets of the twentieth century W. H. Auden (d. 1973) said about one of the greatest poets of the nineteenth century, Oscar Wilde (d. 1900).[13] This is true for all of us in whatever century. We are relational beings brought to life by the touch of another. But that touch is becoming rarer and riskier. The digital world makes us more connected than ever before. But the quantity of those connections seems in inverse relationship to the quality of our connections and the authenticity of our connectedness.

In the digital age's narcotic haze, faces fade to bland masks. Young generations lose the nuance of expression; avoid direct gazes. As psychologist James Hillman laments, "absence of meeting faces" yields no "interpersonal face"—merely isolated visages where "its expression does not matter."[14] We anesthetize against exchanging glimpses into souls. Likewise, cocooned in cars, we need not "prepare a face to meet the faces that you meet," muses psychologist Bernd Jager.[15] Uniformity numbs.

Contacts or Connections: Yet intimacy remains encoded

THE JESUS TOUCH

in flesh—evident in the fervency of teammates clutched in huddles. Bodies bent together toward one goal line. The disciple too yearns for hands joined tight in common mission. In every grasp and clasp, the impulse to touch, be touched, transmits living zeal skin-to-skin. No screen can replicate a look's reciprocal language, nor can virtual emojis match the face's unspeaking eloquence. If we aspire to genuinely see and be seen, naked hands may surpass staring eyes.

At the core, to be is to be in relation—to dwell in bonds that banish aloneness, to turn contacts into connections. We exist not as discrete but enmeshed, strands in a web. Most of life is not a problem to be solved but a relationship to be lived. Therefore, most challenges of life are not problem-solving, but relationship-living. You don't "have" relationships. You "are" relationships. A dog presents no puzzle requiring clever solution—simply a friend to treasure. A dogwood blooms not to vex with botanical analysis—merely to delight our senses through sight, scent, and touch. Are we not creatures wired for engagement?

Our Maker wove us for intimacy. Reality proves not atomistic bits but a tapestry of interlacing hearts and minds. At its best, living means touching the sacred somewhere in each thread. If the divine peeks through every creature tenderly embraced, then love alone illuminates the mundane and vast alike.

We may think we are looking for something, but we all are really looking for someone. To follow Jesus is to bet your life on the fact that we all look for someone, not something:

someone to love, someone to touch, someone to hold on to, someone to follow, some One. Jesus' new community is not about winning or losing, succeeding or failing, but the belonging of the beloved.

There are few more pernicious lies in life than the myth of the "self-made individual," the sovereign individual, or the myth of "self-reliance."[16] Even though three out of four USAmericans think the phrase "God helps those who help themselves" is in the Bible, the phrase is not Holy Scripture and in many ways is anti-Scripture (sorry, Benjamin Franklin). No one is "self-made" or sovereign. No mature human is self-reliant, but fully embedded in connections and contexts. Indeed, to live a disconnected life is to breed violence and live dishonestly.

It would be inexcusably selfish to be lonely alone.
LONDON POET REBECCA PERRY[17]

Jesus is the one who touches—and invites us as he invited Thomas to touch his wounds and the woundedness of others. Wounded lives, a wounded church, a wounded world needs the Jesus Touch. Life flourishes under the Jesus Touch. The Jesus Touch is the ultimate in connection. "Untouched" is the ultimate in isolation and loneliness.

The Jesus life is one that is always "unfinished" and in need of "touch-ups." We don't look for "finish" in ourselves and others, but for the unfinished in need of "touch-ups." If someone appears too "finished" then something is awry.

THE JESUS TOUCH

Picasso was constantly touching up his paintings when he saw them in the homes of those he visited. He could not leave them alone, even after they left his studio and went into the homes of patrons. Nothing he touched was beyond touch-ups, no matter the distance. Jesus is in the business of always touching and touching-up our lives. As soon as somebody dies, we start touching up the portrait. Jesus does just the opposite.

Togethering is Tabling: Disciples are people who leave no one "untouched." And the best place to "touch" is at the table. The space station never planned for a table, but the astronauts insisted on gathering at a common table where they could squeeze together. The astronauts forced the engineers to put a table into the space station.

If you grew up in Appalachian culture, or Asian culture, you know what you're looking at. A lazy Susan was the centerpiece of the table. It included important condiments, like salt, ketchup, sugar, hot sauce, vinegar (vinegar goes on everything, don't ya know?), and pickles. You also knew what was medically wrong with everyone because this was the family's medicine cabinet, and as the wheel went round, you saw what everyone was taking. In Asian culture, the lazy Susan is where the entire meal is often served with everyone sharing in rotating the dish for everyone's enjoyment.

I have written elsewhere about the importance of the table in Jesus' own ministry, and how the table in the home was the replacement for the Temple after it was destroyed in the year 70. But what I failed to appreciate is that it is not just that sharing meals are a big first step in forging faith and improving relationships. But it also matters how that meal is served. A meal taken "family style" from a lazy Susan (central platter) or a set of platters scattered on the table is the best for improving relations, minimizing divisions, reducing competitiveness, and deepening understanding. Formal meals where people are served individual plates by waiters are the worst kind of meals for building bridges between heads of state and deepening relationships among friends, family, strangers, and enemies.[18] The best tables are those with lots of passing of plates, sharing of food, and touching going on. Because touching is togethering.

True communion requires togetherness. Plutarch instructed in his *Table Talk* (c. 100), "do not invite one another merely to eat and drink, but to eat and drink together." Jesus' promise to be present when two or three gather together reveals fellowship's essence. Breaking bread alone nourishes only the body. Breaking bread together nourishes spirits united. There is no true gathering without togethering.

Of course, cultivating such holy togetherness through the Jesus Touch remains an imperfect work-in-progress. We will not always properly convey the healing intimacy Jesus modeled. Yet still we strive for a lightness of touch that avoids controlling manipulation or concealment of truth. Our goal is not "retouching" others with make-up churches and artificial relationships. Rather we share in the sincere ritual of fellowship—gathering in grace—not disguising our flaws but affirming our bonds in God's spirit. Where two or three draw together in trust, touching each other's burdens, there love flows as freely as the wine.

In Irish folklore, lies kill fairies. Every time you host a lie, or tell a lie, or live a lie, a little bit of reality dies. A flower, a tree, a bridge bites the dust. A "retouched" version of Jesus is a lie, and every lie absorbed into the body stamps out life.

> *I cannot stop thinking about Jesus, reading about Jesus, listening to Jesus books and lectures, and praying to Jesus. Jesus truly takes me in, but in the most beautiful and life affirming way. Jesus is the ultimate cleanse and cure.*
> FRIEND AND COLLEAGUE CHRISTOPHER ERIKSEN, ESQ.

In the holiness tradition, there is a song that every child learns in Sunday School: "Let the Beauty of Jesus Be Seen in Me."[19] Modernity's designing of Jesus necessitates heightened emphasis on the designing of Jesus. The modern church designed Jesus and stripped away the signs of Jesus in favor of "Let the Principles of Justice Be Seen in Me" or "Let the Leadership Skills of Success Be Seen in Me" or "Let the Justice of Jesus Be Seen in Me." All of this "retouching" has designed Jesus from our life and churches.[20] We need the designer Jesus, the designing Jesus, the design of the Jesus Touch back in our life and churches.

A "retouched" Jesus, whether the restoration is done by the highly skilled hands of "leadership" or "church growth" or "missional church" or "social justice," does not restore the face and place of Jesus to the church. In their own way they are at best fillers, coverings, and colorings that falsify, things that represent the failure of authentic connection to the person of Jesus, things that botch and block the real healing touch. When not knowing who Jesus is becomes a virtue, and not knowing what one is talking about a homiletic brag, the church ends up where it is today.

> *All these changes did the Merciful One make, stripping off and putting on; for He had devised a way to reclothe Adam in that glory which Adam had stripped off. He was wrapped with swaddling clothes, corresponding to Adam's leaves., He put on clothes instead of Adam's skins; he was baptized for Adam's sin, he was embalmed for Adam's death, he rose and raised up Adam in his glory. Blessed is he who descended, put Adam on and ascended.*
> THEOLOGIAN EPHREM THE SYRIAN (D. 373)[21]

<u>Touch Proves Real:</u> The real Jesus Touch leads to a life beyond transformation, which is outside in.[22] The real Jesus Touch leads to inside-out changes, a metamorphosis into a "new creature" that is changed "from glory to glory" that can only be described as transfiguration and transubstantiation. Sin is an aversive life, but when we touch Jesus, he sanctifies us to touch others.

When you are in love, it is often quite apparent to others because it is said you "beam with joy." You glow. You radiate happiness. Why? Because you've been "touched" by love. Those in love with Christ radiate love and loving touches because you now live life out of what philosopher Henry James called "the strangely accepted finality of relationship," a solid core of inescapable love and indwelling intimacy with God. The Jesus Touch leads to so much more than "transformation."

"Transfiguration." What does this big, fifteen-letter word mean? When a caterpillar enters a chrysalis, it is transformed. When a caterpillar emerges from that silken shroud and becomes a butterfly, it is transfigured. The Holy Spirit is in a bigger business than transformation: the transfiguration business.

Jesus wants us to reach out and understand each other from the inside out, not from the outside-in, as the world does thru CVs, resumes, awards, and categories, but from the inside-out. It is much easier to admire people most for what they do, what they accomplish—not necessarily for what they essentially "are."

To describe the process by which metanoia leads to metamorphosis, there are four better "trans" words than "transformation," depending on the context:

 1) Transfiguration

 2) Transcarnation

 3) Transubstantiation

 4) Transcendence

Once you've been touched by the love of Christ, transfigured into God's image and transubstantiated into a new human, a transcarnation takes place that opens to transcendence. The word "entheogenic" can mean, most widely, anything that generates God within. Not a divine presence from the outside in, but from the inside out. Transfiguration is entheogenic discipleship, and part of a larger framework of entheogenic ecclesiology.

It's natural at first to be awestruck, lovestruck, dumbstruck, breathless, and speechless. Soon you realize, however, that love is much deeper and vaster than a dazzling bright light. But you never get used to new ways of seeing and touching God, the world, each other, and creation that comes from transfiguration. The nuggets of moments you give to someone, your gifts of transubstantiation, or all-thereness—body, soul, spirit—are bouquets of flowers, boxes of chocolates, communion wafers of presence that transfigure everyday moments and transcarnate the most basic elements of life.

High-Touch: Although this seems counter-intuitive at the moment, the more virtual and digital the future gets, the more touch will replace sight and sound as the major cultural interface. When the question of "is it real" pervades all aspect of human existence, and "reality" shows are the ultimate in unreality, the resistance of the real, the pushback of touch, will be a major reality check for identity and integrity. In an iconomic world lorded over by spectral entities like stories and images and sounds which are not themselves real things, touch will be the means by which "real things" are known as "real."

If someone asks you to define sin, try this: Ask the questioner to open their hands as wide as they can. Now ask them to tell you the various things they can do with these open hands and stretched fingers—things like play a piano or violin, plant gardens and pick flowers, style someone's hair, or salve someone's wounds. Now ask them to close their hands as tight as they can, and tell you want they can do with these same hands now—punch, hit, hurt, even kill.

This is sin: a life closed on itself. A life "*incurvatus in se*," as Augustine of Hippo then Martin Luther called it, a life "curved in on itself" facing inward not outward, where mirrors replace lamps, and navel-gazing only reveals the personal lint and never the table linen. Jesus gives us a true "inner gaze" or the ability to see inside another and to look at life from their point of view. You are most YOU when you are least into yourself and most into others.

Couch Christians: Our pews are settled with too many couch Christians—spiritually obese nurslings addicted to sugar-high worship demanding to be "fed" but preferring to gorge on a binge diet of fast-food theology and candy-cane sermons, never properly nourished with veggies and vitamins and visionary fiber. To be a disciple of Jesus is to pick up a fork in order to put on an apron. To be a disciple of Jesus is to keep your hands open, never to be afraid to receive from God's hand, never to be afraid to reach out for the hands of others, always grateful for the hands that God puts in yours.

The Jesus Touch is always making room for others to be, and to be themselves.

The Jesus Touch is always moving over for others to belong and bestow what is uniquely them.

The Jesus Touch is always making us embodied beings,

DESIGNER JESUS

designed to be embedded beings, embedded in relationships. Christ in me needs Christ in you for Christ in us to be Christ for the world.

---

*Sin is not a distance from God,
it is a turning of our gaze in the wrong direction.*
FRENCH PHILOSOPHER SIMONE WEIL (D. 1943)[23]

With lips recently wetted by the wine Jesus served him at the place of honor at the Last Supper table, Judas betrayed Jesus with a kiss. That most intimate of touches, the kiss, is both a symbol of love and a symbol of loving hate, both of which can take hold of a person. The word Judas uses for "kiss" when he talks to the priests refers to the common greeting of the day. But the word used to describe the kiss he and Jesus actually share in the garden is the same word used to describe the kiss shared by the father and the prodigal son.

Yet the early church is known by its kissing, the very symbol of betrayal.

Christians took the kiss, the very symbol of the touch of betrayal which had been heavily invested with history, and turned it into the dominant symbol of blessing that marked their worship.

Christians took the cross, the very symbol of torture which had been heavily invested with history, and turned it into the dominant symbol of blessing that defined their identity.

Christians took the christos oil, not the expensive pistos

oil used for healing and anointing but the christos oil, the very symbol of the cheapest and most modest of oil used for lamps and cooking, and turned it into the dominant symbol of messiahship: Jesu Christos.

Jesus Living uses the language not of transform but of transfigure. You transform outside in. You transfigure inside out. You transform into a likeness. You transfigure into a presence. *Jesus Living* transfigures us into the very personage of Jesus and transmigrates us into the very presence of Jesus himself.

Christianity is not in the information business.
Christianity is not in the communication business.
Christianity is not even in the transformation business.
Christianity is in the transfiguration business.
Christianity is in the transmigration business.

In what can only be called transubstantiation, Jesus shapes form and beauty out of chaos and disarray of our lives. That's why the ultimate ambition of my life: to live a life that emblazons on all its labels, "Designed by Jesus."

Christus Victor: Everyone I touch, whether it's in the form of a handshake or a hug, gets blessed with the Latin "Christus Victor." I cross my fingers, and with the Spirit and Son fingers taking cruciform shape, I say these words under my breath: "Christus Victor" which means "May Christ be victorious in your life." One of my great ambitions in life is to hallow every person I meet, even if it's only for a few seconds, with the Jesus Touch.

Doubt the power of touch? When the flickering shadows

on the screen morph into a snarling monster, when your stomach lurches as the rollercoaster plummets into darkness, when the gaslight in the alley casts grotesque dancing shadows—it's not enough to hear your friend's panicked screams. Your hand shoots out, fingers digging into their arm, grounding you like a lifeline. The warmth seeps through the terror, a tangible reminder that you're not alone, that all is not lost. In that touch, reality snaps back into focus, the nightmare retreating to the edges of your vision. It's a primal language, this desperate clutch for connection, a silent reassurance that even in the face of the unknown, we're not alone.[24]

John L. Bell from the Iona Community has written a modern hymn called "A Touching Place" (1989). Here is one of the stanzas:

> To the lost Christ shows his face,
> to the unloved he gives his embrace,
> to those who cry in pain or disgrace
> Christ makes with his friends a touching place.[25]

Jesus Living makes every life, every community, every family, a "touching place" and a "lazar."

Like Elijah and Elisha,[26] Jesus loved to heal by touch.[27] Even lepers. Recent scholarship has exposed multiple levels of exclusion of lepers in Second Temple society. But there was not the level of social isolation of lepers that most scholars and preachers portray.[28] In fact, the very fact that Jesus' favorite hang-out was in the home of Simon the Leper, whether healed or not, suggests a degree of interchange that was not as severe as the popular reconstruction of the bells, yells, disheveled hair, and torn clothing.

In fact, it is most likely that Lazarus and Simon the Leper were one and the same. If not the same, then a father or a brother. All four gospels tell of Jesus arriving at Bethany six days before Passover, but Matthew and Mark mention Simon, while John mentions Lazarus, as the residence of his home the last week of his life. Abbé Drioux identified all three as one: Lazarus of Bethany, Simon the Leper of Bethany, and the Lazarus of the parable, on the basis that in the parable Lazarus is depicted as a leper, and due to a perceived coincidence between Luke 16:30 and John 12:10—where after the raising of Lazarus, Caiaphas and Annas tried to have him killed.

A lazar was the name of a leper colony, lazarette, leprosarium, or lazar house where people with leprosy (Hansen's disease) were quarantined. The term lazaretto, which is derived from the biblical figure Saint Lazarus, can refer to quarantine sites, which were at some time also "colonies", or places where unwanted people lived or were sent. Many of the first lazarettes were operated by Christian monastic houses.

Every Christian home and heart is a lazar—a hospitality place not for outcasts and outliers, but for fellow human beings. Christians don't look for the good in others. Christians look for the Jesus in them, and invite Jesus in.

There are only two places in the gospels where Jesus calls a living person "Son" and "Daughter." The designation "Daughter" is given to the woman who reaches out of nowhere to touch the hem of his garment, a woman who had been bleeding for twelve long years, and is healed in an instant. "Daughter, your faith has healed you. Go in peace." The designation "Son" is given to the paralytic who with some high-touch friends dares to rip out Jesus' own roof while he is speaking and be dropped down in front of his face. Jesus seems to draw closest to those who most dare his touch.

The Jesus Touch packs a punch in healing each other and showing the world, as Australian poet John Kinsella puts it, the "simple/grace of human contact."[29]

> *And Moses built an altar and called the name of it,*
> *"The Lord is my banner" (Jehovah-nissi), saying, "A*
> *hand upon the banner of the Lord!"*
>
> EXODUS 17:15-16A

<u>Peal Out the Watchword:</u> In the ancient world, when you put your hand upon the banner that belonged to a king or general, it was a pledge of allegiance. It meant you were willing to march under that flag, to give your loyalty to that banner, and even risk your life in fidelity to that person. In the words of a Frances R. Havergal hymn never sung any more:

> True-hearted, whole-hearted, faithful and loyal,
> King of our lives, by Thy grace we will be;
> Under the standard exalted and royal,
> Strong in Thy strength we will battle for Thee.

Disciples of Jesus are those who have stepped forward,

stretched out their hand, touched the banner of the Lord, and marched "under the standard exalted and royal."

Once we have come alive from the Master's touch, a disciple touches the banner of the Lord and hoists the banner high. Disciples constantly unfurl the flag to pass on the banner touch to others. "If I be lifted up from the earth," Jesus promised, "I will draw all people to me."[30] To lift high the cross is to lift high the banner of the Lord for others to touch.

DESIGNER JESUS

STUDIO LIVE

1) How would you respond to this as a sermon title: "Getting into Bed with Other Christians?" Yet every pastor, nurse, and hospice chaplain has climbed into bed with dying parishioners and hugged and sung them into eternity.

   * Discuss our squeamishness about "touching." Is it ever ok to "get into bed with other Christians." How do you give someone permission to touch? How do you want to spend those final moments of human life when we all will face, what Charles Darwin called, the "ineluctable consequences of structural design?"[31]

2) The Spanish poet Fernando Pessoa has written that "The only aristocracy is never to touch."[32]

   * What might that mean? In Jesus are we all peasants? Or is our low-touch, no-touch culture turning us into aristocrats?

   * How would you define true "nobility?" Is it detachment from things? Is it detachment from others? Is it an integrity that comes from within?

   * What made the Jesus Touch so powerful? Was it only his divinity?

3) "If we don't know the satisfactions of solitude, we only know the panic of loneliness," MIT's Sherry Turkle asserts in her *Reclaiming Conversation* (2015).[33]

   * Do you agree that we are losing the ability to have

meaningful conversations because of our obsession with technology?

* Are we using technology to avoid solitude and to connect with others in superficial ways?
* How do we remove barriers to touch while protecting solitude and silence?
* What is the difference between solitude and loneliness?

4) Philosopher and psychologist William James (d. 1910) declared that:

> Of all the senses it is on the skin that the dependence on a foreign object is most immediately felt. The eye and ear can fly free, but the skin stays at home . . . The original sensible totals are skin-totals, and contain coexistent parts; and objective realities which have duration are first emphatically given in the experience of exertion (through the skin and muscles) needed to keep the impression.[34]

James argues that touch sensation relies more on external objects compared to vision or hearing, making it the most relational of the senses, requiring a contact stimulus to function fully.[35]

* What do you think? Would you rate touch above hearing, seeing, tasting, and smelling as our number one relational sense organ?

* Do you think James is right that our other senses, such as sight and hearing, can be fooled by illusions and tricks of the mind. But our sense of touch cannot be fooled in the same way?

5) Might touching extend in time as well as in space? Even touching those in The Cloud, the communion of saints?

    Medieval scholar Caroline Walker Bynum points out the difference in how Muslims and Jews think of holy sites as opposed to Christians. The former both define shrines as those places sanctified by some sacred event that is recorded in their Scriptures. From the very beginning Christians defined shrines differently. They went on pilgrimages to shrines made sacred by the presence of a holy person. At these shrines pilgrims tried to touch, even take away a portion of the dead body of a saint, or of Jesus himself.[36]

* Discuss the role of relics. Do you have any "relics" in your home?

* Is there a difference between collecting relics of celebrities and sports stars and relics of the saints?

6) One of the most touch-sensitive, touch-intensive professions is gardening. God designed humans for a garden, gardeners who conserve and cultivate this garden planet. We are not fully alive until we have been awakened by the organ of the wind playing the trees and water, and the grit and grime of dirt on our hands. It is the touch of dirt, getting our souls soiled, digging down and touching

the muddy, the needy, the toady—that brings humans to life.

* Who are the gardeners in your midst? Ask them share about the benefits of getting dirt under their fingernails.

7) Champagne won't bubble from a glass that is surgically, antiseptically clean. The effervescence, the ebullience, the bubbles of faith come from lives that have been dirtied and then cleaned by hand with paper and cloth. This is what is behind the ancient Japanese art of *shou sugi ban* or *yakisugi*, the making pieces of art and beauty out of charring and scorching wood. You take cedar, maple, oak, or apple, hand-burn and burn-off the soft wood that conceals the natural grain and ligaments and removes the cellulose that insects live on. What remains highlights textures and tones and coloration, as well as turns surface cracks and splinters into deeply defined fractures and fissures that tell a story of their own from the inside out.[37] It is one of the most tactile-rich art forms on planet Earth.

Gardening is best done in a cooperative spirit, as all humans are gardeners communally engaged in improving a common landscape on God's garden planet of the Milky Way Galaxy called Earth. What is often missing in our understanding of the design component is this ecclesial dimension of Christianity, which is much more than "teamwork." The ancients believed that it was the church itself that believed, and that its faith, the faith once for all delivered to the saints, was there to sustain our faith and strengthen it when we falter. Our "trusteeship" of the

Garden is one we share together; it is both an individual and an ecclesial one.

* How does the role of touch factor into your sense of being a "trustee" of this garden planet?

8) The first production in England of Friedrich Schiller's play *Joan of Arc* (1801) features one of the greatest props ever conceived for the stage. While hugging close to the original, the producers add one new prop, the only prop used in the whole production. Joan of Arc sees a helmet just brought in from the battlefield, and exclaims "It is mine!"

This "helmet" is a clump of wet clay molded around Joan's head. It looks like a queen's headdress, but it dirties the hands of all who touch it, who then leave muddy streaks everywhere they go, like in a Br'er Rabbit folk tale. Or like cook Typhoid Mary (d. 1938), who blessed people with food and fever at the same time, the prop symbolized how even the best of us spread the dirt even when we do the divine. From head to toe, we not only have "feet of clay" but a "helmet of clay."

A disciple is both saint and sinner, or in Martin Luther's famous Latin phrase "*simul justus et peccator*," both one who is elevated and one who is tainted. And you can't separate one from the other, the sublime from the slime, the saint from the sinner. The very best in us is woven from tissue-thin thread that wraps around what is the very worst in us.

Every Advent I wonder whether it is Jesus Christ, or

Charles Dickens, who is most responsible for how we celebrate in candy cane and chocolate bark the Christmas season. But Charles Dickens' daughter Katey confided in a postscript to Bernard Shaw her frustration at how her "sainted" father, contrary to how he was being remembered, was not always a "saint," as only a family member could know: "If you could make the public understand that my father was not a joyous, jocose, gentleman walking about the world with a plum pudding and a bowl of punch you would greatly oblige me."[38]

* If we are clay, from top to toe, how can we evaluate our own need for touch compared to others' needs?

9) Captain Cook introduced the word 'tattoo' from Polynesia to the Western world on his return from the South Pacific in the late eighteenth century. There has been a resurgence of tattooing in modern Western culture in the past three decades, with prevalence rates as high as 32% of US population according to a 2023 Pew Research Center survey, including 22% who have more than one. This is up from 21% in 2012.[39] Tattoos are more common among younger adults, with 46% of millennials (ages 26–41) having at least one tattoo. Tattoos are also more common among men (39%) than women (26%). What may be most surprising is that Christians in the US are more likely to have tattoos than the general population.[40]

* How are tattoos inscriptions of identity?

DESIGNER JESUS

- * What tattoos do you have in your midst?
- * If you could tattoo any passage on your body, what would it be? (I might choose Philippians 4:13: "I can do all things through Christ who gives me strength.")

10) Body piercings can come in a variety of shapes and forms. "For the love of money is a root of all kinds of evil. Some people, eager for money, have wandered from the faith and pierced themselves with many griefs" (1 Timothy 6:10).

- * What are some of the "piercings" that can mark us and scar us, for good or ill?

11) "Let the beloved of the Lord rest secure in him, for he shields him all day long, and the one the Lord loves rests between his shoulders" (Deuteronomy 33:12).

- * Discuss God's protective, enveloping touch in your own life.
- * What are some practical ways that we can rest secure in the Lord, even when we are facing challenges?
- * How can we help others to experience the Lord's love and blessing?
- * What are some examples from the Bible of people who trusted in the Lord and were protected by him?
- * How can we grow our faith in the Lord's love and goodness?

Chapter 3: Face
The Jesus Face

The face is the soul of the body.
AUSTRIAN PHILOSOPHER LUDWIG WITTGENSTEIN (D. 1951)[1]

THE GOAL OF EVANGELISM AND DISCIPLESHIP IS NOT merely to inform others about Jesus and call them to repentance. It is to transfigure our lives and the lives of those around us with the image of Christ. Evangelism and discipleship are design issues: imprinting those around us with the face of Jesus on us. Disciples don't "put on a happy face." Disciples put on a Jesus Face. Disciples are incarnators—they pray forth and leak out GBT—the GoodnessBeautyTruth of Jesus. They irradiate the radiance of Christ.

Face of Grace: The face of Jesus is the authentic face of humanity. You can't look into Jesus' face without feeling the need to save face, resolving to change face, and being face-lifted. That's why we "seek the things that are above."[2] The beauty on which we gaze changes us forever. In Jesus' face, we can become the face of grace, the facelift of light, not the drooping gravure of gravity.

Abraham Lincoln is said to have sometimes decided on whether he would meet with someone or not on the basis of their face. He said he would never judge a young person by external features and facial characteristics. But after age forty, Lincoln believed a person's face starts to show their inner thoughts and emotions.[3] Every face is "telling." Lincoln's own weathered face, sculpted by the cares and compassion of life's challenging climates, proved his point.

In 2014, when British art historian T. J. Clark was reviewing Rembrandt's self-portraits on display at the National Gallery, he put it like this: "The face is the form of the brain in the world. It is the human brain presenting itself for inspection and reading."[4] The face is the form of the human in the world.

The lightness of being is not the absence of weight, but the ability to carry it lightly.
CZECH-FRENCH NOVELIST MILAN KUNDERA (D. 2023)[5]

If you can't see the beauty of Jesus in your face, then you need to spend more time looking in the mirror—the sacred mirror of Scripture, God's Holy Story, and your whole life story. Country-singer/comic Ray Stevens tells the truth: "Everybody's beautiful in their own way." Every face is beautiful "in its own way." Some of us are on the underside of beauty; others are on the upside of beauty. But everyone God creates is beautiful. You can't make ugly what God created as beautiful. The aged are especially beautiful, like the leaves of a tree, which reveal in the fall their true colors after having been chlorophylled by youth. Or as the seventeenth-century English philosopher Margaret Cavendish (1623–1673) put it, "Life scummes the Cream of Beauty with Times Spoon."[6]

The ultimate proof that God loves diversity and particularity: God didn't give us all the same face. Each of us has a different face, no matter the color, no matter the place. There is no such thing as "identical twins."

What Did Jesus Look Like? What did an olive-skinned Jesus look like? One of the world's obsessions for the past 2000 years is to speculate what Jesus looked like. Elvis Presley ended his life reading a book on what Jesus looked like. Elvis took a book he'd been reading on the Shroud of Turin, Frank O. Adams' *The Scientific Search for the Face of Jesus* (1972), and went into his bathroom to read on the toilet, and died.

Two cloth legends purport to reveal the face of Jesus. One is the veil of Veronica,[7] a woman who supposedly wiped the face of Jesus with a cloth as he carried his cross, leaving an image of his face imprinted on it. The other is the burial Shroud of Turin. Both cloths purportedly show the face of Jesus, the Veil through direct imprint from wiping his face according to legend, and the Shroud through his burial wrapping. Both "images" portray a bearded man with Middle Eastern features with a musing, solemn expression, nose long and slender, hair parted in the middle, with eyes large and round gazing outward, conveying sadness.

DESIGNER JESUS

The Veronica legend first appears in the apocryphal Acts of Pilate in the mid-fourth century, one of the latest non-canonical gospels. In the Acts of Pilate, the woman who touched the hem of Jesus' robe and was healed of her hemorrhage[8] is identified as Veronica. Jesus reportedly gave her a miraculous cloth, which was allegedly used to cure the Emperor Tiberius of leprosy. No veil relic was documented before the thirteenth century when veils began to circulate in Rome and were used in processions and pilgrimages. There is no historical evidence to support the existence of Veronica, and the veil itself has been shown to be a medieval forgery.

Not so easy to dismiss has been the portrait of Jesus in the Turin shroud, which has been on display regularly since 1694 and became widely known in photographs from 1898 onwards. The hotly-contested cloth in which his body is said to have been wrapped is 14.3 feet (4.36 meters) long and 3.6 feet (1.10 meters) wide. It shows a handsome face, and on the body the marks of torture and five wounds. Jesus would have been 1.78 meters tall, or 5'10", which would have been tall for his day. The Turin shroud image has a long nose, a well-shaped mouth, and abundant hair and beard.

Did Jesus have the serene face shown in Fra Angelico's (d. 1455) paintings or the rigid and hollow-boned look of the Candido Portinari (d. 1962) murals? No one can say. The gospels do not describe the appearance of Jesus.

We know very little about Jesus' face except that it was struck,[9] spat upon,[10] blindfolded,[11] and hit the ground when Jesus "fell on his face."[12] Jesus had an active face that was constantly "looking around,"[13] "looking up,"[14] and "looking lovingly."[15] At the transfiguration, Jesus' face "changed"[16] and "shone like the sun."[17]

Donkey Cross: The earliest image of Jesus is a derogatory piece of Roman graffiti, estimated to date from the second or third century, that depicts Jesus on the cross with a donkey's head. The graffiti was discovered in the 1850s on a wall in a pagan worship space beneath the Palatine Hill in Rome. The inscription reads "Alexamenos worships his god," drawn by Roman soldiers to mock a Christian named Alexamenos for worshiping Jesus. In Jesus' day gods were depicted in physical form with the head of the animal they would most appear as in dreams and visions. It was insulting to the Jews to portray Jesus as a donkey god. Unlike pagan gods, Judaism forbade any physical depictions of God, and did not associate Yahweh with an animal form.

The earliest surviving visual depiction of Jesus himself is a fresco found in the Catacomb of Commodilla in Rome, dating to around the year 240. The fresco depicts Jesus as young, beardless, short, curly-haired, seated philosopher holding a scroll. Without a halo or cruciform or any other symbols, Jesus is portrayed in a stereotypical classical style in line with the Greek idea that youth was an attribute of the gods. Like Moses and David, who were said to have been handsome, Jesus is portrayed in the earliest images as young and good-looking with hair that drapes at the nape of his neck, often in such clouds of curls it looks like clusters of grapes.

Some scholars claim "That Jesus was imagined as being a divinity like Dionysus or Hermes, a son of a god like Zeus, appears to lie behind the earliest image we have of him."[18] I think it is much more likely that another scholar has it right: "Both Judah and David are described in the Bible as handsome men and strong warriors. Although Jesus is not described physically in the New Testament, the earliest readers of the Gospels would think of him with the image of David and of Judah. That image is of a handsome man with dark, mysterious eyes."[19] The psalmist describes the Messiah as "fairer than the children of men,"[20] which is often interpreted as Jesus' physical description. This is underlined by the description of David, the ancestor of Jesus, as having "beautiful eyes and handsome."[21] Fifth century Byzantine art showed Christ as an adult with angular face bones, a thin nose, a penetrating gaze, brown beard, and his hair parted in the center and falling to the shoulders.[22]

Suffering Servant Face: The prophet Isaiah, whom Jesus himself used as the text for his first synagogue lesson, prefigured the Suffering Servant as devoid of attraction, cruelly disfigured, even repulsive.[23] The earliest Christians did not use Isaiah 53 to describe Jesus, but Celsus did. A scholar writing in the mid-second century, in a treatise against the Christians, Celsus used the unattractive, shabby, Isaianic portrait of Jesus against Christians.

Indeed, starting in the second century, a stream of thought featured this side of Jesus—degraded looks, deformed features, destitute garb. Some early Christian texts, such as the Acts of Peter and the Acts of John, describe Jesus as small, ugly, and bald-headed. But a lot of these descriptions of

Jesus' appearances were rhetorical devices used against those who would deny Jesus' human nature. In his treatise "On the Flesh of Christ" (*De carne Christi*) written around the year 210, Tertullian states: "His body did not reach even to human beauty, to say nothing of heavenly glory." And in his work "Against Marcion" (*Adversus Marcionem*) (c. 207), where Tertullian is arguing against a Docetic view of Christ as only divine not human, Tertullian says of Jesus: "He had no form nor comeliness, that we should look upon Him."[24]

The second century saint Irenaeus (d. 203) believed that Jesus had a humble appearance for theological reasons as well. Here is a quote from Irenaeus's *Against Heresies* (c. 180–85) in which he describes Jesus' physical appearance quoting Hebrew prophesies:

> For He was not distinguished by beauty of form or comeliness of appearance, but despised and rejected by men, a man of sorrows and acquainted with grief. We esteemed Him not. Surely He has borne our griefs and carried our sorrows; yet we esteemed Him stricken, smitten by God, and afflicted. But He was wounded for our transgressions; He was bruised for our iniquities; the chastisement for our peace was upon Him, and by His stripes we are healed.[25]

Irenaeus goes on to say:

> For if He had been of outstanding beauty, and His appearance had been comely, He

would have been a stumbling block to those who believed in Him, because they would have come to Him for the sake of His appearance, and not for the sake of His teaching.[26]

However, it is important to note that not all early Christian writers agreed with Irenaeus and Tertullian. Origen (d. 253) defends against charges that Jesus was ugly or deformed, portraying him as having a normal human appearance. Likewise, in *Dialogue with Trypho* (155–161), Justin Martyr refutes claims that Jesus was ugly or deficient in appearance, implying that Justin believed Jesus had a commonplace or unremarkable human appearance.

Origen, writing in the mid-third century, suggests that Jesus could be perceived differently depending on who did the viewing. His polymorphy is attested to in Origen: "Why then should there not be a certain soul that takes a body which is entirely miraculous, which has something uncommon with men in order to be able to live with them, but which also has something out of the ordinary, in order that the soul may remain uncontaminated by sin?"[27] Looked at from the human side, he was without distinction. Looked at from the divine side, he was sublime. After the legalization of Christianity in the 4th century, Jesus was depicted more frequently in art with distinguishing features and in a variety of portrayals.

<u>Nazarene, not Nazirite:</u> Certain things can be said with some assurance. Jesus did not have a long beard. Those who did were Nazirites, who were known for their long beards and abstaining of wine. Jesus was accused of drinking too much wine, and no one ever challenged his beard.[28] So he did not keep a Nazirite vow.[29] Jesus' hair length was probably four to five inches, which today is long hair on a man but in Jesus' day was normal hair for a Jew. Jesus' profession as a tekton, a craftsman or artisan, meant that he was physically active. Combined with his being a walker, wandering around Galilee and in and out of Jerusalem, he was physically fit and probably toward the lean side.

The biblical scholar who has studied Jesus' looks the most suggests that Jesus was ordinary looking—nothing unusual in his color of hair, skin, beard. Like the average Judean male, he was most likely around 5'5",[30] brown-eyed, brown to black-haired, olive-brown or honey-skinned, with lice.[31] In short, he just looked like everyone else, "nothing to write home about," or write up. "Like most of us, he was nether a stunner or stunted."[32] The fact that Judas had to arrange to pick Jesus out of the crowd with a kiss for his arresting soldiers suggests that he didn't look that much different from his disciples.[33] Several times Jesus slipped away into the crowd and could not be found, suggesting that he looked similar to other Jews living in Israel at the time.[34]

Why is the most painted figure in the history of art also the one whose face we know the least about?[35] Jesus wants our face to be his face, "in our own way." In the remarkable words of St. Cyprian of Carthage (d. 258) in North Africa, an early Christian bishop and martyr:

> And the Lord Himself says in the Gospel: "It is in yourselves that you see me, just as a man

DESIGNER JESUS

> looking in a mirror will see his own reflection." For the Spirit of God dwells in us, and the Spirit of God is the image of Christ. Therefore, when we see ourselves and each other, we are seeing Christ.[36]

Jesus himself teaches us that "Anyone who has seen me has seen the Father,"[37] and it is Jesus we serve when we feed the hungry and free the oppressed, since "in so far as you did this to one of the least of these little ones you did it to me."[38]

When the Scriptures speak "Let the light of your face shine on us, O Lord"[39] or "Your face, Lord, do I seek. Do you hide your face from me?"[40] or to "seek the face of God"[41] it is a way of talking about being recognized by God and approved of God. God's face stares us right in the face, and we miss the face of God. Christ formation is facing our face to God's face. The more our faces face Jesus, the more our own faces change into his face.

But there is a paradox here: the more we bear the image of Christ, the more we convey the Abba consciousness, the more our difference shines. Indifference to difference is the ramp to death. We follow the same Jesus differently, each one of us, because Jesus has infinite facets to his beauty which each of us reflect and refract as we live our calling, and for some of us, as we live our call within our calling.

Real Face of Jesus? Why do we not have any images or sketches of portraits of Jesus? Why did not the authors of the gospels describe his physical features?

If we did have such an image, would we worship it or

think that the image was Jesus himself? The essence of Jesus' theology is that each one of his followers can incarnate and impart his life and love. That each one of us is the face of Jesus. That each one of us is an incarnator of the image of Christ.

The real portrait of Jesus is you.

The truth of Christianity is simple. It consists of three-in-one things: Jesus is in you through justifying, sanctifying, and glorifying grace: The Way of goodness, The Truth of truth, The Life of beauty. Jesus' face always radiates the glow of beauty, reflects the luminance of truth, beams the glory of goodness.

The sap of the Spirit is within you, bringing Christ to life daily. In this important quote, Swiss theologian Hans Urs von Balthasar (d. 1988) reminds us that beauty is not a luxury but essential to humanity:

> Beauty demands for itself at least as much courage and decision as do truth and goodness, and she will not allow herself to be separated and banned from her two sisters without taking them along with herself in an act of mysterious vengeance. When we no longer dare to believe in beauty, and we make of it a mere appearance in order the more easily to dispose of it, then we lose beauty itself along with truth and goodness.[42]

Two of the most beautiful women of the twentieth century died the same week in 1997. These were the two most

DESIGNER JESUS

identifiable and written about women of their day. One was known for her glamor, designer clothes, and charity work. The other was known for her plainness, shabby clothes, and charity work. One was named Princess Diana. The other was named Mother Teresa.

You set me before your face for ever.
PSALM 41:12 KJV

Disciples look for the goodness, beauty, and truth (GBT) of Jesus in every face. "Any human face is a claim on you, because you can't help but understand the singularity of it, the courage and loneliness of it," says the veteran pastor in Marilynne Robinson's Pulitzer prize-winning novel *Gilead* (2004).[43] The ability to see and read each other's face is what distinguishes a community from a collective or a crowd. In community, every face is known. A crowd is a faceless hive, a mass mob of glob, which is the source of the anti-humanity of crowds, the mercilessness of masses.

The granularity of the gospel is what scandalized Jesus' family and colleagues. To Jesus, the blind weren't just blind, and the demon possessed weren't just demon possessed, and the lepers weren't just lepers. They were valuable persons, each one a child of God who deserved to be looked in the face and their hurts faced. Sinners were never just sinners. No matter how scandalous—and isn't "scandalous sinners" a tautology—the faceless, broken-faced, and defaced were people to love, to touch, and to face.

True Beauty is Good, and Hopeful, and Loving. Beauty, when untethered from truth and goodness, can take the world in very strange and dangerous directions.[44] GBT (GoodnessBeautyTruth) is the ultimate trump card, even besting indecencies and indelicacies and inadequacies. For example, what some would define as "lying" can be a form of truthfulness, if it is driven by goodness and wrapped in beauty. If you ask me if I like your new haircut, I can tell you how vibrant, vital, and youthful it makes you look even if I hate it and think it makes your noggin look like a burnt chicken nugget.

Beauty Spots: God created each human face as singular—unique, unmatched, unforgettable—but unfinished. Through Christ and the church, we partner in plural toward the fulfilment of God's singular creation. But no life or face is ever "finished." We all lead, and leave, "unfinished lives."

Perfection captivates, yet looms aloof. Perfection beauty does not intrigue. For true allure, a crack must fracture the sheen, peeling pretense to reveal our raw, flawed selves beneath. In brokenness, humanity gleams through. "Scarred for life" becomes the mark of hard-won character, of veils and veneers lifted.

Every face Jesus touched was a landscape of imperfections—wrinkles etching stories, blotches inking memories, crooked noses broken and mended askew. Yet Jesus found beauty within ruined flesh, embracing those society discarded. Until that promised day when the mortal puts on immortality, our flaws remain life's shine—beauty speckled, strewn, and embroidered by experiences. "When that which is perfect is come," the promise is given, "that which is imperfect shall be done away."[45]

"There is no exquisite beauty without some element of strangeness in the proportion," Edgar Allen Poe wrote in one of the most brilliant insights into beauty ever made.[46] Beauty demands some "element of strangeness"—eccentricity that engages our gaze afresh. There is slime in every sublime. Even the commonplace proves resplendent when glimpsed anew. Just as the burls that beautify a redwood trunk are really cancers the tree has had to deal with, so the bruises, breaks, and badness of life can form the most magnetic features and beauteous spots of our life.

I was one of the first to host a learning platform in *Second Life*. My problem with this virtual world and its perfect castles and villas and campuses, is the same problem I had when speaking at Chautauqua Institution in western New York, where I was plunged into pristine Victorian gingerbread and an engulfing ethos of vintage cuteness. After a couple days, I had to leave to break the spell and then come back. I needed to see some imperfection, some dirt, some grime, grit, and litter to remind me that the real world was still there.

Jesus himself seemed strange—this man who dined with rejects, healed lepers, forgave enemies. His revolution lay in daring to be strange enough to be beautiful. What the world deemed ugly, He called beautiful. Designer Jesus disciples embrace the ungainly and unseemly through eyes of grace—finding splendor in our shared scars, thrill in our collective eccentricities, rapture within hearts once broken. Therein beauty flourishes best—not in stale platitudes of perfection, but in boldly bearing our God-graced flaws.

Nathaniel Hawthorne's "The Birthmark" (1843) is a parable of life. It's the story of a husband named Aylmer who thought his wife Georgiana wasn't perfect until she got rid of her birthmark. But when he removed it, making her perfect, she died. As the birthmark faded, so did she.

> Georgiana found the gaze of her adoring husband Aylmer fixed more and more on her tiny birthmark . . . left upon her cheek at birth . . . insistent on perfection, unwilling to see in his love the evidence of any flaw or alien, he persuades his wife to let him remove it. She once saw it as a charm; now an ugly blemish. So he concocted a potion that would remove it . . . and as she drank it, the mark began to fade. But as the stain disappeared from the left cheek, she almost started fading: "My poor Aylmer, you have aimed loftily; you have done nobly. Do not repent that with so high and pure a feeling, you have rejected the best the earth could offer. Aylmer, dearest Aylmer, I am dying!" It was too true! The tiny hand had grappled with the mystery of life and was the bond by which an angelic spirit had kept itself in union with a mortal frame. "As the last crimson tint of the birthmark—that sole token of

human imperfection—faded from her cheek, the parting breath of the now perfect woman passed into the atmosphere, and her soul, lingering a moment near her husband, took its reverential flight."[47]

We don't find the perfect in the present. We find the eternity in the present.

> *Let Christ thy spouse appeare beautiful in thyne eye, since God is beautifull and that he is the Word of his Father . . .*
>
> *Beautifull then, he is in heaven;*
> *Beautifull, upon earth;*
> *Beautifull, in the wombe of his Mother;*
> *Beautifull, in her armes;*
> *Beautifull, in miracles;*
> *Beautifull, in those scourges;*
> *Beautifull, when he inviteth us to life;*
> *Beautifull, in despising of death;*
> *Beautifull, in leaving his soule, when he expired;*
> *Beautifull, when he tooke it againe in his resurrection.*
>
> CONCLUDING WORDS OF ST. JOHN OF AVILA'S *AUDI FILIA* (1556)[48]

<u>Reading Faces:</u> Christ formation is learning to read faces. Every face is different. Every face has a story to tell. Every face reveals something fresh and new about God. Christ followers are unrepentant voyeurs of people's faces, where the vastness of that one word "human" is etched in flesh in such endlessly fascinating and story-telling ways that we explore the diverse manifestations of humanity in each countenance. The fountain of faith is gushing all over the place, all over our faces and places. But the light that flows from God's presence is a "fountain of life" not just for looking, but promotes right seeing and right acting: "For with you is the fountain of life; in your light we see light."[49]

For Jesus, the face had multiple meanings. People deserve to see your real face, because Jesus' disciples look beyond the maw into the marrow. In Jesus' day, one's face presented who you were to the world. Women had to keep their face covered and could not look men in the eye because they were lowly in station and could give men the evil eye (especially blond-haired, blue-eyed women). But the age-old question "Who is my neighbor?" is irrelevant to Jesus for whom everyone, even the lowly, even the enemy, is a neighbor. The only question is, "What does it mean to live neighborly?" or better yet, "To whom are you a neighbor?" and "How are you facing your neighbor?" To see Jesus' face in each other's face is the cure for all divisiveness and nastiness.

During the Last Supper, Jesus said the one who would betray him was dipping in the same bowl. Jesus also looked at each of his disciples in the face and said, "I no longer call you servants but friends."[50] Who was the first disciple addressed as "friend" after Jesus announced the name-change? The double-dipper, double-crosser Judas.

In the Garden of Gethsemane, Jesus embraced Judas as "friend" even as Judas kissed him on the cheek as a signal for his arrest. This act of betrayal is recorded in all four Gospels: "Friend, do what you came for."[51] All of Jesus' disciples betrayed him. We are all double-dippers. But even as we betray Jesus, Jesus still looks double-dippers and double-crossers in the face and tenderly calls us "friend."

In the film *Dead Man Walking* (1995), sister Helen Prejean accompanies Matthew Poncelet as the time of his stay on death row draws to an end and the day of his execution is named.

> I say to him, "If you die, I want to be with you." He says, "No, I don't want you to see it." I say, "I can't bear the thought that you would die without seeing one loving face. I will be the face of Christ for you. Just look at me." He says "It's terrible to see. I don't want to put you through that. It could break you. It could scar you for life." I know that it will terrify me. How could it not terrify me? But I feel strength and determination. I tell him it won't break me, that I have plenty of love and support in my life. "God will give me the grace," I tell him. He consents. He nods his head. It is decided. I will be there with him when he dies.[52]

After-All: As important as the face is, it is not the end-all and be-all but the after-all. In Ernest Hemingway's novel *The Sun Also Rises* (1926), one character is asked how he went bankrupt: "Two ways," he replied. "Gradually, and then suddenly." That's what happens in life. The insides go first, and the surface is the last to go. By the time the Berlin Wall fell, or the Soviet Union collapsed, or the stock market crashed, the insides were so stricken and riddled with disease that the outer layer of skin was the only thing keeping it all together.[53] That's one reason Jesus was famous for not looking on the outward surfaces but for looking beyond the external into the inner depths of life and people.

Every depth has a surface, and every surface a depth. Jesus resisted the temptations of surface clarity that lured others to skate over the underlying problems of the deep. Here's one watermark:

> They came to him and said, "Teacher, we know that you are a man of integrity. You aren't swayed by others, because you pay no attention to who they are; but you teach the way of God in accordance with the truth."[54]

The original Greek for "you pay no attention to who they are" or "you do not look on the outward appearance" translates literally "you do not look on the face" or "you do not look at the face." In other words, Jesus does not look just on the surface. Jesus does not look on faces alone—at face values, at face lifts, "on the face of it." Jesus looks at the vital organs, especially the heart. Jesus looks behind the face at the deeper truths of the heart.[55]

Make your face shine on us, that we may be saved.
PSALM 80:19 NIV

DESIGNER JESUS

A haunting phrase finds its origins in the witness of the saints in the face of persecution. When our ancestors stayed faithful amidst persecution, and refused to betray their Lord, it was said they were "washing the face of Jesus." More recently the phrase refers to the need of each generation to "wash the face of Jesus," to rediscover his original beauty after having "dirtied" Jesus' face by various accommodations and compromises.

---

*When I wash the face of lepers,
I am washing the face of Jesus himself.*
ST. "MOTHER" TERESA (D. 1997)

The cleansing of the face made dirty by sin and unrighteousness is the basic meaning of the Hebrew word for repentance, PNH or paniym. Paniym means a turning of the face, gazing into the face [of God]. When we repent of our sin and separation from God, we "turn and face" God and confront our filth and need for a face-washing. We stand with God face to face, and we "face" our sins and "face" our true selves. The biblical call to repent is the call to face home, to return to where you came from, to turn the face from waywardness, and to turn the whole body toward paths of homecoming and hope.

One of my favorite medieval tales is about a young woman who died early in life, but was a troublemaker in heaven. So much so that she was expelled but told that if she would bring back the gift that is most valued by God, she would be welcomed back.

So she searched the ends of the earth for what God might value most. She brought back drops of blood from a dying patriot. She brought back some coins that a destitute widow had given the poor. She brought back a leaf from the Bible that one of the greatest preachers had used over a lifetime. She brought back some dust from the shoes of a missionary laboring on a remote island. She brought back many things like that, but was always turned away.

One day she saw a small boy playing by a fountain. A man rode up on horseback and dismounted to take a drink. The man saw the child and suddenly remembered his boyhood innocence. Then, looking in the fountain and seeing the reflection of his hardened face, he realized what he had done with his life. And tears of repentance welled up in his eyes and began to trickle down his cheeks.

The young woman took one of these tears of repentance from his face back to heaven . . . and was received with joy and celebration.

A smile is a curve that sets everything straight.
PIONEERING FEMALE STAND-UP COMIC PHYLLIS DILLER (D. 2012)

<u>The Smile That Sets Everything Straight:</u> Can anyone look at a baby and not smile? Can anyone look at Jesus at

DESIGNER JESUS

not smile? Jesus smiles on your face. Do you feel Jesus' smile on you? Will you let Jesus smile on you?

How much would Jesus have smiled? I have always pictured Jesus smiling at the two thieves next to him on the cross while he was suffering and dying. But smiles as we know them were uncommon in Jesus' day. Of course, just as Jesus pushed the boundaries of so many social conventions of his time, he may have violated this one as well.[56] But in the Roman culture of the first century, smiling lacked social significance as a gesture. Laughter abounded in close community, but a gentle Mona-Lisa grin was the norm in public. Whereas few things are sexier today than a white-toothed smile, open smiling that showed teeth in public was culturally problematic in the first century. This is partly because teeth were malformed and decayed (tooth brushes weren't invented until the eighteenth century); partly because baring of teeth used to be a hostile gesture; partly because loose lips and open mouths suggested something salacious more than serious.[57] Attic pictures of our ancestors seldom show them smiling. Over time, people were so resistant to opening their mouths that trigger words were dispatched to get them to smile when photography was invented: "prunes," "money," "delicious," and finally "cheese."

Smile, and the years fall from your face. Frown, and you gain twenty years. The facial gesture that utilizes the most muscles is the frown. It requires seventeen muscles in the face to frown, while a smile only requires ten muscles. But it took fourteen years for Leonardo da Vinci to get those ten muscles right on the most famous smile in history, making the Mona Lisa's smile as interactive as possible so that depending on where you looked on her face, the smile would change.[58]

How much easier is it to imagine God's frown than God's smile? We live in the light of God's smile, not the shade of God's frown. To smile is to accept, to warm up, to recognize a face at the very least, to give a sense of worth. A person that smiles at you acknowledges you as a human being and gratuitously gives you respect. This is the power of Paul's description of Jesus as God's "Yes" or God's "Amen"[59] which I have presumed to translate as God's Smile. A Jesus human can smile with two-thousand years of history in it.

The Jesus Shine: Maybe a better way of talking about God's face is in terms of shine not smile. A smile lights up the face until it shines. In fact, there is something humans need more than smiles. Sunshine. Especially the shine of the Son, where, at Jesus' transfiguration, "His face shone like the sun, and his clothes became as white as the light."[60]

There are multiple references to God's face shining, Jesus' face shining, and other people's faces shining in the Scripture:

> "Restore us, O God; make your face shine
> on us, that we may be saved" is the
> repetitive refrain in Psalm 80.

> "Let your face shine on your servant;
> save me in your unfailing love"
> (Psalm 31:16 NIV).

> "May God be gracious to us and bless
> us and make his face shine on us"
> (Psalm 67:1 NIV).

The Aaronic blessing, also known as the priestly benediction, is the earliest codified ritual blessing in the Bible.[61] It is not the earliest blessing in the Bible,[62] but these words God gave through Moses to Aaron and his sons is the most famous and widely used blessing among Jews and Christians. It is most often translated as follows:

> The Lord bless you and keep you;
>
> the Lord make his face shine on you and be gracious to you;
>
> the Lord turn his face toward you and give you peace.

My personal translation of this blessing changes the last line to read:

> May God bless you and keep you;
>
> may God make God's face shine on you and be gracious to you;
>
> may God's face radiate with joy because of you.

The Aaronic blessing, including an image of God's shining face, appears on two small silver scrolls known as the Ketef Hinnom scrolls that were found in 1979 in a burial cave in Jerusalem. These scrolls, inscribed about 700 years before Christ, contain the oldest existing text of Scripture, predating the earliest Hebrew Masoretic manuscripts by hundreds of years. The metaphor of God's shining face has such power it gave us the earliest confirmation of the antiquity and reliability of Scripture.[63]

> When Moses came down from Mount Sinai with the two tablets of the covenant law in his hands, he was not aware that his face was radiant because he had spoken with the Lord. When Aaron and all the Israelites saw Moses, his face was radiant, and they were afraid to come near him.[64]

Moses had to cover his shining face because of the doxa of the people. The Israelites couldn't stand the shine. The radiance was too beautiful. But that's the promise of the gospel. Here is Paul's version of a "woke" instruction to the Ephesians: "Wake up, sleeper, rise from the dead and Christ will shine upon you."[65] And to the church at Corinth, Paul said "For God, who said, 'Let light shine out of darkness,' made his light shine in our hearts to give us the light of the knowledge of God's glory displayed in the face of Christ."[66] The Revelation of John promises that the "pure of heart" in the heavenly city will "see His face."[67]

The Shining: All these passages, and many more, suggest that shining faces are associated with the glory and presence of God. If you live in the heavenlies, where is the heavenly shine? If you are manifesting the divine presence, does your face shine? Is it an inner-beauty shine that stirs the soul? Or is it a transient, used-car, showroom shine that seduces the senses?

The lamp is a source of light for the path we follow. The ancients believed that in some fashion the eye (hence the "evil eye") itself emitted light, making the face like a flashlight, which enabled you to see. "The eye is the lamp of the body. So, if your eye is healthy, your whole body will be full of light; . . . if then the light in you is darkness, how great is the darkness."[68] People's face should "light up" when their paths cross with a shining. A person's face is "lighting up" when something good passes by, with God's face the biggest "light up" like the sun at dawn, and Jesus dawning in you.

When Jesus begins a series of self-definitions with "I Am,"[69] his hearers would have shuddered from the rumble and the resonance of the identification with God's self-definition to Moses: "I am who I am." When Jesus declares "I am the light of the world," Jesus is proclaiming his oneness with the creator of light itself,[70] and the embodiment of the light of Torah in the face of Jesus which reflects the radiant face of God's very being.

To see the face of Jesus, is to see the light. Or in the words of the Hank Williams gospel song, "Praise the Lord, I Saw The Light" (1948). To live in the presence of the Jesus shine is to incubate in us The Shining, not Stephen King's *The Shining* that gives people telescopic abilities to see things that have happened in the past or will happen in the future, or telepathic abilities to communicate with others using our minds. Rather a "Shining" that beams a shekinah glory that reveals God's abiding presence and indwelling spirit in a person's life and a teleological trust in the providences and promises of God.

Quantum mechanics has taught us the space-warping implications of wave-particle duality, so we know that some light cannot be seen when it behaves like a "wave."[71] Sometimes the shine of Christ's presence is invisible and we don't feel it. Or feel like it.

There will be sunless, dreary days where the shine is more moonshine and the ministerial seems cemeterial. Ask Mother Teresa, now sainted even though she spent the bulk of her life-mission in the dumpster of despair.[72]

Influencer culture monetizes "authenticity," where authenticity is defined as the instant intimacy of obsessively frank airing of fleeting feelings without seasoned or moral reflection. Of course, the failure to feel, to register the "inner touch" of one's own being, is to flunk at being a whole human being.[73] But to make feelings the master sense of discipleship is to swoon in the self more than the Spirit.

Sometimes your joy is the source of your smile, but sometimes your smile can be the source of your joy.
VIETNAMESE ZEN MONK/PEACE ACTIVIST THICH NHAT HANH (D. 2022)

As Ifs or If Onlys: How do we shine when we don't feel like it? We come to faith by the grace of God, not by living faithful lives.[74] But faithful living follows as an expression of our gratitude and love for the God of grace and glory. There are no wrong feelings. There are bad choices, bad decisions, and bad actions on those feelings. But feelings themselves are neither bad nor good. They are feelings. They are what they are. You like what you like. You feel what you feel. Your pain is your pain. There are ways of expressing those feelings that build community, and ways of expressing those feelings that hurt and hamper relationships. How do we shine when we don't feel like it?

Forget the claims of belief, or the feelings of the moment, writes George MacDonald (d. 1905), the nineteenth century dissenting fantasist. Just keep moving, try to do the right thing, and let Jesus shine.

> Fold the arms of thy Faith I say, but not of thy Action; bethink thee of something that thou oughtest to do, and go and do it, if it be but the sweeping of a room, or the preparing of a meal, or a visit to a friend. Heed not thy feelings. Do the work.[75]

Shakespeare was right. In *Hamlet* (1603) Shakespeare wrote, "Assume a virtue if you have it not. . . . For use almost can change the stamp of nature."[76] Cognitive studies and brain science have backed him up. The old adage "It is easier to act yourself into a new way of feeling, than to feel yourself into a new way of acting" is one of the biggest discoveries of brain science over the past twenty years. But it's been long recognized by those like William James, in his *Gospel of Relaxation* (1892), where he calls us to lighten up and loosen up:

> In order to feel kindly to a person to whom we have been inimical, the only way is more

or less deliberately to smile, to make sympathetic enquiries, and to force ourselves to say genial things. To wrestle with a bad feeling only pins our attention on it, and keeps it fastened in the mind, whereas if we act as if from some better feeling, the old bad feeling soon *folds its tent* [italics mine] and silently steals away.[77]

Doing becomes being. Doing precedes thinking. You don't change your character and conduct by thinking differently; you change your character and conduct by acting differently. Action precedes thought.

A lifetime of "as ifs" will prevent a lifetime of "if onlys." Actions create feelings. You want to feel sad? Turn your mouth down. You want to feel upset? Frown. You want to feel happy? Smile. You want to feel determined? Clench your fists.

When you encounter someone in need when you're in a funk and not feeling like shining, don't just think nice thoughts about them and be done with it. Smile at them. Shake hands with them. Shine on them by recognizing them and helping them. Forget "mindfulness" and start some goodness and righteousness.

◇

Preach faith till you have it; and then, because you have it, you will preach faith.
MORAVIAN MISSIONARY PETER BOHLER TO JOHN WESLEY[78]

DESIGNER JESUS

No grain offering in the Temple was allowed to have leaven or honey. But every meal-offering was required to include salt.[79] British rabbi and theologian Louis Jacobs (d. 2006) explains why: "faith is much more than emotionalism, it will be seasoned with salt, signifying that life is grim but can be a stirring adventure."[80] Whether we are feeling sweet, sour, savory, or bitter, we are to be the salt of the world. We are to bring out the God-given flavors of creation through our facial recognition of Jesus in every person we meet.

Humble Confidence: Face and head metaphors convey powerful messages of integrity, intelligence, and identity. From headstrong, hard-headed, head-honcho, head-over-heels, head-start, head-and-shoulders-above, to face-the-music, face-saving, face-value, face-off, face-up, face-time, and face-lift, there is a recognition that the face conveys the essence of the human spirit. And the essence of a Jesus human is one where humility and confidence come together in paradoxical harmony. For example, the *tzitz*, or "frontlet," was positioned on the high priest's forehead to symbolize not only the confidence of the calling but also the humility of service.

Why the forehead? First, the forehead frontlet reminded the high priest of his high and holy calling, which was issued in humility, not pride. The tzitz was inscribed with the words "Holy to God," reminding the high priest that he was set apart for holy service to God. Second, the forehead frontlet was a shield from sin. The tzitz was believed to have atoning power, protecting the high priest from sinning while performing his duties in the Temple. Third, the position of the tzitz on the forehead, the seat of the mind and the will, symbolized the high priest's role as mediator between God and the people. To reflect God's glory. The tzitz was made of gold, which is a symbol of God's glory. It was thought that the tzitz would reflect God's glory to the people, reminding them of God's presence and holiness.

The Aramaic phrase "*tokfa de-mitzcha*" (also sometimes spelled "tokhfa d'mescha") translates to "hardness of the forehead" or "brazen-faced."[81] The phrase comes from ancient Jewish rabbinic literature where the metaphor of a hardened, stiff forehead symbolized a bold, brash confidence about one's beliefs and actions.

But there are nuances that separate the "hard-foreheaded" or "bold-faced" from the hard-headed and brazen-faced. In Hebrew, it is the difference between *azzut metzaḥ* and *azzut panim*.

Azzut metzaḥ literally means "strength of the forehead" or headstrongness and is associated with intellectual chutzpah. This is someone who is convinced of the rightness of their position and is unyielding in their argument. It can be good or bad, annoying and cloying in a frustrating headstrongness but at times a charming and admirable kind of chutzpah.

In contrast, *azzut panim* literally means "strength of face" and is always a detestable feature of any human. Headstrong bold-facedness is not always condemned; impudent brazen-facedness is always a scourge and character flaw. In fact, azzut panim may just be the worst insult you can throw at a Jew,

DESIGNER JESUS

a people who prize bashfulness over brazen-facedness. Azzut panim involves more than the forehead, more than metzah, but the whole face, the azzut panim: "the supercilious glance of the eye, the haughty sniff of the nose, the sneer of the lips, the vulgarity of the mouth, the closing of one ear to all reason, and the opening of the other to all malicious tale-bearing."

What turns *azzut metzah* into *azzut panim*? Take out the humility from *azzut metzah* and you end up with *azzut panim*.

In the construction of the mobile Tabernacle tent (Mishkan), the measurements prescribed for the holiest part of the Tabernacle housing the ark of the covenant (aron) are striking. They are not integers, or complete numbers or full units, but partial numbers: two-and-a-half cubits in length; one-and-a-half cubits in width and height. Why so?

It was God's way of keeping us humble. The German rabbi Nathan Adler (1741–1800) who mentored Moses Schreiber (the famed Ĥatam Sofer) at his yeshiva in the early 1770s, proposed this theological reason for this incompleteness. The people of Israel must also see themselves as incomplete, half-done, unfinished. The pride of accomplishment must always be broken. We are only a portion of what we should be, always in debt to the Lord of creation, and always in need of more knowledge and understanding. Remembering how the holy of holies is itself not made of whole numbers reminds us that we can never see any aspect of ourselves as complete and finished, which keeps us in a state of humble confidence and protects us from the vileness of azzut panim. The Jesus shine is composed of two opposite qualities: humility and confidence.[82]

The point of art is not to reproduce the visible, but to make visible.
SWISS-GERMAN EXPRESSIONIST ARTIST PAUL KLEE (D. 1940)[83]

Live in the Light: Maya Angelou's son was asked what it was like to live in his mother's shadow. "I thought I was living in her light, but what was really happening was that I was living in the light she was shining on me."[84]

In the same way, we are all living in the light that God is shining on us when we see the face of Jesus. God shined the Light of the world on us.[85] To see the face of Jesus is to see the Light, which makes us all beautiful, and live in the light He is shining on us.

STUDIO LIVE

1) Discuss this quote from Milan Kundera's novel *The Unbearable Lightness of Being* (1984):

> On the surface, an intelligible lie; underneath, the unintelligible truth.

The quote is from Part One, Chapter 5, where the character Sabina is reflecting on her paintings and her depictions of the human body and human face. She thinks about how her paintings seem to show a comprehensible lie, while obscuring a deeper, incomprehensible truth about human existence.

* Is that true of your face? The faces you encounter every day?

* To what extent do "surface appearances" conceal or reveal the truth?

* How do we balance appreciating surface beauty with probing beneath for meaning?

* In what ways do our surface portrayals of life often mask deeper realities? When have you experienced this?

* How might art and creativity allow exploration of those hard-to-grasp truths beneath the surface?

* Is it the responsibility of artists to unveil deeper truths? Or simply capture the surface world?

* What role does abstraction play in gesturing toward truths we cannot fully put into words?

THE JESUS FACE

* Do you agree that intelligibility and truth don't always go together? When can truth seem unintelligible at first?

* How might focus on easily-grasped "facts" sometimes distract us from deeper wisdom?

* What are examples of surface lies societies tell themselves versus unsettling realities beneath?

2) There is an old saying: "If you are not pretty at sixteen, you can't help it, but if you are not beautiful at sixty, it is your own fault." Or in the English novelist George Orwell's (d. 1950) supposed version, "At fifty everyone has the face they deserve."[86]

* How can the face be an object of personal identity formation?

* How do you keep your face looking young from the inside out?

3) I posted on Facebook (04 August 2023) "To live in celebrity stereotypes, or to live in someone else's story, is the ultimate in hypocrisy, fraud, and identity theft. It turns you into a play actor and not an active player." To which friend and photographer Jackie Randle replied, "What a slap in God's face when we try to be someone and something other than who and what God created us to be."

* How many times have you slapped God in the face?

* How can we do better at being who God created us to be?

- If God designed each one of us for different kinds of greatness, how do we discover where our greatness lies?

4) St. Teresa used to say she was inspired and aspired to "do something beautiful for God" every day. "I do it for Him," she often said.[87]

- How might it change your life if you began every day with the question: "What beautiful thing can I do for God?"

5) What do you think is the "worst sin?" Playwright George Bernard Shaw proposed: "The worst sin towards our fellow creatures is not to hate them, but to be indifferent to them. That's the essence of inhumanity."[88]

- Do you agree that indifference can be more harmful than hate? Why or why not?

- When is remaining indifferent rather than getting involved most problematic morally?

- What causes people to become indifferent to the suffering or needs of others?

- How can we remain sensitive to injustice rather than numb to it?

- Have you ever witnessed indifference enable harm or indifference be hurtful itself?

- What historical examples of atrocities involved widespread indifference?

- What motivates you to care about people different than yourself? What causes you to tune out?

THE JESUS FACE

* Discuss some candidates for "the essence of inhumanity" as well as "the essence of humanity."

6) Who even remembers a world of Doris-Day optimism where everyone smiled, the sun was always shining, death a taboo subject, and life a bowl of cherries without pits or pitfalls? Is it any accident that Doris Day, who died in 2019, wanted no funeral, no memorial, no remembrance, no markers?

    * Can we not have both a time of mourning and memorializing and a time of celebrating and gratitude for the gift of a life?

    * What was the best "Memorial Service" you ever attended? What made it so memorable?

    * Tell some stories from your own life that compare funeral services and "celebrations of a life." Have you ever attended one that did both mourn and celebrate?

7) The best way to brighten anyone's day and lighten someone's load? Smile at them. The best way to get others to smile? Smile at them. Nothing tingles between the shoulder blades, shivers up the spine, or charges up the spirit, as a smile.

    * The world needs it. Smile! Conduct an experiment of sharing a smile with everyone you see for one week, and report back on what happened (to you and to them).

8) The facing of the face is one of the most contested liturgical issues in the history of the church. In the Latin mass,

priests always face *ad orientem,* toward the East and the returning Christ, with their backs to the congregation. Vatican II's turning the priest's back to God to face the people is still setting teeth on edge.

* Is your church built to "orient" itself to face the East, as early churches were careful to do?

* What direction does your church face?

* Does it bother you when pastors or priests turn their back on you to "face God" together?

* Or do you worship better when the whole liturgy is done facing the congregation?

9) When John "Amazing Grace" Newton (d. 1807) didn't feel right, or as we would say today, he felt "stressed out," Newton would say "my harp is out of tune."[89]

* What causes your harp to go out of tune?

* Pray this prayer together: "Lord, tune my heart daily to sing thy praise. Heal my broken chords to vibrate once more. Amen."

10) I have my own translation of Psalm 16:8: "I have set the Lord always before me" (KJV). I render it: "I have set the Lord always before my face."

* What are the implications of always facing God's face? Not turning back to look what's behind, but always facing the forward and facing the future?

* Does God push us from behind, pull us from the future, or both?

11) Check out the three-minute YouTube video showing rare footage of Pierre-Auguste Renoir (d. 1919) in 1915 as the seventy-four-year-old master seated at his easel is applying paint to a canvas while his youngest son Claude, fourteen, stands by to arrange the palette and place the brush in his father's permanently clenched hand.

Claude Renoir (d. 1969) was the youngest son. As Renoir aged and developed severe rheumatoid arthritis, Claude began assisting him in painting starting from around 1913 when Claude was twelve years old. Claude would help prepare brushes and canvases for his father, and guide his hand to allow him to continue painting despite limited mobility. A number of Renoir's late paintings from 1913–1919 were completed with Claude's assistance in this manner before Renoir's death.

By the time the film was made Renoir could no longer walk, even with crutches. He depended on others to move him around in a wheelchair. His assistants would scroll large canvases across a custom-made easel, so that the seated painter could reach different areas with his limited arm movements. But there were times when the pain was so bad, he was essentially paralyzed. The painter's famous filmmaker son Jean Renoir describes the shock of his father's wasted figure and gnarled hands:

> His hands were terribly deformed. His rheumatism had made the joints stiff and caused the thumbs to turn inward towards the palms, and his fingers to bend towards the

wrists. Visitors who were unprepared for this could not take their eyes off his deformity. Though they did not dare to mention it, their reaction would be expressed by some such phrase as, "It isn't possible! With hands like that, how can he paint those pictures? There's some mystery somewhere."[90]

Henri Matisse (d. 1954) was 30 years younger than Renoir, and he frequently visited the arthritic master for inspiration as he escaped his pain in painting. "I have never seen a man so happy, and I promised myself that, when my time came, I would not be a coward either." Starting in 1917, Matisse talked with Renoir well past sunset as the aged painter faced sleepless nights of arthritic anguish and ailments. Renoir would say, "The pain passes, Matisse, but the beauty remains," as he looked past the interminable night to a new dawn of creativity at the easel."[91]

- * Discuss how Renoir's dictum might apply in your own life: "The pain passes, but the beauty remains."

12) Discuss the variety of smiles that we encounter daily. Diplomatic smiles. Sarcastic smiles. Strained smiles. Frozen smiles.

- * What distinguishes a genuine smile from an artificial smile?

- * How can you discern a sincere smile from a slightly

sinister, menacing grin from a smile that is held for too long?

13) Can you smile, or shine, when you're angry?

* Is your church smiling on the world, or is it so angry at the world it can't shine a smiling face at the world?

* Discuss the dictum of the Roman emperor and Stoic philosopher Marcus Aurelius (d. 180) that "more grievous are the consequences of anger than the causes of it."[92]

14) "You hypocrites! Well did Isaiah prophesy of you, when he said: 'This people honors me with their lips, but their heart is far from me'" (Matthew 15:7–8 ESV).

"Woe to you, teachers of the law and Pharisees, you hypocrites! You are like whitewashed tombs, which look beautiful on the outside but on the inside are full of the bones of the dead and everything unclean" (Matthew 23:27 NIV).

* Is there a bad two-faced and a good two-faced? After all, in Romans 12:15 Paul says you cry with those who cry, you laugh with those who laugh. Isn't this two-faced?

* Are the two faces of Jesus seen on the cross?

15) When a conversation or conference has drifted to a place where even a smile would be a small betrayal, but to speak out would be rude and ugly or to be drawn into what Russians call "*skolka*" (unseemly wranglings), sometimes

the only thing left is the witness of withdrawal with a smile of sadness?

* Have you ever "saved face" this way?

* How do you "save face" in your own life?

16) When you help someone up the ladder, you don't expect to get kicked in the face as they're climbing. But you will.

* Tell some stories of how those you helped the most turned around and slapped you on the cheek or kicked you in the face as a "reward."

* What did Jesus teach us about how to react when we get slapped or kicked?

17) In 1942 a man named Felix Powell sat down at a piano to play an old tune. He had every right to play it, since he had written it himself with his brother George Henry Powell under the pseudonym "George Asaf." It was a very popular song in both World War I and II. Here is the song he was playing and singing:

> What's the use of worrying?
> It was never worthwhile—
> So pack up your troubles in your old
> > kit-bag
> And smile, smile, smile.

Felix Powell finished his song, went to his bedroom, dressed in the uniform of the Peacehaven Home Guard, an armed citizen militia supporting the British Army during WWII, and during guard duty that night shot himself in the heart with his own rifle. Just because you can write a song about smiling, even "the most optimistic song ever written," doesn't mean you are smiling yourself.

* What does it mean when we are smiling in our reframed idea of a smile?

18) Re-read the Marilynne Robinson quote: "Any human face has a claim on you, because you can't help but understand the singularity of it. The courage and loneliness of it." Now look someone in the face, in their particularity—can you hurt someone you truly "face," especially face to face? Some studies suggest increased reliance on electronic communication and social media are hindering face recognition development, thus contributing to the rising cases of developmental prosopagnosia, the inability to read and recognize faces.

How good are you at recognizing and remembering faces? Are you getting better at it, or worse?

Chapter 4: Mouth
The Jesus Voice

The voice is a second face.
ANONYMOUS FRENCH PROVERB

WHEN WE REFRACT HIS VOICE AND WE RADIATE HIS LIGHT, we lengthen Jesus' stride in the world.

One of the little-known stories in the history of Israel is the drama of sibling rivalry. Miriam (sister of Moses) and Aaron (brother of Moses) insist that God speaks through them as much as through their brother. God doesn't like the bickering, so hauls them into the Tent of Meeting and ventilates:

> Listen to my words:
> When there is a prophet among you,
> > I, the Lord, reveal myself to them in visions,
> I speak to them in dreams.

> But this is not true of my servant Moses;
>> he is faithful in all my house.
> With him I speak face to face,
>> clearly and not in riddles;
>> he sees the form of the Lord.
> Why then were you not afraid
>> to speak against my servant Moses?[1]

"Face-to-face" is what you find in most translations of Exodus 12:7, including NIV. But the Hebrew text IS NOT God speaking to Moses "face to face" but "mouth to mouth," as it is translated in the KJV, RSV, ESV, LSV (Literal Standard Version). The Hebrew is *"peh el peh"* where "peh" means in Hebrew "mouth." The Latin of St. Jerome's Vulgate gets it right: "ore enim ad os loquor" ("For I speak mouth to mouth"). God doesn't speak to Moses by dreams or visions or parables. It is "mouth-to-mouth."

<u>Mouth-to-Mouth:</u> The Torah is defined as the "Books of Moses" or the very words spoken by God "mouth to mouth" to Moses. When Jesus opens his mouth, "every word comes from the mouth of God:"

> Man shall not live by bread alone, but by
>> every word that proceeds out of the
>> mouth of God."[2]

> All these things Jesus said to the crowds
>> in parables; indeed, he said nothing to
>> them without a parable. This was to
>> fulfill what was spoken by the prophet:
>> "I will open my mouth in parables; I

will utter what has been hidden since
the foundation of the world."³

Mouth-to-mouth intimacy is so much deeper and richer than face-to-face. God's healing words in the Scriptures are mouth-to-mouth resuscitation of the broken and battered. The Story is truly in-spired, as the movings of Jesus' mouth are the kiss of love bringing back to life those dead and diseased and deluded. How close is God to us in Jesus? As close as a kiss. Just as God breathed "life" into Adam with that first kiss, so The-Word-Made-Flesh kisses us with divine breath and brings us to life. Jesus opens his mouth and heals with the divine breath those breathless and short of breath.

<u>GO THERE!</u> To "adore" God is to use our mouth, and the words from our life, to bring healing and love to the world. The verb "to adore" ultimately stems from the verb "to mouth." Jerome's Vulgate got it right: *ab ore, ad os,* mouth to mouth, suggests breathing in the same breath of the Spirit which comes from the mouth of Christ, from the vital lungs of his own being. When we pray "breathe on me breath of God," we are adoring God.

Within each of us lies an innate calling, a mission of adoration that resonates with the depths of our being. It is in the pursuit of this mission, the living of our adoration, that we encounter God most profoundly, where our hearts align with the divine. Just as God guided Moses, declaring, "THERE I will meet you,"⁴ so too does God beckon us to embark on our destined paths. It is THERE, in the realm of our calling, that we experience the fullness of God's presence, the intimacy of a divine friendship, as Moses himself discovered. "THERE" is where "the Lord spoke to Moses mouth to mouth as a man speaks to his friend."⁵ Jesus-designed humans seek the kiss of life, a profounder connection with the divine, and venture forth into the depths of their calling, where God awaits if we *Go There*. It is God's mission where we find "THERE."

When someone criticizes a person for being "all over the place," I want to defend them and interject "What a nice compliment." Don't we want to be all over the place in a world where any place can be every place? Jesus is not a point, a target, a center, a single place. Jesus is a way of life in every place. Jesus can be heard best in the circumferences and peripheries, the edges and the abysses, even more than the center. Jesus is all over the place, and a Jesus human wants to be where Jesus is. Of course, you can't be everywhere until you first are somewhere. You can't be "all over the place" until you are first some place.

> And the word of the Lord came unto him (Elijah), saying, Get up and turn eastward, and hide by the brook Cherith, that is before Jordan. And it shall be, that you will drink of the brook; and I have commanded the ravens to feed you THERE. . . . Arise, get to Zarephath, which belongs to Zidon, and dwell THERE; behold, I have commanded a widow woman THERE to sustain you. So he arose and went to Zarephath. And when

he came to the gate of the city, behold, the widow woman was THERE.⁶

God provides each one of us with a particular reality, a real THERE. We won't be happy until we are really THERE, and there is something in each of us that knows where THERE is, where home is. There is also a particular THERE that becomes a universal: "Arise, go up to Bethel, and dwell there."⁷

Are you THERE? "There" is the center of God's will. THERE is the place of blessing. THERE is the place of divine appointment to use your voice, the place of divine mission for voicings. THERE is the place for you to BE THERE. Jesus was always "THERE" where God called him to go. There is a Bethel for you.

But sometimes "There" is "Here." Sometimes it's easier to sing "I'll go where you want me to go, dear Lord" than to "I'll stay where you want me to stay, dear Lord."

<u>Attunement:</u> The Jesus Voice that comes from the Jesus mouth resonates with unfathomable stirrings of goodness, beauty, truth. His stories and images form the ideal soundtrack for a life lived in the divine image. Jesus reminds us that all of creation sings in its own unique voice. Every living thing expresses part of the divine poetry if you listen attentively. Mountains, rivers, trees, animals—everything is imbued with a spirit that echoes the voice of the Creator. God's melody courses through the universe, in both words and nature. We need only attune our hearts to hear that heavenly harmony always within and around us.

Each one of us is an instrument in an orchestra, an original instrument voicing the music of creation. Each of us must learn to play our instrument if God's symphony is to play through us and we are to play God's music with others. The more we are skilled at playing our singular instrument, and not fixated on coveting the instruments of others, the more the music of the spheres flows through us. Each life builds a temple of sound, and a temple sounds the voice of the times we are in, the voice of the times past, and the voice of the times to come. The first time the Scriptures mention that someone is filled with the Holy Spirit, my colleague Jorge Finlay reminds me, it was to empower them to be creative so they could create the Tabernacle.[8]

Early in every homiletics or communications course, students are told that they need to develop their own voice. Whether they're told how to develop that voice is another matter. Or whether a voice needs an ear first before it can become a distinctive voice. But the tone of our voice, the timbre of nasal breaths, the speed of our speech, the volume of our voice, the accent we carry, even the tone of our utterance in some cultures, can all convey a wide array of emotions, tics, traits, and even the meanings of the words themselves. Indeed, our voices can be more expressive than our faces.

THE JESUS VOICE

Every element has a sound, an original sound from the order of God; all those sounds unite like the harmony from harps and zithers.

SYBIL OF THE RHINE
(MEDIEVAL MYSTIC/COMPOSER HILDEGARD VON BINGEN'S (D. 1179) PEN NAME)

<u>Find Your Voice:</u> An imprint of an authentic voice is what resonates and humanizes your message. For a Jesus human, authenticity is not being true to oneself, one's values, and one's emotions. Authenticity is being true to the Jesus in you, his virtues and views and values and visions. An authentic voice does not try to sound like anyone else, but is comfortable in its own timbre, tone, tempo, and tessitura. What is required for each communicator is equally true for every Jesus human: Christ formation is voice lessons.

Greek philosopher Pythagoras (d. 495 BC), who believed the universe was a symphony of sound and that "matter is music solidified,"[9] called his disciples "*akousmatists*," literally translated as "listeners who stay tuned."[10] Maybe Jesus akousmatists is as good a name for those who live Jesus as follower or disciple or pneumanaut.

A Jesus human is someone who listens and stays tuned to God's Perfect Pitch: Jesus the Christ, life's tuning fork to the eternal.[11] "The great music beyond reason and reckoning" is how Welsh poet Waldo Williams (d. 1971) names the birth of Jesus and describes the whole doctrine of incarnation.[12] The church is a community of akousmatists, a chorus of people who listen and stay tuned to Jesus' voicings in texts, traditions, and conversations. In the background is a Greek chorus—a great cloud of witnesses[13] who provide constant commentary, perspective, and admonishment through song, dance, speech, and prayer.[14]

<u>The Jesus Voice is Distinct and Recognizable:</u> Jesus living is a manifold witness: "Join with all nature in manifold witness."[15] Manifold means "manyness." In Acts 2, a manifold witness community was born for the first time in history. It is hard to overemphasize how revolutionary this community of manyness and unlikeness really was. The Jesus Voice does not eliminate differences and distinctives but embraces, elevates, and celebrates them.

The cardinal sin is in our failure not to sense the grandeur of the moment, the marvel and mystery of being, the possibility of quiet exaltation.
POLIST RABBI ABRAHAM JOSHUA HESCHEL (D. 1972)[16]

The example of two cities will suffice: Capernaum and Tokyo.

The first world headquarters for Jesus' ministry?[17] Capernaum.

The ancient city of Palestine called Capernaum is mentioned sixteen times in the gospels. Capernaum means Village of Chaos, since "Capernaum" comes from the Aramaic word "capharnaum" (kepar-nā ûm) which translates to "village of Nahum," the Nahum story one of comfort in chaos.[18] A port city situated along important trade routes, the cultural and ethnic diversity of the community yielded a jumble and mix of all sorts of people and things. Capernaum was also the main Roman administrative center for Galilee, and the place where the infamous Roman centurion built a synagogue from which Jesus taught. Jesus' initial headquarters was a potpourri of people.

The largest urban area in the world? Tokyo.

What makes Tokyo such a dynamic, successful city? Unlike Los Angeles, where Edith Stein memorably said: "There's no There There," Tokyo is a place where "There's only Here's There." There is no main street, no urban center, no urban planning, no downtown, not even what we think of as local neighborhoods. There's only particularities, thousands of mini-locales each one with its own uniqueness and character and style and organic architecture. But out of that conglomeration of particularities is born one of the greatest cities of our planet, a truly universal destination.[19]

But the Jesus Voice is still One Voice. The fruit of the Spirit is still One, the fruit of the tree of the cross that brought us back to fruit of the Tree of Life. The Oneness of One like-minded community with many unlike and unlikely components. Not disconnected and discordant manyness, but a oneness out of manyness, a oneness that is stronger for its emergence out of manyness. A healthy singleness needs manyness.

For Hilaire Belloc, a French-born British polymath who could be as wrong about some things as he was right about others, cheese proved the manifold witness of the Trinity. In Belloc's meditation on cheese, the proof of the existence of

God is cheese itself: "Cheese does most gloriously reflect the multitudinous effect of earthly things, which could not be multitudinous did they not proceed from one mind."[20]

Jesus Comes in Surround Sound: A Jesus Voice is comprised of singleness and manyness. It takes many voices to tell a single story, and the story is unfinished without every single voice of the many. The mirror is one, but the reflections are virtually endless. God is one; the human perceptions and interpretations of God are many. The Jesus Voice is a "manifold witness."

To live Jesus is to be a listener who stays tuned to Jesus' voice. Jesus living saves the world with a "both/and" voice that loves not only the world but also each person in it. God gave us two ears to hear voices. Jesus speaks in stereo. Jesus speaks in more than one voice. Jesus always comes in surround sound. A Jesus human learns to speak in multiple registers and multiple voices in addressing the woes and wonders of the world.

> The voice of a Lion and the voice of a Lamb.
> The Alpha Voice and the Omega Voice.
> The divine voice and the human voice.
> The assuring voice and the arresting voice.
> The tender voice and the tough voice.
> The fire-and-smoke voice of thunder, and
>   the still, small voice of whisper.

A Jesus Voice speaks in the universal but also in the particular—the personal voice, unique to every person being addressed. Jesus could speak in a colloquial voice. Or Jesus

THE JESUS VOICE

could speak in a collegial voice, a voice tailor-made to each hearer.

At Sinai, Yahweh is said to have spoken in two voices. In the one voice, the sound came from the heavens. It was an objective voice that everyone heard: "And all the people perceived all the thunderings."[21] From this voice came the last eight utterances of the commandments.[22] The voice was heard in all seventy languages, and went in all directions at once. This is the voice of El! *Ha Sha-may'im*, "The Heavens." The objective voice of content.

At Sinai the other voice was the subjective voice. This was that voice that comes not from outside but inside: the voice of *Makom* (*ma-kom'*), the voice of context or the subjective voice. The voice of the one who spoke to each person intimately according to their needs and abilities: for example, in the voice of his or her parents, or a "little girl" voice that spoke so as not to frighten the child. It was a voice that all hundreds of thousands of people heard in their own distinctive way. This voice uttered the first two commandments . . .

1) You shall have no other gods before Me.
2) You shall not make for yourself a carved image—any likeness of anything that is in heaven above, or that is in the earth beneath, or that is in the water under the earth; you shall not bow down to them nor serve them. For I, the LORD your God, am a jealous God, visiting the iniquity of the fathers upon the children to the third and fourth

generations of those who hate Me, but showing mercy to thousands, to those who love Me and keep My commandments.²³

Though One Voice addressed the entire people, each individual heard that One Voice as if it were addressed individually to him or to her.

How could that possibly be, the rabbis wondered? Rabbi Levi explained by using the metaphor of the omnidirectional painting or mirror:

> God appeared to them in the manner of a picture that seems to face in all directions [or in other versions, "like a mirror in which many faces can be reflected"]. A thousand people look at it, and it seems to look into the direction of each one. Just so, when the Holy One, blessed be He, spoke, every Israelite said, "To me the Lord spoke." That is why it is said: "I am the Lord Thy God" in the singular, and not "I am the Lord Thy God" in the plural.²⁴

Again, in another version:

> The text does not say: "Ani Adonai Elohaychem," "I am the Eternal your God," with the plural form of the word "your." Rather, when it says "Ani Adonai Elohecha," "your God," the text intentionally uses the singular form.²⁵

Every particular person carries universal significance. The more particularized a voice becomes, the more universalized its significance. The way to the planetary is through the provincial, the parochial, the local. Every part of the whole contains the whole, and every whole is greater than the sum of its parts. The particular is of universal importance.

"The clearest way into the Universe is through a forest wilderness; every tree, flower, and rock contains the secrets of Nature,"[26] wrote environmental philosopher John Muir in his reflection on how the partial can contain the whole. To paraphrase Muir, the clearest way to the God of All is through The One Way of Jesus.

Mission-first Mindset: Some of Jesus' last words to us were these: "Go into all the world and preach the gospel to every creature."[27] Jesus living is a life sentence of sentness: "As the Father has sent me, even so I send you."[28] If our mission field is the world, does this not make us all *world* missionaries?

Not so fast on that "world" front. Yes, the "Great Commission" is a global one. And we are called to be "global missionaries," even "global citizens of planet Earth," as some are calling it. But we can be so "global" that we can't see across the street. Or as the rap on academe has it, the more abstract the more alien. Jean Paul Sartre admitted that he loved people in the aggregate and abstract, but hated them face to face. It is easy to love humanity; it is not easy sometimes (most of the time?) to love humans.

DESIGNER JESUS

The procession of great blocks of abstraction, moving across the page as if in some semantic May Day parade, does make one yearn for a joke, a diversion—or an example.

LITERARY CRITIC JOHN CROWE RANSOM (D. 1974)[29]

As much as we loved George Carlin, one was never sure whether Carlin loved the humans he made such fun of. In fact, one of the easiest ways of loving people is to avoid their company. We all need to begin our "world mission" somewhere. The glory of the local church is that it's global. But the only way to the global is through the local. You can't universalize until you first particularize. You can't cross life's Rubicons until you first cross the street.

Clergyman Jonathan Swift joked that he "hate[d] and detest[ed] that animal called man . . . [but he] heartily love[d] John, Peter, Thomas, etc." Swift wrote Alexander Pope a famous letter in November 1725. On the eve of the publication of his classic satire on human nature called *Gulliver's Travels* (1726), he asked his friend to do him a favor:

> When you think of the world give it one lash the more at my request. I have ever hated all nations, professions, and communities, and all my love is towards individuals: for instance, I hate the tribe of lawyers, but I love Counsellor Such-a one and Judge Such-a-one . . . But principally I hate and detest

that animal called man, although I heartily love John, Peter, Thomas, and so forth. This is the system upon which I have governed myself many years, but do not tell.[30]

Hungarian novelist and anti-totalitarian crusader Arthur Koestler built his anti-totalitarian crusades on his opposition to dissolving the single person into the hive mentality of the community and to refuse to believe that the individual "is the result of a crowd of a million divided by a million." At one point Koestler even confessed, "I don't believe any more in humanity. I believe in the individual."[31]

The Greatest Story Ever Told begins with the voice of manyness—two creation stories, the macro creation story in Genesis One, and the micro creation story in Genesis Two. After the unframed Big Picture is revealed in Genesis One, immediately there comes the framed picture which revels in minute details and individual portraits of people, places, and animals.

"Jesus treated everyone the same." No, Jesus treated everyone differently, not as if they were a general thing, but as if they were an original, one-of-a-kind creation of God. For Jesus, every person was an exception. Every person was not like anyone else in the world. Jesus didn't treat people as if they were all alike. There are no interchangeable parts in the kingdom. Jesus did not submerge individuality into a collectivity. Jesus showed contempt for all collectivities.

Jesus did not just spend his ministry dealing with crowds. The gospel story is seasoned with amazing stories of Jesus'

DESIGNER JESUS

voicings for the one, the individual—for children; a deaf and mute man;[32] Greek tourist(s);[33] Herod;[34] a disabled person;[35] Jairus;[36] a lawyer;[37] siblings Martha, Mary, and Lazarus;[38] Nicodemus;[39] a Roman centurion;[40] a paralytic;[41] a hemorrhaging woman;[42] a Samaritan woman;[43] a mentally-ill tomb man;[44] leper(s);[45] Annas, his son Caiaphas, and Pilate;[46] a widow;[47] a Syrophoenician woman;[48] a mother-in-law;[49] a rich young ruler;[50] Zaccheus;[51] and his mother and brothers.[52] Jesus treated every person as unique and precious, capable of finishing the story of their encounter in their own community and context. In nine of these cases, Jesus initiated the conversation. In twenty-five of them, he responded to their initiative. A few of them were initiated by third parties. In each encounter one can find the grand and the intimate, the shout and the whisper.

A Jesus Voice sanctifies the person, as it focuses on Jesus, the savior of the world. A Jesus Voice features the power of the one megaphoned by the many. A singular can revolutionize the universal. Jesus treated everyone as a special case, not as a lump of clay or a bundle of legal codes. He saw the unique beauty and potential in each person, and he loved them as a potter loves each vessel patterned from his wheel. For Jesus, everyone is an exception, not a rule. For Jesus, every voice is a matchless gift to the world.

The Jesus Problematic: This is one reason why people had (and have) such a problem with Jesus. Jesus loved particularity, and with particularity comes peculiarity. We are a "peculiar people"[53] afraid to be peculiar. But called to love all peculiars. The key to "normalizing" difference is not changing brain chemistry but changing the human heart.

Jesus humans engaged in Jesus living are particularly well-suited, if not a family trait, to be mocked as misfits who don't "fit in," to be derided as not "normal," to be attacked, maligned and misjudged. There is no gospel guarantee that following Jesus on the path to Jerusalem will bring applause or acclaim, whether from family, friends or the church. Quite the contrary. There will always be those who look at you as if you were headless, or had four heads, or were harbinger of the four horsemen of the apocalypse.

This is why we long to hear ourselves called by name. "Carve your name on hearts, not on marble," Charles Spurgeon liked to say. "I have written your name on the palms of my hands. I always think about your walls."[54] We are called to call others by name with the Jesus Voice.

Poet and philosopher Vaclav Havel was the last president of Czechoslovakia and the first president of the Czech republic. Havel castigated this tendency toward what he called "complex blindness" in this exchange about academic obfuscation with fellow writers:

> The praiseworthy attempt to see things in their wider context becomes so formalized that instead of applying that technique in particular, unique ways, appropriate to a given reality, it becomes a single and widely used model of thinking with a special capacity to dissolve—in the vagueness of all the

possible wider contexts—everything particular in that reality. Thus what looks like an attempt to see something in a complex way in fact results in a complex form of blindness. For if we can't see individual specific things, we can't see anything at all.[55]

Voice Disorders: This is the academic delusion, or academic fallacy: it dissolves the particular in the application of the universal. Academics tend to live in clouds of theory. They see it as beneath their status to "lower themselves" and do not deign to stoop to particulars. This explains why so many brilliant minds and thinkers have voice disorders on some of the greatest sound offs in history—like slavery, totalitarianism, colonialism, racism, sexism, and genocide. We can't save the word by hating it. The Voice of Jesus, the Sound of Logos, is never one of hate, only love.

Here are some examples of voice disorders from "the best and brightest." In 1933 one of the most influential philosophers of the twentieth century, Martin Heidegger, publicly pledged his support for the Nazis. He even banned Edmund Husserl, on whom he did his dissertation, from using the university library because he was a Jew. Naziism was justified by influential academics and some of the best scholars and theologians of their day because it supposedly broke down social barriers and brought people together in great pageantry and hope. Celebrated novelist and art collector Gertrude Stein canvassed support for Hitler as a candidate for the Nobel Prize of 1938. One of the most widely quoted theologians of the twentieth century, the gentle Jesuit anthropologist Pierre Teilhard de Chardin, thought that the Germans deserved to win the Second World War "because they have more spirit than the rest of the world."[56]

The greatest mass murderer in history? Arguably Mao Zedong, who had a long rock-star list of academic admirers. In fact, the gallery of Mao's scholarly "fans" is a roll call of the most admired and studied intellectuals of the twentieth century. The sacred pantheon of scholars who lauded the plaudits of Mao Zedong include Jean-Paul Sartre, Michel Foucault, Roland Barthes, Jean-Luc Godard, and Andre Malraux. Even the President of France, Valery Giscard d'Estaing, called Mao a "beacon" for humanity. So too did libertarian composer John Cage. Scottish poet Hugh MacDiarmid worshiped Lenin, Stalin, and admitted infatuation with fascism and Nazism.[57]

It is not easy to hold the particular and the universal in tension. Mahatma Gandhi got so caught up in the pursuit of peace and harmony between Hindus, Muslims, Christians, and Jews that he argued, "In my opinion the Jews should disclaim any intention of realizing their aspiration under the protection of arms and should rely wholly on the goodwill of Arabs."[58] When all you look at is the "Big Picture," you can come to justify any indignity and inhumanity. It is the voice of totalitarianism and fascism. It is the voice of the high priest Caiaphas, justifying the murder of an innocent with the mentality of "Let one die to save the many."[59]

When you focus just on the Big Picture and forget the Little Particulars, a logical case can be rationalized for almost anything: "After all, there's seven billion people crowded on this planet. What's the big deal about this one individual? Or this one thousand? The world won't miss them if they're gone. Their absence will be imperceptible . . ." This was the reasoning of Vladimir Ulyanov (better known as Lenin), who like Dostoevsky's Ivan Karamazov espouses intellectual theories about alleviating mankind's suffering in the abstract but is emotionally cold and aloof in his personal relationships. He showed compassion for the suffering of the many in the abstract, but seemed to have little empathy for the emotional needs of the real human beings in his life.

The Jesus Voice weeps and wails over the death of a single human being. Think about that for a minute: Jesus moaned and mourned for a single person, Lazarus. God knows and loves each one of us enough to weep over us. A Jesus Voice particularizes in order to universalize. The Big Picture and the Small Particular must be kept together. In the words of the Swiss theologian Karl Barth, "The God of love is also the God of detail."[60] Or in Oscar Wilde's famous exclamation: "Great God of love, great God of details."[61] There are no resonant abstractions. Abstractions register, and may convey a rhetorical charge, but authentics resonate.

All people should be loved equally. But you cannot do good to all people equally, so you should take particular thought for those who, as if by lot, happen to be particularly close to you in terms of place, time, or any other circumstances.

ST. AUGUSTINE[62]

The Jesus Voice and Dominant Seventh: There are seven dimensions of musical excellence and experience that help us connect to music on its deepest levels: melody, lyrics, rhythm, timbre, novelty, authenticity, and realism.[63]

There are seven gifts of the Spirit that shape our experience of life and help us connect to life on its deepest levels: wisdom, understanding, counsel, fortitude, knowledge, piety, and fear of the Lord. Depending on what key, the dominant seventh chord is built on the fifth degree of a major scale and consists of a root note, a major third, a perfect fifth, and a minor seventh. The strong, unresolved sounds create the tension that propels the harmony of life forward in various genres and contexts.

Receiving the Jesus Voice is a gift. If one is speaking in a Jesus Voice, each musical dimension vocalizes one or more gifts of the spirit into a chord whereby we recognize the Jesus Voice in ourselves and in others. When you speak with a Jesus Voice, the lips mouth utterances that are as distinctive as Elvis Presley's lips, B. B. King's guitar, Willie Nelson's braids, and Frank Sinatra's enunciation.

Thy lips, O my bride, drop as the honeycomb:
Honey and milk are under thy tongue;
And the smell of thy garments is like the smell of
Lebanon.

SONG OF SOLOMON 4:11 ASV

DESIGNER JESUS

Melody: The Jesus Voice carries the tune of peace and joy.

> "Peace I leave with you; my peace I give to you. Not as the world gives do I give to you. Let not your hearts be troubled, neither let them be afraid" (John 14:27 ESV).

> "These things I have spoken to you, that my joy may be in you, and that your joy may be full" (John 15:11 ESV).

The Jesus Voice is a melody of sound and syntax, punctuation and pacing that lifts us up and fills us with hope. The joy of salvation, and the "Melody of Love" (Lawrence, 1997), results in "There's Within My Heart a Melody" (Gabriel, 1907). The "Melody of Life" (Kirkpatrick, 1922) spoken with a Jesus Voice, others hear as "Sweet Melody" (Franklin, 2002) and "The Melody Lingers On" (Dorsey, 1937).

The invention of melody is the supreme mystery of man.
FRENCH ANTHROPOLOGIST CLAUDE LÉVI-STRAUSS (D. 2009)[64]

Lyrics: Jesus' Voice lyrics life with words that speak of love, forgiveness, and hope:

> Love the Lord your God with all your heart and with all your soul and with all your mind. This is the first and greatest commandment. And the second is like it: "Love your neighbor as yourself" (Matthew 22:37–39 NIV).

THE JESUS VOICE

> For if you forgive others their trespasses, your heavenly Father will also forgive you, but if you do not forgive others their trespasses, neither will your Father forgive your trespasses (Matthew 6:14–15 ESV).

We want a blueprint, but God gives us a storyboard and song lyrics—a storyboard of forgiving those who crucified him and instructing his followers to forgive seventy times seven.[65]

We want a "Lord's Program," but God gives us a "Lord's Prayer" and songs to sing ("Song of Mary," "Song of Zechariah"). When two or three gathered in Jesus' name, there was singing. You can't enchant without a chant. Incarnation is chapter. Catechesis means literally "to sound in someone's ear" or "resound" lines of truth. That's why you can't do catechesis without a cantor. You can even be tone deaf and be a master lyricist, as was Alfred Lord Tennyson (d. 1892).

Of course, songs come from the heart, which is why the psalmist pairs head and heart: "May these words of my mouth and this meditation of my heart be pleasing in your sight."[66] Every time we mouth words of calumny and contempt, we are vocalizing the sounds of evil.

In hip-hop lingo, when a rapper's lyrics are considered especially "tight" or "dope" or "outstanding," the response is "That's a bar!" Not Amen! but "That's a bar." When a Jesus Voice speaks the lyrics of love, a refrain with a twenty-first-century charge and vibe is "That's a bar."

DESIGNER JESUS

> *Sing them over again to me,*
> *Wonderful words of life;*
>
> *Let me more of their beauty see,*
> *Wonderful words of life;*
> *Words of life and beauty*
> *Teach me faith and duty.*
>
> FANNY CROSBY (1874)

Rhythm: The Jesus Voice has a rhythm that is both comforting and energizing.

> Peace I leave with you; my peace I give to you. Not as the world gives do I give to you. Let not your hearts be troubled, neither let them be afraid (John 14:27 ESV).
>
> Consider the ravens: they neither sow nor reap, they have neither storehouse nor barn, and yet God feeds them. Of how much more value are you than the birds! (Luke 12:24 ESV).
>
> Blessed are the peacemakers, for they will be called children of God (Matthew 5:9 NIV).
>
> Ask and it will be given to you; seek and you will find; knock and the door will be opened to you (Matthew 7:7 NIV).

Jesus living is a rhythm that helps us keep the beat—staying grounded and moving forward in faith; honoring the past while seizing the future; knowing when to speak and when to be silent, when to fast and when to feast. It is the rhythm of the words of the Book of Common Prayer: "We have left undone those things which we ought to have done, and we have done those things which we ought not to have done."

Every voice has a rhythm. God's voice shook the earth in Moses' day. God's silence shook the earth in Jesus' day. God will yet shake the heavens and the earth one more time.[67]

Sometimes you engage with speech. There is a Gospel According to Words.

Sometimes you engage with silence. Some people never open their mouths unless they have nothing to say. Some people never open their mouths without putting their feats in it. There is a time for a Jesus human to deck themself in decorous silence. There is a Gospel According to Silence.

When God leads us "into deep waters," it is often into deep silence. In troubled waters, Jesus is often silent: "He answered not a word."[68] To whom was he silent? He was silent to Herod. He was silent to Pilate. He was silent to the chief priests and scribes. Maybe we could learn some things from Jesus about whom to argue with and whom to give the silent treatment.

Sometimes you engage with the still small voice. There is a Gospel of the Still Small Voice.

Sometimes you engage with just the stillness, which is the opposite of slouching or slacking. Still waters are the best for seeing and reflecting. The soul quickens and quivers with quietness from the strength of stillness. In the Eastern tradition, they speak less of "silence" than of *hesychia* which means repose or quietness or stillness, not the absence of words—but the presence of integrated wholeness in responding to the world that is unperturbed, unruffled, and deeply calm. Silence is from the outside in. Stillness is from the inside out. There is a Gospel of Stillness.

Sometimes you resemble Jesus best when you have your mouth shut. But I didn't say that. It was first said by Ignatius of Antioch: "It is better for a man to be silent and be [a Christian], than to talk and not to be one. 'The kingdom of God is not in word, but in power.'"[69]

Timbre: The Jesus Voice has a timbre that is both familiar and unique.

> My sheep listen to my voice; I know them, and they follow me. (John 10:27 NIV).

> Come to me, all you who are weary and burdened, and I will give you rest (Matthew 11:28 NIV).

It is a timbre that we can recognize even when it is speaking to us in a new way. It is a timbre of fortitude, courage, and encouragement. In a world where the negative is the norm and the critique is honored, a Jesus Voice finds a way forward in the upbeat and the affirmative.

Written words are musical notation.
PULITZER PRIZE NOVELIST MARILYNNE ROBINSON[70]

THE JESUS VOICE

Yet Jesus had the voice of an iconoclast, which the Pharisees heard as the voice of a heckler. Iconoclasts open windows and doors. Every discipline needs the voice of an iconoclast that others may hear as a heckler. Every orthodoxy needs a dissenter, every celebrity needs a nay-sayer, every establishment needs a maverick. But if you find yourself always playing Devil's Advocate, whose side are you on?

There are few things more revolutionary than opening windows in locked or closed rooms. Fresh air has cost many window-openers their lives. It may be, as Niccolò Machiavelli intimated in this quote from *The Prince* (1513), that Jesus humans even have a gift for being hated: "Hatred is gained as much by good works as by evil."[71]

But the Jesus principles of holy heckling never got personal or reached the level of hectoring. The Jesus Voice could be sharp but always kind, never engaged in cheap shots, and loved the heckled. Holy heckling pulls out a chair, not points to the door. The gates of hell part when Christians open their mouths and out comes carpings and criticizings. Dour, doom-laden wallowing in self-righteous nihilism is unbecoming the name of Jesus. Jesus came to save the world. You don't save the world by hating it or denying that any true progress has been or will ever be made. You hector what you hate; you only heckle what you love. You can't save civilization with incivility or hopelessness.

The future is molded from the sounds of our voices. Let it never be said of a Jesus disciple that they have a gift for hatred, doom-mongering, or scolding virtue-signaling.

DESIGNER JESUS

Novelty: The Jesus Voice does not always voice new thoughts, or embrace the latest trends. Most of what is postured as "new" is simply the reframing, reformatting, and rebooting of the "old."

> Therefore every scribe who has been trained for the kingdom of heaven is like a master of a house, who brings out of his treasure what is new and what is old (Matthew 13:52 ESV).

> This cup is the new covenant in my blood, which is poured out for you (Luke 22:20 NIV).

"See, I am doing a new thing! Now it springs up; do you not perceive it? I am making a way in the wilderness and streams in the wasteland," voices Isaiah.[72] "New things" are those things that are always present but underground or undetected until now, flows of living water that suddenly "spring up" because of changing conditions, treasures hidden "in the Master's storehouse," overlooked by past generations and awaiting discovery by future generations.

The Jesus Voice is always willing to surprise us and challenge us to grow because Jesus "brought with him a total newness," St. Irenaeus (d. 202) stated more than once.[73] The Bible talks about a "new birth" (John 3:3–8), a "new human" (Ephesians 2:15), a "new creature" (2 Corinthians 5:17), a "new life" (Romans 6:4), and "new covenant" (Hebrew 8:6–13). And that's just for starters.

But the novelty of Christianity is Jesus himself: "*Omnen novitatem attulit semetipsum afferens.*"[74] Jesus is another name for "newness" in all of life. "And the one sitting on the throne said, "Look, I am making everything new!" And then he said to me, "Write this down, for what I tell you is trustworthy and true."75

Jesus living is open to new experiences and willing to listen to God in new ways. The Jesus Voice is often found in unexpected, unexplored places. It is even willing to coin new words that jibe with the world that we live in. People ask me, "Sweet, why are you so fond of new or made-up words?" I either say, "new worlds require new words," or "the trouble with old words is that you never know whose mouth they've been in."

<u>Authenticity:</u> The Jesus Voice is always genuine. It speaks from the heart and it is always honest. No haughty carriage and no pretentious airs. To live Jesus is to lead a life of sincerity and authenticity.

Sow your seed in the morning, and at evening let your hands be not idle, for you do not know which will succeed, whether this or that, or whether both will do equally well.

ECCLESIASTES 11:6, NIV

The seven gifts of the Spirit help us to recognize the authentic Jesus Voice.

The gift of wisdom helps us to discern truth from falsehood and sorcery. The gift of wisdom grants discernment, reveals connections, and guides decisions that lead to greater meaning and mission.

The gift of understanding unmasks the deeper dimensions of life and releases the splash of songs and poems that gush forth from creation itself.

The gift of counsel tailors advice that accelerates competency and gives permission slips to skip at least some days in the school of hard knocks.

The gift of fortitude helps us to abide and advance in the face of adversity.

The gift of knowledge helps us to grow in faith by turning knowledge into acknowledgment, to step beyond passive knowledge acquisition and actively engage with what has been learned.

The gift of piety helps us to worship God and to live a holy life.

The gift of fear of the Lord helps us to trust God and in faith. We live in a culture that knows fear and fantasizes new fears. Every day, it seems, we know fear better, and fall deeper in love with "fightings without, fears within."[76] Jesus calls us to know and love not fear but know and love faith—a faith that frees from fear, a love that "casts out fear."[77]

All seven gifts of the Spirit are earmarks of authenticity that open the envelope of creativity and change.

Realism: The Jesus Voice speaks to us in a way that is both real and hopeful. It does not sugarcoat the truth, but it also offers us hope for the future as it "speaks the truth in love."[78] Jesus' realism is heard in his voicings about the realities of human nature, the challenges of living a righteous life, and the consequences of our actions.

Part of the realism is not just to give us a front-row seat in reality's blossoming, but to put us on stage as a participant in reality's betterment.

The Jesus Voice of realism finds expression in many ways, and reaches us through various channels. Extroverts hear Jesus as gregarious and social. Introverts hear Jesus as quiet and retiring. Tough-minded business types hear Jesus as more executive-like. While tender-hearts hear Jesus as cozy and comforting.

Yet all hear him most real at the table. We speak in a Jesus Voice the clearest and profoundest when we are at the table. When Jesus said, "Do this in memory of me," the "this" is the table. In other words, we are instructed to do "table" in memory of Jesus. The Jesus brand is not "do it," as much as the Nike "Just Do It" meme would like us to believe. The Jesus brand is not "do it" but "do this" when "this" is "table." Do table. When anything goes wrong? Table It.

Logos not Logo: The importance of the Jesus Voice in Jesus living is evident in the fact that Voice and Logos are almost the same. Logos is one of the most complex words in existence.[79] Logos itself derives from *legein* which means to say aloud or give voice to. In the case of Jesus, Logos voicings are the GBT voicings of Goodness, Beauty, and Truth. Logos also conveys elements of bringing together opposites, of connecting primordial utterance with contemporary relevance.

Voicings of Goodness, Beauty, and Truth are never

hateful, always hopeful. When Kurt Vonnegut's son Mark claimed conscientious objection status during the Vietnam War, Vonnegut wrote a letter to the draft board. It ends: "He will not hate. He will not kill. There's hope in that. There's no hope in war."[80]

"Hate the sin, love the sinner" is a widely quoted meme that was first articulated by William Law (d. 1761), an important theologian in the eighteenth-century English Evangelical Revival. But the "hate" is muted by what comes next in the full quote:

> To hate the sin, and love the person, is a charitable Christian hatred, which whilst it detests the crimes, yet pities and regards the person, and is always ready to help and deliver them from the evil they are in.[81]

Archbishop Law goes on to say that we should not judge people for their sins, but should instead love them and try to help them overcome their sins:

> We must never judge any person for their sins, but look upon them with the eyes of pity and compassion, as persons that are under the power of a wicked enemy, and that stand in need of our help to deliver them from it.[82]

John Wesley said much the same thing when he sermonized: "Everyone is to give an account of himself to God. Therefore every one of you is to bear his own burden . . .

THE JESUS VOICE

But so far as he is able, (which in numberless instances is far beyond what he supposes) every Christian is to ease the burden of his brother."[83] Yes, sin needs confronting and condemning, but even confrontation is an exercise in care and compassion, not hatred. Maybe "hating the sin" is in part why Christians can be such good haters, all in the name of "speaking truth to power" and "righteous wrath." Hatred is never "charitable" or "Christian" or "righteous." Hatred is never sacred. Christians who speak disparagingly of others with the piety of loving hatred betray with sacred hatred their Lord who loved his haters. Whenever Mother Teresa would meet someone who was particularly obnoxious, or hateful, or mean, or disturbed, or marginal, she would only say that there was Jesus "in a distressing disguise."[84]

I will not permit anyone to destroy my soul by making me hate him.

EDUCATOR BOOKER T. WASHINGTON (D. 1915)[85]

A good image for this is an old television show, one of the few shows my father "watched" on the radio, since having a TV was against our religion. I will never forget the episode where some big man, whenever he met one of the characters on the street, would always slap him in the chest. Hard. Finally, the character lost his patience and said, "I'll fix him. I'll put a stick of dynamite in my vest pocket and the next time he slaps me, he is going to feel it in his hand." Everyone laughed at the punch line, of course, because when the man's hand blew off, it would also blow out the character's heart.

That's what unforgiveness and hatred does to us: blows out our hearts. You can't hold grudges, you can't refuse to forgive, you can't live for revenge and not damage yourself the worst. In the words of the nineth-century Latin prayer ("Ubi Caritas") for unity and peace, asking that God's glory be known and that God's peace be ours,"

> Let strife among us be unknown,
> let all contention cease;
> Be God's the glory that we seek,
> be ours God's holy peace.[86]

The Church's Three-Register Voice: There are three different types of communication that the church needs to master if it is to fulfill its mission to love the world as Jesus loved it. The three registers of voice are as follows:

> Kerygmatic communication (and music): proclamation.
> Koinoniac communication (and music): tradition and table time.
> Leiturgic communication (and music): worship, prayer, praise.

In Kerygmatic communication, one person or a few address the many.[87] A key to kerygmatic communication is that the Jesus Voice be in the vernacular of the culture. When Paul spoke Greek to the crowd, they received his words as "the word of God . . . at work in you." Jesus was brought up in the Hebrew language, thought in the Hebrew language, and sometimes taught in Hebrew. He knew the Hebrew of the prayers and songs, which is a little different from the ancient Hebrew and later Hebrew. But Jesus mostly taught in Aramaic, the language spoken by most Jews in Palestine at the time. Even when he was quoting from the Torah, he read the Aramaic translation which was the custom in synagogues at the time. Most likely Jesus knew Greek, and sometimes taught in Greek, the language of the Roman Empire, but it was not widely spoken by ordinary people in Palestine. The fact that Jesus taught in Aramaic, Hebrew, and Greek means he was reaching out to as wide an audience as possible.[88] You hear Jesus' voice best, and speak the Jesus Voice the loudest, when you know how to read the gospels in the Jewish background of Jesus' day.

In Koinoniac communication, a new verbal and nonverbal mode of communication where all voices were heard, there is not the hierarchy that is present in the kerygmatic.[89] The Jesus Voice transcends every culture, creed, color, and every person's "voice" is of equal value.

In Leiturgic communication, the Jesus Voice speaks the language of liturgy which is marked by formality, dignity, and solemnity. Often archaic and evocative, it can be repetitive and rhythmic, symbolic and metaphorical—but when mixed together in the crucible of sabbathing and silence the elixir releases a sense of awe and wonder that brings new life.

DESIGNER JESUS

---

*God made Adam and Eve on Day Six. The next day,
Day Seven, God made rest, the Day of Sabbath. Adam
and Eve's first day of existence was spent with God.*
PENTECOSTAL THEOLOGIAN A. J. SWOBODA[90]

A case study of the church not speaking with a Jesus Voice is the church's response to abuse. There are many kinds of abuse—child abuse, sexual abuse, spousal abuse, verbal abuse, animal abuse,[91] and bureaucratic abuse (bureaucratic cruelty is administrative cruelty, but still cruelty nonetheless—is there anyone post-Niebuhr who has probed the horrors of system abuse?).[92] The liability of the Catholic Church for cases of child abuse by clergy is the very definition of dereliction of duty and the church speaking with a bad voice.[93]

To be sure, this evil is not just plaguing the Roman Catholic church. Data from American insurance companies suggests that Protestant clergy lead Catholics in the sexual abuse of children, with the SBC (Southern Baptist Church) the worst offender."[94] But the spotlight has been on the Catholic church, which means that more has come to the light. How many of those responsible have been sacked? Resigned? How many are still in office? How should the Roman Catholic church have dealt with the horror of child abuse in its midst? Is a simple "pay-out" the Jesus Voice? The Catholic church in US alone has already paid many billions in compensation to victims of sexual abuse, not to mention bankrupting dioceses and denting collections from disillusioned parishioners all over the world.

A Jesus Voice that addresses all forms of abuse must speak in the three registers of kerygmatic, koinoniac, and leiturgiac voices. The voice starts with speaking the kerygmatic particulars, showing care and concern for those abused, and doing everything to protect them and all others who are vulnerable. But then the particular must go to the koinoniac universal, and for the Pope himself on behalf of the church to repent in leiturgic form and get on his hands and knees and wash the feet of those children and adults who have been victims of abuse by priests.

But there is another particular involved: the priest abusers. And while justice must be swift and sure for pedophiliac priests, the church should never forget that it is in the healing and redemption business, and provide treatments for those with sexual dysfunctions and disorders. If the church had spoken in the three registers of a Jesus Voice in addressing the sexual abuse of particular children, a cancer of long-standing in the church would have been healed.[95]

Water hit by water forms circles around the point of impact. The voice in the air creates the same along a greater distance; even larger ones in fire, and longer still the mind in the universe, but since the mind is finite the impulse does not extend to the infinite.

FROM LEONARDO DA VINCI'S (D. 1519) *NOTEBOOKS*[96]

DESIGNER JESUS

Bonesetter Sweets: I come from a long line of "Bonesetter Sweets" dating back to the sixteenth century, although this form of osteopathic medicine has been around for thousands of years. Artisans by vocation, the science of bonesetting was regarded by the Sweets as an avocation. The inherited skill of bone therapy was passed down from father to son and existed to be exercised for the good of all, never exploited for fame or fortune. Any history of orthopedics includes a section on the "Bonesetter Sweets" clan and their uncanny ability to set fractures, sprains, and dislocations using their hands while aided by herbs, ointments, and skunk grease in massaging the wounds.[97] The secret family recipe for the famous "Sweet's Liniment" is still being passed down from generation to generation. Long lines snaking down many street blocks were common at the home of every bonesetter Sweet, because they were known for succeeding where more learned and "better trained" physicians had failed.

The connection of healing and equipping is made explicit in the Greek word καταρτίζω (katartizō), which has been divorced from its healing or repairing root meanings, as in setting bones so they become whole and well again. What we translate as "equip" as in "equipping the saints for ministry" is originally a medical term that means "to mend," "to make whole," or "to restore to health." It is used in the New Testament to describe Jesus healing people's illnesses and injuries, such as in Matthew 15:31: "So that the crowd was amazed when they saw the mute speaking, the crippled walking, the blind seeing, and the demon-possessed set free.

And they glorified the God of Israel."[98] Here Jesus Is not simply equipping the people he heals, but making them whole again, whether it is broken bodies, broken bones, broken nets, or torn relationships.[99]

George Herbert brought together the healing power of music, bonesetting, and equipping in his poem called "The Reprisal," where he masterfully puns on the word "set" that's outfitting, orchestral, and orthopaedic:[100]

> Thou wilt sin and grief destroy;
> That so the broken bones may join,
> And tune together in a well-set song,
> Full of his praises,
> Who dead men raises.[101]

When the Jesus Voice is heard in all its musicality, there is the setting for healing that is not just a boost to our immune system, or an equipping for our mission, but a balm to our whole being.

The Jesus Voice promises to set us for life, and accompany us through life.

That word "accompany" is packed with meaning. It means to attend and to back up, as in a musical accompaniment. But at its root, "accompany" is a Middle French corruption of the adjoined words "com-panion" or "company," which both derive from Latin words "com" (with) and "panis" (bread). To accompany someone is to break the same bread constantly with someone.

The story of the incarnation is the story of a Jesus Voice which "accompanies" us in good times and in bad, playing the music of God, as it "sets" us in places of healing and wholeness.

STUDIO LIVE

1) Orcas ("killer whales") live in matrilineal pods, each distinguishable by distinctive dialect of its sound system. Each pod has its own soundtrack. Each pod leaves its own acoustic imprint.

   * What's your church's acoustic imprint?

2) Is there anything more unseemly and uncomfortable than elderly married couples who thrive on annoying each other and striking each other with their tongues not to kiss but to kill?

3) A Jesus human voice starts with the particulars, to show care and concern for those abused and do everything to protect them and all others who are vulnerable. But then the particular must go to the universal. Hence the power of the image of the Pope himself on behalf of the church, repenting and getting on his hands and knees and washing the feet of those children and adults victimized by priests.

   But there is another particular involved: the priest abusers. And while justice must be swift and sure for pedophiliac priests, the church should never forget that it is in the healing and redemption business, and provide treatments for those with sexual dysfunctions and disorders. If the church had spoken in a Jesus Voice in addressing the sexual abuse of particular children, a problem of long-standing in the church would have been squelched.[102]

* Discuss how the mystery of the incarnation symbolizes the relationship of particularity and universality. What are the implications for you that the fullness of the divinity dwells in the concreteness of one human, Jesus the Christ?

4) As we see from above, George Herbert liked to use the image of the bonesetter, and combine it with music. Here is his poem "The Collar" where his life is described as "sunder'd music" that has been "scattered" by sin and guilt. God is the bonesetter that puts the "broken bones" back together again.

> Oh, who can tell
> How all this sunder'd music may be set?
> Who can restore
> Unto his place this scattered harmony?
> It may be possible
> In that great Taskmaster's house to find
> A place for all things lost, yea, things destroy'd:
> A place for broken bones.[103]

* How does the poem's image of "sunder'd music" resonate with you?

* What are some ways in which sin and guilt can scatter our lives?

* How does God work as a bonesetter in our lives?

* What are some examples of how God has set your

broken bones and brought back healing and harmony into your life?

* When have you seen God do the same for others?
* How can we learn to trust God as our bonesetter, even when we are feeling broken and scattered?
* What does it mean to live a life of "music" that is pleasing to God?
* What are some practical steps that we can take to cultivate a more harmonious life?
* How can we share the gift of God's healing and harmony with others?

5) On some level, Voice is "mysterious" and can't be neatly analyzed, though we try. Voice doesn't always speak to the Mind, which is one reason English naturalist and biologist Charles Darwin couldn't figure music out. It didn't have any evolutionary significance that he could find. In his *The Descent of Man* (1871), he confessed to his confoundment:

> Music has often been ranked as one of the fine arts; but this is a purely human and artificial distinction. As neither the enjoyment nor the capacity of producing musical notes are faculties of the least use to man in reference to his daily habits of life, they must be ranked amongst the most mysterious with which he is endowed.[104]

To be fair, Darwin did profess to enjoy his wife Emma's piano playing, and sometimes timed his walks to hear the singing inside King's College Chapel in Cambridge, which could give him shivers. But have you ever met someone who simply didn't "get" music? Could it be because music yokes both hemispheres of the brain?

Darwin is not the only one who doesn't "get" music. The Harvard cognitive scientist and public intellectual Steven Pinker calls music "auditory cheesecake," a purely hedonistic evolutionary artifact that "we ingest through the ears to stimulate a mass of pleasure circuits at once." Music, in Pinker's view is a leech on critical thinking and a deterrent to our mental faculties.[105]

* Contrast Darwin's and Pinker's position on music with that of Brazilian theologian Rubem Alves (d. 2014) who claimed that "Hope is hearing the melody of the future; faith is dancing to that melody here and now."[106]

* Do you agree with Darwin and Pinker that music is pointless evolutionarily, or do you think it serves a deeper purpose like Alves suggests? Why?

* Have you ever met someone who doesn't appreciate or "get" music? What do you make of that perspective?

* Why do you think music engages both hemispheres of the brain? What might this suggest about its significance?

* Alves talks about music connecting us to hope and

faith. Do you agree? Can music connect us to things beyond logic and reason?

* If music is an "auditory cheesecake" as Pinker describes it, why do humans persist in making music across cultures and history?

* How might a theologian like Alves view music differently than a scientist like Darwin or Pinker? Do you see those perspectives as opposed or complementary?

* Can analytical thinking or science fully explain something like music? Is reducing music to evolution or neuroscience missing the point?

* What role does music play in your life? Does it feel unnecessary or essential?

* Do you think societies value music enough? Should music be more prioritized in education and culture? Why or why not?

* Overall, what makes music so meaningful yet difficult to explain rationally? What does this suggest about human nature?

6) We are created in the "image of God." That's a visual frame. But biblical faith is more hearing than seeing. So what would be the cognate aural frame for "the image of God?" How about "the echo of God." We are yes, God's image. We are, yes, God's echo.

* What does it mean to you to be an echo of God? Does

your voice echo the divine in all its "echoes of mercy, whispers of love?"

* In what ways can we perceive or experience the divine echoes in our lives?
* How does being an echo of God influence our interactions and relationships with others?
* Are there certain qualities or attributes that exemplify the divine echoes within us? How can we cultivate them?
* Can we also find echoes of God in nature, art, or other aspects of the world? How does this connect to our understanding of being God's echo?
* How does the concept of being an echo of God relate to our purpose and calling in life?
* Are there specific practices or disciplines that help us better attune ourselves to the echoes of God within us?
* What role does introspection and self-reflection play in recognizing our own echoes of God?
* Are there any parallels or differences between being an echo of God and being a reflection of God's character?
* How does the idea of being an echo of God inform our understanding of love, compassion, and mercy?
* Can we unintentionally distort the echoes of God within us? If so, how can we realign ourselves with the true divine echoes?

* Sing together Fanny Crosby's classic, "Blessed Assurance, Jesus is Mine . . . This is My Story, This is My Song."

7) In the monthly magazine *Guide to Christian Perfection* (later called *Guide to Holiness* when Phoebe and Walter Palmer purchased and renamed it in 1864], (January, 1857), 134–140, Phoebe Palmer gave her account of what the "Tuesday Afternoon Meeting" was about (average 120 present in Palmer's home starting at 3 p.m. in the afternoon, usually eight or ten clergy present, that's all, but everyone equal and focus on testimony about what God is doing).

Then there follows these protocols for when to speak and when to be silent, a "seasons" litany that Ellen Gould White picked up and put into her writings and made them famous among Adventists.

Palmer's seven seasons of silence are:
The season of waiting
The season of searching
The season of finding
The season of believing
The season of resting
The season of growing
The season of witnessing

Palmer's seven seasons of speaking are:
The season of being called
The season of preparation
The season of obedience

The season of fear
The season of faith
The season of power
The season of harvest

SEVEN SEASONS OF SILENCE

1. It is never in season to speak until we have a call.
2. It is a season to be silent when we are not rightly informed upon the question to which we must speak.
3. When we know the state of a question, yet must not speak without suitable preparation, either actual or habitual.
4. It is a season to be silent when what we speak is likely to be a snare unto ourselves.
5. As it is a season for silence when the passions and corruptions of others are excited, so we are to be silent when it is thus with ourselves.
6. It is a season for silence, when men are not capable of attending to what we speak.
7. It is a season for silence, when what we speak may be a grief and burden to the spirits of any, especially of those that are already afflicted.

SEVEN SEASONS OF SPEAKING

1. When by speaking we may bring glory to God and good to our brethren.
2. When we have an opportunity to vindicate the honor and truth of God.
3. When we may relieve the credit of a brother that is wronged.
4. When by speaking we may instruct or direct those that are ignorant.
5. When we comfort and support those that are weak.
6. When we may resolve and settle those that are in doubt.
7. When we may duly reprove and convince those that do evil. At such times as these we ought to speak; for then to be silent is our sin and weakness.

8) The Jesus Voice is always the voice of truth. Roger Scruton contends: "A writer who says that there are no truths, or that all truth is 'merely relative,' is asking you not to believe him. So don't."[107]

* Do you agree with Scruton?

* Do you agree that mendacity is always immoral? If your spouse asks, "Does this attire make me look fat?" is it possible to respond truthfully without causing other moral crises? If you were hiding Jews from the Nazis, and you were asked if you had any Jews in your house, is it possible to respond truthfully without conspiring in evil?

9) When you are done reading a passage of Scripture, try out this proem (prayerpoem) by friend Teri Hyrkas as one way to close the reading:

> This is God's Story,
> This is God's Song.
> This is God's Vision,
> This is God's Voice.
> This is God's Mind,
> This is God's Heart.
> This is Meaning,
> This is Mystery,
> This is Miracle.
> This is Truth,
> This is Life.

10) Is your church more worn out from attending to the death throes of the old than energized by the birth pangs of the new? Which is it?

11) Recite together this Unison Prayer of Confession:

> Lord, we admit it. We make allowances and give all benefits of the doubt to those who agree with us and share our beliefs. And we think the worst, take cheap shots at and impugn the motives of those we disagree with. Forgive us our clannishness and un-Jesus conduct. Help us to love those who disagree with us so we can begin to love those who hate us, not to mention our enemies. Amen.

Chapter 5: Nose
The Jesus Nose

> *Another angel, who had a golden censer, came and stood at the altar. He was given much incense to offer, with the prayers of all God's people, on the golden altar in front of the throne. The smoke of the incense, together with the prayers of God's people, went up before God from the angel's hand.*
>
> REVELATION 8:3–4 NIV

The words "God" and "dog" are frequently used in memes and jokes, some of which can put your nose out of joint. But God and dog are alike in a straightforward way: both have an acute sense of smell. It is not just that we have a "smelly gospel," as Drew Doss and Nate Carlson so winsomely put it.[1] Or that we have a "smelly Jesus" as South-African theologian Pierre du Plessis portrays in his award-winning *Myrr and Dust: Tracking the Scent of Jesus* (2024). We have a smelly story from Genesis to Revelation.

God's Nosebleed: Among the Hebrew people, stench

signified uncleanness, disease, danger, and death. Incense and fragrance signified holiness, health, and safety. Prayers are incense before God.[2] God inhales the "soothing odor" or "fragrant smells" (*reach hannihoah*) of offerings, a phrase that the Talmud often uses to describe the loving and protective relationship between God and God's "fragrant friends" known as the people of Israel.

God especially loves the smoky, tangy smell of barbecue, a "pleasing aroma" of atonement that warms God's heart. Noah honored God's sense of smell with burnt offerings as his first act after coming out of the ark.

> The Lord smelled the pleasing aroma and said in his heart: "Never again will I curse the ground because of humans, even though every inclination of the human heart is evil from childhood. And never again will I destroy all living creatures, as I have done."[3]

The ancient Hebrews took the hint, and bombarded the heavens with the charred smells of the grill. Even the Temple opened and closed by the inviting smell of roasted lamb which pleased God.[4]

Jesus was born into a world rich in smell—an olfactory mall of smelly shepherds; sweet, earthy hay; sweaty barnyard animals; strong, ammonia-like odors of manure and urine; not to mention the musky, metallic smells of childbirth. As the Magi presented Jesus with the most expensive perfumes of frankincense and myrrh to anoint his birth, Mary Magdalene lavished on Jesus the most expensive perfume to anoint his death—the sweet, floral fragrance of nard.[5] Jesus was resurrected in a dusty cave smelling of myrrh, chalky limestone, and the exotic early morning scents of garden plants and flowers.

Disciples' BO: Jesus dwells in the nose. So does the divine, as our birth story makes clear when God breathes into Adam's nostrils the divine breath making him a "living being."[6] Or when Job testifies to his friends that he will stay faithful to his God "as long as my breath is in me, and the spirit of God is in my nostrils."[7] For the Hebrew people, what the gut was to compassion, the nostrils were to spirit and life.

> *For while one could avert the eyes, block the ears, avoid touch and taste, one could not stop breathing. And breathing included olfactory encounter.*
>
> HISTORIAN SUSAN ASHBROOK HARVEY[8]

It is not just some people who have "an air" about them. We all squirt a spirit that gives off "an air." And every "air" we exhale has a scent. We emanate a "smell" that sticks as tightly to us as the clothes we wear or the skin we're in. When Christ takes form in us, we take on the air of Jesus and start smelling like Jesus. "For we are the good odour of Christ unto God," Paul told the church at Corinth.[9]

Even your church can give off the odor of Christ. Paul commended the church at Philippi for letting loose in the world "an odor of sweetness, an acceptable sacrifice."[10] A Jesus smellscape is part of the manifestation and impartation

DESIGNER JESUS

of Christ, as the church at Ephesus is admonished to be a fragrance that brings God pleasure.

> And walk in love, as Christ also has loved us, and has delivered himself for us, an oblation and a sacrifice to God for an odour of sweetness.[11]

You smell. Do you give off the odor of Christ?

Your church smells. What does your church smell like? When Jesus is present, there is fresh air, free space, and freedom. When Jesus is absent, there is stuffiness, staleness, and static.

God has a strong sense of smell. After the barbecue of "burnt offerings" like roasted lamb, God loves to smell the aroma of the living Christ, the Lamb of God who takes away the stench of sin.

Biblical phrases like "I will run after the odor of Thy garments, Thy fragrance is better than all spices"[12] or "the scent of your garments is like the scent of Lebanon"[13] expressed for many throughout history the beauty of Jesus[14] and the scentscape of the Messiah.

Praise leaves a sound;
worship leaves an aroma.
NEW ZEALAND SINGER/SONGWRITER BROOKE LIGERTWOOD[15]

Messianic Scentscape: The Hebrew term "Messiah" (in Greek *Christos*) means "the anointed one," and relates to anyone anointed (dedicated to God). The person thus anointed might be a king, a priest, or a prophet. To the ancient Israelite there was no oil or fat with more symbolic meaning than olive oil. It was used as an emollient, a fuel for lighting lamps, for nutrition, and many other purposes. It was scented olive oil that was chosen to be a holy anointing oil for the Israelites.

What scented the anointing oil? The recipe for two fragrances were revealed in the book of Exodus,[16] but their replication for personal use was forbidden. Only the priests were privileged to use these holy incenses. One was for sacred perfumes for the tabernacle, and the anointing of holy vessels. One was for anointing Aaron and his sons as priests and holy vessels. The ingredients for one was myrrh, cinnamon, calamus, and orris, dissolved in olive oil. The ingredients for the other was equal amounts of styrax, onycha, galbanum, and frankincense, ground together into a fine powder. On the Day of Atonement, Aaron was to burn clouds of incense to obscure the Ark of the Covenant to protect him from seeing God and preserve God's mystery.

Fragrance is the fifth dimension of design. A disciple directed to God and designed by Jesus smells like Jesus. Discipleship is in part the parapsychology of the nose, a lost language that lies buried in our brains. Students in training to be perfumers are called "noses." Not "pupils," which features seeing, but "noses" for smelling. Our perception of the world comes as much through the nose as through the eyes and ears. According to Francesca Stavrakopoulou, in the Scriptures God's nose is often used as a symbol of his power and authority: "The nose is a powerful symbol of authority and power. It is the part of the face that is most often

DESIGNER JESUS

associated with leadership and command. In the Bible, God's nose is often used as a symbol of his power and authority."[17] She even goes so far as to say "the God of the Bible was particularly proud of his nose."[18] The relation between the world of fragrance and the aura of faith is the subject of this chapter.

Eau de Jesus: So what does Jesus smell like?[19] What is the Eau de Jesus?

There is an old saying, "Preachers need to smell of the sheep and not of incense." The truth is we all need to smell of both because Jesus smells of both. The most sought-after ingredient in the most expensive, sexy perfumes (Chanel, Gucci, Givenchy) is ambergris, which is essentially sun-dried whale vomit. Ambergris sells for $20,000 per kilogram, compared to the highest quality gold which sells for $44,000 per kilo. If the scent of the manger is not there, it's not a great fragrance. If the smell of the earth is not there, it's fake, it's artificial, it's contrived. The best smells have the whiff of the barnyard.

After it rains, you smell the earth. Petrichor is the name for a new, daring smell to the earth after the rain. You don't smell the rain; you smell the earth. You need the earthy scents of wooly sheep, dewy shepherds, and fecal barns as well as the richly scented, frankincense-festooned Magi to get the whole Eau de Jesus. Jesus was a King, so he needed to smell like a king.[20] But in all the best smells, even kingly ones, there is the scent of nativity—blood, sweat, excrement, and sweet baby smells.

An ancient Jewish tradition was that a mother would

weave a seamless garment for her son when he left home to study with a rabbi or in the Temple. This would have been soaked in the warm, aromatic scent of spikenard first, then in the smells of her own body as she wore it long enough to wrap her absent son in her scented memory and love. His lifetime sacrifice as a rabbi was a sweet aroma to God, and the seamless garment would become one of the most precious possessions of his life.[21]

> *Master, Savior, Jesus,*
> *like the fragrance after the rain.*
> BILL AND GLORIA GAITHER,
> "THERE'S SOMETHING ABOUT THAT NAME"

The Virgin Mary is associated with roses, and Marian appearances are said to be accompanied by the smell of roses. The earliest known image of the Virgin Mary is found in the Catacombs of St. Priscilla on Via Salaria north of Rome, where the Madonna is nursing a child with a companion pointing to the Madonna and holding a book and with two angels offering them roses. The Catacomb of Saints Peter and Marcellinus in Rome depict Mary standing with the infant Jesus in her arms, surrounded by a wreath of roses. Among the five miles of burials there are many frescoes painted by fossores that portray Mary and roses together.[22]

The Roman Curia of the Holy See is famous for its princes in purple. Those who wore purple-colored robes, kings and queens, nobility, priests, and the imperial classes of Rome, Egypt, and Persia, often swathed the fabric in sacred fragrances. Summoned to Tarsus by the Roman General Mark Antony in 41 BC, The Egyptian queen Cleopatra entered the city by sailing up the Cydnus River in a fleet of small ships with purple sails, dressed in the robes of the Greek goddess Aphrodite. The purple sails of her highly decorated barge were drenched in perfume so that the billowing scent would announce her arrival. Aphrodisiac plants, herbs, and other things (red ginseng, maca, alligator testicles) were often ground into powdered form and put into a cloth sachet and worn between a woman's breasts. Whether Cleopatra added this seduction to her entrance is unknown, but with or without it, Mark Anthony was smitten.

> *The dance of predator and prey Is orchestrated by a billion chemical fiddlers. In a unit as large as a forest, a jungle, or a planet, entire symphonies of information resonate through the air, an inaudible behavioral ballet, choreographed by countless biochemical transactions.*
> CULTURAL CRITIC HOWARD RHEINGOLD[23]

Sniff-Invocation: Throughout sacred history, smell has been used to announce the arrival of the divine. Ancient Hebrews believed that the smell of the altar was incense to the divine. God inhales the aroma of burnt sacrifices and offerings.

> Then burn the entire ram on the altar. It is a burnt offering to the Lord, a pleasing aroma, a food offering presented to the Lord (Exodus 29:18 NIV).

> It is a burnt offering, a food offering, an aroma pleasing to the Lord (Leviticus 1:9 NIV).

Incense was burnt on the golden altar every morning and every evening—twice a day most likely around 9 a.m. and 3 p.m., although some argue it was most likely dawn and dusk.[24]

Worshipers prayed in the temple "at the hour of the incense offering."[25] The angel appeared to Zechariah and announced the pregnancy of Elizabeth while he had the privilege of being the priest to preside at the "hour of incense" at the Festival of Pentecost.[26] The altar of incense was inside the Holy Place in the Temple, just outside of the curtain which separated the Holy Place from the Holy of Holies. The twice daily offering of incense was the most pleasing to God of all the offerings.

<u>Covenant of Smell:</u> The call to worship for the Hebrew people was the smell of barbecue. In fact, the smell of barbecue came before the sight of the rainbow in reminding God never to flood the Earth as punishment for human wickedness. The first thing Noah did after he and his family left the ark was to build an altar and make a sacrifice.

> The Lord smelled the sweet/pleasing/soothing aroma and said in his heart: "Never again will I curse the ground because of humans, even though every inclination of the human heart is evil from childhood. And never again will I destroy all living creatures, as I have done."[27]

DESIGNER JESUS

The first thing Noah does after emerging from the ark is to build an altar and offer a sacrifice and minhah that includes frankincense. In fact, the "pleasing odor" of the sacrifice is in Hebrew "reiah nihoah,"[28] a play on words with the name Noah. The smell of Noah, his righteousness and his faith, is like a fragrant incense in the nostrils of the Almighty. Before the rainbow in the sky, there is the smell of "reiah nihoah" that triggers God's reminder never again to flood the world.

Every Jewish home cherished a "spice jar" in which they kept spices for incense (which was made with five spices), herbs, and anointing oils for rituals of prayer and Sabbath. Fragrant oils like frankincense and myrrh would be used for special occasions such as anointings of kings, weddings, funerary rituals, temple and festival rituals, and cleansing rites. Myrrh was a costly incense used to make exquisite perfume.[29] It also had such healing properties they called it "the balm of Gilead." Mixed with wine it was used as a painkiller, an analgesic Jesus refused on the cross.[30]

Sniff-Navigation: It is hard for us to imagine how powerful the sense of smell was to the Jewish faith and to Jesus himself. But let's try. Walking down the street, creeping out of a vent in the sidewalk, or strolling along the mid-way of a carnival or fair, wafting its way from a kiosk: Sometimes an odor will "hit you" and almost send you reeling.

The Jewish faith had official odiferous rituals that some deemed "officious" but identified who you were, what you believed, and how you lived. The word for smell or perceive odor in Hebrew female noun form, "rü'·akh" or "reyach," is derived from the primitive root verb for spirit, "rü'·akh" or "ruach." In Judaism, the sense of scent is considered holy.

Smell was closely associated with purity laws, and the connection between olfaction and holiness was significant. The smells of myrrh, jasmine, frangipani, and lilies of the valley were associated with purity, innocence, and holiness. Martha registered her fear to Jesus about the uncleanness that would come from her brother's decaying flesh when she protested, "Lord, he has been dead for four days. The smell will be terrible."[31]

Our sense of smell is the physical sense most associated with memory. Smells, more than sounds, more than sights, more than touches, transport our minds and bodies back in time to an imprinted memory. Garlic brings you back to your grandmother's kitchen. A wet woolen smell brings you back to the locker room—or to the terror of the day you fell in a frozen pond and almost drowned. Rising yeast smells like every Sunday dinner. Gasoline chokes you with memories of a car crash. Nothing evokes strong emotions, strong memories, strong longings, like the sense of smell.[32] It is a powerful communicator to our inner being.

◇

Taste and smell, like faithful servants, become the Rosetta Stone to the entire structure of recollection.
EDITOR CHRISTOPHER BAMFORD (D. 2022)[33]

Peter betrayed Jesus three times around a fire: not a wood or animal dung fire, which were most common in the ancient cultures of the Middle East, but an expensive charcoal fire.[34] Jesus snuffed out the rancid smell of Peter's betrayal, which would have stalked Peter for the rest of his life whenever he smelled live coals, with a charcoal fire on the shore, where he appeared to his disciples for the third time and gave Peter three chances to restore relationship.[35]

In Jesus' day, when you practiced your faith beyond the home and traveled to the Temple in Jerusalem, the smell of burnt offerings ambushed your senses. Small birds, little lambs, murring calves, great grains—all were sacrificed and burned on the altar. Oil and frankincense were added to the grain before burning it. The smoke that rose from the Temple was a delightful barbecue aroma. Roasted meats, roasted grains, aromatic oils, sweet smoke. No wonder all those sacrifices were referred to by the priests as "fragrant." The aroma around the Temple in Jerusalem must have been like being a Grill-Masters cook-off in Memphis. The sweet smell of roasted richness coupled with the belief in its aromatic atonement made for a heady atmosphere.

Calendar of Scents: There was also in every Jewish household (and still is today) a weekly threshold ceremony called "*Havdalah*" ("separation") that brought the Sabbath to an end once three stars appeared in the evening sky. The ceremony is conducted in the dark except for candlelight. All five senses are invoked in this crossover ritual that ushers you from Shabbat, a day of difference separate from all other days, into the every-days of life.

Havdalah is, at least in part, aromatherapy to get you

through the coming week. Havdalah scents your spirit with Shabbat for whatever challenges and ambushes you might be facing in the future. Havdalah involves the ritual lighting of a special braided candle with multiple wicks (held by a child), blessing a cup of wine, and smelling sweet spices. The highlight of Havdalah is the release of smells, a transition ritual of olfaction that connects the holy with the ordinary, the set-apart from the everyday, the invisible with the visible.

Jesus' resurrection was the ultimate Havdalah celebration, as it ends the seventh day, the holy day, and transitions the world into everyday risings, a life of first days, new days, glory days, even in the midst of rainy days. Because of the risen and rising Christ, we can halo every moment with Havdalah Shabbat. Can you smell the sweetness, taste the tang of eternity in this moment? That's resurrection Havdalah.

Oil and perfume make the heart glad.
PROVERBS 27:9 ESV

The early church resisted the liturgical privileging of smell in the community's worship life, partly to differentiate it from Judaism's adoration of the aromatic and its framing the life of the soul with a cycle of odors in the liturgical seasons. But the metaphor of smell was pervasive among even those like Tertullian and Origen who critiqued its ritual usage. Clement of Alexandria both criticized the olfactory stranglehold on the religious imagination while celebrating a

DESIGNER JESUS

restrained deployment of sacred scents as a proper honoring of God's good gifts.

> *For the first Christians, pleasing smells were a reminder of our Edenic future. The Bible begins in a garden, a paradise of fragrance. The Garden of Eden is most often portrayed in both Jewish and Christian literature as an aromatic heaven. The Bible ends in a garden city made of gold streets, jasper walls, pearly gates, and "golden bowls full of incense." The smell of home (our eternal home) is partly formulated by the accumulative mix of ascending prayers to heaven—prayers that never die but waft their bouquets throughout eternity. The twenty-four elders fell down before the Lamb, each holding a harp, and golden bowls full of incense, which are the prayers of the saints.*
> REVELATION 5:8 ESV

Incense in church signaled the journey of the invisible into the visible, the materialization of the ethereal, the earthy presence of the eternal. You knew God was present when you smelled the divine. Sacred smells in a disciple's life are meant to materialize the presence of Jesus. What makes "thin places" thin, diaphanous to the divine, is that they are thick with the aura and aroma of relationships, stories, symbols, metaphors, heritage.

The dean of science fiction writer", Ro'ert A. Heinlein (1907–1988), was convinced that religion is the most prevalent drive in the human species, and that when it is present you can literally "smell it."³⁶ Historian Susan Ashbrook Harvey, daughter of pioneering neurotheologian (and my professor) James B. Ashbrook, has written a pathbreaking study of the olfactory features of faith called *Scenting Salvation* (2006).³⁷ Harvey cites Athenaeus' observation that gender, social class, and moral disposition were all marked by distinct smells. In Book 11 of his *The Deipnosophists*, or *Banquet of the Learned*, Athenaeus contends that smell was an identifier of social class, gender and moral stature:

> . . . the smell of a rich man is different from that of a poor man, and the smell of a good man is different from that of a bad man.³⁸

In the ancient world, fragrances were more than cosmetics; they were worn by the rich as prophylactics against airborne diseases and the stench of the masses.

Harvey documents how ancient Christians used the sense of smell to experience the divine in a wide array of embodied ways. Christians even borrowed freely from pagan, Jewish, and uniquely Christian sources in their aromatic practices and liturgies. The church in antiquity defined itself in terms of all its senses, which means the community's identity as Jesus followers came partly from the smells. Susan Ashbrook Harvey portrays Syriac Christianity as a "densely textured ritual environment" where one sense was layered on another.

> Their reception of the heightened sensory environment was essential to the ritual process itself. They inhaled the rich scents of incense and holy oil; they gazed upon the

abundant decor that adorned even village churches of late antiquity with fine linens, tapestries, frescoes, and mosaics.[39]

The Russian Church has the true smell: it smells of the poor, of untarred leather, onions, and human sweat.
ENGLISH CATHOLIC ESSAYIST MAURICE BARING (D. 1945)[40]

In the Roman Catholic tradition, there was a spring tradition of women going to their gardens before mass and plucking a bud or blossom from a sweet-smelling shrub, usually the Benzoin spicebush (also known as benjamin-bush or wild-allspice). Devout Catholics would then take this Benzoin (Semitic in origin meaning perfume, which is what it was used for in Asian lands) bud, known for its aromatic fragrance, and wrap it in their handkerchief so that during the sermon, if the preacher got especially long and tedious, they would take out the handkerchief, squeeze the blossom in their hand, and release the spicy fragrance into the air. The jolt of perfume stiffened the body for more of the sermon.

Follow Your Nose: Animals are known for their keen sense of smell. A deer can smell budding roses as far as 100 yards away. They know right when to show up and bite off the perfect rose bud when it's most fresh, fragrant, and tasty. Just ask any gardener. Humans have 5 million smell receptors. A dog boasts 300 million smell receptors. This is the source of the old adage that a dog sees the world through his nose.

The truth is that disciples of Jesus experience others

through their nose too. You don't just nose wine, or nose whiskey. You nose people too. The Nose Knows. The most common translation renders the famous text from Isaiah (11:3 NKJV) "his delight is in the fear of the Lord." But the Hebrew actually says "his scent is in the fear of the Lord" or, more precisely, he has a nose for it, he can sniff it out, it is a sweet aroma to him.[41] We will never enjoy the smell intelligence of a dog, but we are called to nose out Jesus, to track and trek his mission in the world.

The breath is a window into the blood.
RESEARCH SCIENTIST DR. JOACHIM DIETER PLEIL, WHO BELIEVES
BREATH BETRAYS A BODY'S HEALTH STATUS[42]

The #1 predictor of church health and growth is reaching OUTWARD in care and compassion. There are three levels to the ladder of care and compassion: 1) sympathy; 2) empathy; 3) mercy.[43] Irish sister Catherine McAuley (d. 1841), co-founder of the Sisters of Mercy in 1831, identified five core values to mercy: reverence, commitment to the poor, justice, stewardship, and integrity. But Sister McAuley bundled all five together in one succinct definition of mercy, the highest tier of care and compassion: "having an exquisite nose for the sufferings of others."[44] An INWARD focused church exists for the comfort and approval of its members. Every church professes to be an OUTWARD focused church until the church wants to do something a member doesn't like, when suddenly the empathy button has stopped working, the compassion tab is broken, and the nose gets its sinuses plugged.

DESIGNER JESUS

---◇---

You can't conceive, my child, nor can I or anyone the . . .
appalling strangeness of the mercy of God.
ENGLISH NOVELIST GRAHAM GREENE (D. 1991)[45]

<u>The Nose Knows:</u> Scientists now tell us that humans can detect at least over 10,000 unique odors. When you lose your sense of smell, however, it is not just your relationship with food that suffers, since taste and smell are inextricably connected.[46] Your relationship with others suffers. Our bodies talk to each other on a subconscious level through olfactory communication. In fact, "Nose Knows" is one of the most reliable predictors of who you will marry.

Sigmund Freud hypothesized that kids are sexually attracted to parents and siblings, hence the need for the incest taboo. In 1891 the Westermarck Effect was published that argued the opposite from Freud. Family members raised together the first six years of life were characterized by "reverse sexual imprinting." Triggered by the nose we are sexually desensitized to each other in family settings so that our close relatives do not smell sexy.[47] Poet William Wordsworth is famous for being madly in love with his sister Dorothy, who convinced him to marry her friend Mary Hutchinson to give him a sexual outlet. But Wordsworth had no sense of smell. Biologist Lewis Thomas and media philosopher Marshall McLuhan brought back the Westermarck Effect in the 1970s by taking it in genetic directions. They argued that our genes give off a certain odor, and that people are attracted to those whose genes are most unlike their own.

There is an immediate linkup between nose and brain. Odor information works on the brain directly, unlike the indirect route taken by auditory and visual. Olfactory neurons, unlike other nerve cells, regenerate. Each person has an odor-print that is as characteristic as a thumbprint or voiceprint.

How do sperms wend their way toward an egg? Odor receptors.

How does an infant find its mother's nipple? The nose.

How does a mother pick out her newborn from other newborns? The nose.

How does a boy or girl pick out another boy or girl to date and mate? The nose.

Beauty may be in the eye of the beholder, but odor is in the nose of the smeller. Our olfactory sense is the only sense that has a beeline to the parts of our brain that deal with memory and emotion. Smell bypasses the conscious brain and appeals directly to the limbic system. An impaired sense of smell can radically change our relationships with others. Our body odors signal our emotional states, so when we can't smell each other, we can't be sensitive to each other's spirit and emotions. Scents give us subconscious sense and subliminal signage.[48] Humans aren't as good as dogs at reading each other's spirit through scents. But it would not be wrong to say that your dog is not the only one to see the world through its nose.

Jesus followers have "Nose Knows" super-powers. We

bombard the world with missiles from the heavenly realms. Saints are stink bombs of sanctity.

We can learn to "read" or experience a person or a crowd like you "read" or experience cologne, or chocolate, or flowers, or wine, or coffee. How do you "nose out" others? How do you "nose out" the divine?

<u>The Smell Test:</u> Extracting the "essence" of something used to be a carefully guarded secret, an almost alchemical process passed on behind curtains and in whispers. No longer. But every Smell Master insists on four conditions for the best "reading" of wine, chocolate, cologne, or, for our purposes, people.

First, it needs to be at room temperature.

Any conclusion about people formed in strained and alien environments is dangerous and misleading. Don't try to experience someone in the heat or the cold, when they're having to deal with high stress or frigid blasts. Flowers lose their scent while they're refrigerated. The aroma of Christ doesn't fare well when frozen. The true flavor of a person is most often seen as best exposed under stress. But it could equally be argued that one's true flavor comes through most pungently, not in the extremes, but in the absence of distortions and distractions and the everydayness of life.

Second, always give what you are experiencing two passes.

Eat it in two bites. Always give a second chance, which doesn't mean the first time was a failure. Just the opposite. In the first bite, the first pass, you are just getting to know the subject. In the second bite, the return engagement, you are delving deeper and searching out the subtleties and nuances of the person or condition. Wine opens up in the succor of a glass. People open up in the succor of second chances.

Third, be fully present to the experience.

In any "tasting," don't let your mind go anywhere else than where it is. Stay in the experience. And don't start looking at other more favored venues and vessels.

English philosopher and social critic William Hazlitt (1778–1830) decided to get some distance to see England better and visited abroad. After his touring of France and Italy, he described his own nation in 1826 as a people who "do not care about the color, taste, smell, the sense of luxury or pleasure" requiring only "the heavy, hard and tangible." Everything and everyone must be judged in their own terms and conditions and not in comparison with others.

Fourth, there are three stages to every experience, to every taste. There are three levels of sensory excitement in which the nose and mouth partner to describe the taste of something: top note, middle palate, lingering finish.

Top Note: First, breath it in whole. Taste it with air. The beginning taste is called the top note, the first impression. When meeting someone new, is there an initial openness and receptivity, or do judgments break in? In the "top note" of a first impression, is there a sense of curiosity, possibility, and presence? Can you breathe the other in whole as a subject, not in parts you like as an object?

Middle Palate: Second, feel the middle palate of taste on your tongue. Move the experience from the nose to the mouth. Move past first impressions to understand the complexities of the other person. Can you allow their unique essence to impact you deeply? Can you taste their true qualities and better virtues?

Lingering Finish: Third, experience the lingering finish of your encounter, and keep breathing it in. What are the lingering impressions left on you after an interaction? How has the relationship changed you for good? What will be the persistence of their influence?

Jesus-Olfaction: The ultimate scent we are to smell is Jesus, who is "The Living Water." The scent of water signifies the presence of God, and our faith can have scenting skills that alert us to the situations and stirrings of the Spirit.

Though its roots have grown old in the earth and its stump decays, at the scent of water it will bud and sprout again like a new seedling.

JOB 14:8-9 NLT

Elephants can smell water up to twelve miles away. Even in drought conditions, they can smell water underground. Their nostrils are located at the tip of their long trunks, and they literally follow their nose to water and use their trunk to dig for it, suck it up and squirt the water into their mouths. Other animals know that the elephant can smell water, so during droughts, many animals watch and stay near the elephants. Sycamore trees are famous for growing near rivers and streams, and their white bark serves as semaphores for animals looking for water. Tree and plant roots also have a way of detecting water sources and grow in that direction.

Christians are like elephants and sycamores and root systems. We help others become aware of what is already present, but not readily known. And once we help others become aware of the God who is already present, like an old tree stump that smells water, they are able "bud and sprout" new life, new possibilities, new hope, and a new revived relationship with God.[49]

The moment you drink living water, you start smelling like Jesus, the Living Water. Or as Paul puts it, when you walk in the way of love, your life is an Eau de Jesus: "God was pleased for Christ's love for you was like sweet perfume to him."[50]

What does Jesus smell like?

Faith's Fragrance: In Ephesians, we are told exactly what an Aroma of Christ Church, or an Eau de Jesus person, smells like. The aromatic blends of the three transcendentals, in a myriad mix of beauty, truth, and goodness. In other words, no lies, no evilness, no bitterness, no wrath, or wrangling. No lies, only truth. No hate, only love. No condemnation, only embrace. An Aroma of Christ Church is a reflection of God—"imitators" of Christ. Those who embrace and embody these actions and attributes emit a special smell. It is the "fragrance" of Christ, the Eau de Jesus.

How much do we spend every year trying to drown out our own body odors or deluge ourselves in some new fragrance? There is only one odor Christians are called to carry, and it's not Estee Lauder or Tom Ford. It's the "fragrance" of Christ—the essential oils of understanding love, binding mercy, and finding grace. The Eau de Jesus smiles through the tears, as it first wafted its conquering ways on the world by penetrating the putrid garbage-heap road-block called Golgotha.

On the crucible of the cross was pounded out in nails the most attractive scent ever conceived: the fragrance of Jesus' own sacrifice, the bouquet of forgiveness, the corsage of compassion, the aroma of self-sacrificing love. Sniff the peach-fuzzy hair on top of a newborn baby's head and increase it ten thousand times. That is the sweetness of Jesus' sacrificial "fragrance."

The Big Stink: But just as the mission of the light is not to light the light but to light the darkness, so the mission of the Jesus smell is to scent the stink, not scent the scented. The answer to the question of "What does Jesus smell like?" is partly, "Sometimes Jesus smells bad." If all you're smelling is good smells, then something is wrong. If you aren't smelling bad smells, then you're not where Jesus is. Jesus' mission took him where it could be said, as was said of Lazarus: "He stinketh."[51]

We aren't saved from bad smells or fishy smells or "bad chemistry." We are saved to savior bad smells, and savor them as Jesus did beginning with the manger smells and the mangy shepherds.[52] Our sense of smell has been saved so that it embraces the stench of the unclean and dirty. The test of a true messianic smell is the lingering whiff of the mephitic and malodorous. In fact, sometimes when disciples digest hard realities of life, not just tinctures of truth but jaw-dropping enormities of "the hard facts," their fibrous nature can release foul fumes, eructations that evidence our inner coming to terms with fears and the popping of fantasies, the existential flatulence of experience.

The Armpit Effect: A community as well as a person can have a smell disorder. Sometimes the church has not taken the smell of Jesus into the world but has spoiled itself on putting itself first. It gives off unpleasant odors, like those that come from food that has spoiled. Sometimes all you can smell of the church is its armpits. The 2012 buddy cop comedy movie *21 Jump Street* is named after an undercover police post in an old dilapidated church called "The Aroma of Christ Church." The name of the church is intended to be satirical, even mocking. But isn't that what Paul says the church is to be? "For we are to God a sweet smell of Christ."[53]

In fact, is there any higher compliment to a person than "I smell Jesus in you?" Obversely, is there any greater affront to a person than "You stink of the smoke of Satan?" If someone whispers in your ear "You smell good today," you assume they're referring to your perfume or cologne. Are we whispering to each other "You smell good today" or "You smell beautiful today" or "You smell like truth today" when the smell of GBT (GoodnessBeautyTruth) is on them? Is there any better metric for a "successful church" than "the bouquet of Jesus is all over your church." Or how about "the GBT bouquet of Jesus just gets stronger and stronger in your church."

When the Scriptures itemize the ingredients of the aroma of Christ, what's so surprising about the ones spelled out is two-fold. They're familiar, not exotic. They're economical, not extravagant.

First, they're known ingredients. It's as simple as "be loving, giving, and forgiving." It's as familiar as GBT: "generate Goodness, Beauty, and Truth." Or put negatively, "don't be mean," "don't be selfish," "don't be cruel." The repercussions of love, gratitude, forgiveness, goodness, beauty, and truth are life-changing and world-changing.

Second, they're not extravagant. Some people like to douse themselves in perfume or cologne. In fact, the older you get the more likely you are to do this because your decaying sense of smell needs more stimulation to register its presence. But the truth is that smell is perceptible in minute quantities, even as low as one-part-per-billion. Just a little aroma of Christ has transcendent, transfigurational properties.

In meteorological circles, there is a technical term called "near calm." "Near calm" is when there is only one mile per hour of wind recorded. "Near calm" describes a breeze that is just enough to bend a blade of grass. One mile per hour is about what you generate at a slow walk. It appears to be a pretty insignificant amount of pneuma, or wind. But wait: a one mile per hour wind changes the trajectory of a bullet by 15 inches. If you are a soldier standing in the middle of a sniper's scope, "near calm" can save your life. Just a tiny amount of "near calm," just a tiny dab of loving, giving, and forgiving in someone's life, can create huge changes. The aromas of Christ offered by small communities of faith can have massive consequences. The world can be changed by a one-mile-an-hour wind of care and compassion. An Aroma of Christ Church has the power to bend the trajectory of history.

Wake Up and Smell the Spirit: When Christ takes form in us, our lives become aerosol missives, flowers that give off olfactory messages, artworks of beauty, carvings of truth, vessels of goodness shaped to the hand of God. If Christ be formed in us, we have only to breathe deep the fragrance of Christ, and exhale smells of sweetness upon the world. The author of a book that has never been out of print since it was published in 1678 (*Pilgrim's Progress*), said in his memoirs that "For Christians to commune savourly of God's matters one with another, it is as if they opened to each other's nostrils boxes of perfume."[54]

> *When this was noised abroad,*
> *the multitude came together*
> ACTS 2:6 KJV

The Hour of Incense was a key component of the Festival of Pentecost.[55] But at Calvary, Jesus put an end to the sacrificial system of burnt offerings, and turned an "hour of incense" into a life of incense. The flame over the head of each disciple at Pentecost signified that each of our lives is to be a living altar of incense, and the church itself, born at Pentecost, a fragrant offering of Christ's presence wafting in

DESIGNER JESUS

the world by the winds of the Spirit, then sounded forth by the "noising abroad" of God's people.

Noisings: What brought in multitudes? The "noising abroad" of God's continuing presence "on earth, as it is in heaven."

Maybe it's the nose that inspires the noise?

Maybe it's time for God's people to get a little more nosey and noisier?

Maybe it's time to lead by the nose and learn nasal noise, nasal communication?

Maybe it's time to odor print others with the Jesus smell and practice some aroma evangelism?

Maybe it's time for the church to be the perfume that brings others to Jesus?

Maybe it's time to put on some Eau de Jesus.

In the Armenian rite for baptism, they do precisely that. A liturgical rite used by both the Armenian Apostolic Church and the Armenian Catholic Church, it is one of the oldest Christian rites, dating back to the fourth century. The priest presents to God the newly baptized with these words while anointing them with oil:

> Sweet ointment in the name of Jesus Christ is poured upon you as a seal of incorruptible heavenly gifts.
>
> The eyes: This seal in the name of Jesus Christ enlighten your eyes, that you may never sleep unto death.

The ears: This holy anointing be for the hearing of divine commandments.

The nostrils: This seal in the name of Jesus Christ be a sweet smell from life unto life.

The mouth: This seal in the name of Jesus Christ be a guard for your mouth and strong door for your lips.

The hands: This seal in the name of Jesus Christ be a cause for good works and for all virtuous deeds and conduct.

The heart: This divine seal establish in you a pure heart and renew within you an upright spirit.

The back: This seal in the name of Jesus Christ be a shield of strength thereby to quench all the fiery darts of the Evil One.

The feet: This divine seal direct your journey to life everlasting that you may not be shaken.[56]

STUDIO LIVE

1) A benjamin bush is a common name for the spicebush plant which every gardener would love to have in their garden because it has so many uses. The leaves, flowers, and berries make tasty tea, syrup, and jelly. The berries can make wine. The bark of the spicebush yields a spice that is similar to allspice. Wildlife love the berries, and the flowers provide a source of nectar for bees and other pollinators. Most noticeable, however, is the plant's beauty and its sweet, spicy fragrance which odorizes the entire garden.

   * Do you have a benjamin bush? If not, do you have the functional equivalent of a benjamin bush?

2) No person without sight, smell, or hearing would presume to tell music-lovers, artists, and cooks that they are delusional.

   * Why do we so cavalierly dismiss or diminish the religious experiences of others?

3) Our prayers are seen as burnt offerings before God, the fumes of our faith part of the divine ruach (breath) that God breathes in and out. "Prayers are deathless" is the arresting word of E. M. Bounds (d. 1913), a Methodist clergy and lawyer who wrote nine books on prayer, most of which were published after his death.

   * Discuss his comments about the power and enduring nature of our prayers:

The lips that uttered them may be closed to death, the heart that felt them may have ceased to beat, but the prayers live before God, and God's heart is set on them and prayers outlive the lives of those who uttered them; they outlive a generation, outlive an age, outlive a world.[57]

4) How have smells functioned in your life?

* Do some people have a stronger olfactory sense than others?
* What smells can't you tolerate?
* What smells do you really like or cherish?
* Why do smells affect us differently?
* What smells are special to your community?
* Are you attracted to other people by their smell?
* Can you think of your Gramma without smelling her?

5) A mission experience is the going forth into the world and immersing yourself in an olfactory sensation. Your mission is to have fun, to breathe deeply, and to bring back your learnings and share.

*<u>Mission experience #1:</u> Smell the variety of odors the world offers.

Go to a strong-smelling restaurant.

Go to a dump.

Go to a beauty parlor.

Go to a sawmill.

Go to a beach.

Go to a fish market.

Go to the locker room of a sport team (may I suggest a high-school ice hockey one?).

Go to a Russian Orthodox Church.

Go to a coffee house.

Go to a cheese market.

Go to a flower shop.

*Mission experience #2: Smell the essence of the world.

Go get a massage.

Go wash your dog.

Go take a bubble bath.

Go change a baby's diaper.

Go and make bread dough of different flavors.

Go and milk a cow.

Go and cut your lawn/rake leaves/shovel snow.

*Mission experience #3: Smell the sounds of your ordinary world.

What do you smell when the microwave dings?

What do you smell when the clothes dryer beeps?

Do you smell anything when the phone rings?

When your loved one calls your name from the door, what smells do you hear?

6) The Psalmist says God can smell a proud person from

a long way away: "the proud God knows from afar" (Psalm 138:6). Isaiah says explicitly that there is a stench or a stink to a proud person. Different spirits have different smells.

* Can you smell in someone the aroma of arrogance and pride?
* What about the aroma of humility and obedience?

7) Every May stretching into September, in the English countryside of Derbyshire, a series of village festivals offer gratitude for wells, springs, aquifers, and watersheds. Called "Well Dressings," only living material is used to decorate the Derbyshire wells and springs and sheds—flowers, nuts, leaves, berries, moss, bark. These "well dressings" have best been described as "stained-glass windows made of flowers." The smell of these "well dressings" draw visitors back to the festival year after year.

As do the stories, since many of the "well-dressings" tell a story important to the village. Some tell the story of Noah saving the animals from a flood; others tell of Jesus as the Good Shepherd, with Jesus' robe made of pansy petals, and the sky of hydrangeas. Others tell of St. George slaying the dragon, or the plagues of Egypt and dangers faced by the village. Think of a Rose Bowl parade with the focus on the village heritage, not on Disney or Hollywood or celebrities. Each "well dressing" is a stationary "float" that passes on the stories cherished by the community.[58] Of course, every festival needs food, and the food tables are often as amazing as the well-dressings.

* What if your church were to sponsor such a village festival, and invite other churches to join you in honoring the roots and fruits of your common home?

8) Find someone this coming week to whom you can say, "You have the Jesus smell all over you" or "I smell Jesus all over you." Then share the reaction you received.

9) For the past two decades, the world of fragrances (olfaction) has seen a renaissance of "sacred scents."[59] Starting in 2002, when Bertrand Duchaufour captured an olfactory portrait of mass in the French cathedral Avignon, the best perfumers in the world have been capturing sacred scents in both fluid and candle form.

* Here are some of the perfumes your study group could test out, followed by a few of the candles that capture sacred smells from around the world:

<u>Perfumes and Colognes:</u>

JoVoy (Paris), La Liturgie des Heures

The Different Company, Santo Incienso

Comme des Garcons, Incense Series: Avignon, Kyoto, Zagorsk, Jaisalmer, Ouarzazate

HEELEY, Cardinal Eau de Parfum

Tom Daxon, Resin Sacra cologne and shower gel

La Via Del Profumo, Mecca Balsam Eau de Parfum

Candles:

BYREDO, Apocalyptic scented candle

New Moon Beginnings, Sacred Smudge Candles

UNUM, Lavs Candle

Rituals, Black Oudh Candle

Werther and Gray, "Gothic Cathedral" candle

Lisa Carrier's "Cross" and "Cathedral" series

Cire Trudon, Spiritus Sanctus Candle (my personal favorite). Here is the official description of the smell: Splinters of crimson, gold, and olibanum; heady and holy perfume of altar candles; luxurious wake of the senses and perfume-burners where amber splutters: under the nave of a cathedral, the jubilant choir and the holy scents rise into the souls.

One company in particular believes it has brought to earth the "heaven scent" of the Messiah, based on clues in Psalm 45:8 NIV: "All your robes are fragrant with myrrh and aloes and cassia." Some early church fathers thought the odor of the Holy Spirit was "like unto cinnamon and balsam and chosen myrrh." So if you want to find out what Jesus' BO was really like, says the South Dakota couple who founded the company, go to www.hisessence.com for an assortment of whatnots to experience the body odor of Christ. The actual "His Essence" candle turns out be quite a floral experience.

10) Pastors are otolaryngologists: ear, eye, nose, throat, and tongue specialists. You don't have to remind pastors that they're in the ear, eye, throat, and tongue business. Do we forget the nose?

11) What are some of the odor issues of your church? What kinds of aromatherapy can you prescribe? What might it mean to call Jesus the Ultimate Aromatherapy?

12) How can we help the world smell good again? Is one key to becoming a fragrant place becoming a praying place?

13) Therapists who use cognitive-behavioral therapy (CBT) identify something called "stinking thinking."

   * What are some examples of "stinking thinking" or irrational thoughts that distort our perspective? How can these be counterproductive?

   * What cognitive distortions like all-or-nothing thinking, catastrophizing, overgeneralization, etc. do you notice in your own inner dialogue?

   * How might unhelpful thought patterns contribute to increased stress, anxiety, or depression? Have you experienced this?

   * What self-defeating core beliefs tend to drive negative automatic thoughts? How can we challenge these underlying assumptions?

   * What's the difference between thoughts that are

constructive versus destructive for your mental health and life?

* How might negative thoughts become habituated and feel so ingrained? What are tips for shifting out of "stinking thinking" ruts?

* What people or situations seem to trigger unhealthy cognitive distortions for you? How can you better manage those influences?

14) Saints are said to die in "the odor of sanctity," their body giving off fragrant smells as they make their transition.

* Do you use incense in your church? Your home?

* Do you facilitate sacred smells in your life?

* Research and tell the story of the rosary, and how each rose bead was meant to be fondled, and the scent of roses and other flowers released with each prayer. In the Catholic tradition on Rosary Sunday this blessing is said over the rosaries: "You created these roses as a source of pleasant fragrance and gave them to us to lift our spirits."

* How has fragrance lifted your spirit?

15) I write this in 2023 on the sesquicentennial of Proust's birth (10 July), and this book will be published in 2024 on the centennial of Proust's death. Marcel Proust's seven-volume masterpiece *la Recherche du temps perdu* (1913–1927), literally "In Search of Lost Timne" but often translated as "Remembrance of Things Past," which

became a favorite lock-down reading and not just among Proustophiles. In the COVIDian era, we all became Proustians obsessed with the meaning of time—time lost, time off, time out, time wasted, time regained, time bomb, time "of its time."

Proust is famous for his metaphor of the scent and taste of the madeleine. Madeleine is a shell-shaped sponge cake that was dunked in a lime blossom tea infusion which opened the doors of memory and drew the narrator back in time. Proust's early drafts started not with a madeleine but with a piece of stale bread. Then another draft proposed a piece of toast; then another draft proposed a biscotti, a hard biscuit. Finally came the madeleine chosen because the shell referenced the pilgrims on the way to Santiago de Compostela who held out large shells to the townspeople for food donations which were placed in the pilgrims' shells. Saint Jacques is the Gallic name for Santiago, or St. James, the first of the twelve apostles to be martyred. Proust explained why he preferred metaphors like the madeleine to abstract writing in *Le Temps retrouve*, the final volume of La Recherche, "*A work in which there are theories is like an object which still has its price tag on it*" (*Une oeuvre ou il y a des theories est comme un objet sur lequel on laissse la marque du prix*").

* What is your Proustian madeleine, your memory smell?

* What are some of the scents that whisk you away to a specific memory and moment of time, and makes you crazed about a moment?

The high-end fragrance company Mad et Len is playful shorthand for mad-e-leine.

16) Unpack this profession from the *Confessions* of St. Augustine:

> But what do I love when I love You? Not the beauty of any body or the rhythm of time in its movement; not the radiance of light, so dear to our eyes; not the sweet melodies in the world of manifold sounds; not the gentle fragrance of flowers, perfumes and spices; not manna and not honey; not the limbs so delightful to the body's embrace: it is none of these things that I love when I love my God. And yet when I love my God, it is light and melody and fragrance and food and embrace that I love, but the light that is not bound by space; when it listens to sound that never dies away; when it breathes fragrance that is not borne away on the wind; when it tastes food that is never consumed by the eating; when it clings to an embrace from which it is not severed by fulfilment of desire. That is what I love when I love my God.[60]

* What does Augustine mean when he says that he loves "light that is not bound by space," "sound that never dies away," "fragrance that is not borne away on the wind," "food that is never consumed by the eating,"

and "an embrace from which it is not severed by fulfillment of desire"?

* How does Augustine's description of his love for God compare to other descriptions of love that you have read or heard?
* What are some of the challenges of loving God in the way that Augustine describes?
* What are some of the rewards of loving God in the way that Augustine describes?
* How can we cultivate a deeper love for God in our own lives?
* What is the difference between loving God and loving the things that God has created?
* How can we learn to love God with the same intensity and purity that Augustine describes?

17) Select your favorite perfumes and colognes, and share them with each other. As you pass them around for people to sample the smell, explain why the fragrance is so meaningful to you and what memories it brings to mind.

Chapter 6: Groom
The Jesus Groom

[Prayer is] "Man well drest."
POET/PRIEST GEORGE HERBERT (D. 1633), "PRAYER"[1]

SOME SCHOLARS CONTEND THAT THE BEST ENGLISH translation of the Greek word "Logos" is "meaning." Meaning in life comes from living a beautiful, truthful, and fruitful life, which encompasses how one presents oneself to the world.

"Clothes enable us to walk in the sun without getting sunburnt," legendary French fashion designer Coco Chanel (d. 1971) liked to say even as she revolutionized twentieth-century fashion with her groundbreaking styles. Clothing is not frivolous or garnishment or sun screen. It expresses who we are and the dignity of our body in design fashion.

One of the harshest judgments Jesus ever uttered in his parables was to the party crasher who showed up inappropriately dressed for the wedding banquet.[2] Designer Jesus humans do not make dress our principal attention, or a passion for fashion our utmost concern. In the words of Cyril of Alexandria (d. 444), "We must be distinguished not by our clothing, but by what we really are."[3] It is more important to be different than look different. In fact, for Jesus, worry about food and garments denoted "little faith"—an unseemly anxiety that overlooks God's provision and providence.

> Do not worry about your life, what you will eat or about your body, what you will wear. For life is more than food, and the body more than clothing. Consider the lilies, how they grow: they neither toil nor spin, yet even Solomon in all his glory was not clothed like one of these. But if God so clothes the grass of the field, which is alive today and tomorrow is thrown in to the oven, how much more will he clothe you—you of little faith![4]

But just as food was important to Jesus, as any reading of the gospels will attest,[5] a Jesus Groom and garment are not incidental to faith but part of our witness for God and statement of faith.

"Cosmos" comes from the Greek word "cosmos" which is used to describe ornaments on a woman's clothing. The original meaning of the phrase can still be heard in our word "cosmetics." The "cosmos" was created to "ornament" God's clothing or to highlight God's beauty.[6] Ornaments add beauty and wonder. "Let there be light" was an ordaining and ornamenting moment.

This next sentence may be one of the most controversial

I have ever written, given the current state of biblical scholarship. Jesus groomed,[7] combed his hair, and looked nice.[8] Jesus was well-kept. Not frumpy, fusty, or slovenly. Face washed and fresh, not gloomy and grim. "When you fast, anoint your head and wash your face and do not look gloomy," Jesus said in his Sermon on the Mount.[9] Look up. Cheer up. Or in another translation,

> When you fast, do not look somber as the hypocrites do, for they disfigure their faces to show others they are fasting. Truly I tell you, they have received their reward in full. But when you fast, put oil on your head and wash your face, so that it will not be obvious to others that you are fasting, but only to your Father, who is unseen; and your Father, who sees what is done in secret, will reward you.[10]

Jesus is doing more here than telling us to look our best. He is warning against any lifestyle that makes a show of our piety, or "all hat and no cattle" to use an old Texan metaphor for hypocrisy. But he is also telling us not to look better when we're broadcasting our fasting than when we're enjoying our feasting. We are to present ourselves to the world without pretense and in a fashion befitting the Savior.

Sacrament of Dirt: Jesus revolutionized the holiness code of his day. Instead of elaborate and extensive purity rituals that kept one uncontaminated by the world, Jesus emphasized the importance of touching and serving the unclean and marginalized. He showed that true holiness comes from a clean heart, not clean hands.

Handwashing was required before eating any meal, especially bread. Before washing his hands, Jesus would cup his hands together and pour water over them three times. He would then wash his palms, the backs of his hands, and fingertips, and then dry them on a clean towel. Other handwashing rituals he kept included washing his hands before entering the Temple, or washing his hands after touching a diseased or dead body.

Foot washing was typically performed by a servant upon entering a house. The filthiest part of the body—dusty and dirty feet—were washed thoroughly with water and soap, then dried with a clean towel.

Face washing was also required before eating a meal and before praying. Jesus' face would be washed with water and soap, and then dried with a clean towel.

Jesus flipped the holiness code on its head as decisively as he flipped the tables in the Temple courtyard. Instead of extensive handwashing, face washing, and foot washing rituals that kept you from touching the unclean, for Jesus these rituals made sure you had pristine and holy hands when you did touch the unclean. Jesus got his hands dirty touching lepers, touching women who were considered to be unclean, touching food with tax collectors and sinners, and touching dirty feet. In fact, for Jesus the sign of holy living and a proper approach to God was not clean hands themselves but clean hands made dirty by touching the outcasts and outsiders.

Getting one's hands dirty in loving others almost became a sacrament—a sacrament of dirt. In the early church, foot washing was either seen as a necessary preparation for the Lord's Supper, or it was seen as a separate ordinance in its own right. The sacrament of water (baptism) was always first and foremost, but the sacrament of dirt (foot washing) existed alongside the sacrament of bread and wine (eucharist) until cultural changes left it behind. A sign of holiness for Jesus was every gardener's trademark: dirty hands. Dirty hands became the sign of a clean heart.

Skin Care: The naked truth? The first Adam was born naked.[11] The last Adam died naked.

> *Clothes make the man. Naked people have little or no influence on society.*
> HUMORIST MARK TWAIN (D. 1910)[12]

Humans had a problem with body image from the very beginning. When Adam and Eve knew they were naked, they immediately tried cover-ups. The Bible says it was a fig leaf that they used, one of the biggest leaves in the world. But fig leaves are not comfortable, and get hard quick.

God re-clothed them with animal skins (the first time the killing of animals is referenced). But one day we would be covered by more than animal skin. God put God's own "skin in the game" and clothed us with Jesus skin. Jesus didn't just save our skin. He adorned us with his own skin so that we too might be "all things to all people."[13]

The first Adam was clothed in the skin of the animals God had created. After dying naked and in his own skin, the last Adam would clothe us in his own skin. One could see Adam's being clothed through the death of an animal as the very first sacrifice for one's sin. God killed to cover Adam and have him "restored to his original life."[14] When you are wearing Jesus skin, and enveloped in him, beauty is skin deep, a deep that goes from skin to soul.

> *I say more: the just man justices;*
> *Keeps grace that keeps all his goings grace;*
> *Acts in God's eye what in God's eye he is—*
> *Christ.*
>
> THEOLOGIAN/POET GERARD MANLEY HOPKINS (D. 1889)[15]

<u>Clothed in Christ:</u> On the cross, we were clothed in Christ. "For those of you who were baptized into Christ have been clothed with Christ."[16] Our clothing is Christ. A Jesus human is someone who has been cut from the same cloth as Christ. Garmented in God's glory, we are layered in radiance both inside and out, Christ's splendor seeping from flesh down into bone.

Being clothed in Christ is a controlling metaphor in early Christian thought. It appears several times in Paul's letters: clothing with Christ,[17] clothing with the new human,[18] and clothing with the resurrection body.[19] Paul speaks explicitly of being clothed in Christ through baptism.[20]

Clothing and baptism go together within the backdrop of "putting off" the "old man" and "putting on" the new.

Being "baptized into Christ" and being "clothed with Christ" are fundamentally the same thing. Nude baptism of various forms was practiced in ancient times.[21] Proselyte baptism in Judaism involved taking off one's clothes, immersing oneself fully in the water, hearing commandments read by mentors and rabbis, and then coming out of the water and putting on new clothes. A baptized person was seen as a new man, as a "little child just born." New clothing in Christ means living as sons and daughters of God and heirs of the kingdom.[22]

At sixteen, a Roman boy went from wearing the toga praetexta to the adult toga virilis, accompanied by a special ceremony attached to the transition into adulthood as a full Roman citizen. The boy removed the purple hem from the white robe to signal he had become a man with a place alongside his father in the councils of the family with full citizen rights. The "man's toga" or toga virilis was a plain white garment signaling he could vote, wear the purple-striped tunic, marry, and perform other civic duties. Both men and women could wear versions of it.

Christian baptisms were similar: the new convert stripped naked, took off the clothes of the old man, then trampled and stomped on the old clothes with his feet and immersed himself in water, "naked and unafraid," putting on new clothes when he emerged.[23] In the mind of these first Christians, the symbolism had less to do with Roman rituals of manhood than with Adam and Eve being restored to their original state in the Garden of Eden.

Some baptisms included oil anointing as well, variously called "oil of exorcism" or "oil of thanksgiving." Other accounts of the first baptisms are united in one thing: the ritual involves the taking off of old clothes and putting on of new clothes, which was almost as symbolic for the early church as the water. A new identity was put on; an old identity was cast off.[24] There is no sign or smell of death in the new linen clothing, as in the old skin clothing. The pure white linen of the baptismal robe symbolizes release from the "shame" and "guilt" of the old Adam which the new Adam covers with himself.

Paul reminds Christ followers to put off their old self and put on the new self after the likeness of God—God clothing us with a new self.[25] Paul discusses being further clothed by God in terms of our heavenly dwelling.[26] Paul makes the connection with the new self that we are clothed directly with Christ when he says to, "put on the Lord Jesus Christ."[27] This clothing in Christ is again connected with the covering up of one's old self with a new one which can be thought of in terms of covering one's nakedness or sin.

Baptism creates a "garment of praise instead of a spirit of despair"[28] or "filthy rags"[29] of dirt. Every tattered shred, every frayed fabric of life can be transformed to beautify the whole garment by drawing each thread, every strand through the eye of the needle of Jesus. Jesus then covers us with his robe of righteousness, a hand-stitched elegance of the finished raiment. In Revelation nineteen, the white linen given to the Bride of the Lamb for her wedding banquet is the life experiences of the saints which God graciously transformed into activities which pleased Him.

The contextual unpacking of the metaphor in the

Galatian letter would suggest that "to be clothed with Christ" is to adopt a new sense of identity as a "child of God," a new view of community life as "all one in Christ," and a new view of the telos of life as "heirs to the inheritance."[30] Once clothed in Christ, we join creation in being oriented toward divinely ordered ends.

> All of you who were baptized into Christ have clothed yourselves with Christ. There is neither Jew nor Gentile, neither slave nor free, nor is there male and female, for you are all one in Christ Jesus.[31]

When we're clothed in Christ, we have all the clothing we need. You don't find your identity in what you wear, but in whom you wear. The crowds that followed Jesus didn't follow him because he looked like a rock star or a model, but they loved his style, his stories, his signs, his healings, his teachings.

Noah's sons Shem and Japheth covered the nakedness of their father.[32] The covering and clothing of the naked is part of the fast that God describes as pleasing.[33] God's self-description of Israel's calling is the clothing of her nakedness.[34] Moses' sin and circumcision being covered is part of a larger theme of sins being covered and righteousness being connected with the covering of nakedness whether one's own or others.

New Garments: The prophet Joel makes a point about going beyond throwing off the outer, visible "garments"—symptoms such as negative emotions or behaviors—and addresses the root issue: the inner condition of our hearts. Isaiah tells us to put off our "clothes of sorrow and distress" and put on "the cloak of the integrity of God."[35]

Jesus stops for the social misfits, the politically useless, the disabled, the pariahs, the unmentionables. In the story of the blind beggar Bartimaeus, one of the "onlys" of the Bible (the only story of someone who is healed by Jesus and named), Jesus stopped and said, "Call him over!"

> They called out to the blind man and said, "Don't be afraid! Come on! He is calling for you." The man threw off his coat as he jumped up and ran to Jesus.[36]

Like blind Bartimaeus, how many of us are actually in this fight to throw off our old "cloaks?" Thankfully, on this side of eternity, we have already been given a new set of "garments" that truly spark joy. From the passage Jesus chose for his inaugural sermon at his hometown of Nazareth, Isaiah tells us what some of these garments are:

> The garment of praise instead of a spirit of despair (Isaiah 61:3).
>
> The garments of salvation and the robe of righteousness (Isaiah 61:10b).[37]

In Christ, we have a choice of which garments we want to wear.

No longer am I a blind Bartimaeus resigned to the cloak that identifies me as a beggar or someone unclean, contemptible, or immobile. Because of Jesus, I am no longer bound to any of these identities. I am who Jesus says I am.

The cloak was Bartimaeus' tent, his tool, his tribute, his only treasure. Am I able to throw off the familiar cloaks of identity I've worn for so much of my life in order to put on these new garments of identity? Bartimaeus trusts Jesus enough to toss it all aside, and follow Jesus. No longer would he be defined by his past, only by his future.

Like Bartimaeus, Jesus discarded his clothing in the tomb to symbolize his transition to a whole new life. At the beginning Jesus is clothed in rags ("swaddling cloths"). At the end Jesus is shrouded in "linen cloths," where linen is a fine garment worn by nobility, priests and rich. In their priestly duties priests wore fine linen, which Jesus is here throwing away.

When the crowds threw their cloaks down on Palm Sunday, they were giving up one of their most prized possessions. Usually made of wool, the thickness of the cloak doubled as a blanket at night. It was so valuable that bandits would steal it,[38] and creditors would accept it as payment for debts or collateral for loans.

Herod ridicules Pilate by sending Jesus back to him with "an elegant robe on him,"[39] what biblical scholar Robert L. Brawley calls a "carnivalesque" moment where Jesus, the King of Kings, is mocked in royal robes as a pseudo king.[40] Clothes don't make the man, but sometimes they reveal him.

At the Transfiguration, Jesus' "dazzling white"[41] clothing reveals his majesty and glory. Might this be a foretaste of future clothing? Biblical scholar James L. Resseguie and

DESIGNER JESUS

historian Gildas Hamel unearth the significance of those two words, "dazzling white." A white garment is one that is thoroughly washed and "fulled" (i.e., bleached in a special clay to make it as white as possible). Fulled garments, which are costly and take a long time to process, would normally "have been the prerogative of priests and for contacts with the gods in general."[42] Common people, the poor, and slaves wore "unfulled" cloth, "that is, in its natural color which was grey for linen and 'black' (i.e., dark), brown, or greyish to white for other materials."[43]

Jesus' post-resurrection look is not specifically described in the accounts. An angel at the tomb is described as wearing dazzling white raiment, but not Jesus himself.[44] The focus is on the garb of his glorified body and identity, not the clothes themselves, which seem to fit into the style of what others were wearing in his day to the point where he did not stand out.

Clothing for a Christian: Duke professor Lauren Winner asks a thought-provoking question regarding Paul's clothing metaphor of "putting on Christ:"

> If to change clothes can be to change one's sense of self; if to change clothes is to change one's way of being in the world; if to clothe yourself in a particular kind of garment is to let that garment shape you into its own shape—then what is it to put on Christ?[45]

How would you answer that question?

Paul answered that question by outlining the best gear for

the deep struggles of life: "Our struggle is not against enemies of blood and flesh . . . but against . . . spiritual forces of evil in the heavenly places."⁴⁶ We are to stand firm and "fasten the belt of truth around your waist and put on the breastplate of righteousness."⁴⁷ We are sent to proclaim the gospel of shalom wearing the helmet of salvation, the sword of the Spirit, and the sandals of peace.⁴⁸

This is our garment for everyday encounters, no matter the season of life or weather of the day. Irish molecular biologist J. D. Bernal fruitlessly kept trying to give meteorological advice to the British Army during WWII until they finally shut him down by reminding him "soldiers fought in all weathers."⁴⁹ Jesus humans wear clothes for an all-weather mission.

In the story of the prodigal son, the father clothes his son with the best robe, or in the Greek, "the first robe."⁵⁰ The "first robe" is of uncertain origin. Most scholars claim it to be the finest, foremost, or best quality robe in the house, often reserved for the oldest son. Whatever this "first robe" refers to, it frees the son from his disgrace and literally graces him with honor of restoration to his previous standing in the family.

When the son first sees his father, he is likely covered with the earthy hues of a hog-pit, which represents the dour nature of his disgraceful past. But the father's robe will cover him in vivacious tones that speak of a renewed season of celebration and joy. The father was, after all, dressing his son for a party. New Zealand biblical scholar Joan E. Taylor suggests that the fabric of the robe would have been emblazoned with bright colors: "The ordinary people of Jesus' time loved color and their clothing has beautiful shades of red, green, and types of purple." They favored colors that were "vibrant" and not "earthy hues."[51] The nobility were full of color, as colorful as the passage that describes them in Lamentations 4:7–8 (KJV): "Her Nazarites were purer than snow, they were whiter than milk, they were more ruddy in body than rubies, their polishing was of sapphire: Their visage is blacker than a coal; they are not known in the streets: their skin cleaveth to their bones; it is withered, it is become like a stick."

The prodigal is also given a ring (gold or silver) and sandals when he returns home.[52] In the ancient world, rings were often used to seal official documents or contracts. Perhaps the ring that the prodigal son received was not just a piece of jewelry; maybe it was a symbol of his authority and responsibility as a son of the family. The ring may also have been a symbol of the prodigal son's inheritance. In ancient Jewish culture, the eldest son was typically the one who inherited the father's property. However, the fact that the father gave the prodigal son a ring suggests that he intended to treat him equally with his older brother.

In the ancient world, slaves and servants went barefoot, while free people wore sandals. By giving his son sandals, the father was saying that he was no longer a slave or a servant, but a free man. The sandals are also a symbol of the prodigal son's new journey. He is no longer the same person who left home; he is now a changed man. The sandals are a reminder of his journey back to his father and his new life in the family.

THE JESUS GROOM

> *I am going to send you what my Father has promised; but stay in the city until you have been clothed with power from on high.*
> JESUS[53]

<u>Dress Code:</u> Jesus gave his disciples a dress code for ministry. He allows one tunic to the twelve, but no money belt, begging bowl, or staff.[54] "Don't take any money with you, nor a traveler's bag, nor an extra pair of sandals."[55] After all, "When I sent you out without a purse, bag or sandals, did you lack anything?"[56]

This dress code symbolizes many things. First, it is another embrace of dirt. Clothes get dirty quick, and not to have back-ups to wear while you're washing away the spots is to risk appearing impure.

Second, it is an embrace of an unassuming carriage that identifies with the marginalized, since only the very poor lacked a change of clothes.

Third, it is a symbol of total dependence on God, almost as if each day were a Sabbath day.

Fourth, it is a recognition of a mission life that is light and unencumbered, so that they can move quickly and easily from place to place.

Finally, if you're robbed, turn the violent theft into a nonviolent "absurd exchange of gifts" by throwing back at them more than what they took from you and breaking the cycle of violence by creating the possibility of a new relationship.[57]

DESIGNER JESUS

Jesus instructed his newly-formed team that they needed to wear the right clothing before they went out into the world as his apostles: "Stay in Jerusalem" he commanded them until "clothed with power from on high." Disciples don't go anywhere or do anything without wearing the right clothes.[58] Fitness for mission requires being "outfitted" for the task. The ultimate clothing is to be "clothed from on high" or "clothed with power from on high" which is the gift of the Spirit.[59]

The Jesus life demands mission digs—the vesture of vision, the raiment of righteousness, the tog of truth, and the garment of light. Without this missional apparel, we are unsuited for our witness and work in the world.

The Holy Spirit tailor-makes this clothing to match our character, our context, and our circumstances. In Genesis the first humans aim to clothe themselves in synthetics. But God stages an intervention and re-clothes us in authentics, the kind of relational composites God designed humans to be.

The apostles needed to wait for God to clothe them in Jesus pants and Jesus shoes for their mission in the world. The Master Tailor would outfit them in an authentic style that not only would cover their outside, but stitch together their insides as well, even knitting and latticing the hidden recesses of their hearts. "Clothed in light," colored with the glow and glamor of the gospel, "armored" by the protective plating of the Spirit, they were now suited for the task they were about to undertake. They were now decked out in robes of righteousness as authentic disciples of The Way, uniformed to "wear their hearts on their sleeves" for a hurting and broken world.[60]

How do you create a robe of righteousness? Every tattered shred, every frayed fabric of life can be transformed to beautify the whole garment by drawing each thread, every strand through the narrow eye of the needle of Jesus.

DESIGNER JESUS

STUDIO LIVE

1) What might a fusty, fuddy-duddy, frumpy faith look like?

2) In elementary education Carol McCloud is very popular. She is the author of "Have You Filled a Bucket Today?"

   To answer the question "How Full is Your Bucket?" she uses the metaphor of the dipper and a bucket. Positivity fills your bucket and lets you fill others from the overflow. Negativity empties your bucket and empties the buckets of others. People can empty your bucket or fill your bucket. In other words, your bucket's state of being is dependent on you getting it filled from others.

   * To what extent is a positive attitude and upbeat spirit a part of the Jesus Groom?

   * Do we dip into the bucket and scoop things out? Or do we fill other people's bucket? Do we look to people around us to fill our bucket?

   * What if only Jesus can fill your bucket? What if only Jesus can fill your emptiness?

3) Bonnee Hoy was a gifted Philadelphia pianist and composer who died in the prime of her life. At her memorial service, a friend said that there was a mockingbird that used to sing regularly outside Bonnee's bedroom window on summer nights.

   Bonnee would stand at the window, peering into the darkness, listening intently and marveling at the beautiful songs the mockingbird sang. Then, being a musician, Bonnee decided to respond musically. So she whistled the first four notes of 'Beethoven's Fifth Symphony.' With amazing quickness, the mockingbird learned those four notes and sang them back to Bonnee. Then, for a time, the bird disappeared. But one night, toward the end of her life, when Bonnee was very sick, the bird returned and, in the midst of its serenade, several times sang the first four notes of Beethoven's fifth.

Then the friend said:

"Think of that now! Somewhere out there in this big wide world there is a mockingbird who sings Beethoven because of Bonnee."[61]

* Go around the room, and one by one complete this sentence:

There is someone out there in this big wide world who sings of love because of [then give a name].

4) The husband-and-wife team of Philip and Carol Zaleski, who write books on faith and culture, assert that "Theology may explicate the ways of God, but art clothes sacred truth in concrete form, escorting us . . . into the felt presence of the divine."[62]

- What do you think the Zaleskis mean by "sacred truth?"
- How does art "clothe sacred truth in concrete form?"
- How does art escort us into the "felt presence of the divine?"
- Can you think of any examples of art that have had this effect on you?
- How can we make art more accessible to people who are not typically exposed to it?
- What are some of the challenges of using art to communicate sacred truth?
- What art do you have in your church? Your home?
- What are some of the ways in which art can help us to grow in our faith?
- How can we use art to build up the body of Christ?

5) Here is an early description of a baptism from Bishop Hippolytus of Rome (d. 236). Read it carefully and compare how our first ancestors baptized with how we baptize today.

> [1]At the hour in which the cock crows, they shall first pray over the water. [2]When they come to the water, the water shall be pure and flowing, that is, the water of a spring or a flowing body of water. [3]Then they shall take off all their clothes. The children shall

be baptized first. All of the children who can answer for themselves, let them answer. If there are any children who cannot answer for themselves, let their parents answer for them, or someone else from their family. ⁵After this, the men will be baptized. Finally, the women, after they have unbound their hair, and removed their jewelry. No one shall take any foreign object with themselves down into the water.

⁹When the elder takes hold of each of them who are to receive baptism, he shall tell each of them to renounce, saying, "I renounce you Satan, all your service, and all your works." ¹⁰After he has said this, he shall anoint each with the Oil of Exorcism, saying, "Let every evil spirit depart from you." ¹¹Then, after these things, the bishop passes each of them on nude to the elder who stands at the water. They shall stand in the water naked. A deacon, likewise, will go down with them into the water.[63]

* What are some of the similarities and differences between baptism in the early church and baptism today?
* What does the fact that people were baptized naked tell us about the early church's understanding of baptism?

- * What is the significance of the renunciation of Satan and the anointing with the Oil of Exorcism?
- * What can we learn from the early church's practice of baptism about how to baptize people today?
- * What is the significance of the time of day (cockcrow) at which baptism took place in the early church?
- * Why do you think it was important to use pure and flowing water for baptism?
- * What is the significance of the fact that children were baptized first?
- * What is the significance of the fact that women were required to unbind their hair and remove their jewelry before baptism?
- * What are some of the challenges that the early church faced in practicing baptism?
- * How did the early church's practice of baptism reflect its understanding of the gospel?

6) After twenty-five years on the job, Alexandra Shulman counted the clothes in her wardrobe as a hook to write her memoir. Thirty-seven skirts, twenty-two coats, thirty-seven handbags, eighty-one pairs of footwear, and four fur shawls, was just a sampling of the 549 clothing items she listed. Of course, her job was editor of British *Vogue*, so surely the quality of items in that wardrobe was way above the normal content of a closet.[64]

- * What is your reaction to the number of clothes in

Alexandra Shulman's wardrobe? Do you think it is excessive, or is it understandable given her job as editor of British *Vogue*?

* How does Shulman's wardrobe compare to your own? Do you have more or less clothes than her? What factors contribute to the size of your wardrobe?

* Do you think the number of clothes we own is a reflection of our values or priorities? What does it say about our society that people like Alexandra Shulman have such large wardrobes?

7) In the past, men's fashion was as important as female fashion. Take the eighteenth-century time of John Wesley, just one century as an example. There was the "fop" fashion of the early-eighteenth century, then came the "macaroni" mode of the 1760s,[65] then came the Regency dandy. After the Seven Years' War in 1763 which brought people from all over the Continent together, men started wearing striped stockings, spotted waistcoats, and embroidered suits of velvet and silk, with lilacs, pinks, buffs and silver trimmed with sequins, satin, shell, ermine and metal threads.

* What are some of the similarities and differences between eighteenth-century men's fashion and men's fashion today?

* How do you think our own society's views on men's fashion have changed over time?

* What are some of the factors that influence our own personal fashion choices today?

* What are some of the challenges that men faced in dressing in such elaborate and flamboyant styles?

* What are some of the ways in which men's fashion has become more simplified over time?

* What are some of the ways in which men's fashion has become more expressive and diverse in recent years?

8) Scholars of material culture talk about "technologies of selfhood"—the devices and rituals by which we "fashion ourselves for the inspection of others."[66]

* What does the term "technologies of selfhood" mean to you? How do you interpret the idea of "fashioning ourselves for the inspection of others"?

* Can you think of any specific examples of technologies of selfhood in our society today? How do these devices and rituals shape our self-perception and the way we present ourselves to others?

* How do technologies of selfhood differ across cultures and historical periods? Are there any universal aspects of self-fashioning that can be observed?

* Do you believe that technologies of selfhood have both positive and negative effects? What are some potential benefits and drawbacks associated with these practices?

* How do technologies of selfhood influence our

relationships with others? Do they enhance or hinder genuine connections and understanding?

* How can Jesus humans maintain authenticity and conform to societal expectations when engaging with technologies of selfhood?

* Are there any ethical considerations that arise when examining technologies of selfhood? How might these practices impact privacy, consent, and societal norms?

* Can you envision any potential future developments or changes in technologies of selfhood? How might these advancements shape our understanding of self and our interactions with others?

9) Joan E. Taylor is a New Zealand ancient historian who specializes in early Christianity, the Dead Sea Scrolls, and Second Temple Judaism. In her valuable resource exploring "What Did Jesus Look Like?" she starts her exploration from the John Dominic Crossan view of Jesus as a Palestinian peasant (see his *Jesus: A Revolutionary Biography* [1994]) and builds a portrait of Jesus from that perspective. In my view she over-emphasizes Roman influence on Jesus' looks while underplaying his Jewishness. She also dismisses Christian sources too hastily in favor of non-Christian texts. Her interpretation of Jesus' seamless garment for which the soldiers cast lots (John 19:23–24) also makes one pause. She rightly sees this as strange, "because mostly tunics were made of two pieces sewn at the shoulders and sides. One-piece tunics

in first-century Judaea were normally thin undergarments or children's wear. We shouldn't think of contemporary underwear, but wearing a one-piece on its own was probably not good form. It was extremely basic."[67] The problem with this interpretation is that a seamless garment was a costly garment, often worn by priests and royalty, not "children's wear." The soldiers would not fight over kid's underwear.

* That said, here are some of her observations for you to deliberate and debate:

> From the Bible (for example, Mark 6:56) you can discover that he wore a mantle—a large shawl ("*himation*" in Greek)—which had tassels, described as "edges"; a distinctively Jewish tallith in a form it was in antiquity. Usually made of wool, a mantle could be large or small, thick or fine, coloured or natural, but for men there was a preference for undyed types. He walked in sandals, as implied in multiple Biblical passages (see Matthew 3:11; Mark 1:7, 6:9; John 1:27), and we now know what ancient Judaean sandals were like as they have been preserved in dry caves by the Dead Sea. He wore a tunic (*chitōn*), which for men normally finished slightly below the knees, not at the ankles. Among men, only the very rich wore long tunics. Indeed, Jesus specifically

THE JESUS GROOM

identifies men who dress in long tunics ("*stolai*", Mark 12:38) as wrongly receiving honour from people who are impressed by their fine attire, when in fact they unjustly devour widows' houses.

10) St. Clare of Assisi (d. 1253) had a famous crop cut and monastic tonsure, her golden locks cut by St. Francis (d. 1226) himself. When her father tried to rescue her from her vows, she finally proved her commitment when she ripped off her habit and revealed her crop cut and tonsure. Her locks cut off by St. Francis are supposedly preserved in a reliquary.[68]

* Why do you think cutting her hair held such symbolism and significance for Clare in demonstrating her commitment?

* When in your life have you made a major personal sacrifice or change to prove dedication to an important cause, belief, or loved one?

* What are some modern examples of people using their hair or appearance to make a statement of conviction?

* If you were in Clare's father's position, how would you have responded to witnessing such a dramatic act of conviction?

* Does preserving relics like the hair serve a purpose even though the act itself is most meaningful? Why or why not?

* What lessons can be learned from Clare's willingness

to eschew vanity and comfort in order to live out her values?

* When have you stood firm in your beliefs despite pressure from family to conform or change paths?

* Why do you think such tangible rituals and symbols can help solidify abstract faith and convictions?

11) Here is a description of Jesus at the end of time from Revelation 1:14–15 NRSVA:

> Then I turned to see whose voice it was that spoke to me, and on turning I saw seven golden lampstands, and in the midst of the lampstands I saw one like the Son of Man, clothed with a long robe and with a golden sash across his chest. His head and his hair were white as white wool, white as snow; his eyes were like a flame of fire, his feet were like burnished bronze, refined as in a furnace, and his voice was like the sound of many waters. In his right hand he held seven stars, and from his mouth came a sharp, two-edged sword, and his face was like the sun shining with full force.

* This vivid image of Jesus accents his divine authority and majesty, although portrayed in human form. Are you more comfortable with the divine or human Jesus?

Most scholars see the symbolism as follows:

> The long robe and golden sash indicate his priestly role and dignity.
>
> The white hair symbolizes wisdom and purity.
>
> The fiery eyes represent penetrating perceptiveness and judgment.
>
> The burnished bronze feet suggest strength and stability.
>
> The voice like the sound of many waters signifies power and authority.
>
> The sharp, two-edged sword represents the Word of God.

* What else do you see in this symbolism, or where do you see it differently?

Chapter 7: Appetite
The Jesus Appetite

This is God's Prayer:
That you have my grace,
That you desire my grace,
That you at least desire to desire my grace,
Given freely and abundantly: that this
will be your desire,
So that I might be born in you.

MEISTER ECKHART (D. 1328)[1]

JESUS EXHIBITED A RAVENOUS APPETITE FOR LIFE. Jesus was witty, playful, whimsical, unpredictable—a person who loved surprises, cherished celebrations, and was fully alive.[2] Jesus called his disciples to "follow me," but he didn't tell them where they were going. Jesus' appetite for adventure was contagious.

We know next to nothing about Jesus' childhood (birth to six), except we do know something about how children in Jesus' day played. If Jesus played with other children, then he played with whistles, rattles, toy animals on wheels, hoops, and spinning tops, all of which have been found by archaeologists. Hopscotch and jacks were popular. In addition to checkers, other popular board games of the time included senet, mancala, and backgammon ("*ludus duodecim scriptorum*" or the "game of twelve lines"). These games were often made from simple materials such as wood, clay, and stone. Jesus' playful interactions with his disciples, and his playful nature, makes it difficult not to imagine Jesus as a child have a strong appetite for play.

The biggest appetites of a Jesus human are for the five things Jesus commanded us to do in no uncertain terms: help the sick, awaken the lifeless, embrace the rejected, care for the mentally ill, and give freely.[3] Jesus shifted his disciples away from a legal code of living to a love code of living. Jesus shifted appetites from self to others, turning human appetites outward without denying the "innards," as my Gramma used to say. After all, both the outward appetites and the inward appetites are part of the same hunger and thirst for God.

Jesus showed how the exaltation of the self-code's "what-do-I-want" and "what-can-I-have" appetites becomes purified and satisfied in the exultation of Jesus and others in the outward love-code appetites. Instead of finding ourselves in our own exaltation, we find ourselves in the exultation of Jesus, and in his appetites for saving the world.

*All who exalt themselves will be humbled,
and all who humble themselves will be exalted.*
JESUS[4]

Jesus Energy: Design is everywhere, including our appetites. When our desires and pleasures embody Jesus energies, doors unlock that reconnect our destiny with God's design. A design bundle of "Sursum Corda."

The simple phrase "Sursum Corda" is like a shot of adrenaline to the soul. It is a Latin phrase that means "Lift up your hearts" but it opens a call and response between the priest and the people that introduces the celebration of The Lord's Supper. The two Latin words invoke the whole exchange:

> Priest: Lift up your hearts!
> People: We lift them up to the Lord!
> Priest: Let us give thanks to the Lord our God.
> People: It is meet and right so to do.[5]

To live the "Sursum Corda" designed life is to live a "meet-and-right" life of giving thanks to God. You want to thank God? You want to praise God? Eat, live, love with gusto and grace. Live completely in each moment. Drink deeply of the living water. Savoring the Savior's gifts is the sincerest gratitude. Life is Short. Be swift to love, live, enjoy, forgive, take the long view, and the long way home.

"*In-carnate*" is Latin ("*in carne*") for "in the meat." God is found in both the "meet" of human flesh and blood, and in the "meat" of bread and wine. Jesus is found in the meat of meals and the meeting at tables. Jesus taught with more than words. He used meals and feasts, signs and symbols as favored ways of teaching in a holistic way of knowing God.

The First Eve hungered for knowledge about good and evil. Not more relational knowing of the Creator, but more theoretical knowledge of the thinking behind creation. The Last Adam hungered not for knowledge about the good and evil of his disciples, but hungered for knowing and eating with his friends, both his good and evil friends. The sacred texts of faith can be read only bodily, and incarnation goes straight through all our senses, especially appetite and hunger.[6]

I will give you a new heart and put a new spirit within you; and I will remove the heart of stone from your flesh and give you a heart of flesh.

EZEKIEL 36:26 AMP[7]

Meet and Meat: People are nervous and unprepared for Incarnate Truth, truth "in-carne," truth in-the-flesh, truth inscribed on the heart. They much prefer Truth "in-lapis," in the stone, truth carved in stone tablets. But the gospel story is one where Jesus wants truth to be written in our hearts—not in-lapis, but in-carne. Every Jesus human must decide which it will be. A heart-of-stone Jesus or a heart-of-flesh Jesus? A Stone Tablet Jesus or a Beating Heart, Living Stone Jesus? For how many Christians has the prophesy of the prophet Jeremiah still not come to pass in their lives:

"The days are coming," declares the Lord,

> "when I will make a new covenant with the people of Israel and with the people of Judah. It will not be like the covenant I made with their ancestors when I took them by the hand to lead them out of Egypt . . . This is the covenant I will make with the people of Israel after that time," declares the Lord. "I will put my law in their minds and write it on their hearts. I will be their God, and they will be my people."[8]

A Jesus designed life is one of teleological discipleship, not eschatological discipleship. "Telos" means "end," and that word "end" is a powerful one. It means not just termination but telos, the purpose and raison d'etre for which something exists.[9] Telos is the belief that natural processes and objects have inherent purposes or goals, and that creation is oriented toward certain divinely ordered ends.

For John the "end" was the eschaton: the end of times which were coming to judge and indict the present. For Jesus the "end" was the telos, the ultimate end and purpose of life: to glorify God and enjoy God forever.

For a Jesus human, the ultimate "end" or telos of life? To glorify God and enjoy God forever with "meat" and "meet:" "meaty meetings" that include a sandwich, a cup of coffee, and conversation with family and friends. One thinks of the character Clevinger in *Catch-22* (1961), who knows "everything about literature except how to enjoy it."[10] How many Christians know everything about Christianity except how to enjoy it? How many Jesus followers know everything about Jesus except how to enjoy him?

The kingdom of God is a "gift," a "presence," a Jesus reign which we receive and then gift others with its blessings. The kingdom is a teleology that starts at the end and plays backwards from an end of God's making. The future is an eschatology that starts now and builds to an end of our making. Jesus humans receive and then gift the kingdom, thereby creating the future, both at the same time.

It is God's gift to us that everyone should eat and drink and take pleasure in all his doings.
ECCLESIASTES 3:13

<u>Mission and Mates:</u> God gave our lives two coordinates: Mission and Mates. Some things to do (mission) and some ones to do it with (mates). The mission was "tend and till the garden." The mate was a partner who was "bone of my bones, blood of my blood." The basic necessities of life are more than food and drink. They are also kith and kin where everyone is "kinning" and turning strangers into "kinfolk." Keep faith with these coordinates and you live the telos life. But we go off course quickly and follow other lights (which explains the importance of Lucifer's name as "light-bearer").

Why are followers of Jesus not temperamentally allergic to Christians who do not do fun, have fun, or are fun? Even though it was the Protestant Reformer Martin Luther who is widely credited (falsely, I suspect) with the couplet "Who does not love wine, women and song/Remains a fool his whole life long,"[11] Protestantism's overriding cerebral focus often promoted a grim modern version of Christianity that suppressed play, pleasure, style, joy, ecstasy, festival, form, and privileged sins of pride over sins of passion. For Jesus, sins of passion are no worse than sins of pride. The sulky, smug self-righteousness of the older brother was as bad as the pigpen lifestyle of the younger brother.

Of course, a strand of ascetic discipleship was there from the beginning, even to the point where some fifth-century bishops had to restrain their clerics from castrating themselves. One notable eleventh-century ascetic was renowned for his terrible personal hygiene, floor-length hair that mopped the floor wherever he walked, and two pet snakes.[12] When you look at how rapidly USAmericans are walking away from Christianity—in my lifetime we have gone from 90% to 64% who call themselves Christians—it seems we are more a sea of broken spirits than a windsurf of Mt. Carmel/Pentecostal fire.

To be sure, there are seasons of abundance for different expressions of the abundant life. Abundant living embraces the ritual year's complimentary festivals of Lent and Carnival, the mysteries of dying as well as daying. Abundance does not exclude seasons of fasting, penitence, lamentation (one-third of the psalms are lamentations), sobriety, gravity, and self-denial. To live the Jesus life is to occupy paradoxical conditions all the time. St. John Climacus (d. 649), an anchorite at the Mount Sinai monastery known for his ladder of devotion, called this the "charmolupe" life after the hybrid mythical beast that combined contrary features. We might call charmolupe a "bright sadness" or "joyful sorrow" which issues in tears of both mourning and joy.

But a sour, dour faith sends all the wrong symbols. John fasted because fasting was a sign of preparing for the coming of the Messiah, an appeal to God for the coming of the messianic age.

Jesus feasted because he is the Messiah, and the Messiah is here. To fast is to deny the Messiah. You fast in the bridegroom's absence, not his presence. Can you imagine going to a wedding and fasting to celebrate the marriage?

Jesus humans pass the torch, not the ash pan. Vases of brightly colored flowers festoon funerals for a reason. And flowers are brightly colored for a reason too: in order to attract pollinating insects.

Even Calvinists could let it rip in ways that belie Puritan reputations as pious prigs. For example, Genevans loved their vineyards. When the grapes were gathered and new wine pressed, it was party time with round-the-clock dancing, singing, and drinking. John Calvin gave the details of the revelry: "There they sit, as if stunned, unable to turn away to relieve their reeking stomach: they throw up all over the table and the glasses, or else, if they still manage to turn aside, they vomit on their robes and there is no corner that is not filled with their spew."[13] What astounds Calvin, and astounds us to read it, is that no one else complains about this debauchery. Calvin doesn't forbid the merriment, but demands that the religious function of the celebration be remembered by those Genevans who "capered about like calves that are let loose."

The ancient usages was to celebrate harvest and vintage with songs. And such an usage was not bad in itself, if only they would address their canticles to God in thanksgiving. For since we receive all good things from his hand, we have a good reason to rejoice, provided it be in him.[14]

John Wesley could be a bit snarky. He brushed aside Calvinist revivalist George Whitefield's "amorous style of praying and luscious style of preaching"[15] that he felt cloyed the appetites for truth. But he himself told his followers to "sing lustily."[16]

For both John Calvin and John Wesley, anything that becomes an end in itself becomes an idol. Even good things, when made into ends, become bad things. When family becomes an end, it becomes an idol. When wealth becomes an end, it becomes an idol. When food and feasting become an end, they become an idol. Jesus is the only end. Only Jesus is "Alpha and Omega, the Beginning and the End."

Whole-Life, Wholesome Living: God lives in laughter, lightness, loyalty, love, spontaneity, imagination. Uprightness and uptightness do not go together. Have some of us misread "hate" for "have" in John 10:10: "I have come that you might hate life and hate more abundantly?"

DESIGNER JESUS

> *If the least significant is excluded,*
> *it is no longer a celebration.*
> CANADIAN CATHOLIC JEAN VANIER (D. 2019)[17]

It's time Jesus humans be known for their zest and appetite for life. Our default setting is one of abundance, not scarcity. A culture of scarcity will be a culture based on acquisition and possessiveness and consumption. A culture of abundance will be a culture of generosity and grace, "full of God dwelled,"[18] filled with the "riches of God's glory in Jesus,"[19] replete with an "abundance of grace,"[20] and boasting "the boundless riches of Christ"[21] and "all the treasures of wisdom and knowledge."[22] The church's romanticization of poverty is amiss. Jesus was forever turning the water of eking out existence into the wine of exuberant and abundant living.

In the Hebrew tradition, if it were possible, a fatted calf (beef was feast food) was on hand and constantly being fed in case an "angel unaware" or other divine visitor might show up and require a meal. There is another little-known Hebrew tradition prescribing a special tithe to be set aside every three years specifically for celebrating and rejoicing. This "tithe of rejoicing" is described in Deuteronomy 14:22–27. The Hebrew Bible commands "a tithe of rejoicing" paid every third year on top of the standard annual tithe. Whereas the annual tithe went to the Levites, this special one was set aside within each town to host and fund celebratory feasts and celebrations, holidays and hospitalities for the whole community including the Levites, foreigners, orphans and widows. The purpose was to rejoice before the Lord, celebrating the harvest and God's provision. It was seen as charity, spreading joy and including everyone in the festivities.

The "abundant life" promised in John 10:10 doesn't mean "nonphysical life" but all of life—whole life, not half-life, or term life, but whole and wholesome life. "Wholesome" is a good summarial word for a life where style and substance are the same, content and form are the same, meaning and matter are the same, inner and outer are the same. A wholesome life is an as-above, so-below life. A whole life is a wholesome life is a holy life.

To die for God is not what we live for. That's perverted faith. To live for God is what we die for. That's pure faith. Some days require part of you. Some days require most of you. Some days require all of you. Some days require more than the whole of you.

That's a Holy Spirit Day.

A Jesus Appetite does not take for granted this splendid gift of life. To live for God is to put back in the church's dreary eyes that dreamy glint. I yearn to see the dreamy glint in Christian eyes again, as did apologist G. K. Chesterton:

> Christianity is itself so jolly a thing that it fills the possessor of it with a certain silly exuberance, which sad and high-minded Rationalists might reasonably mistake for mere buffoonery and blasphemy; just as their prototypes, the sad and high-minded Stoics

of old Rome, did mistake the Christian joyousness for buffoonery and blasphemy.[23]

Jesus loved life and loved people more than anyone else ever. How are we doing as his disciples at loving life and loving people? A "new Christian" friend says "I don't ever want to be anything other than a 'new Christian.' When I am no longer 'new' it means I have taken Jesus for granted."[24] That's an appetite for God.

There are a lot of ways to take the Lord's name in vain. To call yourself a Christian and not to have a sense of humor is one of them. A sour spirit is to take the Lord's name in vain. Humor and comedy presuppose faith in a framework of Providence and Purpose. I suspect this is what G. K. Chesterton was getting at in his famous quote: "In a world where everything is ridiculous, nothing can be ridiculed . . . If life is really so formless that you cannot make head or tail of it, you cannot pull its tail; and you certainly cannot make it stand on its head."[25]

Humor is, in fact, a prelude to faith, and laughter is the beginning of prayer . . . The intimate relation between humor and faith is derived from the fact that both deal with the incongruities of our existence. Humor is concerned with the immediate incongruities of life and faith with the ultimate ones . . . Laughter is our reaction to immediate incongruities and those which do not affect us essentially. Faith is the only possible response to the ultimate incongruities of existence which threatens the very meaning of our life.

THEOLOGIAN REINHOLD NIEBUHR (D. 1971)[26]

The Good Life: The gospel celebrates human life at the same time it changes human lives. The good news says "good" to life as it holds out the "news" of better and changed lives. But look what we've done to that phrase "good" in "the good life."

Take "a good Christian." What does that mean? Is to say someone is a "good Christian" is to say that they're trying hard not to have fun? I don't want to be a "good Christian" if that's what you mean by "good." The church has too many "good Christians" running around trying to be "good" rather than letting Jesus live in them. When people see me, I don't want them to say "What a good Christian he is." I want them to say "This guy loves Jesus."[27]

What is heaven like? John's vision of heaven is a tableland featuring a global menu of tastes, textures, traditions, and colors not melted together in some gray gruel or boiled pottage but placed on the same table for everyone to enjoy the delights of its diversities. A portent of what heaven is like, and the possibility of experiencing the kingdom of God now, is the very essence of Jesus' first miracle, his coming-out miracle, in Cana of Galilee where no sermon was preached, no one was healed, no one was saved, but where everyone had a good time singing, dancing, and feasting.[28] Jesus never performed a wedding: he could have done it, but all he did was perform one miracle just for pleasure and make between 144 and 216 bottles of wine.

Early Christianity was a meal society. Worship and liturgy were organized around the table, where joy and love became the dominant ethos of life. At the table God was celebrated as the dancer:

> Yahweh . . . will exult with joy over you,
> He will renew you by his love;
> He will dance with shouts of joy for you
> as on a day of festival.[29]

In Jesus' day to rejoice was almost synonymous with dance. You can sing and read with your feet nailed to the floor. And you can sing and read when you're in a bad mood. But to dance is to act yourself into joy. Saul danced so hard with Samuels' prophets that he passed out for many hours.[30] One Jewish exposition of the Song of Songs declares that God will lead the dance among the righteous in the new age.[31]

My Wesleyan holiness preacher mom insisted that Jesus turned water into grape juice. As much as I love my mother,[32] wine is wine. The Bible records how Noah "drank some of the wine and became drunk."[33] You don't get drunk on grape juice. The Hebrew word for wine (*yayin* pronounced yah'·yin) is used for wine throughout the New Testament. Paul scolds the Corinthians because they even got drunk during the Lord's Supper, turning it into a toast to Jesus: "Here's to Jesus."[34] Again, Corinthians are not getting drunk off of unfermented grape juice.

Jesus and his followers drank wine at these meals, and at the Last Supper there is a symbolic significance to the wine being wine. Giving thanks over the wine, Jesus says, "This cup is the new covenant in my blood."[35] The last words of

Jacob to his twelve sons reveals the mysterious wine of Judah, the tribe to which Jesus belongs, and connects the wine with blood:

> Judah, your brothers shall praise you;
> . . . He washes his garments in wine
> and his robe in the blood of grapes;
> his eyes are darker than wine,
> and his teeth whiter than milk.[36]

We can learn from the Catholic understanding that the closest we come to the resurrection body of Jesus is the eucharistic elements of bread and wine. It symbolizes a rich life of simple appetites and pleasures, as symbolized in the toast of the twelfth century *Rubaiyat of Omar Khayyam*: "A loaf of bread, a jug of wine, and thou."[37]

Jesus used water, not wine, as the symbol of his teaching. But in turning water into wine at the wedding feast in Cana, he uses wine, not water, as the symbol of his Messiahship.

Life Essentials, Life Pleasures: The sign of the Messiah's coming is a wedding feast where Cana becomes Canaan and which erases the boundaries between the two types of trees in the garden from which God instructed humans to "Eat Freely."[38] "The LORD God made all sorts of trees grow up from the ground—trees that were beautiful and that produced delicious fruit."[39] Some trees were meant for food, the essentials of life. Some trees were meant for beauty, the pleasures of life. In the words of Psalm 104, which is based on the Genesis creation story:

> You cause the grass to grow for the cattle,
> and plants for people to use,
> to bring forth food from the earth,
> and wine to gladden the human heart.[40]

Notice how plants are primary and essential for life, while wine is a gift of God for pleasure and joy that will "gladden the human heart." Both are God-given, one for use and one for sheer beauty and delight—like the two kinds of trees in the garden.

Children ask God for things, telling God what they want. As we grow, we start listening to God and shift our me-focus to God-focused prayer. But there is one more step, and it's the biggest one. The height of prayer is listening "for" God, not just listening "to" God. This movement from "for" into "to" removes us from the question-answer, receive-give formats (as if we even knew the right questions or what's best for us) and brings us to the place of prayer as the premier appetite and posture of life: pleasuring in God's presencings and listening to God's heart.

Jesus spent the last night of his life eating and drinking with his friends. He didn't try to escape his destiny and slip out of the city under cover of darkness. He stayed in charge of his future, not as a hopeless victim but as a Messiah in charge: "I have a new commandment for you: love one another as I have loved you . . . no one has greater love than this, to lay down your life for your friend."[41] A Jesus human lives in that love, lives loving life and friends enough to die for them, to die for love.

> *Do not be overcome by evil,*
> *but overcome evil with good.*
> PAUL[42]

Jesus was attacked personally on two fronts: 1) depraved indifference to rules (he was a repeat offender of Sabbath-breaking); 2) a moral reprobate who ate too heartily, drank too openly, and attracted attention-grabbing "friends in low places." What if the church had spent the last 2000 years embracing these accusations rather than running from them?

Even if you deem someone a sinner (i.e., chronic liar, racist, sexist, homophobe, pervert), that does not mean they are a lesser being unworthy of respect and relationship. Zaccheus was a despised billionaire, a member of the 1%, but Jesus prefers to spend time with him than with the religious people and power establishment. When you thought of tax collectors in the first century, the first thing that came to your mind was not the 1% of power, wealth, and influence. You thought of corruption, crookedness, greed, abuse of power, and degeneracy. If you are known by the company you keep, Jesus didn't seem to care about whom he kept.

Jesus humans have a huge appetite that enjoys life. Not a miserly, meager appetite, but a generous appetite for life, appetite for love, appetite for change. The Jesus "ask-and-you-shall-receive"[43] vision is one of abundance. We begin in a garden where there are fruit trees galore, all free. Eden is a place of plenty, a palace of abundance. Even after humans get kicked out, there is the Promised Land of abundance, a land of Canaan "flowing with milk and honey." But even in exile there is the promise of abundance and "overflowing streams."[44]

The story ends with a meal . . . the marriage supper of the Lamb. The vision of future is a banquet table where all is full and free, all our appetites are met, above and beyond all our expectations. Jesus provides—not just promises—abundance. Even in the desert places, abundance can flow. There are sins of commission, where you live life badly. But worse are sins of omission, where you're afraid to live life fully and abundantly.

A good measure, pressed down, shaken together, running over, will be put into your lap.
JESUS' SERMON ON THE MOUNT, LUKE 6:38 NRSVA

<u>What Matters?</u> The real marker of "mattering" is not how many things you have, or how many things you get done, but the spirit in which you have them and do them, especially the smallest and lowliest of things. Abundance is not material wealth, but an openness to receive the gifts of God that come day by day, moment by moment, especially the gift of the indwelling Spirit. In choosing scarcity over abundance, many Christians are living accordingly, with no verve or vision.

Sometimes it's the rituals, not the beliefs, that are the

comfort. Food is a ritual and a thing. Sometimes doctrines and creeds are no longer the things we need. Sometimes the thing is the thing we need . . . the things of fabric, candles, rosaries, mirrors, embroidery, statuary, food. My house is a thing, but it is more than that. It is a living manifesto. It is not a dead object, but a living memoir, and I want it to make you smile.

The appetite for things, or what I call "thingys," is confused and clouded by the fact that we live in a sensorially subdivided universe. A Jesus human has an appetite spread across the sensory spectrum, with all senses beckoned to the worship of God. The "eye gate" and the "ear gate" are no longer enough. There must now be as well as smell gate, a taste gate, and a touch gate.

The appetites for truth are not just for the ears, eyes, hands. The appetites for truth are sensory transactions for the whole body. Can you imagine jazz without the haze of smoke and scotch? Can you imagine country music without the crackle of hay and the scrape of barn-wood floors? Classical needs the starch of caviar, candles, and champagne.

Thingys: Every religion will have its holy things, its holy objects and relics.[45] Especially a religion where the first time we meet God, we meet a God who is a Gardener (God the Gardener) and a Potter (God the Artist). Both flowers and pottery are things. One of the most holy relics in Christian history was the navel (or *umbilicus*) of Jesus Christ, which symbolizes the humanity of the divine and the corporeality of our common human condition.[46]

Medieval supplicants felt and touched the religious image in a visual-tactile presence of things. Remnants and traces of holy men and women—pieces of their clothes, their hair, objects which they had worn, touched, or associated, even their trash—became ritualized and coveted. These items were traded for huge sums, even celebrated for their miraculous healing potential. John Calvin, of course, called such relics "precious rubbish," the same John Calvin that gave a bounty for every piece of Christian art destroyed (paintings, curtains, wood carvings, stone sculptures, etc.). But you can't live without holy things. The only question is: will it be an icon relic or idol relic.

A signature in a book makes it a relic. The "aura" of original art objects, which gives them authority and authenticity, makes it a relic.[47] A selfie is a new form of relic. Celebrity merch is a relic market, where some of our holiest things are traces of celebs—a Marilyn Monroe dress, an Elvis ashtray, a Mickey Mantle bat. The more venerable the provenance, the more valuable the relic.

Russian czar Nicholas II's army was being beaten by the Japanese in 1903. His solution was to ship to the front lines thousands of holy icons. What the soldiers thought when, instead of ammunition and weapons and clothing, they got religious relics to fight with is anyone's guess. But they were totally crushed by the Japanese.

The Love Code: Love is a seditious, subversive word in the

Jesus vocabulary. It's not some soft, cozy, cuddly word that brings out starry eyes and romantic kisses. To "love your enemy" to the point where, if they demand your cloak, you strip it all off[48] and go naked is not simply "give-them-more-than-they-ask-for" generosity. It is turning the tables on the oppressor, shaming the creditor, upending the system, and undermining the reigning power dynamics.[49] To "go the second mile"[50] is not to carry a soldier's gear for twice the distance required by law, but to gum up the power system,[51] even making the soldier chase after his gear, not by violence or by inaction but by a third "way," the Jesus Way of overcoming, overpowering love.

Jesus' appetite for love was endless. But love isn't a weakness. Love is a holiness and rebelliousness against the powers and principalities of the world. Love is a whole new way of living in the world that brings goodness, beauty, and truth to break us open, only to make room for grace and to fill the breach with healing forgiveness and love.

Love is tabletime. Mealtime at the family table is first huddle/cuddle/play time, second story time, third give-and-take time, finally thanksgiving time.

All those dinners around the table? It's not just a dinner.

DESIGNER JESUS

My God, my Lover, my Love, my Joy, my Beauty, my Spouse, my Father, my Mother, my Comforter, my Counselor, my Teacher, my Nourishment, my Life, my Light, my Hope, my Strength, my Refuge, my Peace, my All!

AUGUSTINE, CONFESSIONS, BOOK I, CHAPTER 4

STUDIO LIVE

1) This "Table Talk" litany was written by writer/composer Laurie Klein ("I Love You Lord") after she read *Tablet to Table*. It is used by permission.[52]

    * Designate one person the Leader. Invite those present to read the bolded responses. If you're alone, read both parts. Use different voices. Or arrange to read with someone you love via phone or Zoom.

    ALL READ:

    "Eventually, all things merge into one, and a river runs through it. The river was cut by the world's great flood, and runs over rocks from the basement of time. On some rocks are the timeless raindrops, under the rocks are words and some of the words are theirs. I am haunted by waters." —Norman Maclean

    LEADER:

    It's also true that, eventually, all things merge into One because God's Table runs through it. The first table was conceived by grace for those in the Garden, and it extends, literally and figuratively, across our world. Come to the table prepared by God, our timeless Host. The invitation stands, long as there are clocks and long after their chimes shall cease.

ALL:

> **All good things—time as well as eternal salvation—come by grace.**

LEADER:

> We remember today the Periodic Table of the Elements and earth's bounty.
>
> We remember the multiplication tables and the multiplied loaves and fish.
>
> We give thanks for every table of contents in every book that has helped us find our way.

ALL:

> **All good things—provision as well as eternal salvation—come by grace.**

LEADER:

> We remember "Wisdom has also set her table."
>
> We remember the psalmist's table prepared by God, in full view of his foes.
>
> We give thanks that "It is not the one who reclines at table who is greatest, but the one who serves."

ALL:

> **All good things—wisdom as well as eternal salvation—come by grace.**

LEADER:

> We remember Martha, lovingly arraying her table for Christ.
>
> We remember the Canaanite woman, shrewdly arguing "Even the dogs feast on the crumbs from the Master's table.
>
> We give thanks for the worried mother at Cana; the Son who was willing to help; the wine steward's awe; and all those oblivious, thirsty, hungry guests, who, like so many today—ourselves included—show up for the food.

ALL:

> **All good things—hope as well as eternal salvation—come by grace.**

LEADER:

> We remember the Temple tables, upended by Christ.

ALL:

> **All good things—both those actions we understand and those that perplex us—come by grace.**

LEADER:

> We remember the woman who anointed Jesus, pouring out her all.
>
> We remember the meal at Emmaus, Jesus revealed in the sharing of bread.

We give thanks for Jesus presiding over his last earthly table: wine and bread, blessed. Broken.

ALL:

All good things—reconciliation as well as eternal salvation—come by grace.

LEADER:

We remember God's call to set a table for the strangers among us. And we anticipate the forthcoming Marriage Supper of the Lamb, all of us together, feasting . . .

ALL:

Blessed be God, our Host, in whom all things merge, eventually, into One. From the first shared meal in the Garden . . . through this moment we share now . . . until well beyond what we mean by forever, may we be haunted by Love.

2) Terence Eagleton is a British literary theorist, prolific author, and Distinguished Professor of English Literature at Lancaster University. Without professing to be a Christian, he is one of greatest apologists for Christianity on the worldwide intellectual scene today. Discuss this summary of Jesus' uniqueness in Eagleton's *London Review of Books* take-down of atheist Richard Dawkins, who sees God as some monster:

Jesus hung out with whores and social outcasts, was remarkably casual about sex, disapproved of the family, urged us to be laid-back about property and possessions, warned his followers that they too would die violently, and insisted that the truth kills and divides as well as liberates. He also cursed self-righteous prigs and deeply alarmed the ruling class.... The central doctrine of Christianity, then, is not that God is a bastard. It is, in the words of the late Dominican theologian Herbert McCabe, that if you don't love, you're dead, and if you do, they'll kill you.[53]

* What parts of this summary of Jesus do you agree with? What parts leave you uneasy?

3) Pastor and linguistics professor Andrew Farley has a unique slant on Jesus' parable of the traveling merchant in search of fine gems in Matthew 13:45ff. Here are some of his insights. What are your reactions and reflections after reading his interpretations:

> This parable calls to mind various passages in wisdom literature, above all those that encourage the search for wisdom (e.g., Proverbs 2:1–4; Wisdom 7:1–8:21). Yet Jesus took up this theme of search in his own way and did not merely borrow from the Scriptures he had inherited. What we read there, among other things, are poetical descriptions of Solomon's desire to have wisdom as his bride (Wisdom 8:2, 9. 16).

Solomon values her more than 'any precious gem', not to mention an abundance of gold and silver (Wisdom 7:9; see Job 28:1–19). Yet the theme Jesus chose for his brief parable about the traveling merchant was the search for a priceless gem, not the search for the perfect bride (see Proverbs 18:22; 30:10). Dare we hazard a guess about his choice and the motives for his choice?

Could it be that he did not feel attracted to the image of a man traveling around the world in search of the perfect bride? Despite its positive possibilities, this image might demean women and reduce them to the object of a male search. Whatever the reason, Jesus preferred to use the image of a merchant searching for fine pearls and not that of some latter-day Solomon out and about checking the marriage market.[54]

* Why do you think Jesus used the metaphor of a merchant searching for a pearl rather than a man searching for a bride?

* What does this suggest about how Jesus viewed women versus how they were culturally regarded as "objects" to obtain?

* How might the pearl represent something different

than earthly riches or romance? What else could its meaning encompass?

* Why might seeking the Kingdom of Heaven be better represented by a precious jewel versus a human bride?
* How might this parable have been more controversial and countercultural in Jesus' time versus today?
* What other biblical metaphors use jewels and precious metals symbolically? What do they represent?
* How does this parable represent the immense value of the Kingdom for those who seek it?
* In what ways is the Kingdom like a priceless treasure that merits selling everything else? In what ways might it differ?
* What might this parable say about the fundamentals of true fulfillment and meaning in life?

4) Here is Mennonite historian Alan Kreider describing the changes that occurred in the early church to move it away from a "meal society" to a worship/sermon society:

> Other changes were equally far reaching. The service times had changed. Typically the earlier churches held their primary meetings in the evenings, but by the first half of the third century most had their main services in the morning. The churches had moved from being a meal society to being a worship assembly, and their primary meeting had

moved from dinner to breakfast. Another change had to do with the food that was served in the liturgies. The full meals that had characterized early Christian services were being replaced by symbolic tokens of bread and wine in a cultic meal. And the words that were spoken were changing in character: from spontaneous utterances spoken by many after the evening meals to monological addresses given by clergy to morning congregations worshiping in larger assemblies.[55]

* What would it mean for your church to be a "meal society?"

5) When do you stop filling the punch bowl? Right when the party gets going good. Otherwise the punch bowl becomes the party.

* When have you seen a good thing go bad by going overboard rather than quitting while you were ahead?

* What are some signs that you've reached the point of diminishing returns in an activity where more is not better?

* Why do you think moderation and balance can be so difficult to maintain sometimes?

* What is an area of your life you need to be cautious about indulging too much in?

* How can we keep the focus on people rather than getting distracted by activities or substances? How do you

let the guests and social interactions take center stage, not the particular refreshments. How do you make sure the party is about the people, not the punch itself?

* What advice would you give someone struggling with excess right now?

* How can you be present and mindful even while engaging in an enjoyable activity, so you know when enough is enough?

* What does wisdom look like in discerning when the party has peaked and it's time for a change?

6) The ultimate in wine tasting, besides terroir, is known in the trade as "nervosity." This is the shimmering edginess and nervous excitement that comes from the anticipation of tasting a rare or highly regarded wine.

* Have you ever experienced "nervosity" when it comes to a meal or a gathering?

* Have you ever experienced "nervosity" before worship?

* Can nervosity be a positive or negative experience? Positive when it enhances the enjoyment of the meal by making the experience more memorable and meaningful? Negative when it makes it difficult to focus on the experience and to appreciate its rich nuances?

7) Why do we call wedding celebrations "receptions" and not "feasts?" What is the difference between attending a wedding where there was an abundance of food, favors, and wine provided for guests, and one where everyone

got punch and cake? Might not the family who cannot afford a catered dinner be celebrating with more abundance than the egoic dad showing off his bride price?

* Discuss different wedding "receptions" and "parties" you've attended.

* Which ones do you remember the most? What makes them so memorable?

* What are the pros and cons of having a large, formal wedding reception versus a small, informal wedding party?

* What are some ways to make a wedding celebration more meaningful, regardless of the budget?

* What are some ways to celebrate a wedding without spending a lot of money?

8) Jesus always provided more than those present could possibly consume. Jesus always has leftovers. Why do you think this is so? Did Jesus want his followers to know that God's provision is limitless? When Jesus multiplied the loaves and fishes, was he not just feeding the physical hunger of the crowd, but also feeding their spiritual hunger and showing them that God would always provide for their needs? If "there is always enough for one more," there will always be left-overs.

* What should we do with leftovers?

* Might there be a theology of leftovers?

- What are some of the ways that we can share our leftovers with others?
- What are some of the challenges of sharing our leftovers with others?
- How can the theology of leftovers help us to be more generous and compassionate people?
- What are some of the creative ways that we can use leftover food?
- How can we reduce food waste in our homes and communities?

9) Jesus had immense empathy for women and appetite for lifting them up. Here is one example: "When a woman is in travail, she has sorrow; but when she has recovered, she no longer remembers the anguish, since a child is born by her into the world."[56]

- How might Jesus have known that the pain of childbirth is the hardest pain to endure but the hardest to remember? What is the essence of compassion?
- Do you agree with that old saying?
- What is the essence of compassion?
- Have you ever experienced a pain that was physically and emotionally exhausting, but that was also followed by a deep sense of joy and satisfaction?
- How can we support women who are going through the pain of childbirth?

- * What are some ways that we can celebrate the gift of new life?
- * How can we create a more supportive world for women who are pregnant or giving birth?
- * What are some ways that we can celebrate the unique gifts and contributions of women in our society?

10) Some people don't start life at ground zero, or plus with plush, but at minus four or minus five. These are the people with whom Jesus spent the most time.

- * Who do we spend the most time with?
- * Do we spend any time with people born below ground zero?
- * How might we do better?

11) Here are some specific examples of how our desires and pleasures can embody Jesus energies:

a) When we desire to serve others, not just ourselves, we can find fulfillment in ministering or being generous givers.

b) When we find pleasure in spending time with loved ones, or strangers, we can strengthen our relationships and build a healthier community.

c) When we are passionate about learning and growing, we can open ourselves up to new experiences and expand our horizons.

The possibilities are endless.

- * Give some more examples of what happens when we allow our desires and pleasures to be guided by Jesus energies, thereby creating a life that is both meaningful and joyful.

12) Do you want to know what love is? Try listening to Schubert's "Impromptu in G Flat Major," and then reveal to one another what you heard and how you felt about this nonverbal expression of love.

* What emotions, images, or memories came up for you while listening to this piece? What did it evoke?
* How would you describe the "tone" or "mood" of the music? What does that convey about love?
* What moments in the piece resonated with you most deeply? What did those parts communicate?
* How did the music physically make you feel? Where in your body did you experience reactions?
* Did the music tell a narrative about love? What journey did it take you on?
* How was love expressed through the variations, dynamics, and tempo of the music?
* What aspects of love do you think the music captured well? What did it miss or leave unexpressed?
* How was experiencing love through music different than talking about it? What unique insights did this provide?
* Has a piece of music ever helped you grasp something in a new way? What core human truths can music convey?

Chapter 8: Style Cool
The Jesus Style: Cool

*It is art that makes life, makes interest, makes importance
. . . and I know of no substitute whatever for the force
and beauty of its process.*

ENGLISH NOVELIST HENRY JAMES (D. 1916)[1]

EACH YEAR, THE OXFORD WORD OF THE YEAR CAPTURES a word or phrase that reflects the current zeitgeist. In 2023, the winner wasn't "Swiftie" or "parasocial," but rather a term straight out of Gen Z vernacular: "rizz."

Rizz, a shortened and punchier version of "charisma," refers to the magnetic ability to attract and charm others. It's more than just good looks; it encompasses style, wit, confidence, and an unblushing cool.

But what if I told you that living with "rizz" wasn't just a social skill, but a spiritual calling?

This might sound surprising, but hear me out. Imagine a life infused with the qualities of rizz: exuding genuine kindness, radiating confidence, and inspiring others with your unique spark and cool. That's the essence of the "Jesus designed life."

Rizzing is not about superficial charm or manipulation, but about cultivating a life of authenticity, compassion, and positive influence. It's about living "rizzily" through acts of kindness, genuine connection, and standing up for who and what you believe.

The Jesus revolution is a rizzolution that inspires others to "rizz on." A Jesus human embraces the spirit of "rizz" that radiates kindness, inhabits your unique strengths, and makes a positive impact on the world around you. Who knows, you might just inspire others to "rizz on" themselves.

Rizz reminds us that discipleship is a design vocation, especially when it comes to style. Jesus is a style of life. The Jesus lifestory has a distinct lifestyle. But Jesus is more than a lifestyle. The Jesus life is style, and the Jesus style is life.

Cicero (d. 43 BC) celebrated Socrates (d. 399 BC) for calling "philosophy" down from the heavens and forcing it to enter the towns and villages, the hearths and hearts, the lives and loves of actual people. Cicero was wrong. It wasn't Socrates who brought philosophy down to earth and muscled anthropology out of cosmology. It was Jesus, for whom the "love of wisdom" (Greek philo-sophia) was found in the "love of God" (theos-philia) more than the "study of God" (theos-logia). There is a difference between loving God (theo-philia) and studying God (theology).

THE JESUS STYLE: COOL

The proper study of humanity is the science of design.
ECONOMIST/PSYCHOLOGIST HERBERT A SIMON (D. 2001)[2]

Style is the way to be love inside and out. The Jesus Style encompasses every aspect of human existence, including and especially economics. Jesus brought economics and teleology together stylistically. The "end" of our economic activity is human be-ing, not income betterment. One of the theologians to have gotten this is Thomas Aquinas. In the eight million words Aquinas wrote, economics is never about how best to satisfy our desires, but how best to civilize ourselves to desire what is good, beautiful, and true. If the "fruits of one's labor" are not dedicated to making humans grow and flourish and bear fruit themselves, then such behavior is in "bad form."

Bad Form: If something is in bad form, it does not mean it is wrong or immoral. It means it is unbecoming to someone becoming a Jesus human. For example, cruelty is wrong. Cheap shots are not wrong, but unbecoming. They are beneath the dignity of any self-respecting Jesus human. At least this is what I was taught, and still teach.

After checking social media or listening to the news, one wonders if the tide has turned to normalize cruelty and cheap shots and abnormalize giving others the benefit of the doubt and the refusal to turn clever repartee into cheap snipes. Whatever the Zeitgeist, the Heiliger Geist (Holy Spirit) is firm: Cruelty in pursuit of the good and just is still cruelty,

DESIGNER JESUS

and cheap shots even taken at your enemies are still unseemly and bad form.

Oh, those Greeks! They knew how to live: what is needed for that is to stop bravely at the surface, the fold, the skin: to worship appearance, to believe in shapes, tones, words—in the whole Olympus of appearance!

LATIN AND GREEK SCHOLAR FRIEDRICH NIETZSCHE (D. 1900)[3]

Form is more than function.[4] Form is content. Style is now substance.[5] Style tells who you are and reveals the essence of your character. The Jesus style is not a gum-chewing, lip-smacking style but neither is it a formal, ornate style that can snap under the weights of its adornment. The Jesus Style is the epitome of "cool."

Cool has nothing to do with being trendy, or hip, or relevant. Jesus calls disciples of every age to be both in their time but also out of time. That is why so many hipsters aren't hip, and why so many "cool churches" aren't cool. Cool is fitting together not fitting in, living as a one-of-a-kind classic not a copy or clone. "Cool" for you may be sandals or stilettoes, cold shoulder or hot halter, hoodie or helmet, low-rise jeans or over-all jeans, boot-cut jeans or skinny-leg jeans, capris or Carhartts. Cool is finding your style, being comfortable in your style, and living your style. To call Jesus "cool" is to use original definition of "cool," which comes from Nigeria.

THE JESUS STYLE: COOL

Love does not act in an unseemly fashion
APOSTLE PAUL (D. 64)[6]

Mystic Coolness: Sociologists and linguists are surprisingly of one voice in where we got the concept of "cool." This concept that took root in the mid-twentieth century actually had its roots in the culture of the fifteenth-century Nigerian Yoruba tribes. The Yoruba described tribal leaders, warriors, and persons of authority as possessing "itutu," literally "cool."

"Itutu" meant to be calm, steady and confident as cool water. "Itutu" was actually a combination of character qualities. An expression of nobility and character, a sense of certainty and confidence, was termed "ashe." This "ashe"–ness was enhanced by what they understood as "mystic coolness," which is the literal translation of "itutu." This combination of "ashe" and "itutu" was expressed by those individuals who could always respond with grace under pressure, who expressed confidence in any situation, and in whom goodness could prevail even under the most difficult circumstances. "Itutu," "coolness," was an individual gift, but was always intimately connected to the community it served, where it was received as a communal gift.

"Itutu" or "mystic coolness" was also part of Yoruba artwork. "Itutu" was expressed in art with the color blue or indigo. African American musical culture created the "blues," and in 1957 Miles Davis declared that jazz culture was the "Birth of the Cool." Blue is "cool." Jazz is "itutu." Saxophonist

Lester Young loved to talk about "cool jazz," which he saw as saying the same thing twice.

For too long we have had a western classical Jesus. Maybe it is time for the jazzing of Jesus. A jazzed Jesus is less simple linearity than complex circuitry, less a Carnegie Hall Jesus than a coffee-house, dance-floor Jesus.

Keep Your Cool: No one consistently "kept his cool," "stayed cool," or "lived cool" more than Jesus. Jesus conducted his ministry in a crucible of cool. "Itutu" or "mystic coolness" was named by the Yoruba. But it was a style honed and perfected by Jesus throughout his ministry.

Of all the stories of the gospel, the encounter with the Canaanite woman seems to put Jesus in a definitely uncool light.[7] Leaving behind both a successful healing ministry and a confrontational disagreement with the local Pharisees and scribes over the issue of ritual cleanliness, Jesus journeys to the district of Tyre and Sidon. Tyre and Sidon were fortress ports riddled with pirates, the hallmark of pagan or Gentile territory.

Suddenly Jesus is approached by a Canaanite member of the local community. It is unclear from the text whether Jesus is actually still outside of Gentile territory and the woman comes out to meet him, or if Jesus is inside what is generally deemed Gentile uncleanness.

This Gentile woman does not exactly exhibit genteel manners. She shows up shouting at Jesus, demanding action from him: "Have mercy on me, Lord, Son of David; my daughter is tormented by a demon."[8] Her forthrightness might be a bit brash and presumptuous, but she has all the names right. Even though she is a Canaanite, an indigenous "pagan" of unholy lands, she addresses Jesus with accurate accolades: He is "Lord" and he is the "Son of David"—messianic titles that imply the presence of wisdom, power, or in other words, the "ashe" and "itutu" of "mystic coolness."

At first Jesus does not seem "cool" one bit: "he did not answer her at all." Even the disciples start complaining about her request and dared to order Jesus to "send her away, for she keeps shouting after us." But Jesus does not deal with her as a pain-in-the-neck penitent. Instead, Jesus "cools off" this confrontation by pointing the disciples in a different direction. Jesus asserts his prime directive: "I was sent only to the lost sheep of the house of Israel." In other words, his mission is to be focused on the Jewish people, not on others.

As Jesus gradually cools off the situation, he shows us the four features of "itutu," the four marks of mystic coolness.

Jesus Cool #1: The first mark is self-transcendence. You must transcend some of your initial emotions and cool off by letting go some of those immediate, instinctive, knee-jerk reactions. Jesus doesn't just listen to the Canaanite woman's pleas. He works hard to hear what she is saying. To go beyond "listening" to "hearing" takes a moment for some "intimate distancing." He steps forward and leans back at the same time. He takes a beat. He does not respond emotionally, but he respects her voice while responding with the traditional mission of one who is both "Lord," and "Son of David."

But the Canaanite woman is undeterred by the distancing.

She kneels before Jesus and specifically asks, "Lord, help me." Again, Jesus does not tell her no, but reiterates the basic premise of his promise and his priority of mission—to the children of Israel.

The softening of Jesus' rhetoric is slight but significant. He suggests that Gentiles are "dogs" by using the diminutive "*kynarion*"—"puppies," suggesting house dogs, not feral beasts of the wild who consume all flesh. Yet while dismissing pagans as "domestic pets," Jesus engages this Gentile woman face to face. He speaks to her as a person to be respected and whose desire is reasonable and cannot be dismissed.

Jesus Cool #2: The second feature of "cool" is to embrace one's own authentic, distinctive style. Every style has some edges. Vanilla pudding is smooth and sweet. Anyone can eat it and I love it. But vanilla it is not cool without the edginess of the added bean. It doesn't matter so much what your style is but that you have one—especially in this culture where style is morphing with substance. "Good taste" is integral to a Jesus identity. More than any other sense, taste bridges the gap between external stimuli and our internal world. What we ingest literally becomes part of us, and it's no surprise that our preferences, reflected in the word "taste," reveal so much about who we are.

Jesus' second response to the Canaanite woman is definitely edgy. Jesus distinguishes between the Jewish community he felt called to serve, and the Gentile community that was not his prime focus. Again, Jesus in no way personally attacks this woman or her requests. Jesus "keeps it cool" by

THE JESUS STYLE: COOL

simply continuing to engage her in dialogue and keeping her in his concern. His style is to keep talking, keep listening, keep looking the woman in the eye. But he never loses his edge, a real reveal about who he is.

◇

There is no elegance without a certain nonchalance.
FRENCH FASHION DESIGNER, BUSINESSWOMAN COCO CHANEL (D. 1971)[9]

Jesus Cool #3: The ultimate in living with style is best expressed in an Italian word that is almost untranslatable: Sprezzatura. Sprezzatura is the art of making the difficult look easy.[10] Sprezzatura is when you pull off an all-nighter writing a paper, turn it in, grab coffees for friends or coworkers, and remember to pick up your dry cleaning. You do it all, make it look easy, and do NOT make a big production about what you have done. Doing hard things and making them appear easy is the art of sprezzatura. Duke Ellington's 1931 hit gave it another name: "It don't mean a thing (if it ain't got that swing)."

Renaissance scholar and Italian diplomat Baldassare Castiglione (d. 1529) defined sprezzatura as "a certain nonchalance, so as to conceal all art."[11] The art of concealing art, or making something difficult look easy and effortless, is the highest expression of style.

You know you are in the presence of a great tennis player if they make the most impossible shot and make it look leisurely. That's sprezzatura. You know you are in the presence of great hosts if in the midst of an unexpected disruption they

341

remain unflappable and every time you ask "What can I do?" they wave you off with "Just relax, everything is good" and make hosting in a hurricane look easy. "Cool" is sprezzatura.

Just because you have a style that puts people at ease doesn't mean you're an easy touch. This is what makes "Lizzy" one of Jane Austen's most endearing characters of all her six major novels and one of the most popular figures in the history of British fiction. *Pride and Prejudice's* (1813) Elizabeth Bennet, or "Lizzy," is so unforgettable and adored because of her style of sprezzatura, which she maintained in the most difficult of circumstances and conditions.

Jesus is confronted for the third time by the Canaanite mom who just won't quit and shows her own form of sprezzatura. Her third confrontation with the man she has already called "Lord" and "Son of David" is to remind him wittily that "Lord, yet even the dogs eat the crumbs that fall from their masters' table." You might have even paraphrased her words in the once famous phrase from Cool Hand Luke: "what we have here is a failure to communicate."

With a sprezzatura that masks the immensity of Jesus' sudden redirection, Jesus makes his abrupt about-face seem like no big deal. Addressing her in the same intimate way he tenderly addressed his mother Jesus says, "Woman, great is your faith! Let it be done for you as you wish."[12]

When the Canaanite woman's daughter is healed, the gates of heaven are opened to all the peoples of the world. Jesus makes it look easy, but it is a huge upheaval. From this point on, Jesus is clear about the focus of his message and mission. It is for all the people of the world. He is the

THE JESUS STYLE: COOL

long-awaited Jewish Messiah, but he is also the Messiah for the world. Jesus is Torah-True, but the embodiment of Torah-True. In one sprezzatura motion, Jesus "cools out" the conflict between Jews and Gentiles, the chosen and the outsider. In one sprezzatura motion, Jesus turns mountains and valleys into one level playing field.

Jesus Cool #4: The final feature of "coolness" is to aid everyone and everything in moving forward, not backward. We are coming through a period where a style of ironic coolness was chic, which meant no one could take anything seriously enough to fix it. That's the coolness of death, not life; mortal coolness, not mystic coolness.

When Jesus heard the Canaanite woman in front of him, he was moved and moved himself and everyone around him forward: "Great is your faith!" In welcoming her into the family of the faithful, Jesus took all his disciples "around go." Suddenly the situation between Jews and Gentiles changed, and changed for the better. No longer was there a great divide between the Jew and Gentile. No longer was his mission focused on one group but on all people. No longer did the kingdom of God have restricted entrance—it now was an open-door policy, inviting all who would enter into a new relationship with God and each other. God's favorite time was "the cool of the day."[13] God's people are to be "the-cool-of-the-day" people, people who dew this world with "mystic coolness."

DESIGNER JESUS

You remove my sackcloth and clothe me with joy.
PSALM 30:11

The Lord is clothed with splendor.
PSALM 104:1

<u>Dress as Address:</u> No garment or gown comes alive until it is worn. The most beautiful Armani suit can be made ugly by the person wearing it. Similarly, the ugliest outfit, or room, can be made beautiful by the person who spreads out within its space. It is not true, as Mark Twain liked to put it, "Clothes make the man." But clothes do make something, as the forgotten rest of the Mark Twain quote reminds us: "Clothes make the man. Naked people have little or no influence on society." Shakespeare caught this important distinction when he had Polonius say in *Hamlet*, "apparel oft proclaims the man."[14]

Style is different from Skin. We put on Jesus Skin which is in some fundamental sense consistent. Dress is more diverse. Style is not an identity. Our identity is in Christ. But style sends a signal of our identity, and where our identity is found. When you make a fashion statement you also make a faith statement.

When you put on a piece of clothing, when you buy a product, when you attend an event, you are sending a signal, a political signal of your preferences as much as your personality characteristics. Fashion can be a carpe manana[15] political form of expressing faith and emotion. I leave the house each day appareled as a hamper of oddly assorted goodies. But all the goodies can tell the same story in color, pattern, texture, and design, one way or another—the Jesus story.

Pinstripe piety is not the enemy. Bland, blank, and boring is the enemy. Jesus humans live in color. Some in washed out pastels, some in subtle hues, some in blazing tinges and rainbow glares. We could learn a few things from our Generative Organizing Designer. God plants churches like a gardener outfits flower beds: in colors and smells, sounds and shapes that attract pollinating insects.

The Jesus Style is not found in "keeping up with the times," but in keeping up with Jesus and opening to God's presence in the times we're in. Those who do not adapt end up as fossil exhibits in a museum cabinet of curiosities, but the adapting is not to the constantly moving Zeitgeist but to the constantly moving Heilige Geist.[16] That's why fashion statements of a Jesus human living amidst today's deepfakes and disinformation may be prone to be more fashion understatements in a world of fashion overstatements.

When Augustine was reading 1 John 2:16 NIV, "For everything in the world—the lust of the flesh, the lust of the eyes, and the pride of life—comes not from the Father but from the world. The world and its desires pass away"—he paused to give a name to conformity to the Zeitgeist spirit of the age: *ambitio saeculi*. The Latin phrase "*ambitio saeculi*" meaning "worldly ambition"[17] is part of this sentence: "*Ambitio saeculi est contraria charitati tuae.*" Which translates to: "The ambition of the age is contrary to your charity."

We must always be reminded that the "ambitions of the

DESIGNER JESUS

world" (materialism, consumerism, hedonism, celebritism, scientism, imperialism) are not holy ambitions, but often prohibitions and exhibitions that are at odds with the holiness of divine goodness, beauty, and truth.

The time is coming [future], and now is [present]
JESUS[18]

"I don't fit in." You're not supposed to "fit in." Jesus' disciples were not made to fit in to their times, but to fashion and forge a new time. Our identity is found not in empurpling ourselves in old dignities but emboldening others with new directions and appearances. We are not here just to hold a mirror to the world and reflect it back, but to construct a new world. In a world becoming more and more android, we be a metanoid. Live the metanoia life, a life of repentance, about-faces, mind-cleanses, and turn-arounds. Live the metanoid life, Jesus said, for the time of your life.

Think about it: to be a fashion trendsetter is never to wear what is currently in fashion anyways. Mix and match to create your own fashion that reflects who you are and lets your unique light shine. We are not bystanders in our own story; we are the authors and architects of our future.

Trend Starters: There is nothing publishers like more than a trend. The church is not far behind publishers in its derivative directions, especially if the trend comes from corporate culture. There is nothing Hollywood likes more than a sequel. Studies have shown that original movies typically

THE JESUS STYLE: COOL

make a profit of two to three times their production costs, while sequels can make a profit of three to five times their production costs. A Jesus-designed human is more interested in starting trends than conforming to trends. You can be "in trend" but not "of trend" without being "out of trend" if you use Jesus' incarnational formula of being in/not-of/but-not-out-of the world either.

How do you do "start" a trend? One way is to pick out the weak signals in the culture. All trends start out as weak signals. Each one of us will pick up different weak signals, signals that are emitted on our particular frequency.

Take the wearing of hats, for an example. In the last half of the nineteenth century and the first half of the twentieth century, hats were as much a part of a man's apparel as socks, ties, handkerchiefs, jackets, and gloves. The kind of hat a man wore—fedoras, Stetsons, berets, bowlers, boating hats, baseball caps, cowboy hats, panamas, trilbies—spoke volumes about the identity of that person. While he was on the campaign trail, John F. Kennedy read some weak signals coming from various cultural arenas: the rise of the automobile and the migration from cities to the suburbs, changing fashion trends, the increasing informality of the workplace. Kennedy started going hatless and at his inauguration he wore no head covering. Kennedy started a trend that set the future and eventually killed hats and haberdasheries.

Toward the end of the first decade of the twenty-first century, I picked up some weak signals of a men's shirt company that obsessed over obscure details, was design intensive with colorful patterns, hidden images, and tender buttons.[19]

DESIGNER JESUS

Each no-tuck shirt tells a unique story and spotlights contrasting cuffs and collars made to be rolled up. I decided it was time to change my "look" and create an original "Robert Graham" look. Once Robert Graham shirts became identified with the character Cameron Tucker from the television sitcom *Modern Family* (2009–2020), I have given away more and more of my shirts to people who say how much they like them. It may be time for a new "look." But it's a constantly adaptable "look" that has stood me well for the last fifteen years as I have tried to make the case for learning the vernacular of a culture that is steeped in story and image.

Robert Graham is a New York City clothing company named after its co-founders, a fashion designer (Robert Stock) and a textile designer (Graham Fowle). On every item it sells, whether shirt, pants, jacket, or underwear, whether standard release or limited edition, there is etched somewhere the brand's trinitarian mission motto: "Knowledge Wisdom Truth." My personal daily "look" is an unchanging palette of black, brown or blue t-shirt over which is layered a Robert Graham shirt, and/or vest, and/or jacket. Since I can't afford a new Robert Graham product off the shelf or out of the catalogue, I routinely patrol eBay for RG's that come up for auction and seem to speak my language. These often are priced at ten percent of the original listing. When it arrives, I take a moment, bow my head and give thanks for the person who once wore this item, as well as his family's re-gifting of the dead man's clothes.

Often when I'm preaching or lecturing, furtively bedecked in the clothes of the dead, I braille the stitched

THE JESUS STYLE: COOL

words with my fingers to remind me of what business I'm in: "Knowledge Wisdom Truth." In this "my truth" culture, I want "my truth" to be the Jesus story which is The Truth. Not many people would judge it "cool" to parade yourself in public and on platforms in dead people's clothing. But it's my style of "cool." It's Jesus cool. It's "my truth" about The Truth.

> *When you're hot you're hot.*
> *When you're not, you're not.*
> 1970S COMEDIAN FLIP WILSON (D. 1998)

Ice and Fire: You have just read something about which almost nothing has been written: what does it mean to be a "cool" church or a "cool" disciple? The lament over the lukewarm church of Laodicea is twofold: "you are neither cool nor hot."[20] "Hot" and "cold" are different forms of the same thing: kinetic energy. The higher the vibrational molecular motion, the higher the scale of "hotness." The slower the vibrations, the more the slide into "coolness."

In the paradox of style, better "cool" or "hot" but never mild, middling, mediocre, middle-of-the-road, tepid, average, or normal. Just because Zillow reports that buyers will pay $2512 more for a house where the walls are painted gray doesn't mean that you have to live in a bowl of oatmeal.[21] Unfortunately, gray is most often how Jesus is portrayed—as a bouillabaisse of banalities—and the church faithfully lives out that portrayal.

So if the essence of "cool" is "mystic coolness," what is the essence of "hot?" You can't be a Jesus hotspot without being hot. But will we have the contrarian courage to be "hot" in a world that defines "hot" differently?

THE JESUS STYLE: COOL

STUDIO LIVE

1) Paul Valery (d. 1945), one of the most important French poets and thinkers of the early twentieth century, liked to say that "Taste is made of a host of distastes."[22]

   * What do you think Valery means by this quote?

   * How can our distastes shape our taste?

   * What are some examples of how your own distastes have shaped your taste?

   * How can we learn to appreciate things that we may initially find distasteful?

   * What is the role of criticism in developing our taste?

   * How can we be more open-minded and accepting of different tastes?

   * What are some of the challenges of developing our own taste in a world where we are constantly bombarded with messages about what we should like and dislike?

   * How can we resist the pressure to conform to mainstream tastes?

   * What is the relationship between taste and identity?

   * How can we use our taste to express ourselves and connect with others?

   * What is the role of taste in promoting social change?

   * Do you agree that we have to know what we don't like

before we know what we do like? Or can you know the positive without first experiencing the negative?

2) Is the point of art to be perfect and pure and objective and true to itself? Or is the point of art to convey a GBT experience of goodness, beauty, and truth?

* How do you react to the slogan "art for art's sake?"

* Look up some art that is the opposite of "art for art's sake," and is intended to give the BGT messages of ethics, aesthetics, and social change—like Pablo Picasso's *Guernica*, or Kehinde Wiley's portrait of Barack Obama, or Banksy's street art, or Nina Simone's music, or the films of Spike Lee and Ava DuVernay.

3) You can never be Christian enough for some people, who aspire to be more Christian than Jesus. The problem is that Jesus was never a Christian. Jesus was The Christ. "Christianity" and "Christian" is what we made Jesus into.

* Do you think Jesus intended to establish Christianity as a distinct religion, or did that evolve later?

* Does focusing on the label "Christian" sometimes distract from simply following Jesus? Why or why not?

* How might competition around who is more "Christian" conflict with Jesus' message of grace, acceptance, and humility?

* If Jesus wasn't a "Christian" as we know "Christian," what implications does that have for us today?

THE JESUS STYLE: COOL

* What problems or hypocrisy have you seen arise from Christians judging who is Christian enough?

* How can we refocus on Christ over human-defined religion or criteria?

* Are there areas where Christian institutions have lost sight of or even contradict Jesus? Examples?

* What might it look like to follow Christ in spirit and action rather than adhering to the "Christian" label?

* Will there be any Christians in heaven? Or will heaven be a home for those who live and love Jesus? What's the difference?

* Is it getting more and more difficult to say the word "Christian?"

4) Do some people watching.

* When you see someone who does not look typical, do you respond positively or negatively? Do you think "What's wrong with them?" or "Good for them?" Do you think "Why would they do that?" or "What if I did that?"

* What thoughts might glorify God in our people watching?

5) Socrates' famous dictum "The unexamined life is not worth living" is often cited in tandem with the Delphic oracle's injunction: "Know Thyself." But didn't Jesus teach that self-analysis can be the way of delusion and

fantasy if it's done without knowing God first? Aren't we supposed to know God as the way to know ourselves?

* Check out Jeremiah 17:9, which warns that the heart is deceitful above all things. Can looking inward alone be misleading without God?

* Check out 1 Corinthians 3:18, which advises against deceiving oneself. Can relying on worldly wisdom rather than God provide a distorted self-view?

* Check out Matthew 22:37–39, where Jesus emphasizes loving God above all and loving others as yourself. Should focusing on God first shape self-knowledge?

6) What would be Jesus' favorite emoji? Or meme?

* What would Jesus think of social media?

* What would Jesus' favorite streaming service be?

* What would Jesus' favorite video game be?

* What would Jesus' favorite band or musician be?

* What would Jesus' favorite sports team be?

* Here are some True or False statements. There are no "right" or "wrong" answers here, only your perception of whether these statements are T or F?

   1) Jesus would use his social media platform to spread messages of love, compassion, and social justice.
   2) Jesus would watch streaming services to learn about different cultures and perspectives.

THE JESUS STYLE: COOL

    3) Jesus would play video games to connect with people of all ages and backgrounds.

    4) Jesus would listen to music and go to concerts to experience the power of art and community.

    5) Jesus would cheer on his favorite sports team and use his platform to promote sportsmanship and fair play.

7) "Do I have any pleasure in the death of the wicked?" declares the Lord God, "rather that he should turn from his ways and live."[23] The wicked are not there as a perfect opportunity for us to feel better about ourselves and superior in our morality, but for us to pray for, call to repentance, and re-examine our own hearts.

    * What prevents compassion from being the calling card of every Jesus human?

8) What do you think of this thesis: The *"joy en kurio"* (joy in Christ) is not a joy that finds its object in Christ but a joy that finds its subject and source in the story of Jesus and in communion with Jesus?

    * What is the difference between finding our joy in Christ as an object and finding our joy in Christ as the subject and source of our joy?

    * How does the story of Jesus and communion with Jesus bring us joy?

    * What are some examples of how the joy of Christ is not just a feeling, but a way of life?

- How can we cultivate joy in Christ even when we are facing difficult circumstances?
- How can we share the joy of Christ with others?
- How does our understanding of the joy of Christ compare to the way that joy is often portrayed in popular culture?
- What are some of the challenges of maintaining our joy in Christ in a world that is often hostile to Christian faith?
- How can we create a community where people can experience the joy of Christ together?
- What are the implications of the joy of Christ for our understanding of mission and evangelism?
- How can we use the joy of Christ to incarnate the gospel in the world around us?

9) Economist Friedrich von Hayek (d. 1992) says there are two kinds of institutions: designed ones, which begin and end in a blueprint, and organic ones, which come without maps. The first is "top down" and managed by a designer; the latter is "bottom up" where change happens gradually and unplanned.

- What are some examples of designed institutions that follow a set blueprint versus organic ones that evolve more freely? Which do you think the church should be?
- In what ways can top-down designed systems fail to

anticipate real needs on the ground? When are they preferable?

* How might organic, grassroots structures allow more trial-and-error and customization? What are the tradeoffs?

* When have you seen misalignment between institutional plans and real community needs? What worked better?

* How can organizations like the church harmonize structure with openness to uncontrolled innovation and change? Discuss the old saying "The Spirit's fire needs a fireplace."

* What conditions best enable "bottom up" organic development vs requiring "top down" design?

* What risks or downsides might emergent, uncontrolled institutional growth introduce?

* How could technology impact the balance between centralized and decentralized organizations?

* Isn't the view from below as one-dimensional as the view from above? What if we saw life in all its multi-dimensionality? Just as life is an accumulation of experience, so aren't the best paintings layers upon layers, built up over time, both "top down" and "bottom up?" What if the ideal is one that is design-intensive but one that an unsuspecting visitor would look on as natural?

10) Werner Richard Heymann (d. 1961) was a German-Jewish

film composer of popular songs who was banned from working in Germany when the Nazis came to power in 1933. He emigrated to London and later the United States to continue his film composing career. Heymann returned to Germany and applied for the restoration of his German nationality in 1951. The deciding body was asked to sing a popular German song to authenticate his nationality. He sang "*Das gibt's nur einmal*," familiar to all the German officials dealing with his case. That was enough to receive his nationality back.

Heymann never mentioned the fact that he had written the song.

* What does it take to be that humble? What if a song could be a password? What if everyone were that humble?

Chapter 9: Style Hot
The Jesus Style: Hot

*And I, when I am lifted up from the earth,
will draw all people to myself.*

JOHN 12:32 NIV

IT USED TO BE AN ADAGE THAT YOU CAN'T "BUY STYLE." A whole style industry exists today on the proven track-record that you can buy style. But while you can't buy real style, you can conjure a "that's divine" style from Jesus. To be sure, Jesus is not a flat mirror for us to imitate. But Jesus is a window to God, a doorway into eternal life, the DNA of the divine, and The Way to a Way-Truth-Life lifestyle.

Fashion changes like politics changes. But not style. The new person in Christ has a gracious and authentic style (graceful authenticity) that could be shorthanded as "hot." It is hard for Christians to hear this kind of talk because we have been taught that words like "flesh" and "carnal" and even "body" are "bad" words. The problem is that all those movements that made them "bad" words—Gnostics, Docetists, Manichaeans, Albigenses—have been officially denounced by the church as heresies. The official position of the church is we are enfleshed beings. In the incarnation, God sanctifies matter.

It is easier to talk about the style of Jesus cool, as we did in the last chapter, than the style of Jesus Hot, which we do here with tremendous trepidation as we explore both sides of the Revelation 3:16 challenge: "So because you are lukewarm, and neither hot nor cold, I will vomit you out of my mouth" NASB. What might a Jesus hot church look like?

We have been taught that while our bodies may be the "temple of the Holy Spirit,"[1] that temple needs to be well-covered and camouflaged. Discomfort around the human body was spotlighted in the 2002 edict to cover up the nude male and female Justice statues in the headquarters of the U. S. Justice Department by former Attorney General John Ashcroft, a devout Christian who found nakedness embarrassing, even if it was only above the waist and in cast aluminum.

Let's clear something up. When Genesis 3:7 reads "Then the eyes of both of them were opened, and they realized they were naked," it has nothing to do with sex. It means Adam and Eve suddenly realized that they were vulnerable, exposed, and in need of protection from unknown threats and terrors. It does not mean the corruption and wrecking of sex. We are the ones who conflate sexuality and sexual activity.

A Jesus being that is "being sexy" encompasses more than the physical. To be alluring transcends the corporeal. The

THE JESUS STYLE: HOT

"draw" is more through charisma, charm, and confidence than physical beauty, a subtle dance of intrigue and desire. An alluring person seduces with style, grace, and authenticity as much as sensuality. Attraction is stoked by mystery and layers of depth, not just surface displays of sensuality.

Jesus embodies this allure of "hot" not through physicality, but through the richness of his teachings, empathy, and wisdom. Divinity's appeal operates on multiple registers, at once spiritual, psychological, and sensual. Reducing the erotic to the explicit diminishes its poetry and power. Allure at its best is a tapestry woven of many threads.

Paul's famous flesh vs. spirit dichotomy[2] is one of the most misunderstood passages of Scripture. In this passage Paul refers to "flesh" not as "body flesh" but as natural desires corrupted by the fall. Sexual desire (good) gets corrupted into "fleshy" lust and lechery (bad). The desire for excellence and greatness (good) gets corrupted into "fleshy" pride and vanity (bad). The perversion of the best (the original, natural desires of the "flesh") yields the worst (the toxic, vile desires of the "flesh" profaned by sin).

The incarnation reverses the worst and returns it back into the best. The very word "incarnate" is based on the word "carnal," which literally means "to put flesh on" or "to put skin on." In Jesus God became carnal: Jesus the Christ is Creator Con Carne. In the incarnation God blessed matter, God romanced the material, and God chose to be known to us as spirit wrapped in matter, glory wrapped in flesh.

DESIGNER JESUS

> *When I enter my house, I shall find rest with her,*
> *for companionship with her has no bitterness,*
> *and life with her has no pain, but gladness and joy.*
>
> WISDOM 8:16 NRSV

<u>Some Like It Hot:</u> These are eggshell times. Truth and trust are seriously corroded. People have hair-trigger tempers and get their dander up at the smallest provocation. One scholar sums up the essence of Jewish humor with these words: "To be truly offensive and blasphemous, to be deeply vulgar, i.e., easy and artless. To be meaningfully so, in a way that enlightens—that has a long tradition. And it's done with love."[3] So let's get a bit blasphemous and go offensively "carnal," "meaningfully" and incarnationally ("*incarn*" or "put on flesh") carnal, and talk about that part of Jesus' style that made it so alluring.

It is disquieting to put the words "Jesus" and "hot" or even "Body of Christ" and "sex" together, especially in a religious tradition that is uncomfortable about sex and nervous about sexuality. So nervous, in fact, that it leaves its children on their own to figure everything out. Sixty percent of British students now look to porn for their sexual education.[4]

We may not have been as severe as the early Christian theologian Origen (d. 253), who got so conflicted over sexuality he castrated himself. But in our three reigning attitudes towards sexuality—1) give it the death dismissal and ignore it; 2) "dead to me" and be done with it; 3) hide it and hide

THE JESUS STYLE: HOT

from it—the effect is the same. Any faith that castrates itself rather than integrates sex into daily life is not a Jesus faith.

True sex is a sacred act. We live in a world of faux sexy and the love drug. Sexuality is measured in terms of goods and services and not mutuality and vulnerability. But the apex of sex is intimacy not orgasm. To be fully human you have to express your sexuality, not primarily in terms of intercourse but in terms of interconnections and interior design. Jesus bequeathed this interior design to the church, making the Christian faith a quite sexy religion.

What makes the Body of Christ, The Church, The Total Package?

> *Though made of body and soul, man is one. Through his bodily composition he gathers to himself the elements of the material world; thus they reach their crown through him, and through him raise their voice in free praise of the Creator (cf. Genesis 1:6; Wisdom 2:23). For this reason man is not allowed to despise his bodily life, rather he is obliged to regard his body as good and honorable since God has created it and will raise it up on the last day.*
> SECOND VATICAN COUNCIL (1965)
> GAUDIUM ET SPES ("JOY AND HOPE"), 14

---

1) Brainy Church: A brainy church is not a know-it-all church, but a book-smart and street-smart and people-smart church. A hot Christian is a bibliophile and a sapiophile—a lover of learning and a lover of minds. Underlining books, highlighting eBooks, journaling meditations, cut-and-pasting quotes into notebooks, is a spiritual practice.[5]

Every book on a shelf romances the reader, flirting to be swept into one's arms and lap. Those left behind live on the edge, waiting their moment in the sun of the reader's attention. That makes a library a bedroom of desire and coquetry. Venetian author Casanova (d. 1798) is one of the most complex characters in the Italian Renaissance. The child of an actor and dancer, he started out as a violinist who played in a Venetian orchestra. He spent the last thirteen years of his life as a librarian. Librarians are hot.

Every trade has tools: a surgeon has a scalpel, a carpenter has a hammer, a plumber has a wrench, a preacher has a book, The Bible, and a library of books about the subject of that book, which include living books. For we all are authors who write a book, some with words, all with actions. It's called the book of life. For the designed-by-Jesus disciple, the book of life is a fifth gospel, a Third Testament.

If Jesus is the head of the church, the brain is a primary reproductive organ. Smart is always hot, and power is smartly exercised or it loses power. The church has a crisis-level reproduction problem partly because its brainpower has atrophied. The power of the brain to influence the rest of the body is illustrated in "The Placebo Effect," which doesn't mean a drug doesn't work, but that the mind ("Placebo") has such power it measurably alters our bodies and sense of health.

Few things are as arousing as spending time in the company of a beautiful mind. Unlike Woody Allen, who was fond of calling his brain "my second most favorite organ," a

Jesus human first and foremost puts on the "mind of Christ" because Christ is the "head" of the church[6] and it is that "head" that steers the rest of the body. Disciples of Jesus don't live life just from experience but from memory, learning, and a mind-meld with Christ. Those who live in and live out the life of Christ are less interested in showing something or telling something or teaching something than in giving others the feeling of what is it like to be alive.

But when intelligent becomes merely intellectual, what was once alluring quickly becomes repulsive, even obscene. When the brain goes rogue and becomes disembodied; when reason is isolated from emotion and experience: the brain can be the motherboard of manifold injustices and iniquities. Some of our "best and brightest,"[7] our most brilliant "minds," have embraced war, tyrants and totalitarianism.

Setting aside his creation in Geneva of a theocratic form of fascism, a Christian version of Sharia Law, that executed dissenters and disgraced the body of Christ,[8] John Calvin (d. 1564) authored arguably the greatest theological tome in Christian history. Setting aside Scottish philosopher David Hume's (d. 1776) shameful racism, his skepticism reset the future course of philosophy. Setting aside their unrepentant defense of Hitler, Martin Heidegger (d. 1976) and Carl Schmitt (d. 1985) stand as two of the most influential philosophers of the twentieth century.

There is always a "setting aside." Find one character in the Bible other than Jesus that doesn't need a "setting aside." All humans require a "setting aside" caveat to separate the luring and the lurid in each one of us. Setting aside his inexcusable love for Stalinism and Stalin's Soviet Union, Walter Benjamin (d. 1940) penned some of the most influential essays on literary theory ever written. Setting aside his romance of Maoist China and Islamist Iran, Michel Foucault (d. 1984) is one of the most important social theorists in the world of academe.

There is no colossus in history that is not in some things a colossal jerk. Irish novelist James Joyce, one of the most celebrated writers of the twentieth century, was famous in the neighborhood for pelting stones at local dogs. His rationale was rational, he insisted: "They have no souls," therefore he could do as he willed. To the end of his life, Ezra Pound was a rabid anti-Semite for all sorts of "rational" reasons not unlike those found in Martin Luther's 1543 tract "On the Jews and their Lies," an embarrassing and disgusting antisemitic pamphlet which makes every Christian hang their heads in shame.[9] One of the most widely quoted theologians of the twentieth century, the gentle Jesuit anthropologist Pierre Teilhard de Chardin, thought that the Germans deserved to win the Second World War "because they have more spirit than the rest of the world."[10] The bigger the brain in your head, the more love you need in your heart.

The Enlightenment enthroned reason as the foundational pillar and highest peak of civilization. Thomas Jefferson, the very definition of a "Renaissance man" who espoused Enlightenment ideals with greater eloquence than any of his contemporaries, could still own slaves. The first attempt in the history of the world to stamp out religious practice entirely was done in the name of reason. In the last months of the French Revolution in 1793, Notre Dame Cathedral was renamed the "Temple of Reason" and dedicated to memorializing the virtues of atheistic republicanism. The heights of irrationalism are found most frequently in hyper-rationalism.

The assumption that people of faith who are most "intellectual" are capable of rational discussion is a problematic one, as anyone who has ever attended a church board meeting or a seminary faculty meeting can attest. Some of the most sophisticated specialists in insult fests and razor-bladed religions are religious "intellectuals," titillating critics whom social media has turned into unappealing crusaders.

For Christ to form in us, we put on "the mind of Christ"[11] which is less a mindset than a mind-meld with Jesus. When mind, body, and spirit are harmonized, each to the other, all with God, you enter a state of what some call health and wholeness, others call holiness, still others call shalom. And there is nothing hotter or more alluring than shalom.

Conversely, there is nothing more off-putting than a nondesigner disciple who thinks they know it all. "You shall know the truth," Jesus said," and the truth shall make you . . . know-it-alls." That's the stylistic reading of John 8:31–32 from many Christians.[12] With the possible exception of a Soviet-style apartment block, there is nothing uglier nor more unattractive than a non-learning, know-it-all spirit. A Jesus human is a lifelong learner with intellectual humility.

If you think you understand, it isn't God.
PARAPHRASE OF SØREN KIERKEGAARD (D. 1855)[13]

DESIGNER JESUS

2) Leggy Church: The Body of Christ has legs. Good legs. The most prominent features of this legginess are its longs legs, and its willingness always to give a leg up.

The long legs of the church are revealed in how Jesus played the long game. His truth has long legs, not only persisting over time but getting brighter and more beautiful over time. There are many more things Jesus said and did than we know.[14] Some of the things he said he admitted we wouldn't get right away, or were hard for us to understand at this point in time.[15] As time went on, the promise is, more would be revealed to us, and the Spirit of truth would guide us into all truth until his return.[16]

The light of Jesus' "truth" was strung on such a long fuse that much of its impact wouldn't be felt for centuries. In his literary classic *Invisible Man* (1952), Ralph Ellison talked about how we can sometimes pick up things "on the lower frequencies" that resonate beyond what words can say. To be a disciple was to learn these "lower frequencies" and to understand the ways of God beyond the limits of our times. Jesus' teachings were on such long wavelengths that it would take millennia for some of their symphonic melodies and meanings to play themselves out. Jesus waits and endures with an unchanging love, even in the face of our rejection and violence, until we are able to and awakened enough to hear and see the truth.[17]

Jesus even claimed that his disciples would be able to do "greater things" than he did when they maintained the headship of Christ and the leadership of the Spirit. When Paul

THE JESUS STYLE: HOT

arrived in the Athens harbor from Berea of Macedonia about the year 53, and then arrived in Rome about six years later, roughly one-third of the population of Athens and Rome were slaves. It took another 1800 years for the legginess of Paul's "in Christ-no-slave" credo to be realized in those very places of Athens and Greece. Jesus' disciples of the eighteenth and nineteenth centuries, in their leading of various abolitionist movements, did what he predicted: "greater things."

We honor a father or mother when we live our best life and do greater things than they did. We honor Jesus when we live our best Jesus life and do greater things that he did: "This do in remembrance of me." What do we miss most about those who have gone before us? "You being here." We miss them being here. We miss them being themselves. Not being with us in all their perfection. We miss them being with us in all their imperfections. We honor them by being here with others and being ourselves in all our imperfections. We honor them by being ourselves here.

The "legginess" of the Body of Christ is also its readiness to give a "leg up" to anyone in need of getting to higher ground. The phrase "leg up" comes from the days when people needed help in mounting a horse or getting over a high fence. The "leg up" spirit means that a disciple is living the Jesus story with broad shoulders and long legs, living the perfect love of Christ that casts out fear, and leaking Jesus love out of every nook and cranny of that story, carrying the weight of the weak, infirm, sick, disabled, and hurting.

Members of the Body of Christ esteem others more highly than themselves, which means they are not looking for ways to get a "leg up" on others but ways to give others a "leg up"—especially those whose legs may be weak and wobbly—the elderly, the child, the impaired of body and mind. This is the true meaning of all Christian "comfort," a word built on *com fortis* or "with strength." The Christbody community's own leg muscles are built up by giving others a "leg up"—whether it's in the form of leg squats, curls, lunges, extensions, presses, or raises.

To give someone a "leg up" is a form of hospitality that does not drag others down to your level of understanding and conversation, or make them taper their life to the points that fit your principles. Leg-up hospitality lifts people up beyond personal horizons into realms that widen our own conversations and participations. A "leg-up" disciple becomes stepping stones and turning points in the plot-lines of others' life stories.

A "leg-up" church boasts a soft spot for lost causes, even though it cannot always recognize them. But lost causes in the long run are the winners. And the winners in the short run are the lost causes of the future.

The righteous are not afraid of bad news;
their heart is firm, trusting in the Lord.
PSALM 112:7

Before the twentieth century in North America, it was not unheard of for clergy to be the primary art dealers of a community. In the twentieth century, art dealership became

THE JESUS STYLE: HOT

a profession, and clergy turned away from the arts and looked to the business world for its inspiration and models. The most influential art dealer of all these professionals was Joseph Duveen (1869–1939). Duveen had an eye for art works that were underappreciated and gave them a "leg up" by taking them on and lifting them up personally. In fact, when you got an artwork from Duveen, even though it was Renaissance, Baroque, Rococo, Neoclassical, or Modern, it was henceforth a "Duveen." The ultimate compliment you could pay a collector was to say, not "that's utterly divine," but instead "that's utterly duveen."[18]

Duveen not only gave artists a "leg up," but he played the long game as well with collectors like Henry Clay Frick and Andrew Mellon. With Mellon, he rented the apartment directly under Mellon's own place and decorated it with paintings and tapestries and carvings. He gave Mellon the key and invited him to come down whenever he liked. Eventually, Mellon moved in and bought the whole collection.[19]

When the Body of Christ is most "leggy," giving others a "leg up" and playing the "long game" in its investment in and trust of the truth, the response is not "That's utterly duveen" but "That's SO Jesus."

3) In-Your-Skin Church: Skin is hot. To show some skin is to reveal that you are comfortable in your own skin, that you have some skin in the game, and that you are not so thin-skinned that you must hide behind the fabric and the coverings, but will risk revealing the real thing, even those warts and scars that make you vulnerable.

Jesus showed the most skin at his baptism and crucifixion. God continues so show the most human skin in the sacramental skin of baptism and communion. Those traditions that keep the early church's ritual of foot washing know the seeing and smelling and feeling of dirty skin at foot-washing.

The church, conceived from the side of Christ, came before everything else. Born at Pentecost, the church came before the New Testament. In fact, the first writings that circulated twenty years after Pentecost were quires of sheets of papyrus or parchment folded together to form a group of leaves, or pages that made up a codex. The pages of the New Testament are the true vestures of the body of Christ, the sheet coverings of the skin of the body of Christ. No wonder the church is most sensuous ("smells, bells, chants") in its sacramental adoration and adornments. But all veneration of the elements of bread, wine, and water must point us to the beauty of Christ, not to the elements themselves.

The world can make the words "I love you" a meaningless void of absence. But when "I Am" says "I love you," they become a life-saving vortex of continuing presences, breathe-easy places of composure. Your very presence, the nuggets of being-all-there moments you give to someone, are bouquets of flowers, boxes of chocolate, communion wafers of sacramental life.

Our skulls beneath the skin are so similar. The skin that clothes our skulls is so different. Through the incarnation,

Jesus is already in an intimate relationship with all flesh, through our flesh.

The church's unease around all things "carne" is paradoxically expressed in its hedging of the Sistine Chapel. Before any man or woman is allowed entrance, they are required to cover past the shoulders and knees, with many venders hawking on the requisite scarves, shawls, and coverings. Once inside, one is surprised by the presence of the five sibyls, female prognosticators that parallel the seven prophets. Both sibyls and prophets are looking to the future, but the viewer is ambushed by the fleshiness of the Last Judgment Scene, said to be Michelangelo's greatest work. The whole wall is of naked people in vivid colors. The only ones not naked are the angels, who are partially clothed. But the whole wall is of one naked body after another. In other words, the Vatican requires visitors to cover up in order to see naked people.

For the Apostle Paul the Body of Christ was most comfortable in its skin and most "in-its-skin" when "all things [were] done decently and in order."[20] Both Greek words Paul uses here for the true composure of the body, "*euschamonos*" and "*kata taxin,*" are complex and full of nuance. What is usually rendered here as "decently and in order" is better translated "with decorum and a sense of proportion," or best yet, "gracefully and authentically."

The skinny on Jesus? Jesus followers have a style that is graceful ("*euschamonos*") and authentic ("*kata taxin*"). The Jesus Style can be edgy in appearance, but conservative at heart.

3a) In-Your-Skin is Graceful

> *Grace is the beauty of form under the influence of freedom.*
> GERMAN PHYSICIAN/POET/HISTORIAN FRIEDRICH SCHILLER (D. 1805)[21]

Graceful means decorous, gracious, and grace-filled, at all times and to all peoples. A finish of poise is missing from the lives of too many Jesus humans. At best we are like unsalted bread—grammatically correct but lacking in flavor. At worst, we have a style as prickly as porcupines. Jesus tolerated no arch elitism or aristocratic dandyism from his disciples.

Grace is not some celestial seasoning we sprinkle on life. Grace is what we're made of. Grace is what we're crammed with. Or as Portland storyteller Brian Doyle (d. 2017) puts it, "Maybe we're stuffed with the stuff."[22]

This is why Martin Luther believed "A Christian must and should be a cheerful person."[23] Even though Luther found himself often plunged into pits of depression—"In the teeth of death we live"[24] is how he liked to put it—he would repeat over and over to himself the mantra "I was baptized" and the joy of God's grace would overpower his sagging spirit. The worst thing you could say of a Christian, as Nietzsche knew and used to his advantage, was "Where's the joy?"

Martin Luther got his doctorate in theology in 1512, at which point he took the doctoral vow of being a preacher. He took this preaching vow with lifelong seriousness. He would

THE JESUS STYLE: HOT

later renounce his monastic vow and his vows of celibacy and poverty, but he always cherished his preaching vow. In fact, the headwaters of Reformation amounted to a clash about preaching. We are accustomed to designating the trigger of the Reformation Tetzel's sale of papal indulgences in an effort to raise money for the Pope's building projects, including the Sistine Chapel. But what bothered Martin Luther the most was not the indulgences themselves (as offensive as he found them) but the fact they instead of the Scriptures were being preached to the people. Johan Tetzel's fame as a great preacher made his proclamations on behalf of indulgences all the more persuasive and powerful. Luther was so incensed at the fact that the people were hearing fund-raising sermons and not gospel sermons that he nailed the 95 theses to the Wittenberg door.

Tetzel died in Leipzig in 1519, a broken and bruised man. His reputation was ruined by the Protestants who hated him. His own colleagues in the friary and in the church turned on him and shunned him because of the trouble he had caused the church and the order. The trauma of these double rejections and betrayals ruined his health. When Luther heard about the pending death of his old adversary, Luther penned the broken man a magnanimously pastoral letter. The letter is not extant (at least to my knowledge). But Luther comforted his old enemy by telling him "not to be troubled, for the matter [Reformation] did not begin on his account, but the child had quite a different father."[25] What grace. What graciousness. What gratuity. "Gratuity" is not a tip one gives for good service. Gratuity is a life of Jesus style and service itself.

DESIGNER JESUS

The Jesus style of grace and gratuity values variety and harmonizes difference. Sameness is not saneness or stylishness. For Jesus, who chose an apostolic team noteworthy for its oppositional style, diversity is divinely healthy and healing if there is oneness in Christ. To be "of one accord," though, is an accordion-like complexity of differing keys, buttons, and bellows requiring both hands, all deployed simultaneously in the unfolding of one song.

This organizational style of bringing together opposites and forcing them to sit down together, breathe the same air, and participate in the same mission, is a gratuitous form of play and humor and the most powerful generator of creativity. Friction, not fiction, is the best doorway to the imagination. When cognitive dissonance is embraced, not excluded, there are explosions of creativity. Some of my friends are more brilliant than I am, but they have positions that are the exact opposite of mine. Yet I love them, learn from them, and am better for the repartee.

When opposites are in play and not in combat, the dance of concatenation (not the bout of conflict), the grace of harmonious difference (not the choose-your-own-key diversity) draw everyone together into a chorus of joy.

Coincidences are spiritual puns.
G. K. CHESTERTON (D. 1936)[26]

3b) In-Your-Skin is Authentic

> *Beauty, to me, is about feeling comfortable in your own skin.*
>
> ACTRESS, BEAUTY ENTREPRENEUR GWYNETH PALTROW

Authentic means true to the original while fitting to a time and place. Authentic means letting the Holy Spirit put the Spirit of the Age in its place.

Every circumstance has a stance, and our stance makes all the difference in difficult circumstances. Paul preached to the Jews differently than he preached to the Gentiles, but he never preached a different gospel. He always started from Scripture when he was speaking to Jews. He always started from culture when he was speaking to Gentiles. But he always ended with Jesus.

The manner in which we conduct ourselves inevitably communicates identity and integrity. If Christianity has a "politics," it is the politics of living justly, beautifully, truthfully. "Whatever happens, conduct yourselves in a manner worthy of the gospel of Christ," Paul urged.[27] This Greek word for "conduct" is where we get "politics" (*politeuomi*). The answer to fractious identity politics may be cultivating a GBT aesthetics of goodness, beauty, truth—reflecting the sacred transcendentals in our composure. This requires the sturdy yet gentle virtues Jesus embodied: listening fully, enduring humbly, touching sensitively, standing resolutely, serving steadily, thinking clearly, loving warmly, seeing keenly, speaking truly, smiling gently. In style and substance, we can reflect the GBT transcendentals of goodness, beauty, truth. In other words, we need what Jeus had: big ears, thick skin, a soft touch, strong back, steady hand, cool head, warm heart, keen eyes, trusty tongue, and a gentle smile.

4) <u>Ripped Abs Church:</u> The "abs" of the body are four parallel abdominal muscle groups running vertically along each side of the stomach, covering up the internal organs. These are the core muscles of your body, the muscular column that protects and preserves the upper body. The four "abs" include:

1. transversus abdominis—this deepest layer of muscles secures and stabilize the trunk and keeps constant the internal abdominal pressure.

2. rectus abdominis—popularly known as "the six pack," in rare cases "the eight pack" or "the ten pack," these muscles contract as they move the body between the ribcage and pelvis, thus displaying the well-defined bulges and bumps between the ribs and public bone.

3. external oblique muscles—on each side of the "six pack," these muscles enable the trunk to turn and twist in the opposite direction. The right external oblique contracts to turn the body to the left, and vice versa.

4. internal oblique muscles—these flank the rectus abdominis and are located just inside the hipbones. They operate in the opposite way to the

external oblique muscles. For example, twisting the trunk to the left requires the left-side internal oblique and the right-side external oblique to contract together.

The Body of Christ has multiple ways of talking about its four abdominal muscle groups. There are four classic cardinal virtues in Christianity: temperance, prudence, courage, and justice. The word "virtue" literally means power or strength. The Spirit brings "virtues" that empower us to triumph in our struggle against distorted desires and deformed values, one of the most prevalent of which is the world's default position of objectifying people and not treating them as subjects.

Virtuous is hot—goodness, kindness, politeness, honor, and loyalty. And the ultimate in virtuosity is respect for and intimacy with every person, regardless of rank or title or credentials.

Four Discipleship Abs: There have been many attempts to characterize what personality characteristics are central to the human species. For example, psychologist Geoffrey Miller (University of New Mexico) has identified "Central Six" personality characteristics that encompass the human species and help explain a wide range of human behaviors: 1) general intelligence; 2) openness to experience; 3) conscientiousness; 4) agreeableness; 5) stability; and 6) extraversion.[28]

By contrast, a Jesus Style has a "Muscular-Four" style with characteristics that play out in a myriad of ways in each personality but that are imperatives in a Jesus Style. All four of these distinctive discipleship imperatives are found in this one passage from Paul: "I can do all things through Christ who gives me courage."[29]

> I can do ALL THINGS (Confidence)
> THROUGH CHRIST (Humility)
> who gives me (Connection)
> courage (Courage).

The "Muscular-Four" style elements for a Jesus disciple are as follows: The gospel keeps . . .

> your heart humble (heart in the kitchen),
> your head confident (head in the sky),
> your hands courageous (hands in the dirt),
> and your heart-head-hand connected to
> those in need (bread in the oven).

"I can do all things"—you can't get more confident than that.

"Through Christ"—you can't get more humble than that.

"Who gives me"—the ultimate connection.

"Courage"—the three courages: 1) the courage of holding on; 2) the courage of letting go; and 3) the courage of going where angels fear to tread.

Courage is almost a contradiction in terms.
It means a strong desire to live taking
the form of a readiness to die.
G. K. CHESTERTON[30]

The pairing of the first two (Humility-Confidence) with

the second two (Courage-Connection) are the two rails of the ladder, each rung in between an ascent of grace, by which we step by faith (justification) and ascend in holiness (sanctification) to book an entry ticket into the Pearly Gates.

We might also talk about these "Muscular Four" style elements of a Jesus lifestyle in more biblical language: "I can do all thing through Christ who gives me courage."[31]

1) plerotic (*plerosis*) is confidence: "With Christ all things are possible."
2) kenotic (*kenosis*) is humility: "Without Christ I can do nothing."
3) koinoniac (*koinonia*) is connectedness: "Who gives me" is the connection to one another and to God.
4) kerygmatic (*kerygma*) is courageousness: the courage of one's convictions as reflected in Peter's and John's courage in speaking the gospel: "When they saw the courage of Peter and John and realized that they were unschooled, ordinary men, they were astonished and they took note that these men had been with Jesus."[32]

Sons of Adam and daughters of Eve have a design flaw that interacts to counteract these four style elements. We refuse to bend at the knee for the divine. We do, however, bow down before ourselves. We come to believe our "success" is wholly merited. We pat ourselves on the back for "pulling ourselves up by the bootstraps" (or bookstraps) when we know deep down it is impossible to pull ourselves up by our own efforts, bootstraps, or hard work. We all "arrive" by the grace of God and the gifts of others. True success is not haughty lordliness but humble unworthiness.

We also drop down and bow before every fad and fashion. People may say there is no God, but they don't live no-God lives. They live lives that worship food, fashion, fads, celebrities, politics, principles, intellectual and social trends, self, etc.

How do we overcome this design flaw and live out of our design intent of drop down and wash feet?

1) Plerotic Style [Filling/Maximum]: Confidence The Greek philosopher Heraclitus of Ephesus is also known as the Logos philosopher, since he is the first to talk about "logos" as the unity of opposites. All of Heraclitus's writings have come down to us in fragments. One of the most elegant and imposing fragments consists of just three Greek words: *ethos anthropoi daimon*. Literally it translates, character, for humans, is fate. Or more pointedly, character is destiny.

Christians have the plerotic confidence that our character can be the character of Christ, embodied in the context of any culture. A Jesus Style is a matter of both imagination and intellect, character and conduct, emotions of the mind, motions of the spirit. Our "self-confidence" is not based on self but on a surrendered life, which gives us God-confidence, not self-confidence.

The ultimate, the sublime, the glorious confidence of every Christian? All our losses and lostness, all our closedness and closetings, all our looseness of thought and loose ends of life, will one day find their home in Jesus. Heaven, beginning here and now and one day there and then, is the final fulfilment where the totality of all dwells in Christ, the Plerotic of God.[33]

> *There is a place called 'heaven' where the good here unfinished is completed; and where the stories unwritten, and the hopes unfulfilled, are continued. We may laugh together yet.*
> J. R. R. TOLKIEN TO HIS SON MICHAEL IN 1941[34]

Plerotic confidence is a foolhardy confidence that enables the disciple to hold nothing back. A disciple throws in "all," and throws all in. We are designed to dedicate our whole being in loving God (with ALL our heart, mind, soul, and strength), and neighbors. We are commanded to love our neighbors, not to agree with our neighbors or to pedestal our neighbors or to have high opinions of our neighbors. Love them. Period. When we face any challenge, including that of loving our neighbors or loving our enemies, we find surprising strength we didn't know we had. That strength comes from God.

Plerotic confidence is a foolhardy confidence that derives from the fact that there is never only one of us. Always there are at least two—and "two are better than one."[35] With two, when one of the two is God, "ALL THINGS ARE POSSIBLE." Plerotic confidence is not in ourselves, but in God. In the words of Scripture, "for those who are with us are more than those who are with them"[36] and "for the one who is in you is greater than the one who is in the world."[37]

Plerotic confidence is a foolhardy confidence that implies a fulfilment that is running over, that overflows and abounds in abundance. This is one of the unique features of Jesus' miracles: he loved to leave leftovers. I love left-overs. I love it when you need a treasure map to find out where things are in the refrigerator. This theology of left-overs is what Thomas Aquinas was referring to when he wrote, "Whatever is delightful is in heaven in superabundance."[38]

You cannot aspire to the maximum without bending to the minimum, a self-emptying where out of the dregs only God can be seen for who God is—Love—and where God only is the filling who can bring the maximum. In the Jesus Style, the Plerotic is always found with the Kenotic.

2) Kenotic Style [Emptying/Minimum]: Humble

> *Eat your humble pie . . .*
> *If you're too big to clean the 'throne'*
> *you're too small to sit on it.*
> MABEL BOGGS SWEET (D. 1993)[39]

Many of the prophets had visions and other encounters with the divine, but Moses stood apart. Only Moses spoke to God "face to face" or more precisely, "mouth-to-mouth."[40] So how did this singularly close relationship with God shape Moses' life? God anticipates our question, defending Moses against criticism from his siblings by touting him as "the most humble of men, the humblest man on earth."[41] The one person with the right to possess lordly arrogance and egoistic vanity was instead "the humblest man on earth." Intimacy with God imbued Moses with a humility that defied the expectations of his position and authority.

John Masefield, Poet Laureate of the United Kingdom from 1930 until 1967, was a sought-after author whose name dignified any publication. But in an unsolicited act of humility, Masefield always enclosed a self-addressed stamped envelope with his essay submissions to *The Times*, one of the most prestigious and influential newspapers in the world, should they opt not to publish his work.[42] He honored the oldest continuously published daily newspaper in the world by humbling opening himself to rejection.

So many Christians have not just a chip on their shoulder, but the whole tree (and sometimes an entire forest). The only chip on our shoulder should be the cross, which we carry humbly and gladly. On the cross-beams, Jesus united us vertically to his Father and horizontally to one another. To paraphrase Augustine, it was pride that turned angels into devils, and it is humility that turns humans into something greater than the angels.[43]

The Bible knows a double *kenosis*, a double "emptying:" once in the incarnation, once on the cross.[44] In one kenosis, the divine humility, Jesus came down. The God who filled the universe emptied Himself and came down to Earth. In the other kenosis, the God of all power and might gave it all up and refused to come down. Jesus refused to come down . . . from the cross. Love kept Jesus on the cross.

Humility is the biblical word for transparency. Humility is the virtue of knowing yourself so well you know how unvirtuous you are. Arrogance is the self-made delusion that we can stand on our own and don't need anyone. Humility is the God-made recognition that we are needy creatures, totally interdependent on creation and others, and we each conceal unique "creature features" that crawl out from under our skin periodically, scaring us and others.

Humility is as much a requirement as intelligence to perceive the world as it is. Asked when he first suspected that Wittgenstein was a genius, G. F. Moore famously replied: "When he was the only one who looked puzzled during my lectures."[45] No one should be more humble in style than preachers. Preachers must always preach better than they are, all the while praying hard for God to make them better than they preach.

---

*God does not choose the same people
to keep his word as to fulfil it.*
FRENCH NOVELIST GEORGES BERNANOS (D. 1948)[46]

In seeing ourselves as we are, shattered and tattered, wretched and weak, we can see others as they are, shattered and tattered, wretched and weak. Rent garments and ripped shirts are not pleasing displays of contriteness, however. In the words of Prophet Joel, "Let your hearts be broken not your garments torn."[47] St. Bonaventure liked to put it like this: "Humility is what cleans and polishes the mirror of our soul."⁴⁸ Humility's daily prayer is a simple one: Keep my mirror clean and polished. Help me to see myself for what I really am.

The kenotic style is a daily lesson in littleness. St. David of Wales (d. 589) spoke these dying words to his monks: "Be joyful, keep the faith, and do the little things"⁴⁹ based on an ancient Welsh proverb "*Gwnewch y pethau bychain mewn bywyd*" ("Do the little things in life"). God is large in life's littles. It is the little things that reveal our great love for the one who loved us first and that bind people into a community of faith, love, and service.⁵⁰ You can't knock someone down without puffing yourself up. That's why personal attacks and condemnation are so dangerous to the kenotic life.

> *Not great deeds, but small deeds done with great love.*
> ST. TERESA OF CALCUTTA (D. 1997)⁵¹

3) *Koinoniac Style: Connection* Connectedness to one another and to the God "who gives me" is a design imperative of the koinonia life. A Jesus human learns the art of human connection, which means the ability and flexibility to be always "between" since that is where connection takes place. You can't be a Jesus human without being well-connected.

Wikipedia was launched in January 2001 less to acclaim than to ridicule and derision. Some universities refused to allow any use of "wacky wiki." By December 2005, *Nature* published a peer-reviewed article which stated that

Wikipedia, the peer-produced encyclopedia made possible by the fact that half a billion people can connect to it and contribute to it (and, through it, to each others' thoughts and expertise), was very nearly as accurate as that gold-standard reference work, *Encyclopedia Britannica*.[52]

Wisdom (or the lack of it) is always "proven" in the crucible of connections. Every biblical indicator that someone is not living in wisdom comes through the way they relate to others (bitterness, jealousy, anger, etc.).[53] Conversely, every indicator James lists that a person is "in" wisdom (basically the fruit of the Spirit) is also verified in relationship.[54] In other words, relationships become the proving ground for wisdom and the schooling ground as well.

Wisdom is manifest and cultivated in relationship. Without relationships wisdom is an impossibility. We've tended to see wisdom as disembodied principles, but really wisdom can only emerge as she is incarnated in connection.

Aquinas built a theology on the pedagogy of the question (*quaestio*)—or, in other words, theology formed out of asking questions of the universe. Moderns built a theology on the pedagogy of the thesis and the proposition—"dogmatic" theology was the result. It is time to build a theology on the pedagogy of the relational and the connectional.

It is less that one "finds" one's self and more that one's self is found in the nexus of chosen relationships. Self is the space between, not within, with the boundaries of the self the boundaries of the universe. There is no such thing as an "autonomous self." We are all cultural artifacts.[55] Sin

THE JESUS STYLE: HOT

is that which limits us from locating God in the world of relationships.

Nobel-Prize winning French-Algerian author Albert Camus (d. 1960) is quoted as saying "I believe in justice, but I will defend my mother before justice." This quote is often paraphrased as "Between justice and my mother, I choose my mother."[56] Healthy relationship trumps and triumphs over everything in life, especially if that relationship is with Jesus the Christ.

Embodied beings are designed to be embedded beings, embedded in relationships. Christ in me needs Christ in you for Christ in us to be Christ for the world.

4) Kerygmatic Style: Courage Courageousness is the courage of trendsetters to escape living under the tyranny of trends and to set new trends in motion.

We need enough security to give us the courage and confidence to take risks to be insecure, and not too much to make us so comfortable in our cocoons we will never want to fly. The key to moving forward is the courage to move.

The divine invitation is "Call to me and I will answer you and tell you great and unsearchable things you do not know,"[57] not "call on me and I'll reassure you with comforting thoughts about what you already know." If it is God, expect to have your horizons blown up, your hopes expanded, and your knowledge overturned. As the Apostle Paul warned, "Eye hath not seen, nor ear heard, neither have entered into the heart of man, the things which God hath prepared for them that love him."[58] If your eyes are not bugging and your ears not buzzing and your head not spinning, you haven't yet entered into the heart of God.

I have never met a person who lacked problems to solve or predicaments to endure. Maturity is knowing in life the difference, and the courage to connect the two.

These four style elements come together in what might be called the theology of the Ferris wheel.

> *You'll never know how great a kiss can feel,*
> *'til you're stuck at the top of a Ferris wheel.*
> "PALISADES PARK" (1962) WRITTEN BY CHUCK BARRIS,
> RECORDED BY FREDDY CANNON[59]

<u>Ferris Wheel Theology:</u> The cyclic nature of the Ferris wheel lifts us in some form of community (connection) so that together we are brave enough (courage) to see farther than we have all day (confidence) yet we accept that we'll descend together (humble) and could not have gotten there without each other.

The Ferris wheel is a symbol of Jesus Style. No wonder it is the venue of many a first kiss? Somehow young lovers know that the ecstasy and the trepidation of riding together on the Ferris wheel is an echo of the love they're flirting with, and a deeper echo of the love of their Creator's style of creation. Hugh of Saint Victor (d. 1141) says that the whole of the universe is like a book, written by God's finger.[60] Mother Nature has a Father who has stamped the divine style in all of creation, from the smallest fairyfly to the largest star.

<u>5) Backboned Church:</u> A hot church has a strong spinal

THE JESUS STYLE: HOT

column of character. Jesus was not a threatening person. But he was strong and sure and always displayed the firm backbone of mission.

> *To succeed in life, you need three things:*
> *a wishbone, a backbone and a funny bone.*
> "QUEEN OF COUNTRY" SINGER AND ACTRESS REBA MCENTIRE

Estimates are that 97% of all living animals on Earth are invertebrates.[61] In other words, most creatures are spineless. We are surrounded by lemming-like jellyfish creatures, no-backbone beings and wussified churches. Backbones must be grown, and Jesus shows us how.

Authentic disciples of Jesus are known for their vertical pillars, not their horizontal herdings. Let's just say it about a digital culture: mobiles create mobs. The mobs are back. As is common with mob assessments, mob judgments, mob conclusions—they were wrong. There is an old saying: "Put it to a vote, and they'll always vote to go back to Egypt." There is something about the anonymity of crowd decisions, the headlong, headstrong energy of "the pack," that makes wrong decisions seem so right, bad choices seem so flawless, cruel actions seem so sensible. Time and again in scripture, in story after story, when the crowd spoke and its majority vote was taken, it was a big mistake.

The trend today is to treat people as part of a crowd, a group, not as persons. How many listen to what is being said, not just who is saying it? A backboned church always protects the freedom to resist the herding of large groups, mob mentality, and groupthink.

The word "maverick" comes from nineteenth-century ranching, where it refers both to: 1) a range animal that refused to follow the herd; and 2) an animal unbranded. Cattleman Samuel Augustus Maverick thought branding a cruel practice, and so refused to impose a brand. If that's a maverick, why aren't all disciples of Jesus "mavericks" in that there is no brand on us but Jesus, and his followers don't follow the masses only the Master. Let the culture have its mobs; let the church have its mavericks.

The wussification of the church is one of its ugliest features. In the story of the raising of Lazarus, there is a clear division of labor that requires a church with backbone.

Note who does the rising from the dead: Jesus.

Note who does the unbinding and unwinding: We do.

"You unbind him," Jesus instructed his dumbfounded disciples.[62]

It is God's power alone that can bring the dead to life or save sinners. But it is up to us to have the backbone to untie those bound by sin, to free those chained to addictions, to heal the ravages of despair, depression and disease.

God frees us from the grave.
> But we must take the grave-clothes off.

God releases us from being wrapped up.
> But we must have the initiative and industry and integrity to take the wraps off.

God initiates the freeing.
> We participate in the freedom.

THE JESUS STYLE: HOT

God gives us breath.
> We give each other mobility.

I liberate him, Jesus says.
> You loose him.

"Lazarus, come forth.
> Disciples, unwrap him."

God will work in us.
God will work with us.
God will work through us.
But God will not work for us.

God will not do for us what we can do for ourselves. God will not do for others what God gave us a backbone to do for each other.

The Italian Renaissance painter Titian's great altarpiece depicting the red-robed Virgin and child is located in the church of Santa Maria Gloriosa dei Frari (otherwise known simply as the Frari) in Venice. A blue-robed Peter is on her left side, with one hand in a book, and a key chained to his right ankle. The key, of course, is a symbol of Peter's "keys of the kingdom" and his binding and unbinding power. But the keys of the kingdom are not given just to Peter, but to all the disciples, and to all of us, for the confining and unbinding of all peoples found by sin.[63] Jesus humans are keepers of the keys, stewards of the mysteries of God, that can unlock and unbind people from what traps and ensnares them through the releasing power of the Spirit.

What are we too wrapped up in? Are our own backbones so tightly swaddled in safety and security and selfism that we can't unwrap each other? Are our backbones unwrapped in all-thereness or wrapped up in out-of-itness? Do we have the backbone to look at the world with alert eyes, innocent eyes, keen eyes, and romance the sinner in the moment? In the midst of sin and guilt and dirt and grime, do we have the backbone to sing with eye-to-eye contact "I can't take my eyes off of you," or to sing to the lost "Jesus only has eyes for you" right now—not with eyes darting around to see who else is in the room or who might hear you? Do we have the backbone to skin-kiss, not air-kiss, the sinner?

It's always dangerous to quote one of the most quotable thinkers and artists in history: William Blake (d. 1827). When commissioned to illustrate biblical passages, William Blake was totally orthodox. But when he was off doing his own thing, he wandered far into fantasyland, and believed that all religions were different spores from the same source. He desperately tried to get back to that source and forget the spores, but he never had the backbone to do it without the tether of a church commission.

In the Ashkenazic tradition, at the end of reading a Book of Torah you stiffen your spine for mission and say *Chazac*: "Be Strong." The ancient war cry of the Hebrews "Rak Chazak Amats" (pronounced rock cha-zack) was a battle hymn that literally means "Be Strong and of Good Courage."[64] Rak means humble and tender. Chazac means strength and confidence. Amats means the holy courage of prophesying forward a promised victory.

For someone to have the courage of humble confidence ("Rak Chazac Amats") the phrase was "That takes amats." Today the phrase is "That takes backbone."

It takes a backboned church to move forward in the midst of much sloth and such wussification.

6) *Adam's Apple/Eve's Apricot Church:* Both men and women have an "Adam's apple," the bump in the front of the throat that is part of the larynx, a voice box that contains the vocal cords. The laryngeal prominence is larger in men than in women because of the thicker layer of fat that covers it. But you can see the Adam's apple in both men and women.

Since the Adam's apple moves as we laugh, it has become a symbol of humor and laughter. Humor and charm are the ultimate aphrodisiacs. A good sense of humor is crazy hot. Often cited as the number one reason people say they fall in love with someone? "He/she made me laugh." To be a serious Christian means you don't have to take everything so seriously, especially yourself. Humor stands as one of best evidences the brain is working well. In fact, laughter can save your life. Laughter releases enzymes necessary for health and wholeness in self-organizing systems.

The proof that "poetry is a part of the structure of reality," as Pulitzer-prize winning poet Wallace Stevens (d. 1955) liked to put it?[65] The first words out of the First Adam's mouth? Poetry and a Pun. First the poetry of "Bone of my bones, flesh of my flesh." Then Adam names his bride with a pun: "ish" (man) will be called "ishsha" (wo-man).

Likewise, the last Adam, Jesus, was a Master Poet and Punster. What were the first recorded words of Last Adam? Aramaic poetry: "This is the time of fulfillment. The kingdom of God is at hand. So μετανοεῖτεα, and believe the gospel."

DESIGNER JESUS

Jesus founds his bride, the church, on a pun: "Cepha, on this cepha (Aramaic), Petros on this petra (Greek) I will build my church."[66] How symbolic is it that the church is founded on a pun? Jesus is punning Peter's name "Rock" where the Greek "Petros" which means the giant "chief cornerstone" of Herod's Temple is paired with the "Petra" or little boulder upon which even a house couldn't be built.[67]

The whole Road to Emmaus is Jesus pulling a fast one on his aunt and uncle. Jesus loved humor and used it constantly. His wordplay on gnat and camel is mostly missed because no one knows the Aramaic *galma* and *gamla*. The "speck" of sawdust versus "log" of lumber in the eye is another word-play.

Grant me, O Lord, a sense of good humor.
Allow me the grace to be able to take a joke.

PRAYER OF SIR THOMAS MORE (D. 1535)[68]
PRAYED DAILY BY POPE FRANCIS

Even the earliest disciples of Jesus enjoyed a rich and invigorating laugh life, which sometimes got them in trouble. In his fifteenth Homily on the Letters to Hebrews, John Chrysostom (d. 409) confronted his fourth-century congregation with their habit of laughing in church at what he deemed inappropriate moments.

> For the Church has been filled with laughter. Whatever clever thing one may say, immediately there is laughter among those present: and the marvelous thing is that many do not

leave off laughing even during the very time of the prayer.⁶⁹

Chrysostom scolded them while reading out, in disgust, a list of biblical episodes at which his congregation was prone to laugh out loud. He even complained that "there are some persons so dissolute and silly as even during this very rebuke to laugh." Yet without laughter how can we "become like a child," as Jesus instructed his disciples, in order to enter the kingdom?⁷⁰

Humour is, in fact, a prelude to faith, and laughter is the beginning of prayer. Laughter must be heard in the outer courts of religion, and the echoes of laughter should resound in the sanctuary, but laughter cannot have the last word. This is why humour generally seems to be more congenial to religious understanding than wit.
THEOLOGIAN REINHOLD NIEBUHR (D. 1971)⁷¹

Humor is theme of Umberto Eco's historical novel *The Name of the Rose* (1980), where the nefarious monk Jorge poisoned anyone who came upon the one book in the monastery library that proposed that God laughed. The investigator who uncovered this malice in wonderland asked Jorge the question on the reader's mind: "But what frightened you in this discussion of laughter? You cannot eliminate laughter by eliminating the book." Jorge defended himself by claiming: "Laughter is weakness, corruption, the foolishness of our flesh [but] the function of laughter is reversed [in this book]: It is elevated to art, the doors of the world of the learned are opened to it, it becomes the object of philosophy, and of perfidious theology."[72]

From Jorge's point of view, the possibility of anyone learning anything from laughter could not be tolerated. "I accept the risk of damnation," Jorge boasts. "The Lord will absolve me, because He knows I acted for his glory."[73]

> *So when God speaks through the prophet Isaiah and says, "My bowels shall sound forth like a harp for Moab," isn't the Creator just telling us, "I love you" with a good old fashioned air biscuit?*
> PASTOR/HUMORIST STEVE CASE[74]

Might laughter be a subliminal form of glossolalia, of "speaking in tongues?" Laughter is a public confession of the limits of language, and a public profession of the indispensability of utterances that come not from speech, but from deep inside and from the spirit. Whereof we cannot speak, thereof we can laugh.

John Lennon, the Beatles founder, said that he gave up going to church after the vicar threw him out for laughter. After that he said he went to church every morning, "in the temple of his own head."[75]

> *Your speech should always be gracious, flavored with wit.*
> COLOSSIANS 4:6

THE JESUS STYLE: HOT

The Jesus Laugh: One of my Th.D. students, Nathan Nordine, wrote a dissertation on Jesus' laugh life and subtitled it "The Church Has a Serious Problem." Sometimes the Jesus smile erupts in a Jesus laugh.

There is laughter throughout the Bible, though it often takes expression in forms different from our own. One example: Isaac is literally named "Ha, Ha, Ha." We translate it as "One who Laughs." But in Hebrew, the name Isaac (Yitzchak) means "he will laugh" or "he will rejoice." This comes from the Hebrew root tzchok, meaning "to laugh" but is an onomatopoeic word that sounds close to "Yuck Yuck." The name is sometimes translated more broadly as "happiness" or "laughter." Hence the most common translations of the name Isaac from Hebrew are "he will laugh/rejoice," "laughter," or "happiness," relating to the incredulous laughter in the biblical account of Isaac's unlikely birth. The very name Isaac reflects themes of joy, laughter, even sarcasm.

Perhaps we can learn about Jesus' laughter from other cultures. In Navajo culture, for example, a child is seen as formally leaving the Spirit world and becoming fully human at the point of their first laugh, since laughter evidences relational recognition and thus human being-ness. The first laugh is commemorated with a First Laugh Ceremony, also called "Laughing Baby Ceremony," a traditional celebration held when the newborn is a few weeks old to welcome the new human into the community. Close friends and relatives gather to pass the baby around in clockwise fashion multiple times as each person holds and rocks the infant while

DESIGNER JESUS

joyfully laughing, talking, singing, and praying with the child. Laughter and humor are seen as means of blessing the child with happiness, lightheartedness, and positive energy as they start their life's journey. Feasting and dancing conclude the ceremony, as small gifts are left for the child as keepsakes. The parents wash the infant's hair with yucca root during the ceremony, and sprinkling with salt plays a symbolic role in bringing the Navajo First Laugh Ceremony to an end.

Maybe our baptismal ceremonies should require some laughter as part of the ritual, preparing the child to experience comedy in the face of life's calamities.

7) Cleavaged Church: The word "cleave" is one of those rare contronyms that convey two opposite meanings at the same time—to bring together and to keep apart, to unite and to split apart. All contronyms are seductive and mysterious, but cleavage may just be another name for the art of seduction, from which comes all reproductive, creative, and generative progeny. That is why baptismal fonts were often structured as yonic art because at your baptism, your church was mothering you and birthing you in the faith.

Now I a fourfold vision see
And a fourfold vision is given to me
Tis fourfold in my supreme delight,
And threefold in soft Beulahs might
And twofold Always, May God us keep
From Single vision and Newtons sleep.

POET, PRINTER, MYSTIC WILLIAM BLAKE[76]

THE JESUS STYLE: HOT

Christianity is cleaved: there are always dual poles of reference. Christianity inherits this from Judaism, where the nature of God is both singular and plural (in ancient Hebrew the One God *Elohim* is plural)[77] and where the Talmud blesses contradictions with these words: "both of these are the words of the living God." Orthodoxy is paradoxy.

Christianity mystically marries perceived polarities into paradoxical harmony. "The arrival of Christ puts apparent oppositions into relationship" is how Emma Mason puts in in her wonderful essay on Christmas poetry.[78] Jesus is the all-embracing lover who passionately romances opposites. Like the "humble confidence" of the abs. The shadow of the cross is a paradox. Not a plus, but a paradox. To be a follower of Jesus is to learn how to dream in two languages, to dream both human and divine dreams because it takes the divine to be human.[79] Dream as though you would live forever; live as though you would die today.

In the "overlap" of the opposing circles is the mandorla, the sweet spot and dance floor of life.[80] The mandorla is the almond-shaped aureole that often enclosed medieval representations of Mary. The open arch and long narrow interior of Gothic church architecture with musically pounding processionals was intentional: it represented the continuing divine penetration of Mary's virginal body so that new life can be born in the Body of Christ and new incarnations of divine presence conceived.

Some call this juxtaposition of opposites into a paradoxical harmony a creation of tension. The allure of drama stems from the simmering friction of tension. Audiences lean in, hooked by the promise of resolution. Take star-crossed lovers. As anticipation peaks for their first on-screen kiss, ratings skyrocket. Once passions ignite, interest soon fizzles. The yearning often eclipses the romance. This holds true across genres: the cryptic cliffhanger hooks more than orderly dénouements; the cold case grips more than the conviction. Tension conjures engagement, and its dissipation cedes to disenchantment.

For compelling storytelling, tension must not dissolve completely but regenerate in new forms. Each answered question spawns new mysteries. The insoluble tension between desire and fulfillment, problem and solution, is the engine that drives our dramatic voyeurism. Skillful stories stoke tension perpetually, granting temporary reprieves before ratcheting up the pressure once again. For tension relieved begets boredom, while tension prolonged captivates. Tension is the fuel of pleasure, the fire that burns bright and fierce.

> *You make known to me the path of life;*
> *you will fill me with joy in your presence,*
> *with eternal pleasures at your right hand.*
>
> PSALM 16:11 NIV

The universe exists because it brings God pleasure. Humans exist to bring God pleasure, and the ultimate in pleasuring God is taking pleasure in God's gifts and presence. English novelist Ian McEwan observed how literary critics "can never really encompass the fact that some things are on the page because they gave the writer pleasure."[81] Neither can

THE JESUS STYLE: HOT

some theologians. Faith is not a matter of pleasant feelings, but pleasuring in God's presence and hosting others in the pleasure of service in the kingdom of God. If you want to go through life with joyfulness in your spirit and the freedom to play and explore stirring your heart, you need consciousness of God's pleasure that comes with living in tensity.

Holiness is the ultimate pleasure zone. Holiness is not about getting better at doing what God commands us to do. Holiness is about getter better at enjoying God and pleasing God.[82] True holiness is rapture, not restriction; wholehearted devotion, not dutiful obedience. True holiness seeks not to perfect performance for a divine audience, but to deepen intimacy with the divine presence. Pleasing God arises not from grimly following the rules, but from freely lavishing love upon Love itself.

Holiness is thus the ecstasy of full presence—of being so engulfed in worship that analysis ceases. Like a kiss too pressing for thought, it is consummation beyond critique. In these timeless moments of rhapsodic reverence, we are fully known and adored by the Source who adores all creation. We rest in the romance of reciprocity. The false divide between sacred and sensual collapses. Holiness becomes celebrating the divine in the beauty of being. A hot church embraces the passionate play of praise without pomp, inhabiting holiness through exultation not evaluation. For God is only pleased by gladness given gladly, in love's rapture.

DESIGNER JESUS

The very word paradox is paradoxical. Let the paradox be. Remember, after all, the Gospel is full of paradoxes, that man is himself a living paradox, and that according to the Fathers of the Church, the Incarnation is the supreme Paradox.

FRENCH JESUIT THEOLOGIAN HENRI DE LUBAC (D. 1991)[83]

Dance of Tradition and Improvisation: You can't have "style" without tradition. Every "style" entails simulation and staging, both of which implies tradition. You are taking something that someone has done before you (tradition), and either adopting it or mixing and matching it with your own twists and turns (innovation). That's combining tradition and improvisation.

Tradition is inescapable unless it's ex nihilo, and the only one who creates ex nihilo (out of nothing) is God. What already exists (tradition) is played with in a new way. That's why tradition is inherent in any style. The "old" can either become "old-fashioned" and "old-fogeyish" or it can become primed, well-timed, advanced, tempered, and seasoned. There is a certain dated dignity and tattered charm to the old-fashioned and unfashionable. Besides, one cannot escape the presence of "old" in "new" in Jesus' new-world, ancient-future style.

Jesus followers have a unique aesthetic, not an aesthetic of things as they are, but an aesthetic of things as they are not. "So we fix our eyes not on what is seen, but on what is unseen, since what is seen is temporary, but what is unseen is eternal."[84] The Jesus Style always has one eye on the future, not seeing to fit in but to fit together and to fit forward.

Jesus beckons us to join him in what he's already doing in the future. Jesus is always ahead of us. Gregory of Nyssa insisted that faith goes from beginning to beginning for all eternity. "Such a fast/God, always before us and/leaving as we arrive" is how Welsh poet/priest R. S. Thomas puts it.[85] We romance the dance and glance of God's back, as Moses did on the mountain. Faith means we live life forward.

Compline is the last of the seven daily hours of prayer in the Christian tradition. Typically a brief prayer service lasting about fifteen to twenty minutes, compline includes prayers for forgiveness, thanksgiving, and protection as well as hymns, readings from the Bible or other spiritual writings, and a time for meditation or silent prayer. Compline can be prayed individually or communally, but many churches and monasteries offer compline services every evening.

From the seventh century onward, the church has sung this compline hymn called the "Night Prayer" at the final service of the day.

> 1) To you before the close of day,
>   Creator of all things, we pray
>   that, in your saving constancy,
>   our guard and keeper you would be.
> 2) Save us from troubled, restless sleep;
>   from all ill dreams your children keep.

DESIGNER JESUS

> So calm our minds that fears may cease
> and rested bodies wake in peace.
> 3) A healthy life we ask of you:
> the fire of love in us renew,
> and when the dawn new light will bring,
> your praise and glory we shall sing.
> 4) Almighty Father, hear our cry
> through Jesus Christ, our Lord, most high,
> Whom with the Spirit we adore
> forever and for evermore. Amen.

The last two lines of the first verse are "in your saving constancy,/our guard and keeper you would be." Or in the original Latin, "*ut solita clementia sis praesul ad custodiam.*" But Trappist monk and bishop Erik Varden has recently reminded us that the word "*praesul*" which is most often translated as "protector" literally means "someone who leaps or dances in front" like David did before the Ark as he moved it the seven miles from Kiriath Yearim to Jerusalem.[86] As Varden puts it, to be a custodian of a tradition is "not to lag behind but to go ahead" and dance the past into the future. Or more epigrammatically, "Custody is a function of constancy in clemency."[87] Once again, we move forward fearlessly at the same time and only because we are good trustees of what lies behind. Tradition is a verb that brings together conservation and innovation.

A great life happens by design. The Jesus design. The Jesus style is hot.

THE JESUS STYLE: HOT

STUDIO LIVE

1) Can Jesus come to us, not just from the church, but from the wider human story and the whole human panoply?

   * Do you think Jesus can manifest in unexpected places and through diverse people, not just formally religious figures? In what ways?

   * How might focusing only on Jesus in the church limit our understanding of who he is? What is gained by seeing Jesus in the full human story?

   * Does the church hold any contradictions with Jesus' actual lifestory? If so, how should those be addressed?

   * How might the church evolve or expand its perspectives by learning from the way Jesus influences culture and humanity?

   * Is there value in spiritual insights from non-Christian sources? Can these offer fresh perspectives on Jesus' teachings?

   * Does the church risk becoming isolated from society if it does not look for Jesus in the broader human experience? Why or why not?

   * Where do you gain your deepest sense of connection to the essence of Jesus—church or the wider world/society? Why?

   * Overall, how can the church stay dynamically engaged

with Jesus' living spirit outside its own walls? What needs to change?

2) I love gardens that don't look like gardens, but look like nature at play—a dialectic between human initiative and divine purpose, between agency and acceptance, between growth and decay, between conservation and cultivation, between tradition and innovation. That's why I want my house to disappear into the landscape of trees, rocks, dirt, and water. "Houses were built to live in, not to look on" (Francis Bacon).[88]

God has given each of us a garden. It's called the garden of life. I want the garden of my life to be seen by others as ecopoetry, a natural wilderness of God at play with the transcendent elements of truth, beauty, and goodness. Poesis means "making" and "eco" means household or dwelling place. An ecopoetic life is one where an unsuspecting visitor would discover a natural wilderness with scenic vistas of an expanded universe, not a look-at-me youniverse.

If prayer is walking and talking the garden with God, when The Creator of the Universe whispers in my ear "Len, how does your garden grow?" I want to be able to say, "You tell me please, Master Gardener. Do you see Me, or We?"

* Look at the person next to you and say: "How does your garden grow?"

3) If we truly believe that the missional life of self-giving and self-sacrifice is the path to virtue and joy, how do we

THE JESUS STYLE: HOT

convey that to our children/grandchildren and to this culture?

* How can we help our children/grandchildren to understand the importance of serving others and putting others before themselves?

* What are some ways to model a missional life to those around us?

* How can we create opportunities for our children/grandchildren to experience the joy of serving others?

* What are some challenges that we face in raising generations to live a missional life in our culture?

* How can we support each other as parents and grandparents in raising missional children/grandchildren?

* How can we challenge the cultural values that emphasize materialism and selfism over self-giving and self-sacrifice?

* How interconnected are the exercise of deferred gratification and the embodiment of the missional life?

* Rate these suggestions about passing on the baton of the missional life in order of importance:

 ___ Talk to future generations about the importance of serving others. Explain that serving others is one of the best ways to show love for them and to make the world a better place.

 ___ Model a missional life yourself. Volunteer your

time to a cause that you care about, and invite your children/grandchildren to join you.

— Create opportunities for your children/grandchildren to experience the joy of serving others. This could involve volunteering at a local soup kitchen, homeless shelter, or animal shelter. It could also involve simply helping out a neighbor or friend in need.

— Teach your children/grandchildren about the importance of giving back to their community. Encourage them to donate to charities or to volunteer their time to help others.

— Challenge the cultural values that emphasize materialism and individualism over self-giving and self-sacrifice. Talk to your children/grandchildren about the importance of putting the needs of others before their own.

4) Might not one of the problems the church faces today be that its ideas of what it means to be a "Christian" are in fact "too easy," i.e., trite, tasteless, undemanding.

* Discuss your favorite jazz masters, and what makes them so memorable to you? Did any of them NOT work their buns off to make cool blues?

* Discuss your favorite pop musicians, and why you listen to them. How much of a soundtrack does this music provide for the story of your life?

THE JESUS STYLE: HOT

* What is your favorite genre of Christian music? How important is your growing up context to determining your musical tastes? For example, I am a product of mountain culture (Alleghenies, Adirondacks), and hence am convinced the kind of music the angels listen to is southern gospel–the more raw, nasal, and rootsy the better.

5) Colin Powell displayed in his office as Secretary of State this quote from Athenian historian and general Thucydides (d. 400 BC): "Of all manifestations of power, restraint impresses men most."

* How important is "restraint" to a Jesus Style?

* How do we teach our kids the art of "restraint," and the need for self-discipline and deferred gratification?

* Do you agree that exercising restraint can demonstrate power more than using force? Why or why not?

* When has someone you know or a leader impressed you more by showing restraint than dominance?

* What internal qualities allow someone to demonstrate restraint in the face of provocation or aggression?

* How might restraint require more wisdom and discipline than impulsiveness?

* In what scenarios might immediate restraint backfire by enabling bad actions? When is intervention required?

* How might restraint be interpreted as weak rather than impressive by some people or cultures?

* How can restraint be used strategically and purposefully versus just passive acceptance?

* How might you need to practice greater restraint in your own life? What would the benefits be?

6) Listen to the story of Gnaeus Pompeius Magnus (d. 48 BC), commonly known as Pompey the Great. He was a celebrated Roman general and statesman who moved Rome from republic to empire. But his lack of restraint led him to being despised by the masses, even when he was lavishing them with "bread and circuses." Here is one historian's assessment:

> No loser in ancient history had more successes or received more insincere eulogies than the unlucky and unloved Gnaeus Pompeius. Even at the peak of his powers, he misjudged the mood of the people by staging triumphal games in which, as a novelty, he had elephants abused to death, for fun, in the arena. The animals' pitiful bewilderment at the cruelty visited on them excited the pity of the usually callous Roman plebs; Pompey was hooted for his generosity. Not one of the many writers who looked back with nostalgia at the old Republic (and its well-distributed dividends) referred with respect or affection to the sorry figure who died friendless and unadmired, the leader of a caucus of aristocrats whose authority he had, in the

THE JESUS STYLE: HOT

days of the first triumvirate, disempowered. Pompey's reputation never received as much as a quotable epitaph.[89]

* Why do you think Pompey lost the affection of the people, even when he provided "bread and circuses"?
* How might Pompey have misjudged what true leadership requires beyond just material benefits?
* What does this story reveal about the kind of legacy leaders want versus the one they actually leave?
* Why is restraint and wisdom so important for leaders if they want to earn lasting respect?
* How do you think Pompey's lack of restraint led him to become "friendless and unadmired"?
* Why is it not enough just to have success if you want to leave an honorable legacy?
* Does a tragic ending invalidate the positive things a leader accomplished earlier? Why or why not?
* What qualities make for a leader who is both effective and honored? Which matter most to you?
* Are there certain sounds that haunt you? What are they? How do you feel about those who are responsible for these stalking sounds?
* What sounds might your church be sending out that the wider culture mishears as the cries of tortured elephants?

7) Here are some passages about the "headship" of Christ.

> Colossians 1:18 ESV: "And he is the head of the body, the church. He is the beginning, the firstborn from the dead, that in everything he might be preeminent."

> Ephesians 1:22 ESV: "And he put all things under his feet and gave him as head over all things to the church."

* If Jesus is the head, what role do clergy and church members play? How should we operate in relation to Christ's authority over the church?
* What kind of leadership model did Jesus himself demonstrate during his ministry? How might church leaders emulate this?
* What are the risks if church leaders overemphasize or misuse their own authority versus pointing toward Christ's headship?
* How can churches today ensure they are staying intimately connected to Jesus as head rather than operating by human agendas?

8) Do your own Bible study on Revelation 3:16, where God tells the tepid, lukewarm, middle-of-the-road Laodicean church that "You make me sick, church." And then goes on to warn that God will "spew" or literally "vomit" out such fetid-faith churches. I call this Barf-bag theology and have collected dozens of "barf bags" from various

airlines with signature sayings on them that reveal the dangers of fetid-faith religiosity.

* Would you say about the thesis that mediocrity is the swan song of the church?

* What approaches other than the ones here would you suggest to cultivate a "hot" or even "cool" faith, just not a "moderate" or "lukewarm" faith?

* A popular phrase critiquing the church is "the bland leading the bland." How accurate is that barb? How do you react when you hear such a description of the body of Christ?

9) Amazon's Jeff Bezos sees the role of a CEO as "gardener—seeding, nurturing, inspiring, cultivating the ideas coming from below." In fact, the word "neighbor" originally meant person gardening the next strip of land to your own.[90]

* How does the gardening metaphor apply to leadership? What are the parallels between nurturing ideas/people and tending a garden?

* When have you seen a pastor or other front-line person effectively take a "gardening" approach versus just designing from above? What was the impact?

* How can leaders strike the right balance between structure and organic cultivation? What are the risks of too much top-down control?

* What might it look like to "garden" ideas among your peers and neighbors rather than just work in isolation?
* How could you adopt a gardener's mindset of caring for and nurturing the ideas and talents around you each day?
* What might be the benefits in your workplace, community, or family of taking a gardening approach of seeding and inspiring growth?
* What creative partnerships or projects could emerge by collaborating with your "gardening neighbors"?
* How can we better appreciate both individual growth and our shared interconnectedness, like neighboring garden plots?

Chapter 10: Mind The Jesus Mind

Have this mind among yourselves, which is yours in Christ Jesus.

PAUL THE APOSTLE (D. 64)[1]

A JESUS MIND KEEPS THE WORLD POINTED IN THE right direction.

"Put on the mind of Christ" is how Paul described this design feature of a Jesus human life. The "mind" was important enough to Jesus himself that he added "and with all your mind" in his version of the Shema.[2] Jesus doesn't just set our hearts on fire, but our feet on fire, our hands on fire, our minds on fire—a firecracker faith for a dynamite gospel.[3]

What Were You Thinking? When the Jesus human "puts on" the Jesus Mind, it is the highest of life's triumphant symmetries. To begin each day basking prayerfully in the sunshine of God's presence, and opening the blinds to let the light of God's Story to shine forth, is the essence of the

DESIGNER JESUS

solar-powered life. A Jesus frame of mind gives the human mind the freedom to play and explore in the midst of epistemological chaos, and the means to resist the homogenizing forces of contemporary existence.

John Wesley was an Oxford don while a leader of two revolutions of the eighteenth century: the Reading Revolution and the Methodist Revolution. Wesley's most favorite phrase to quote in his sermons (fifty-two times at least) is "Put on the mind of Christ."[4] It was his eighteenth-century way of talking about *Alter-Ipse* Christus, or the real AI (Alpha Intelligence).

You don't have to showcase the five wounds of Jesus on your body to be "alter Christus" like St. Francis of Assisi did after spending time on Mount La Verna in 1224. You just have to put on the "mind of Christ" and show a willingness to share in Christ's suffering.

The mind of Christ is the fulfilment of ASICS, the Latin acronym "*Anima Sana In Corpore Sano*" translated as "a sound mind in a sound body." The mind of Christ is a well-furnished mind that is full of fire, ravenous in reading, industrious in curiosity, rigorous in reflection, valorous in virtue, vigilant in compassionate awareness, not indolent in living off the conceptual achievements of its ancestors or embalmed in past dreams and stale cliches but pioneering new paths into the future where Jesus is calling us to join him.

<u>Talking Heads and Tall Tales:</u> When guests visit my house, I can always count on the question, "Have you read all of these?" It is said with a twist of irony, as if I must have something wrong with me to surround myself in every room with books like this. But these books of talking heads and tall tales are my friends and companions for life.[5]

Umberto Eco argued that the point of libraries is not to find the books you already know, but "to discover books whose existence we never suspected, only to discover that they are of extreme importance to us."[6] This is why I love open stacks, the kind I had when attending Colgate Rochester Divinity School (whose library has since been sold), and the kind I didn't have when researching at the Library of Congress.

Mind is the matrix of all matter.
PHYSICIST MAX PLANCK[7]

The hunger to know God and discover more about God's nature is what fueled and fired the scientific pursuits of Copernicus, Kepler, Galileo, Newton, Leibnitz, and Collins. They reproduced the Jesus Mind in their research and discoveries.

A Jesus Mind is always on the edge of its seat, waiting for some new illumination or more information, as Jesus' encounter with the Canaanite woman demonstrates. If theoretical physicist Richard Feynman (d. 1988) could admit "Nobody understands quantum mechanism. If you think you do, you don't," how much more do we not understand this one word "Emmanuel" or "God with us."

It's not just a mystery. It's a Christ mystery, or Chrystery. And over time more and more of the mystery of Christ, the

DESIGNER JESUS

Chrystery, is revealed depending on how much we can take. A fluff-brained, mordant mind of atrophied attitudes, know-it-all judgments, and idle verdicts is the very definition of frigidity. The problem with a no-romance, frigid faith? It can't reproduce.

The Jesus Mind is based more on questions than answers. Even Jesus feigned ignorance in the greatest understatement of all time—"What things?"[8]—because he cared more about hearing the Emmaus Road disciples tell his story than showcasing his own resurrection.

The deeper our faith, the more intense and profound our questions. The more inquisitive our faith, the less inquisitorial we become. Theology has seldom provided satisfactory answers to many things, but it has provoked many "do-I-dare-disturb-the-universe"[9] questions, quests, and discoveries. Latvian philosopher Judith Shklar (d. 1992) prefaced her book *Ordinary Vices* (1984) by calling it "a ton of perplexities, not a guide for the perplexed."[10]

These scientific geniuses didn't boast comprehensions but were buffeted by apprehensions. What's the difference between comprehensions and apprehensions?

1) Apprehension is a mode of consciousness wherein one is aware of something but cannot pass any judgment on it, while comprehension is a psychological state of mind wherein a person is aware of something, is able to think about it, and knows how to deal with it.

2) Comprehension requires knowledge, while apprehension does not.

3) Comprehension is deeper than apprehension.

4) Apprehension is a state of mind wherein a person does not fully grasp the meaning of an idea or object presented to him, while comprehension is a state of mind wherein he is able to fully understand the meaning of the idea or object presented to him.

In sum, apprehension means partial understanding. Comprehension boasts full and often imperious understanding. Even the primary languages of truth, whether paradox or silence or song,[11] is more apprehension than comprehension. Beethoven sonatas take us up to God; Bach chorales bring God down to us.

<u>Headstrong and Headlong:</u> The ultimate in mindfulness is putting on the "mind of Christ." There are all sorts of mindfulness techniques, many of which will be presented to you daily on your Apple watch and its mindfulness app.[12] The irony of getting digital "notifications" to unplug and meditate and pay attention doesn't seem to have registered with Apple. But mindfulness leaves us marooned in our own mind unless our mind is headstrong and headlong with the mind of Christ.

An opening roll call of scholars who explored the deep connections between narrative, identity, cognition, and the brain and have highlighted the role of story in how the mind works include Carl Jung, Joseph Campbell, Jerome Bruner, Marshall McLuhan, Eleanor Rosch, Roger Schank, Antonio Damasio, Paul Ricoeur, Oliver Sacks, Alan Newell, Judith F.

DESIGNER JESUS

Kroll, George Lakoff, and Iain McGilchrist. If the mind is made of metaphors which it turns into stories, then to put on the mind of Christ is to live in the Jesus story, stay in the Jesus story, and trust the Jesus story.

This is why meals over a table are so important.[13] Identity is forged from shared stories, symbols, images, and ideas that resonate across a constituency. With no shared narratives and metaphors, there is identity confusion, collapse, and disjunction function.

Story makes us fully human and until we become fully human we will not be ready for home.
MADELEINE L'ENGLE[14]

Live in the Jesus Story: All life is lived in story. The only question is what story and whose story. Stories are not simply entertainment. They are the way humans make sense of the world and find our place in it. A Jesus designed life derives a sense of self from the narratives of the Scriptures, and the stories we tell about ourselves and our experiences.[15] The Jesus story is an unending adventure, an abiding advent, and the most mind-bending adventure of your life.

If the Jesus story isn't taking your breath away, leaving you blown away, taken aback, taken by surprise, amazed, and astonished, you're not living it right. The Jesus story turns the world upside down so that we live life the right way up.

Jewish literary scholar Erich Auerbach (d. 1957), one of the foundational figures of comparative literature, draws our attention to the stunning contrast between the stories of the Bible and the ancient literature of heroes and battles like what you find in Homer, Virgil, Sophocles, and Aristophanes. Auerbach compares Homer's Odyssey to the Book of Genesis, and finds that the biblical representation of reality is a world apart from that of Homer.

The Bible is not interested in telling stories about heroes and battles, but rather in depicting the everyday lives of ordinary people. Auerbach compares the Bible's exploration of the relationship between God and humanity, especially the nature of good and evil with Homer's Odyssey, where a hero travels the world and performs great deeds. The Odyssey is not interested in exploring the everyday lives of ordinary people, and it does not deal with the same complex moral and theological issues as the Bible.

> The biblical narrative does not know the heroic style. Its world is not a world of heroes and battles, but of ordinary people and their everyday lives. It does not describe the external world in detail, but concentrates on the inner lives of its characters. Its language is not elevated or poetic, but simple and direct.[16]

In other words, the story of a nobody fisherman named Simon Peter, having an encounter with a person like Jesus, and it leading to a metanoia life-change based on that personal encounter, has no parallels or place in the world of classical tales.

DESIGNER JESUS

> *The Incarnation prepared the way for Christians to discern value in small, even crude, things, just as Christ took lamp stands, a mustard seed, a bit of money, or a wineskin to symbolize great spiritual significance. Such a perspective prevents all likelihood of artistic snobbery.*
> WHEATON COLLEGE PROFESSOR CLYDE S. KILBY (D. 1986)[17]

Jesus taught us to ore the ordinary, find the hum in the humdrum, discover eternity in the earthbound, or in John Updike's haunting phrase, give "the mundane its beautiful due."[18] In a 06 May 1998 commencement address at Mills College (Oakland, California), *A Wrinkle in Time* author Madeleine L'Engle unveiled her own version of the Auerbach thesis: "Jesus focused on very ordinary people doing ordinary, mundane things. You see his love of the 'mundanes' in his story-telling."[19]

French philosopher Paul Ricoeur, who explored how narratives configure human understanding and make meaning, had this to say about the parables of Jesus: "The Parables are radically profane stories. There are no gods, no demons, no angels, no miracles, no time before time . . . but precisely people like us: Palestinian landlords traveling and renting their fields, stewards and workers, sowers and fishers, fathers and sons."[20]

By the way, "mundane" comes from the Latin word "mundanus," which has a double meaning of earthy/worldly but also elegant, beautiful, and precious like gemstones. For

Jesus, the mundane of life, even the mud of life, is beautiful, elegant, and precious. The common is uncommon if you live the Jesus story.

"What's the love of your heart?" is an important question. But equally so is the question, "What's the love of your mind?"

For to set the mind on the flesh is death, but to set the mind on the Spirit is life and peace.

APOSTLE PAUL[21]

Stay In the Story: It's not easy to master the geography of thoughts that keep us focused on the Jesus story, awash as we are in a sea of influencers and celebrities and hormones. The mind is constantly buffeted by the limbic system, which is itself controlled by emotion and metaphor. Or the mind is controlled by the Spirit of God.

Each of us lives in a state of frantumaglia,[22] an Italian word for the jumble of fragments and contradictions and scattered story-lines in the mind waiting for coherence. We are enticed to outsource our thinking to culture and brands, which are now sacred entities in this iconomic world. We fall prey to the trends of the times and to commercials that rape the imagination. We become co-opted by a historical moment, or politicize the faith in the service of popularity or polemics. But to live in celebrity stereotypes, or to live in someone else's storyline, is the ultimate in hypocrisy, fraud, and identity theft. It turns you into a play actor and not an active player.

> *Nine out of ten people have intrusive thoughts that distress and shock them. Many of us, in a high place, get an urge to jump. Half of all women and 80% of men have involuntary thoughts of strangers in the nude.*
> BRITISH FICTION WRITER SEAMUS SWEENEY[23]

James constantly warns against being "double-minded."[24] To have half-a-mind for Christ, and half-a-mind for Beelzebub, is to be split in half and pulled apart from the inside. They're not going in the same direction. As offensive as this statement from Paul may seem, it coincides with James' view of double-mindedness: "The mind of sinful man is death, but the mind controlled by the Spirit is life and peace."[25]

The siren songs of self-realization, self-actualization, and self-fulfillment leave the door open for the ghost of narcissism. Jesus cures the "I, me, mine" mindset in his insistence that we find our identity in him, not in ourselves. The best way to find yourself is to lose yourself in self-sacrifice and service to others. Or as Jesus put it, "Whoever finds their life will lose it, and whoever loses their life for my sake will find it."[26] Classical pianist Arthur Rubenstein (d. 1982) was playing a difficult piece for some friends in 1975 when they began to applaud his skill. Suddenly he stopped, looked them in the eye and said, "Friends, please do not applaud. Your applause directs my thoughts from the music to myself, and then I cannot play."²⁷ We play life the best when we focus on self the least.

Whenever a disciple of Jesus responds reflexively in ways shaped by cultural stereotypes, lazy slogans, placard cliches, or corporate codifications, we need to do a double-take about our double-mindedness and think again, back up, and replant our minds in the Jesus storyline. One of the best wake-up calls to other Jesus humans whose definitions and perceptions are being shaped by the world's definitions of life is a simple one: "Whose story are you in?" Or more directly, "That's not my story." Or you can quote Paul: "Set your minds on things that are above, not on things that are on earth, for you have died, and your life is hidden with Christ in God."²⁸

Jesus once asked his disciples "Have you understood all this?" They answered him in a way that flushes red on the cringe-meter: "Yes." We don't know whether Jesus smirked or shook his head after hearing their glib response, but he let it pass and continued on: "Therefore every scribe who has been trained for the kingdom of heaven is like the master of a household who brings out of his treasure what is new and what is old."²⁹

We are all called to become scribes, scholars, masters of The Torah, masters of the Story. The Greek word for "disciple" is *mathetes*, which literally means pupil, student, follower, disciple, learner. Jesus even went further and instructed his followers to "Consider the lilies of the field"³⁰ where the verb for "consider" means to *katamanthanō*: to learn thoroughly, to research seriously, to ponder to the depths of one's being, to understand by standing under. It takes *manthánō*, "learn," to the next level of intensity. Whether *manthánō* or *katamanthanó*, we are being invited to enroll for life in the Jesus Seminary where everyone is a mentor, everyone is mentored, and reverse mentoring is the norm. Do you wear the mantle of a mentor?

You are standing firm in one spirit,
striving side by side
with one mind
for the faith of the gospel.
PHILIPPIANS 1:27 NRSV

The global youth organization called Young Life has a "Chief Learning Officer," which is a corporate name for what we are all called to be. As lifelong learners, what you acquire in this Jesus Seminary is wisdom and understanding. But an understanding of what? Jesus. Jesus was sent by God to be "our wisdom, our unhindered access to God, our holiness and our atonement."[31] In Jesus we learn a new lifescape of beauty, truth and goodness as our "new self is being renewed in knowledge according to the image of its creator."[32] In that new lifescape, "there is no longer Greek and Jew, circumcised and uncircumcised, barbarian, Scythian, slave and free; but Christ is all and in all!"[33]

The church is a learning community. The question is not "how much do I know?" but "how much am I being stretched?" and "how much am I learning?" And since the half-life of education is now about six years, "how much am I unlearning?" Sixteenth-century Catholics fought the Protestant notion that since each of us had "the mind of Christ" we could be guided into truth and read the Scriptures for ourselves without being told by the church what to think and how to interpret. They had a point. The Scriptures are best read in community and in the context of the community.

The deeper my walk with God, the tighter my hold on the cross, which is the "whole armor of God" that enables me not just to "withstand" but "stand" against and stride over the "principalities and powers" that would blow us off course.

Let the morning bring me word of your unfailing love,
for I have put my trust in you.
Show me the way I should go,
for to you I entrust my life.
PSALM 143:8 NIV

Trust the Story The trouble of trust has been with us from the very beginning. In the first human story, God trusted Adam and Eve to trust and obey God's command to eat freely of all the trees in the garden except the one where the cost of gaining knowledge was too high. Eve and Adam trusted the scheming Serpent over God and went for the one knowledge that came at whatever cost.

There is nothing new under the sun, but the sun is burning brighter and hotter when it comes to trust. We are living in a time of deep suspicion and division. The epidemic of distrust makes it difficult to solve the big problems we face.[34] Trust in institutions is at an all-time low. People are less likely to trust their neighbors and strangers than ever before. There is a growing distrust of the media, politicians, corporations, clergy, and police.[35] The highest trust level that physicians have historically held has been on the downswing since 2020.

Every blink is a reset reminder that you can't trust your own eyes. Sleep is a deep reset that reconnects to the within so you can see the without—without illusions, hallucination, mirages, and lies. With all the hallucinations coming out of AI platforms like ChatGPT, Claude, and Bard, maybe we ought to impose some sabbath laws on AI intelligence.

Identity requires narrative form, but our stories are losing their narrative significance and becoming commodified and commercialized. In a world where every commercial is inviting us to trust our lives to this story or that story, and every celebrity is saying "live my story," the only story worth trusting your life to and turning your life into is the Jesus Story. The old, old story works on a subliminal as well as supernatural level, sending out wordless signals to trust and obey.

The religious establishment mocked Jesus on the cross with words that were more a tribute than a sneer: "He trusts in God. Let God rescue him now if he wants him.[36] "He trusts in God." The Last Adam trusts in God like the First Adam failed to do. Can we trust in God as Jesus did? Even knowing that the "trust" in God will end in results that the world will not comprehend or understand, or may even laugh at?

One reason I trust The Story with my life is the lapidary maxim and axiom—If it reads too good, it's probably not true and not to be trusted. The Story tells the truth about humanity from the start, but with the promise of redemption. From the very beginning of The Story, the first human family is a mess like every human family since, suffering shame, expulsion, violence, betrayal, excommunication, embarrassment, turmoil of thought, and punishment. In Jesus' own family tree, he has two women of ill repute (Tamar and Rahab) and two women of unusual sexual circumstances (Ruth and Bathsheba) as part of his generative story.[37] Rahab the Canaanite brings back the Canaanites into the genealogy of Jesus. Ruth the Moabite brings back Esau who founded Moab into the mainstream story of Jesus.

Autobiography is only to be trusted when it reveals something disgraceful.
ENGLISH NOVELIST GEORGE ORWELL (D. 1950)[38]

Too perfect, too flawless, too clear a story-line doesn't add to its reliability as truth, but to its implausibility and probability as fiction. Truth is messy, contradictory, ragged, and doesn't always "make perfect sense." That is why the gospels ring so true, so authentic, and can be trusted. They were not written by storytellers trying to prove something as "true," but by truth-tellers trying to tell the story of what really happened.

In the words of second-century theologian Tertullian about the Jesus story, "It is certain because it is impossible."[39] Part of the impossibility and implausibility is that nobody could "figure" Jesus out. Not the religious establishment. Not the political establishment. Not the economic establishment. Not even the disciples had Jesus figured out. That's what made everyone so mad, even why they called him "mad." Jesus didn't fit with any of the labels of his day. If you think you've figured Jesus out, or "made sense" of him, it's not Jesus.

Jesus is beyond our figurings and configurings. So too should be his disciples: beyond labels and tags, categories and configurations. What enabled him to do this was what A. N. Wilson has called his "almost suicidal addiction to paradox."[40]

Even further, Jesus tantalized his disciples to trust him with new perceptions to come. "I still have many things to say to you, but you cannot bear them now. When the Spirit of truth comes, he will guide you into all the truth."[41] Trust is a moral muscle that gets stronger with use and substantiation and weaker with disuse, abuse, and betrayal.

The Spirit helps us "bear all things"[42] and trust the story, including the truth that is far beyond our culturally boxed brains. We are always being led towards truth, but we must "ripen" (Irenaeus' word) into wisdom and truth. As a child grows in perception, so do we in relationship to God. But this "ripening" takes place in time ("in the fullness of time") as well as in space.

Life is short, and art is long;
opportunity fleeting,
experimentation perilous,
and decision difficult.

APHORISM #1 OF ANCIENT GREEK PHYSICIAN HIPPOCRATES (D. 370 BC)[43]

Part of trusting The Story is never looking for finish in the story, or resisting the temptation to apply too much "finish" to the story itself. Finish strong. But the strongest finishes are unfinished.

Every truth story is an unfinished story. The Jesus story is a time-released capsule of dynamite that sets loose new explosions of understanding and activity as it moves through time: "greater things will you do," Jesus promised his disciples.[44] This is not like Leonardo da Vinci, who had a problem finishing projects. He started lots, but we only have fifteen finished paintings that survive today. It is more like Picasso, who had a problem constantly touching up his paintings when he saw them in the homes of those he visited. He could not leave them alone, even after they left his studio and into the homes of patrons. Nothing he touched was beyond touch-ups, no matter the distance in time or space. A "classic" by definition is something "that has never finished saying what it has to say."[45] Every Jesus story is an unfinished symphony of truth.

In Jesus is Truth revealed, and authenticity displayed, not just his but ours. Only in the Light do you see the Truth. Have you ever tried looking for something lost in the dark? You need a little bit of light in order to see where something is. The more light, the more you can "see" and "discover" what is around you, and see the relationships between objects and people. As degrees of light increase, the better you can see. Light reveals what is hidden.

When we are "in the dark" about God, Jesus the Light helps us to come closer to God and see God. But "all the truth" takes an eternity to see. Indeed, you and I can't handle "all the truth" even if it were revealed to us. Can you imagine living in the time of Poldrake or Outlander or Sanditon and being told the truth about the next 250 years? Just that little bit of truth would give you a heart attack, forget the fullness of "all the truth."

Paul was "raptured" into Third Heaven, where he saw things of the future he was "forbidden" to reveal.[46] "Forbidden" is a weak word for "under penalty of law" or legally bound not to reveal. Some things in the future are so far beyond our immediate comprehension that we are under legal compulsion not to share them under penalty of severe consequences ("not lawful for man to utter" is how the KJV puts it). He had never mentioned for fourteen years even the existence of this experience in his life, and now only drops the bombshell in passing and keeps moving.

Another way we don't stay in the story or stray from the story is to give up our control to our emotions or feelings. Feelings are biased, based on the short term rather than the long term and often prejudiced in favor of oneself and one's context.[47] Also called the "myside bias,"[48] this is all about feeling good about doing good without bothering about whether the good you are doing is actually doing any good. When the emotional highs of the best of intentions in virtue-signaling reign supreme over the more disciplined and deliberative constraints of value-rendering, political puritanism will find itself tacitly accepting ravaged wastelands like San Francisco, California; Chicago, Illinois; Seattle, Washington; and Portland, Oregon.

In the ancient Greek worldview, compassion, pity, mercy, and other visceral emotions were associated with the bowels and digestive organs rather than the heart. The Greek word "*splagchnon*" meaning both "gut" and "compassion" reflects this ancient perspective on emotions.[49] Maybe in our feeling-dominated culture, where knee-jerk feelings and drum-roll outrages override mindful reflection and rational deliberation, it's time for some gut checks.

The Jesus Mind is a whole brain mindset. It pays attention in a way that requires both sides of the brain. We trust our feelings and emotions to give us information about ourselves and the world around us. But we should never give our emotions control over our story or to undermine trust in the story.

*The Christian life itself should be
our greatest work of art.*
FRANCIS SCHAEFFER[50]

If Jesus himself "increased in wisdom and stature"[51] as he matured, to put on the mind of Christ is to be like Jesus: to grow over a lifetime in wisdom, knowledge, and grace before God and others.

God did not design us to have the same opinions, but to have the same mind—the sound mind, the renewed mind, the one mind—of Christ. To put on the mind of Christ, though, is not to put on a cloak of one color but to put on a many-colored, many-splendored cloak. Not a monotonous monochromatic cloak, but an explosive, expanding kaleidoscopic cloak.

I like spinach on my sandwiches. My wife loves spinach, but never on her sandwiches. Diversity of opinion is a gift from God, and it allows us to learn from each other and to grow in our understanding of God and the world.

THE JESUS MIND

STUDIO LIVE

1) Why is getting history right, and knowing the traditions of the faith, so important to the mind of Christ? Novelist and essayist James Baldwin (d. 1987), who still shapes the national conversation on race and social justice, answered the question like this:

   > For the roots of the Black man's identity plunge deep into the hidden places of American life, far deeper than the roots of the white man's identity. The force of history comes from the fact that we carry it within us, are unconsciously controlled by it in many ways, and history is literally present in all that we do. It could scarcely be otherwise, since it is to history that we owe our frames of reference, our identities, and our aspirations.[52]

   * How do you respond to Baldwin's portrayal of the importance of knowing the past? How important is the past to you?

2) One day during her years at Radcliffe (1893–1898), Gertrude Stein sat down to write a philosophy exam. She just wasn't in the mood, though, so instead of answering its questions she penned a short note to her professor, William James: "Dear Professor James, I am so sorry, but really I do not feel a bit like an examination

paper in philosophy today." In due course Stein received a response from James: "Dear Miss Stein, I understand perfectly how you feel. I often feel like that myself."

He ended up giving her an excellent grade.[53] Why? William James rewarded her for her philosophical insight that summarized his own philosophy: one's own feelings in the moment are the paramount value and the ultimate arbiter.

* What grade would you have given Stein?

3) In the sixteenth century, everyone regarded Augustine as an authority on almost everything. Whether Protestant or Catholic, the authority was Augustine. In fact, one of the insults you could hurl at someone was "You seem not to have read St. Augustine."

This is what William Fulke hurled at Edmund Campion in the Tower, whereupon Campion challenged him to an intellectual duel in any university of his choosing, but especially a dispute "in St. Augustine in the University of Cambridge."[54]

* Why do you think Augustine was considered such an authority on almost everything in the sixteenth century?

* What are some of the potential benefits and drawbacks of having a single authority figure on religious matters?

* What are some of the challenges of interpreting the writings of a church father from a different historical and cultural context?

- How can we learn to read the writings of the church fathers in a way that is both respectful of their tradition and critical of their limitations?

- How can we learn from the debate between Fulke and Campion to engage in more productive and respectful dialogue on theological disagreements today?

4) Everyone seems to be seeking the secret of this or that—the secret of living to one hundred, the secret of fighting obesity, the secret of a happy marriage. Woody Allen professed to have found the secret of the universe in something very simple: "not to yodel," Woody Allen said.

- What if the secret of the universe is something as simple as saying "Yes!" to Jesus, "God's Everlasting Yes." Read and reflect on 2 Corinthians 1:20.

- Why do you think we make things in life so difficult?

5) There is no gospel guarantee that following Jesus on the path to Jerusalem will bring applause or acclaim, whether from family, friends, or the church. Quite the contrary. There will always be those who look at you as if you were headless, or had four heads, or were harbinger of the four horsemen of the apocalypse.

- Discuss some times when following Jesus was not easy, when you were misunderstood, or maligned.

- What area of your faith or values has been most difficult for your family, friends, or church community to understand or accept?

DESIGNER JESUS

- * When have you felt pressure to compromise your biblical convictions to avoid disapproval or rejection? How did you handle that?
- * What scriptural examples come to mind of faithfulness being met with opposition rather than acclaim? How do those stories encourage you?
- * Why do you think Jesus living often elicits criticism, even sometimes from other Christians?
- * What has helped you stand firm when you felt misunderstood or maligned for following Christ?
- * How can we grow in our willingness to obey God rather than seek human applause or approval?
- * What advice would you give someone struggling with feeling rejected for their faith?

6) God gave us rational knowing, but God also gave us intuition and imagination. Might these be our deepest, highest and least developed form of knowing? What might a sacred imagination, or a sanctified imagination, look like?

7) In the last act of Tristan and Isolde (1865), Richard Wagner pits a lone harp against ten woodwinds, the entire string section, four horns, two trumpets, three trombones and a tuba.

- * Ever know how that harpist feels . . . to play against almost the whole orchestra?
- * Do you have a story of when you felt like that harpist?

8) Ludwig Wittgenstein was haunted by the question of what makes the difference between "I lift up my arms" and "My arms go up"?[55] There are some people who can't tell the difference and don't care.

   * Do you think the church attracts more than its share of left-brained people who have trouble with metaphors and narratives and only want bullet points and fill in the blanks?

   * Why have we played whack-a-mole with more right-brained people like artists and creatives?

9) We can unwittingly be surrounded by beauty and live in a wonderland, only to discover one day what a beautiful and wondrous place it is.

   * How does Jesus open our eyes to the beauty around us and within us?

   * How often have you missed the wonder, the moment? How do you stop yourself from missing it?

10) In another book I put it like this: "To put on the mind of Christ doesn't mean we'll all end up thinking alike or that we'll merge and submerge all our differences; but it's a true coming together where the manyness of the Body of Christ can truly emerge in our oneness in the mind of Christ. When the Church Universal turns away from business models of organizational leadership and instead begins to trust and obey the Spirit, the global church will not march in step but dance in sync."[56]

    * Do you see more evidence of Jesus humans "marching

in step" or "dancing in sync?" How can Jesus humans learn to dance?

11) Do your neighbors think you are a Christian? Is that good enough? How well do you know your neighbors? What prevents you and them from becoming more neighborly?

12) Discuss this quote from Samuel Taylor Coleridge (d. 1834).

> In wonder all philosophy began, in wonder it ends, and admiration fills up the interspace; but the first wonder is the offspring of ignorance, the last is the parent of adoration.[57]

* If theology is the true "parent of adoration," have we made it the parent of argumentation?

* How can we make theology not sticks and stones to beat opponents with but a baton to conduct conversations with?

* What do you think Coleridge means by the "first wonder" versus the "last wonder"? How are they different?

* When have you experienced wonder that stemmed from ignorance versus a deeper awe rooted in understanding?

* How might retaining a sense of wonder prevent cynicism, even as knowledge grows?

* Does education and learning diminish wonder, or transform it into something more meaningful?

* How has your sense of wonder about life evolved

throughout different stages of your intellectual and faith journey?

* How could cultivating more wonder lead to deeper worship and appreciation of creation or the divine?

* In what ways does childlike wonder persist even in the midst of adult intellect and experience?

* How can we kindle more wonder about the ordinary? What practices help nurture it?

* Why is maintaining wonder important for continuing growth and having reverence for the mysteries of existence?

13) Which of these statements characterize you? The people in your church? Your community? Your denomination?

> I create, therefore I am (Adam and Eve)
>
> I eat, therefore I am (Fred and Wilma Flintstone)
>
> I think, therefore I am (Descartes)
>
> I feel, therefore I am (Spinoza)
>
> I have sex, therefore I am (Freud)
>
> I selfie, therefore I am (Kim Kardashian)
>
> I shop, therefore I am (Barbara Kruger)
>
> I doubt, therefore I am (Thomas Didymus)
>
> I believe, therefore I am (Billy Graham, David Copperfield)
>
> I do, therefore I am (John Macmurray)

> I act, therefore I am (Laurence Olivier)
>
> I act, therefore I am (Moses)
>
> I love, therefore I am (Jesus)

14) Marshall McLuhan wrote an 1967 article for *LOOK* magazine called "The Future of Education: The Class of 1989." In this article he predicted that the future would be one where everyone would no longer "earn a living" so much as "learn a living."

* How might the pace of technological and social change support the idea of needing to constantly learn new skills?

* What are some key areas of knowledge or skills you think will be most crucial to "learn" moving forward?

* How might the traditional model of education during childhood need to shift to support lifelong learning?

* What challenges do you think the transition to "learning a living" rather than just having a job presents for people?

* How can we make continual learning accessible and achievable for all people in society?

* What role does unlearning outdated assumptions play in this constant learning process?

* How might the idea of "learning a living" make you think differently about your own growth and that of future generations?

15) The "art" of healing refers to the skills, knowledge, and wisdom that require a lifelong pursuit of learning, unlearning, adaptation, and innovation.

   * What would it mean for the church to be a "healing place" again?

16) Read selections from *The Confessions of Saint Augustine* (circa 397–400), *The Imitation of Christ* by Thomas Kempis (circa 1418–1427), and *The Summa Theologica* (1265–1274) by Thomas Aquinas.

   * How difficult was it? How enriching was it?

   * How did it feel for you to acquaint yourself with some of the classics of Christianity?

   * How important is it to immerse yourself in the classics of the faith if we are to "put on the mind of Christ?"

17) "There are no dangerous thoughts; thinking itself is a dangerous activity."[58] Do you agree with this thesis from Hannah Arendt (d. 1975), a German-American political theorist and philosopher who is widely considered one of the most influential political thinkers of the twentieth century. Is there even such a thing as a "thought crime?"

   Arendt goes on to say that "Thinking without a banister means thinking without the security of a tradition, without the comfort of a fixed system of beliefs. It means confronting the world without a net."

   * How strong a banister of tradition do you think we need?

* How dangerous can it be to climb unknown stairs without a banister?

* Do you always need to hold on to a banister when climbing stairs, or is knowing that it's there enough?

* What is your banister?

18) One of the most important and influential novels of the twentieth century, which has been translated in forty languages and sold millions of copies worldwide, is Milan Kundera's *The Unbearable Lightness of Being* (1984). Discuss Kundera's own summary of his thesis at the end of his first chapter: "The lightness of being is not the absence of weight, but the ability to carry it lightly."

* What do you think Kundera means by the "lightness of being"? How might it differ from just superficiality?

* When in your life have you experienced a feeling of lightness, in spite of or amidst carrying burdens? What enabled that?

* How might holding things too lightly be detrimental? When does depth and commitment bring meaning?

* In what ways has modern life added to the "lightness" of existence for good or ill?

* Kundera connects lightness with eternal return and recurrence. Why might lightness feel unbearable when continuity is broken?

* What gives your life substance and stability even amidst the unpredictability of existence?

- Is the tension between lightness and weight an internal or external struggle? How do you manage it?
- How might this concept of existential lightness versus weight apply to your own life?

19) Repent ("metanoia") also means "change your mind." A Christ mind is one that can "change its mind."

- How often do we use our minds to justify our own stubborn opinions and not be open to changing our minds?
- How has your mind changed over the years?
- How good are you at repenting?

20) Pneumaplasticity is the Spirit's ability to move us beyond our current limits to adapt and rewire to negotiate new realities.[59] It is an expansion of neuroplasticity, the scientific name for our capacity to develop new pathways in our brains to replace or compensate for what has been damaged. Jesus gives us a pneumaplasticity (pneuma is the Greek word for spirit or breath) that enables us to see and hear and live in new ways.

For example, people who can't hear can lip-read, which the deaf call "hearing" not "seeing." Blind people can develop a sense of touch so sophisticated that they can braille and identify things that sighted people miss or can't see.

- Can you come up with some examples of pneumaplasticity, both from the Bible and from your own experiences? Here are some examples to prime the pump:

A vision gave Peter pneumaplasticity[60] after he had lived his entire life believing God's salvation was meant only for Jews. In the vision he discovered that "In truth . . . God shows no partiality. Rather, in every nation whoever fears him and acts uprightly is acceptable to him."[61]

The Son of God, Jesus himself, had pneumaplasticity when he submitted to the baptism of John in the face of his protests, assuring him, "Allow it for now, for thus it is fitting for us to fulfill all righteousness."[62]

*Discuss how God has worked around your blocked pathways to give you pneumaplasticity.

Chapter 11: Heart
A Jesus Heart

Wait for the Lord;
be strong and take heart
and wait for the Lord.

PSALM 27:14 NIV

As a child growing up in Bavaria, future Pope (Benedict XVI) Joseph Ratzinger liked to play being priest with his brother and sister. The two brothers would say mass while their sister, or the girl next door, would serve the elements. In Bavaria children didn't write to Santa but to the Christ Child. Here is one "Dear Christ Child" letter little Joseph Ratzinger wrote in old German script:

> Dear Christ Child, you will soon float down to earth. You want to bring joy to children. You also want to bring me joy. I wish for the Volks-Schott (missal), a green Mass

vestment, and a JESUS heart. I will always be good. Best wishes from Joseph Ratznger.[1]

One of the design features of a Jesus disciple is a "Jesus Heart." The ultimate signature of designer Jesus may even be a "Jesus Heart."

Take Heart: The art of the heart in a designer—Jesus' life is built on a real person and a figurative image: a Messiah and a metaphor. Jesus the Christ, Messiah, and the human heart, metaphor.

Ever since the Greek physician Galen upended Aristotle's conviction that the heart was secondary to the liver, the organ which Aristotle taught was "the principle seat of life," we have understood that the heart is a real muscle, a cardiac pump with four chambers that shoots blood throughout your body. But in Christian theology the heart is more than a muscle. This anatomical organ is a centering and controlling metaphor without which it is hard to imagine faith and practice.[2] The heart is a metaphor of such complexity and subtlety that if you get the metaphor wrong, a lot can go wrong.

Augustine warned about this when he said that the heart was more than the seat of our emotions, or our best impulses whether intellectual or moral, both of which are metaphorical uses of the heart. The bilobed heart is who we are—it is the core of our being.

Rice University philosopher Timothy Morgan believes emotions are from the future, while ideas are from the past.[3] I'm not sure he's right, but if he is then the head is the wellspring of the past and the heart is the wheelhouse of the future. "It is from within, from the human heart, that evil intentions come,"[4] Jesus warned. The heart is the seat of the divine within us. The God who comes to us from the future inhabits the human heart. God knows the human heart. The art of the heart is the essence of Designer Jesus in human formation.

<u>The Love Beat:</u> Love is what races the Jesus Heart. The realization has never sunk into some people that the heart of Christianity is not a creed, or philosophy, or morality, or set of ritual practices but a person who enables and ennobles us to love with Jesus' heart. This whole book is based on the premise that what we call "spiritual formation" is best described as Paul did, "Christ formation." Or in a more global-friendly and universal format, "human formation" with the particular proviso that Jesus is the fullest expression of what it means to be human.[5] Every human heart is designed to beat a Jesus Heart.

The gospel changes the heart, charges the body, channels the mind, channels the spirit—all the better to chalice the good and deliver us from evil. The life of faith is the life of Christ. It is not some sugary, sticky, sickly Cinnabon-glaze or fluffy buttercream frosting you smear on the surface of life. To live the designer Jesus life is to home the head in the heart, to locate the life of the mind in the hands of the heart.[6] Theology in the head stagnates into something stale and stinky unless it circulates as doxology in the heart and praxeology in the hands.

Discipleship is the name given to the phenomenon of falling deeper and deeper in love with Jesus.

Justification is the occupation of that love.

Sanctification is the maturation of that love.

Glorification is the coronation of that love.

Or to put the same thing differently:

Justification is the activation of Jesus. Sanctification is the animation of Jesus. Glorification is the celebration of Jesus.

Trust your Jesus Heart. That tingling spine, fluttering heart, gnawing stomach, clutching throat are some of the most trusted guides in the journey of faith.

If you should ask me what are the ways of God, I would tell you that the first is humility, the second is humility, and the third is humility.

WIDELY ATTRIBUTED TO ST. AUGUSTINE[7]

For God So Loved You: Jesus loves each of us from the inside out. One of the most astonishing statements in all of Scripture is seldom quoted: "He knew all people and needed no one to testify about anyone; for he himself knew what was in everyone."[8] Jesus proved his heart-art knowing in the story of the woman at the well. The Samaritan woman tells everyone, "Come and see a man who told me all that I ever did."[9] Philip's friend Nathaniel, the initial skeptic ("Can anything good come out of Nazareth?") later asks Jesus in amazed belief, "Where did you get to know me?"[10]

Jesus knows our hearts. When we sing "Since Jesus came

into my heart" we are singing metaphor theology. We don't literally mean that Jesus dive-bombed into our heart. We don't stuff Jesus down the caves of our cardiac. And if we get a heart transplant, or a mechanical heart, we are not removing Jesus from our lives.

But the figurative metaphor of the heart is more than a metaphor since without it we cannot understand the meaning of that actual figure who lived, died, and rose again. Nor can we understand human formation. To lose heart, to stray from the heart, to hurt heartfulness, is to lose our very being, to lose our humanity. When you turn away from God, you turn away from yourself. You "lose heart" and even "abandon heart." Or in the words of Augustine, "Why do you want to drift so far away from yourself? Turn back from your idle wandering. Return to your Lord. He is waiting. You have become a stranger to yourself. You do not recognize yourself. And you seek for Him who created you."[11] How quickly we can become "strangers to ourselves" when we lose sight of Christ.

Look within. Look at your heart. The brand identity of the divine is a signature "written on the heart."[12] "Designed by Jesus" is penned in the ink of the Holy Spirit, inscribed by a permanent marker that cannot be erased. As we have seen, just as the monogram "Knowledge, Wisdom, Truth" adorns the flap of every Robert Graham shirt, the monogram of the Messiah "Designed by Jesus" is the tattoo on every human heart.

God created the world to be more like a great song than a great machine or a "great chain of being." A world out of tune cannot listen to life in ways that lead to wellness and wholeness. A church out of tune cannot listen to the Spirit in ways that bring Jesus fully to life in their midst. Music tuned to a 432 Hz frequency is best for the heart. A-432 Hz is a little lower than the international standard pitch of 440 Hz, but that small difference of less than a third of a semitone can convey significant physical, psychological, and even spiritual consequences.[13] Some say a song tuned to 432 Hz is heart therapy.

<u>For God So Loved the Church:</u> Jesus designed his church to be more like a beating heart than a flowchart; a musical score more than a performance scorecard. Nothing causes the heart to beat faster and stronger than the sound of the name of Jesus. What rejoices and fortifies the heart of the church is the lifting up of the name of Jesus. A church is a community of "good hearts" whose breathings and heartbeats are in sync with the very heart of God. The heartbeat of Jesus is love.

This does not mean the church is perfect. Paul called David "a man after God's own heart,"[14] quoting Samuel's words in his rebuke of Saul.[15] But Jesus says little about David. The Davidic line is a mixed bag of rogues, reprobates, and shady characters. We all have compromised ancestors. Even Jesus. Like the church, we can both scorn David's violence, rapacity, and his proclivity toward the abuse and abandonment of women, while also treasuring his devotion, his tenderness, his poetic sensibilities, and his penchant for the posture of repentance. Love can be a "pain."

Jesus is proud to claim his "bride," the church, in the

same way God is proud to claim "I am the God of Abraham, Isaac and Jacob." If you know the story of these three characters, you are stunned that God would want to be associated with any one of them, much less all three. Their lives are a total disaster. They make a total mess of almost everything they touch, and most of the time can't seem to make a right decision. But God is not ashamed to be associated with them. In fact, God says that I'm proud to be the God that bears their name. I have entered their story, and their story is now my story, for better or for worse. Sin is at the heart of being human, which is why "while we were still sinners, Christ died for us."[16]

It's the same with the church, which often strays from the light, can get so little "right," and whose "issues" and "fusses" seem so far from the heart of God. The default heartbeat of a Jesus community is a drumbeat of love. A Jesus Heart thumps life and thrums love. If you don't see Jesus in the love-life of a person and a community, there is desperate need for a retuning and tune-up. Love is the heartbeat of being, the hammering of a Jesus Heart. When you're running from Jesus, you're running from your natural heartbeat.

Alexander the Great sought out worlds to conquer.

Star Trek sought out worlds to discover.

Jesus sent us forth to seek out worlds to love and heal.

It must be acknowledged that a religious organization is not inherently the same as a church. The designation of "church" refers to more than just a faith-based institution. A community of believers becomes the Body of Christ when it continues Christ's mission in the world and strives to be a powerful force for moral good, beauty, and truth in its immediate vicinity.

When the driving purpose of such a congregation shifts focus onto itself—becoming a religious country club, an exclusive family chapel, a political advocacy group, a members-only hospice providing private chaplaincies, or a platform for social climbing—has it not strayed from the essence of a church? In those cases, it shapes itself around a self-serving mission rather than God's healing mission in the world. This begs the critical question of whether God's global mission can indeed have a dedicated "church" as its steward and vehicle.

For God So Loved the World: A theory, made into John Guare's 1990 play *Six Degrees of Separation*, talks about six degrees of separation. In other words, a chain of connections can be made to link any two people in the world in a maximum of six steps or five intermediators.

Designer Jesus disciples have only two degrees of separation. The two degrees of separation are these:

1) I don't know you. But I know Jesus.
2) Jesus knows you and knows your heart.

Therefore, if I know Jesus, then I know you. Wherever you are in the world, I know you in our Jesus connection. Life is less what you choose to see, hear, taste, touch, and smell than what you choose to connect. And connection is a matter of the heart.

We have misread "The Greatest Commandment" passage and made two commandments out of what Jesus said was really One Commandment with two sides. Here is the passage for the Grand Commandment that should always be paired with the Great Commission:

> And one of the scribes came, and having heard them reasoning together, and perceiving that he had answered them well, asked him, Which is the first commandment of all?
>
> And Jesus answered him, The first of all the commandments is, Hear, O Israel; The Lord our God is one Lord: And thou shalt love the Lord thy God with all thy heart, and with all thy soul, and with all thy mind, and with all thy strength: this is the first commandment. And the second is like, namely this, Thou shalt love thy neighbor as thyself. There is none other commandment greater than these.[17]

Did you catch that "like?" Or as other translations put it "like unto it" but which some newer translations omit entirely? By "like unto it" Jesus is really saying that he is saying the same thing twice, just in a different way. So "The Greatest Commandment" or "You shall love the Lord your God, with all your heart, soul, mind, and strength" is saying the exact same thing as what is too often seen as the "next greatest commandment" but is in reality the flip of the same coin: "You shall love your neighbor as yourself."

We cannot separate our relationship with God from our relationship with each other, with Jesus even extending the definition of "neighbor" to include "enemy." We live out our union and communion with God, not just in a safe sanctuary but in the streets and corridors, websites and walkways of life. Nor can we "shave off" either side of "The Great Commandment."

God's Love Is an Extreme Love: I am worried. We are losing some good words, and baptizing some bad words as if they were good. It may be too late to do anything about it. The words I'm talking about? For example, the words "extreme" and "radical" have been hijacked by the culture. Resistance may be futile. "Extreme" and "radical" have now become bad, and "moderate" has become good. Extremism in common parlance is not simply "bad," it is reckless self-righteous hatred and destruction—the opposite of love.

But in a final, desperate sortie of rescue, let me make a case for why the world needs extreme love. The world does not need more moderate love or affectionate fondness.

Unconditional love is extreme. There is no other way to put it. Jesus loves with wild abandon. Jesus was a radical for his day. Mediocrity and lukewarmness have brought us to where we are today; they quickly dampen the spirit, sap motivation, and erode enthusiasm. Who would read a book entitled "Embrace Mediocrity." Or "How to Be a Second-Rate Disciple." Too much of the story we write with our lives today is this one: "God bless mediocrities everywhere" as poor Antonio Salieri curses God with an obscene gesture at the end of Peter Shaffer's play *Amadeus* (1979).[18]

Extremism is not evil in itself, something to renounce.

A JESUS HEART

Evil is what we denounce. For example, racism is evil. Racism is wrong, a lie. Extremism is not the problem. Evil is the problem. Racism and its vile offspring remain the true poisons we must expunge. Extremism is often virtue's burning spear that pierces racism.

Anyone want to celebrate lukewarm lovers? Anyone get married because they were moderately in love? Anyone get promoted because they had a mediocre job rating? Anyone want a half-hearted friend? The Medal of Honor graces no moderate acts of valor, and institutions reward no mediocre work. Ardent spirits need tempering and training, not killing. Within righteous extremism lies salvation; within blasé moderation lies decay. If we would inspire humanity, best to set brushfires of justice over firecrackers of compromise.

To be moderate in the face of God, would be profane. The goal is not accommodation but a transformation. A mediocre response to immensity is offensive to eternity.
RABBI ABRAHAM HESCHEL (D. 1972)

The clarion calls for "moderation" are sounded everywhere. Imam Feisal Abdul Rauf said in a speech at the Council on Foreign Relations: "The real battlefront, the real battle that we must wage together today, is not between Muslims and non-Muslims. It is between moderates of all faith traditions, against the extremists of all faith traditions."[19] Even our best minds, like Fareed Zakaria, are framing the problem in the context of radical vs. moderate:

> But let's be honest: Islam has a problem today . . . There is a cancer of extremism within Islam today. A small minority of Muslims celebrate violence and intolerance, and harbor deeply reactionary attitudes towards women and minorities. And while some moderates confront these extremists, not enough do so and the protests are not loud enough. How many mass rallies have been held against ISIS in the Arab world today?[20]

To take another example closer to home, the number one Catholic periodical in Europe, *The Tablet*, defines radicalization as the willingness to die for one's faith. Well, wait a minute. Am I willing to die for my faith in Jesus Christ? Yes. Jesus teaches me how to live, but also how to die. And there are some things I am willing to die for. Notice I didn't say kill for. I said die for. So this idea that "Radicalization produces people who are terrorists, willing to die for the cause" gives me pause.[21]

I refuse to say "Radical Islam." I refuse to say "Extreme Islam." But not for the reasons everyone is giving for not saying it.

I refuse to say "Radical Islam" and "Extreme Islam" because the words "radical" and "extreme" define the extent of God's love and forgiveness. In fact, I am a radical Christian, even an extreme Christian, if I claim Jesus living. Why can't we say instead "Mutant Islam" or "Mutant, Militant Islam" instead of "Radical" or "Extreme" Islam?

A JESUS HEART

The very concept of "tolerance" itself is the offspring of radicals and extremists. The pioneers of Western toleration were passionate Christians. They were radical Christians. They were known as extremists. If I don't want to be "moderate" in my faith I can't expect others to be "moderate." There are a lot of other faith traditions out there. If you're going to be a Jew, or a Muslim, or a Buddhist, or a Hindu, be passionate about it. Be a passionate Muslim. Don't be a lukewarm Buddhist, or a moderate Jew. Be passionate about your faith. If you are going to be a person of the atheist faith (and atheism is a faith system—I believe it takes more faith to be an atheist than a Christian), then be passionate about your faith. Don't be moderate about your faith. Passion and moderation cannot live at peace with one another, whereas moderation and indifference are casual bedfellows.

Or as the Apostle Paul confessed, he and others like Stephanas and his family were "addicted" to "the ministry of the saints."[22] In today's jargon, Paul was a Jesus junkie. Mother Teresa was an extremist and addicted to the poor. So too was Martin Luther King, Jr. When King was accused of being an extremist, he embraced the term. In his *Letter from Birmingham Jail* (1963), the tide-turning document of civil rights movement, King defended extremism:

> The eighth-century prophets were extremists in their contexts. Jesus was an extremist in his own context. Paul, an extremist in his context.[23]

After a roll-call of extremists, King asks the church in the famous paragraph 20: "What kind of extremists will we be? Will we be extremists for the preservation of justice, or will we be extremists for the cause of justice?"

Martin Luther King, Jr. also once said that in the dramatic scene of Calvary's hill, three people were crucified for the same crime: the crime of extremism. Two were extremists for immorality; the other, Jesus Christ, was an extremist for love.

"If any human being, man, woman, dog, cat or half-crushed worm," wrote Virginia Woolf, *"dares to call me 'middlebrow' I will take my pen and stab him, dead."*[24]

<u>Debased Gospel:</u> Jesus-brand extremism doesn't harm the heart, but plenty of other things too, starting with a debased gospel. So we guard the heart, the wellspring of life.

When coins were still made out of precious metals, people used to debase the currency through "coin clipping" or shaving. The debaser would cut off a piece of the precious metal and, after collecting a certain amount, he or she would then melt it down and either sell the precious metal or turn it into a new coin.[25] When someone "shaves off" either side of The Great Commandment, they have debased the coinage of the gospel.

A debased gospel will call people to "love God" yet will make room for people to treat their neighbors badly.

A debased Gospel will call people to "love their neighbor"

while forgetting this love for neighbor is based upon the *imago Dei* in which all of humankind has been made.

A debased gospel mutes the story of God's love affair with marginals and mavericks, those who don't follow the rules of culture and convention but the rule of God.

A debased gospel serves the wealthy and powerful, forgets the rejected and neglected, and mocks the true markings of a Designer Jesus disciple which are dirty hands, sore knees, soiled reputations, and tilted halos. Coin clippers in times past were considered as bad as counterfeiters today and would serve prison time if caught.

Those who clip away from either side of The Great Commandment may find themselves locked inside prisons of hatred, anger, and unforgiveness which may last for an eternity.

To be a church means baptizing the heart of a community's life into the Jesus life which is a *tov* life of beauty, goodness, and truth.

<u>Healthy Heart Beats for Treasure:</u> And treasure hunting. The designer life of Jesus hunts for Jesus treasures. "For where your treasure is, there your heart will be also."[26] Jesus' mother Mary was famous for her heart for treasure collecting. Before he was born, "Mary treasured up all these things and pondered them in her heart."[27] When he was twelve, "Mary treasured all these things in her heart."[28] The Greek word for "ponder" is *sunballousa*, which is Greek for "placing together for comparison."

What were "all these things" that Mary was treasuring in her heart?

The angel Gabriel's words.

Her cousin Elizabeth's words.

The shepherds' words.

The Hebrew Scripture's words about the Messiah's coming.

Every developing event, every new word, might yield more light to this astonishing unfolding.

So she kept adding to her treasure chest. She kept storing her treasures. She held all that was happening in a precious "casket" (originally a jewelry box). Over and over again, she unpacked it and spread it out on the table of her heart. Each time, she would arrange the pieces anew, placing the various elements in fresh configurations and making new connections. Today she would, perhaps, place the shepherds' words beside a passage from a Hebrew prophet. Tomorrow she might place the shepherds' words beside the words of Gabriel. On Thursday she might consider the shepherds' words as they related to Elizabeth's greeting. Mary reverently held each word of promise and providence to the light of God's Story, and compared it with other stored treasures in her story bag.[29] Somehow, she knew that "In [the promise of the Messiah's birth] are hid all the treasures of wisdom and knowledge."[30]

You can keep from making up your mind about some things. You can put off making up your bed until a tomorrow that never comes. But you can't abstain from making up your life and living out your dreams. The "treasures" we collect in our heart are the bricks and mortar of our dreams. The "treasures" of the heart are stones that become living stones, the sand in the oyster that becomes pearls and gemstones. Through the everyday press and pressures of living the story of God's love affair with marginals and mavericks, there is a permanent press of the heart.

A Healthy Heart Is a Racing Heart for Christ: Paul uses the phrase "in Christ" at least 164 times. To live "in Christ" is not to inhabit an altitude so high there is perpetual sunshine. To live "in Christ" is to find and live the light in every landscape of life and every topography of truth.

The phrase "heart calls to heart" is built on the proverb "Each heart knows its own bitterness, and no one else can share its joy."[31] The more you live with someone, the more you share each other's life and love and thoughts, the less you need to spend your time monitoring and analyzing the relationship. You come to share a silent heartbeat.

To be "in Christ" is not to have to analyze constantly the relationship, but to trust that shared heartbeat. Too much "spiritual formation" yields the "paralysis of analysis" for this very reason. The best explanation of the "paralysis of analysis"?

The plight of the centipede . . .

> . . . happy, quite,
> Until a toad, for fun,
> Enquired which leg came after which

> Which brought his mind to such a pitch
> He lay bewildered in the ditch
> Forgetting how to run.[32]

With all our heart we are to "run the race" to "win" the race. The world thinks of "winning" as:

> From nobody to UPSTART.
> From upstart to CONTENDER.
> From winner to CHAMPION.
> From champion to DYNASTY.

Jesus thinks of "winning" as:

> from nobody to somebody;
> from somebody to everybody;
> from everybody to everything;
> from everything to nothing;
> from nothing to nobody.

> *May God grant me to become nothing.*
> SIMONE WEIL

Victory in Jesus: To live in Christ is to inhabit the reality that the victory has already been won by faith. We are saved by hope. But the victory is by faith. Faith IS the victory. Not a victory we win, but a victory already won on the cross.

That's why when you start seeing mushroom clouds swelling out of the Scriptures, run for cover, not from the Scriptures, but from those working the fog machines. Followers of Jesus are high hopers who sound the alarm, not herald the apocalypse. Abandon hope, enter hell. Dante was right in his proposed sign over the entrance to hell: "Abandon hope, all ye who enter."[33]

The hope of the church is not in better people, or better preaching, or better worship, or better facilities. The hope of the church is not even in hope. The hope of the church is the Holy Spirit. There were no converts between Calvary and Pentecost. No healings, no miracles, no stories. Just two months' time of holing up, huddling, and hiding behind closed doors. What unlocked the doors? What unbolted the gates? What loosed the tongues? What opened the heart?

Wind and Fire.

When I pray—
a new heart create in me O Lord
that the bones which you have broken may
a while, rejoice.

JOHN F. DEANE, *A LITTLE BOOK OF HOURS* (2009).

When my mother died, her wings were ready but my heart was not. My spirit slumped into a tailspin. For months people would say to me, "Are you OK?" "Something's off." "What's wrong?" "Your spirit doesn't just seem right, Sweet."

So I started praying with King David, "O Lord, put a right spirit within me." Psalm 51:10 had been one of the last verses of Scripture I read to Mother as she fought valiantly congestive heart failure: "Create in me a clean heart, and put a right spirit within me." It took me a while, but suddenly I realized David goes on to identify and indemnify some of features of a "clean" or "pure" heart. A pure heart is a broken and bleeding heart. A sacred heart is a broken and bleeding heart: "a broken and contrite heart God will not despise."[34] My prayer changed: "Contrite my heart, O God, that it may not contract but contact with your broken heart."

Bible translator Eugene Nida says that there is a word for "love" in the language of the Miskito Indians of Nicaragua that literally means "pain in the heart." Love is a pain in the heart. Sometimes a pain in the neck too. Some things can light up the heart and break the heart at the same time. A child lights up your life. But is it possible to have a child without having your heart ripped out, your back broken, your gut inflamed, and your brain fried?

What is so "amazing" about "amazing grace?" Precisely this. The more your heart breaks, the stronger your heart gets, and the more vigorous your love. That's "amazing grace." Sometimes you meet someone whose heart is so big there is no room for ego. When that happens, you take your shoes off and kneel—in the presence of amazing-grace holiness.

A Jesus Heart keeps humanity at its heart. Where does your "heart go out?" The Jesus Heart races when its field of vision looks with the eyes of love at the world, not scoping out the powerful and scouting the successful, but scanning for the meek and marginal, the poor and pure, the persecuted and peacemakers. There is a direct connection between the state of the heart and the state of the world.

But what "breaks" the heart is different from what "harms" the heart. What is harmful to a Jesus Heart?

Harmful to Your Heart: Religion can be harmful to your heart. Faith will take the form of a religion, but religion is not faith but the architecture faith takes. Jesus is God's corrective to all of religion's mistaken images and notions of God.

Unforgiveness leads to a hardening of the heart. Every heart grows a shell; every cardiac muscle has grown a carapace. Forgiveness frees us from the cold caves of our cardiacs.

"Pride of heart" will kill the heart. Jesus is a paradoxical "servant king" with a Lamb's heart that was "completely humble and gentle"[35] and a Lion's heart that was confident and certain. Not a "heart of gold" as in the golden calf, or a prideful heart as in a pride of lions. But one heart with two opposite chambers: humbleness and confidence. The systole and diastole of the divine heart are humility and confidence. Jesus, Lord of mercy and grace, is gracious and humble in all things. He would never force or impose himself on anyone. He shows great courtesy in knocking at our door, and will go away if we insist. But his mercy endures forever. So count on this: He'll be back.

To seek the fulness of truth is not to claim a monopoly on truth. In fact, the more you travel on the path of knowledge towards wisdom and towards truth, the more humble and less haughty you are.

A critical, carping spirit can clog the arteries of the heart. When you listen to any kind of performance such as a voice from a singer, turn off the critical evaluation, and turn on the crucible which conceived the "event" in the first place. The tone of the heart behind the performance is more important than the tonality and technique of the voice in the performance.

Hesitancies of the heart cause all sorts of arrhythmias, which over time can de-form your heart. Jesus frees us from the cold caves of our cardiac and warms the heart with fires of courage and faith.

Spite. No spike can pierce the human heart, seizing it and freezing it, as icily as spite.

When sorrow strikes, solemnity and sobriety can put your heart on hold. Sadness without laughter is the solitary confinement of the soul. After his only son Hamnet's death in 1596, William Shakespeare sought solace in writing comedies. In weightlessness lies sacred power—the grace to elevate and levitate out of grief's mire, if only momentarily. Laughter leavens life's heaviness. Smiles stir hope's embers under stone-cold burdens. Though no facile cure for fissured souls, a dose of laughter's lightness bears its own healing.

In the darkest nights, the human spirit yearns for counterweights to life's gravity—wisps of wit and whimsy hinting at dawn's glow. Before critiquing positivity literature as "sunshine enemas," perhaps we should craft more works of bullish buoyancy as ballast against life's buffeting. Never ignoring or invalidating suffering, we yet honor life by drawing touches of light and lightness along its via dolorosa. If you would comfort the downcast, gift glimpses of beauty, silliness, giddiness, and gladness—lighten loads, even if only by even a fraction, awaiting the morning.

Take Heart: I am a person of faith. My faith is in Jesus

A JESUS HEART

Christ. If Jesus is in my heart, why do I hide my heart? Why do we hide from God what's on our heart? Why do we cloak our hearts from the One before whom all is laid bare? What keeps us from unburdening ourselves fully to the Lord who already sees and knows us utterly? Do we doubt that God can handle the heat of our rawest emotions—the scalding pain, the chilling doubt, the constricting fear? Why do we reduce our cries to tepid whispers, policy speeches for the divine?

Our mediocre minds and namby-pamby faith are reasons why we are afraid to tell God what's on our minds and hearts. Do we think we have a feeble-minded, faint-hearted God? Christ welcomed the cripple and the contrite, the zealot and the harlot, without flinching. God remains unshaken by the tremors of our hearts. However they may quake with joy, ache with sorrow, or smolder with anger—Jesus asks only that we offer every trembling piece of our true selves. God can handle whatever we bring. Peter himself went from saying "Teacher, do you not care if we perish?"[36] to "Cast all your cares on him, for God cares for you."[37]

Jesus connects our hearts to him, and through him to one another. Even to the point that when you are celebrated, and due honor is paid to someone else, a living Jesus disciple feels honored and takes pleasure in their honoring. This is the opposite of how the world works: "Every time a friend succeeds a part of me dies," Gore Vidal admitted in one of his novels.[38]

A rabbi taught his disciples to memorize and contemplate the Torah and Talmud. He studiously instructed them to place the prayers and holy words on their heart. One day a student asked the rabbi why he always used the phrase "on your heart" and not "in your heart." The master replied: "Only time and grace can put the essence of these stories in your heart. Here we recite and learn them and put them on our hearts, hoping that some day when our heart breaks they will fall in."[39]

"Take heart. It is I. Do not be afraid."[40] Jesus said this to his disciples as he comes to them walking on water.

Take Heart.

Designer Jesus disciples can take heart even when the world's heart is bursting and breaking because they share the same Jesus Heart.

STUDIO LIVE

1) How strong is this critique of the church today?

    > Ecclesiology is inseparable from Christology in the Pauline corpus. And that needs emphasizing, especially in evangelicalism in the US where what it means to be church often seems to have little connection with the story and character of the Jesus of the Gospels.[41]

* Do you agree that many churches today seem disconnected from the example of Jesus? Why do you think that is?

* What are some key values and behaviors of Jesus that you wish were better reflected in churches today?

* How might overly institutionalizing church undermine the organic community of followers Jesus modeled?

* What are some ways we could repivot our idea of church around Jesus' life and teachings?

* Does your current church community feel more defined by human traditions or the model of Christ? Examples?

* How can we harmonize necessary structure with recapturing the spirit of Jesus' ministry in churches?

* What does it look like practically for a church to align itself with the life of Jesus?

* How could our church better emulate the way Jesus

treated outcasts, sinners, women, children, and the vulnerable?

* Does the word "church" carry baggage today that obscures Jesus' vision of a faith community?

2) Discuss the Emic/Etic principle of "As above, So Below" or "In Here, Out There."

> There is a Wesleyan principle that "in here" and "out there" cannot be separated. For example, in a Jesus Peace, inner peace and "peace on earth, good will to all" are connected in a "peace that passes all understanding." The path to peace "in here" cannot bypass "out there," and vice versa. Another emic/etic example is the way personal holiness and social holiness are opposite sides of the same coin.

* In what ways have you experienced your inner spiritual growth being connected to outer action and service?

* How might focusing only on personal piety or only on activism both fall short on their own?

* What practices like prayer or meditation help ground you inwardly to live Jesus outwardly?

* How have you seen personal and social holiness intersect in your faith journey or in leaders you admire?

* What biblical examples model bringing inner devotion and outer action together in harmony?

- What causes the gaps between inward devotion and outward mission in believers?
- How might institutions lose sight of emic foundations while pursuing etic programs?
- What advice would you give new Christians on integrating inward and outward faith from the start?
- How have you struggled to overcome barriers between inner and outer spirituality in your walk?

3) God created us for fellowship with Christ and fellowship with his body—which includes all generations and all cultures. To be "out of fellowship" with one is to be "out of fellowship" with the other. For the past 1800 years the church has consistently taught that you can't have God as Father without Church as Mother.

- How important is the church in your life?

4) Wonder where that phrase "eat your heart out" came from? It doesn't come from anything having to do with envy or jealousy.

Some of the Aztec victims who had their heart ripped out and held before the people were volunteers. Positively Aztecan. Estimates of the number of people the Aztecs sacrificed a year ranged between 15,000 and 250,000 . . . They believed the sun would stop beating if there wasn't blood . . . so they'd drag anybody to the top of the mountain, and while they were still alive, cut open their chest and yank their bleeding heart out of them, take a bite out of it, and hold it up to the sun.

- Why do you think people volunteer for things that are bad for them?
- What are some examples of people volunteering for things that are bad for them?
- What are the potential consequences of volunteering for things that are bad for you?
- What are some ways to help people who are volunteering for things that are bad for them?
- What are some of the social and cultural reasons why people might volunteer for things that are bad for them?
- How can we create a society where people feel supported in making healthy choices, even when it comes to volunteering?

5) The Father's heart is filled with love. If Jesus, who shares his Father's heart, loves anyone and everyone, what does that make him? Does your church have a promiscuous reputation on account of its love for anyone and everyone? Or do you find such language offensive? If so, what language would you use that better defibrillates the church's heart to beat with the Father's heart?

6) Say this prayer, and explore its implications in everyday life:

> Lord, save me from my propensities, either for self-promotion or self-deprecation. Give me honesty and clarity of vision about who and whose I am, and help me receive others as a gift, just as they are, not as I would like them to be. Amen.

7) The Greeks didn't like extremes. They celebrate what they called *enkrateia* (self-control) and they lambasted the opposite they called *akolasia* (licentious excess). We are familiar with the first Delphic aphorism "know thyself." But there were two aphorisms inscribed on the lintel at the entrance of the Temple of Wisdom: *Gnwqi seauton* (Gnothi seauton): "know thyself;" and *Mhden agan* (Meden agan) "nothing too much" or "everything in moderation."

* If everything is to be taken in moderation, shouldn't that include moderation itself? In other words, "Everything in moderation, including moderation." How would you live this motto in everyday life? Is it still good advice to live by today?

* What are some areas of life where too much moderation can actually be harmful? Where should we indulge?

* If the ancient Greeks were right, what is one area of your life where you need more moderation?

* What do you think "know thyself" means for finding inner moderation and self-control? How well do you know your own limitations?

- Is moderation mostly about external behavior or internal character? Which is harder to cultivate?
- How would your life be different if you practiced more moderation? Would it be better or worse?
- Should principles like pursuing justice or peace be moderated? When is moderation not a virtue?
- How might technology and social media challenge living a moderate life today?

8) Faith is bringing three things together: head, hand, heart.

> Orthodoxy is right belief: Head
> Orthopraxy is right action: Hand
> Orthopathy is right feelings, right passion: Heart.

- Discuss how many have heard of any of these words. Most likely, people will know the word orthodoxy, and a few will know the word orthopraxy. But almost no one will know the word orthopathy. Why do you think this is? Why is faith more associated with the head and hand over the heart?

9) In Luke 21:34–35 ESV, Jesus said "But watch yourselves lest your hearts be weighed down with dissipation and drunkenness and cares of this life, and that day come upon you suddenly like a trap. For it will come upon all who dwell on the face of the whole earth".

- How do you "watch yourself" so that you don't become weighed down with life and your heart heavy?

10) Claire Carlisle has written a biography of Soren

Kierkegaard titled *Philosopher of the Heart* (2020). Who in your life has understood your heart the best? To whom have you bared your heart the most? How hard (or easy) is it to share your heart?

11) Ancient Romans invented the anatomical myth of the *vena amoris*, a tiny vein tying your fourth finger to your heart. This is the origin for the placement of the wedding ring on your fourth finger. But it wasn't until the late sixteenth and early seventeenth century that love became a primary basis for marriage, and petitions for annulment started reading "I said yes with my mouth but not my heart."

* Do you think the symbolism of wearing rings to signify love and marriage still matters today, or is it an outdated tradition? Why?

* If you could pick a different finger to wear a wedding ring on, which would you choose and why?

* Do you think marrying for love is still as valued today as in the past, or have priorities shifted?

* What are some other interesting historical wedding traditions you would have liked to experience? Which are you glad have changed?

* Do you know any stories about the origins of your own or your family members' wedding rings?

* What symbols, items, or traditions would you invent to represent love and commitment in a modern wedding?

Antiphon: Jesus Living

Beauty is to the spirit what food is to the flesh. A glimpse of it in a young face, say, or an echo of it in a song fills an emptiness in you that nothing else under the sun can. Unlike food, however, it is something you never get your fill of. It leaves you always aching with longing not so much for more of the same as for whatever it is, deep within and far beyond both it and yourself, that makes it beautiful.

AUTHOR, PREACHER FREDERICK BUECHNER (D. 2022)[1]

"This is my God and I will beautify him with praises."

What does this passage from Exodus 15:2 mean? The rabbis tell us:

> Adorn yourself before him by a truly elegant fulfillment of the religious duties, for example a beautiful tabernacle, a beautiful palm branch, a beautiful ram's horn, beautiful show fringes, a beautiful scroll or the

> Torah, written in fine ink, with a fine reed, by a skilled penman, wrapped with beautiful silks.[2]

When you blow the shofar, a ram's horn, don't just blow any horn—blow a beautiful horn. When you read the Torah, don't just read any Torah scroll, read a beautiful Torah scroll. When you sit down to eat at table, don't just eat any food, enjoy some exquisite cooking. When you become a disciple of Jesus, don't just become any disciple. Become an original Jesus disciple. Historian Lauren Winner has reminded us of the Jewish principle of *hiddur mitzvah*, the idea that "one does not just do the commandments, one 'beautified' them" in how one lived every aspect of one's everyday life.[3]

We are all marvels of design, one-of-a-kind masterpieces from the Master Beautician. God didn't make us to be a key that fits in the lock of every door it tries. We are made to make the most of the doors that open, to expect some doors to be closed, other slammed in our face, and to learn to pick out The Doorpost and The Door. Most of all, we are to learn to live life through the Narrow Door, the way of the cross, the cruciform life.

That Narrow Door is what opens life to its widest and weightiest landscapes and legacies. The beam for all crucifixion crosses, including the one carried by Jesus with help from the African Simon of Cyrene, had to be the heftiest weight-bearing timber of the exceptional trees ("cursed is he who is hung on a tree").[4] It was on this cross-beam Jesus shed much of his blood, just as at Passover the doorpost "lintel" on which the blood was sprinkled with a hyssop branch was the weight-bearing beam for the whole house made from the strongest beams from the most prominent trees.

◇

I say more: the just man justices;
Keeps grace that keeps all his goings grace;
Acts in God's eye what in God's eye he is—
Christ.

THEOLOGIAN/POET GERARD MANLEY HOPKINS[5]

Jesus is not a brand. Jesus is not a cause. Jesus is not a metaphor. Jesus is not a principle. Jesus is not a worldview. Jesus is not a religion. Jesus is Messiah, the One anointed to save the world. The culminating document of the Second Vatican Council was *Dei Verbum*. On 18 November 1965 it received the approval by the assembled bishops by a vote of 2,344 to 6. In the words of the document, "Jesus Christ himself is both the mediator and the sum total of revelation" (n.2). Jesus is All in All. And it is our mission to make him all in all and continue his mission.

A cancer cell is not a toxic cell, or a diseased cell, or an evil Pac-Man out to engross everything in its path. A cancer cell is a normal cell, just like every other cell in your body, with one difference. It is a cell without a mission. It has no assignations or assignments. It is disconnected from any organ, a rogue cell unrelated to all the other organs and functions, and thus can't contribute anything to the organism but to grow. It's only purpose in life is to grow. It has no other mission than growth. So it feeds on the food that comes in, stealing nutrients from the mission-driven cells, and grows and grows until it takes over the whole body and starves all the other cells that have functions and purposes and missions.

When the human mission becomes other than a God mission, humans become sub-human and in-human, and enter the chaos zone.

<u>Tohuvavohu Chaos:</u> *Tohuvavohu* (Tohu wa-bohu) is a Hebrew phrase found in the Genesis account of creation. The KJV translation of the phrase is "without form, and void," corresponding to the LXX ἀόρατος καὶ ἀκατασκεύαστος, which means literally "unseen and unformed." In a world where the forces of decreation and deformation are returning us to chaos, the need for human formation or Christ formation is greater than ever.

It started in cricket, then spread across the sporting world—the language of a player being "on form." What does it mean for a disciple of Jesus to be "on form?" How do you find "form?" What happens if you lose form, and how do you maintain form or regain it? Loss of form can mean the end of a career.

It is high praise to honor someone with the words "good form." What is the Jesus form? When you live the Jesus life, what does it look like? That is the question that has driven the writing of *Designer Jesus*.

JESUS LIVING

> *May all my life be sacrificed to the sublime.*
> *May it be a sanctuary of art.*
> BEETHOVEN[6]

The language of the Scriptures is less Christ being "in us" than our being "in Christ." To live "in Christ" is to live the Jesus life, to so allow his story to become our story that we become the literal meaning of "Christian"—"little Christs"—and Jesus lives his resurrection life in us and through us.

The "good news" of the gospel is God in Christ born, restored and resurrected in and through us as members of his body, the church. To live the Jesus life is to live the Jesus story. Don't need to say any more since Jesus in his ascended state is at the "right hand of the Father," where he lives in, through, and as us. That's why "it is good for you that I go away." We become "a new creature" (2 Corinthians 5:17), a "new person" (Ephesians 4:24, Colossians 3:10) as we let Jesus author our story and become our authority for living. Our new identity is "in Christ."

Christophany: The influence of Thomas Merton (d. 1968) is even greater now than when he was celebrated upon his death as the greatest spiritual leader of his time. Merton was once asked to speak to the novices at the Trappist monastery called The Abbey of Gethsemani near Bardstown, Kentucky. "Fr. Louis," as he was known because of his baptismal name, was living in a Hermitage at the Abbey that had been built for him by his brothers in 1960. The words of welcome to the novitiates focused on the nature of a Christophany:

> What you came here for is to become yourself, to discover your complete identity, to be you. But the catch is that of course our full identity as monks and Christians is Christ. It is Christ in each of us . . . I've got to become me in such a way that I am the Christ that can only be the Christ in me. There is a Louis Christ that must be brought into existence and hasn't matured yet. It has a long way to go.[7]

A Christophany is an expression or manifestation of Jesus Christ, either in physical form or as a vision. The term comes from the Greek words *Christos* ("Christ") and *phainesthai* ("to appear"). The term Christophany most often has been used to describe visions of Christ reported by Christians throughout history. Some visions have been private, while others have been witnessed by multiple people.

In the companion volumes of *Jesus Human* and *Designer Jesus*, we have argued that each human is designed to be a christophany: Love imaged in human form, a manifestation of Jesus living. But participating in the divine nature, or "union with Christ," does not mean we become "gods," which would be polytheism. Nor does it mean that we become God as Father, Son, and Holy Spirit. A Christophany means that we share in the divine "energies," not essence. Christ is represented in us, embodied "in us" and enfleshed "as us:" "As

He is, so are we in this world."[8] A Christophany means Jesus living, and a disciple is precisely that: a Jesus living life.

The highest epitaph at the end of my life would be this one:

Here was Jesus Christ in Len Sweet form.

Connect with Leonard

For more from Leonard Sweet:

Websites:
    www.leonardsweet.com
    www.preachthestory.com
    www.sanctuaryseaside.com

Instagram: @leonard.sweet

Facebook:
    facebook.com/lensweet
    facebook.com/preachthestory
    facebook.com/sanctuaryseaside

Twitter: @lensweet

YouTube: www.youtube.com/@leonardsweet1

Podcast: www.leonardsweet.com/podcasts

Napkin Scribbles Podcast:

    Spotify:
    https://open.spotify.com/show/2vt6wEi70dQEpW37CypfvY

    iTunes:
    https://podcasts.apple.com/gb/podcast/napkin-scribbles-a-podcast-by-leonard-sweet/id1436743015

Scripture Versions

Scripture quotations marked NIV are taken from the Holy Bible, New International Version®, NIV®. Copyright © 1973, 1978, 1984, 2011 by Biblica, Inc.™ Used by permission of Zondervan. All rights reserved worldwide. www.zondervan.com. The "NIV" and "New International Version" are trademarks registered in the United States Patent and Trademark Office by Biblica, Inc.™

Scripture quotations marked KJV are taken from the Holy Bible, King James Version.

Scripture quotations marked NASB are taken from the NASB® New American Standard Bible®, Copyright © 1960, 1971, 1977, 1995, 2020 by The Lockman Foundation. Used by permission. All rights reserved. lockman.org

Scripture quotations marked NKJV are from the New King James Version.® Copyright © 1982 by Thomas Nelson, Inc. Used by permission. All rights reserved.

Scripture quotations marked ESV are from The Holy Bible, English Standard Version® ESV®, copyright © 2001 by Crossway, a publishing ministry of Good News Publishers. Used by permission. All rights reserved.

Scripture quotations marked NLT are taken from the Holy Bible, New Living Translation, copyright ©1996, 2004, 2015 by Tyndale House Foundation. Used by permission of Tyndale House Publishers, Carol Stream, Illinois 60188. All rights reserved.

Scripture quotations marked AMP are taken from the Amplified Bible, Copyright © 2015 by The Lockman Foundation. Used by permission.

Scripture quotations marked CSB have been taken from the Christian Standard Bible®, Copyright © 2017 by Holman Bible Publishers. Used by permission. Christian Standard Bible® and CSB are federally registered trademarks of Holman Bible Publishers.

Scripture quotations marked MSG are taken from The Message, copyright © 1993, 2002, 2018 by Eugene H. Peterson. Used by permission of NavPress. All rights reserved. Represented by Tyndale House Publishers.

Scripture quotations marked CEV are from the Contemporary English Version Copyright © 1991, 1992, 1995 by American Bible Society, Used by Permission.

Scripture quotations marked ASV are from The American Standard Version of the Holy Bible which is in the Public Domain.

DESIGNER JESUS

Scripture quotations marked DRA are from the Douay-Rheims 1899 American Edition which is in the Public Domain.

Scripture quotations marked LEB are from the Lexham English Bible. Copyright 2012 Logos Bible Software. Lexham is a registered trademark of Logos Bible Software.

Scripture quotations marked YLT are taken from the 1898 YOUNG'S LITERAL TRANSLATION OF THE HOLY BIBLE by J.N. Young, (Author of the Young's Analytical Concordance), public domain.

Scripture quotations marked PHILLIPS are from the The New Testament in Modern English by J.B Phillips copyright © 1960, 1972 J. B. Phillips. Administered by The Archbishops' Council of the Church of England. Used by Permission.

Scripture quotations marked TJB are from The Jerusalem Bible © 1966 by Darton Longman & Todd Ltd and Doubleday and Company Ltd.

Scripture quotations marked NRSV are from the New Revised Standard Version Bible, copyright © 1989, Division of Christian Education of the National Council of the Churches of Christ in the United States of America. Used by permission. All rights reserved.

Scripture quotations marked RSV are from Revised Standard Version of the Bible, copyright © 1946, 1952, and 1971 National Council of the Churches of Christ in the United States of America. Used by permission. All rights reserved worldwide.

Scripture quotations marked NRSVCE are from the New Revised Standard Version Bible: Catholic Edition, copyright © 1989, 1993 the Division of Christian Education of the National Council of the Churches of Christ in the United States of America. Used by permission. All rights reserved.

Scripture quotations marked NRSVA are from the New Revised Standard Version Bible: Anglicized Edition, copyright © 1989, 1995 National Council of the Churches of Christ in the United States of America. Used by permission. All rights reserved worldwide.

Scripture quotations marked BSB are from The Holy Bible, Berean Standard Bible. Scripture quotations marked BLB are from The Holy Bible, Berean Literal Bible. They produced in cooperation with Bible Hub, Discovery Bible, OpenBible.com, and the Berean Bible Translation Committee. This text of God's Word has been dedicated to the public domain.

Scripture quotations marked NEB are taken from the New English Bible, copyright © Cambridge University Press and Oxford University Press 1961, 1970. All rights reserved.

Scripture quotations marked TLB are taken from The Living Bible, copyright © 1971 by Tyndale House Foundation. Used by permission of Tyndale House Publishers, Carol Stream, Illinois 60188. All rights reserved.

Notes

FRONT MATTER

1. Augustine, *Confessions*, Book 8, Chapter 1.
2. Thomas Merton, *New Seeds of Contemplation* (1962), 41.

INVOCATION

1. Galatians 4:19 ASV
2. See Michael Mott, *Thomas Merton: The Seven Storey Mountain* (1999), 545, and the whole section on Merton's death.
3. See F. F. Bruce, *The Epistle to the Galatians: A Commentary on the Greek Text* (1982), 212. With thanks to colleague Jorge Finley for pointing me to this reference. For a sermon which helps us come alive to the meaning of this metaphor, see Ken Ulmer's farewell sermon "I Did My Best" to his congregation of 41 years at Faithful Central Bible Church, https://www.youtube.com/watch?v=eMzFiZ_jn9k. Accessed 09 January 2024.
4. John 1:14 NIV
5. 2 Corinthians 13:5 NIV
6. Romans 8:10 KJV
7. Galatians 2:20
8. Galatians 4:19 ESV
9. The phrase "wardrobe malfunction" was coined and popularized by Justin Timberlake and USAmerica's CBS network after the 2004 Super Bowl halftime show incident where Janet Jackson's breast was exposed by Timberlake.
10. Romans 13:14 NIV
11. See Leonard Sweet, *I Am a Follower: The Way, Truth and Life of Following Jesus* (2012).
12. The first time I encountered this phrase was in Leighton Ford, *The Attentive Life: Discerning God's Presence in All Things* (2008).

13. Shakespeare, *Othello*, act 1, scene 1.
14. Scot McKnight calls this "Christoformity." See his *Pastor Paul (Theological Explorations for the Church Catholic): Nurturing a Culture of Christoformity in the Church* (2019).
15. Hebrews 5:11–12 NEB
16. Hebrews 5:12 NEB
17. Leo Tolstoy, *War and Peace* (1869), translated by Rosemary Edmonds. Book 1, Chapter 2, 23.
18. John 15:4 NKJV
19. "Bond" was John Calvin's word to describe how the Spirit attaches Jesus to us. "The Holy Spirit is the bond by which Christ effectually unites us to himself; so that we are not only partakers of his benefits, but also made one with him, and so ingrafted into his body, that as the head lives, so do the members also" (*Institutes of the Christian Religion* [1536], 3.1.1). See also Calvin's *Commentary on Ephesians* 1:13–14, *Commentary on Galatians* 3:27, *Sermon on John* 15:4–5.
20. Galatians 2:20 ESV
21. Tom Chivers, *The AI Does Not Hate You* (2019).
22. John 8:12 ESV
23. Matthew 5:14 NIV
24. Early documented uses of this phrase are in the writings of biblical translator Saint Jerome (d. 420), who applied the phrase to priests, as did Thomas Aquinas in the thirteenth century. But Augustine used it first to describe all Christians, not just priests.
25. There are many "alter-ipse" passages in the Scripture, including Romans 8, where the Christian is referred to as "the mouth . . . by which the Father spoke." But perhaps the most contentious of all is John 7:37–39, an "alter-ipse Christus" passage that has divided scholars, but more importantly, divided Christianity itself into eastern and western branches. "Rivers of living water will flow from within them." Who's the "them?" "Out of his belly shall flow rivers of living water." Whose "belly" is it? The Eastern Church said that the "belly" is all disciples living in the Spirit. The Western Church said that the "belly" is Jesus himself, or, as John Wesley argued, it was the "effusion of the Spirit by the Messiah." But both the eastern punctuation and the western punctuation understand the Spirit as the "effusion" of Jesus. The eastern interpretation focuses on the stream and flow of the Spirit of Christ in the life of disciples. The western

NOTES

interpretation focuses on the sourcing of that stream of the Spirit in Jesus, the new center of the messianic community and the eschatological temple. The outpouring of the Spirit flows from inside the glorified Jesus (western) through the insides of every disciple (eastern). The literature is extensive, but see Joseph R. Greene, "Integrating Interpretations of John 7:37–39 in to the Temple Theme: The Spirit as Efflux from the New Temple," *Neotestamentica* 47 (2013), 333–353.

26. St. Augustine, *Tractates on the Gospel of John* 21.8, 100.

27. For a soundtrack to this teaching, see *Christ is Mine Forevermore* sung by The Worship Initiative.

28. See Leonard Sweet, *Rings of Fire* (2019).

29. Paraphrase of a passage from the Gospel of John, Chapter 15, verses 4–5: "Abide in me, and I in you. As the branch cannot bear fruit by itself, unless it abides in the vine, neither can you, unless you abide in me. I am the vine; you are the branches. Whoever abides in me and I in him, he it is that bears much fruit, for apart from me you can do nothing."

30. For John Wesley, the founder of my tribe, the basic meaning of "holiness" was wholeness, completeness, perfection. Personal holiness is harmony of the physical, mental, social, and emotional components of human existence. In other words, holiness was an aesthetic term that had less to do with keeping God's commandments than with glorifying and pleasing God by living the ongoing life of Christ. Wesley could not have been more clear: perfection was "loving God with all our heart, mind, soul, and strength." That word "all" became the source of the passion of holiness. Holy is to have the restoration of God's image in us and to hear the words "very good" spoken over the harmony of relationships between us and God, ourselves, each other, and creation. Holiness is a state of shalom between this quadrilateral of relationships.

31. The twenty-first century began with a design renaissance. By 2010, it was hard to find a company that had not climbed aboard the design bandwagon. In 2004 *Fast Company* identified the trend by featuring twenty designers and design advocates: "Design shapes a company's reason for being; it has become an undeniably transformative force in business and society." But much of the "design revolution" in the corporate world involved incentivizations revolving around efficiency, not design. In current pursuits of sustainability and accessibility, the design focus has stalled somewhat in the business world even though design has assumed an importance in the culture unexpected and in some ways unprecedented except perhaps in the Victorian era. *Designer Jesus* introduces a more

encompassing, more expansive view of design than a skeuomorphism or neumorphism.

32. My use of "aesthetic" is almost the opposite of how Kierkegaard used the word and critiqued the concept: "the flight into imagined possibilities, into fantasy, is the essence of what Kierkegaard calls the 'aesthetic' attitude to life. It is a way of keeping life at a distance, a result of not being willing to acknowledge the claims which life makes upon us." G. Pattison, "Soren Kierkegaard and Imagination," *Theology*, 87 (1984), 10.

33. The poet Richard Wilbur is the first one I know of to bring together the words habitude and hebetude. See his poem "Grace," p. 455 of *Collected Poems* (2006).

34. As quoted in *The Tablet*, 14 April 2018, 9.

35. For an excellent application of design thinking in the local church, especially those in the liturgical traditions, see Lorenzo Lebrija, *How to Try: Design Thinking and Church Innovation* (2021). For a short history of design thinking, see pages 9–10.

36. The concept of "iconomy" comes from Peter Szendy in *The Supermarket of the Visible: Toward a General Economy of Images* (2019).

37. Matthew 15:8–9

38. Ron Mehl, *God Works the Night Shift* (1994), 31.

39. Virginia Woolf, *Orlando: A Biography* (1928), 15.

40. Physicist Brian Greene uses the acronym GOD to refer to "Grand Organizing Design" in his marvelous *The Elegant Universe: Superstrings, Hidden Dimensions, and the Quest for the Ultimate Theory* (2003).

41. For more on the MRI design as the Operating System for life, see my *So Beautiful: Divine Design for Life and the Church* (2009).

42. Genesis 3:21. Paul's profession of tent-making was really sewing leather to make tents.

43. Jonas Holst, "The Fall of the Tektōn and The Rise of the Architect: On The Greek Origins of Architectural Craftsmanship," *Architectural Histories*, 5 (2017), 5. "We should be careful not to announce wood to be a kind of singular prima materia of tectonics."

44. 1 Corinthians 3:10

45. One time in the Bible archi-tekton or "architect" or "master craftsman" or "master assembler of materials" is used, and Paul uses it of himself: "According to the grace of God which is given unto me, as a wise

masterbuilder (architect), I have laid the foundation, and another builds thereon. But let every man take heed how he builds thereupon" (1 Corinthians 3:10 KJV).

46. Aristotle, *Nicomachean Ethics* 1141a.
47. *Nicomachean Ethics* 1141a.
48. Jonas Holst, "The Fall of the Tekton and The Rise of the Architect," 4–5.
49. Dan Hooper, *Nature's Blueprint: Supersymmetry and the Search for a Unified Theory of Matter and Force* (2008), 5.
50. John 2:11–12. "*Doxa*" can mean "beauty" or "glory" or "radiant splendor."
51. Adam Ford, *Universe: God, Man and Science* (1986), 78.
52. . . . for your business or meetings or baby's birth https://www.ritualdesignlab.org/. Accessed 09 January 2024.
53. Sigal Samuel, "A Design Lab is Making Rituals for Secular People," *Atlantic*, 07 May 2018, 36–38.
54. Kursat Ozenc and Margaret Hagan, *Rituals for Work: 50 Ways to Create Engagement, Shared Purpose, and a Culture that Can Adapt to Change* (2019), 118.
55. A. S. Byatt, *A Biographer's Tale* (2000), 156–7.
56. G. K. Chesterton, *The Everlasting Man* (1955), 21–38.
57. J. K. Elliott, "Beyond the Bible," *Times Literary Supplement*, 16 December 2016, 15.
58. Genesis 1:4, 10, 12, 18, 21, 25 KJV
59. Genesis 1:31 KJV
60. E. Stanley Jones, *In Christ*, as quoted in Whitney J. Dough, ed., *Sayings of E. Stanley Jones: A Treasury of Wisdom and Wit* (1994), 35.
61. Philippians 4:8 KJV
62. George Fox, the founder of the Quakers, is known for referring to Jesus as the "Inner Light," but he also liked to refer to Jesus as "The Seed." See Fox's book *Some Principles of the Elect People of God Who in Scorn are called QUAKERS: For all People throughout all Christendom to Read over, and thereby their own States to Consider* (1661), Section XII on "The Higher Power."
63. John Keats, "Ode on a Grecian Urn." *Annals of the Fine Arts*, 4 (1820),

444–450. The quote appears in the final lines of the poem's fifth and final stanza.

64. For the trust-worthiness of the three transcendentals, see Iain McGilchrist, *The Master and his Emissary* (2019), 443: "We can't remake our values at will. There may of course be shifts in art theory, but that is distinct from beauty itself, and we cannot rid ourselves of the value of beauty by a decision in theory. In this, beauty is like other transcendental ideals, such as goodness. Societies may dispute what is to be considered good, but they cannot do away with the concept. What is more the concept is remarkably stable over time. Exactly what is to be considered good may shift around the edges, but the core remains unchanged. Similarly, exactly what is to be called beautiful may vary a little over time, but the core concepts of beauty remain, which is why we have no difficulty in appreciating the beauty of mediaeval or ancient art despite the passage of centuries."

65. https://www.nobelprize.org/prizes/literature/1970/solzhenitsyn/facts/. Accessed 09 January 2024.

66. Susanne Sklar, "How Beauty Will Save the World: William Blake's Prophetic Vision," *Spiritus*, 7 (2007), 30, 30–39.

67. The global beauty industry was valued in 2017 at 523 billion, with expectations to reach 800 billion by 2025. Irina Dumitrescu, "We're All Jessica Rabbit Now," *Times Literary Supplement*, 23 October 2020, 10.

68. Letter to Theo, 1 June [1882], in *The Complete Letters of Vincent van Gogh* (3rd ed.; 2000), 1:379.

69. Third Apostolic Exhortation, 19 March 2018, *Gaudete et Exsultate (Rejoice and Be Glad)*, 13.

70. For more on this see my *The Well-Played Life: Why Pleasing God Doesn't Have to Be Such Hard Work* (2014).

71. Sociologist Edward Carpenter quoted a Balinese villager, as cited by Edwin Schlossberg, *Interactive Excellence: Defining and Developing New Standards for the Twenty-first Century* (1998), 32.

72. *The Essential Rumi* (1995), Coleman Barks and John Moyne, translators.

73. Luigi Perissinotto and Begoña Ramón Cámara, *Wittgenstein and Plato: Connections, Comparisons and Contrasts* (2013).

74. Austrian philosopher Ludwig Wittgenstein, *Tractatus Logico-Philosophicus*, trans. D. F. Pears and B. F. McGuinness (1961). Originally published in 1921.

NOTES

75. Mark S. Burrows, "Raiding the Inarticulate: Mysticism, Poetics, and the Unlanguageable," *Spiritus*, 2004, 173–204.

76. For more on Miami's starchitects and their car parkitecture, see "Pile 'em in Style," *The Economist*, 07 January 2017, 66.

77. See Virginia Postrel, *The Substance of Style: How the Rise of Aesthetic Value Is Remaking Commerce, Culture, and Consciousness* (2009). Also see special report in *The Economist* on "The Beauty Business" called "Pots of Promise." (24 May 2003), 69–71.

78. William Wilberforce, "Letter to John Newton dated October 20, 1787." In *The Letters of William Wilberforce*, edited by John Stephen Taylor (1860), 17.

79. Quoted in *The Tablet*, 10 September 2016, 15.

80. 1 Peter 2:25 NIV

81. Ephesians 4:11–12

82. This is the concept devised by German philosopher and sociologist Theodor Adorno (1903–1996), a concept best elaborated by Josh Robinson, *Adorno's Poetics of Form* (2018).

83. 1 Corinthians 14:10

84. H. A. Williams, *The Joy of God* (1979), 20.

85. Ephesians 5:23b LEB

86. Psalm 36:9

87. In a 1750 edition of *Poor Richard's Almanack*, Franklin wrote: "His tools must be proportioned to his work, or his work can never be completely performed." This is as close to the quote I have been able to find.

88. *Fast Company*, October 2015, 17–18.

89. People don't always know what they want. For example, focus groups hated the clear plastic bins that showcased the dirt in Dyson prototypes. Engineers loved it and voiced their preference with such vociferation that the company ignored the data from the focus groups and went with the engineers.

90. See *Poems of Gerard Manley Hopkins* (1918), 44.

91. Richard Dawkins, *River Out of Eden: A Darwinian View of Life* (1995), 131–32.

92. As quoted by William Wootten, "Flying Ant Day at Jam Tree Gully," *Times Literary Supplement*, 26 May 2017, 31.

93. Here is the link to the video: https://www.youtube.com/watch?v=-6hUsnOkdOA. Accessed 09 January 2024.

94. α or alpha is the "magic number," also known as "the fine-structure constant" that has a fine-tune value making life possible and the universe "fine-tuned for life." It's a deep mystery of physics how it came to be. What makes it even more mysterious is that it's a number that varies from place to place depending on where in the universe you place it.

    The exact number is the result of starting with the square of an electron's charge, divide it by the speed of light and Planck's constant, then multiply that number by two pi. What you end up with is a pure dimensionless number. The result is 1/1370.036.

    Alpha doesn't carry through time, only thru space. In other words, maybe there are "higher dimensions" that elude us, and that physical laws are not the same everywhere.

CHAPTER 1

1. "Walk It, Talk It," Migos and Drake (2018).

2. John 14:16. Recently I was struck to read how literalist an atheist biblical scholar could be. British professor Francesca Stavrakopoulou has written a disturbingly literalist interpretation of "God's anatomy" in Scripture. When the Bible says that God "loved Israel," this University of Exeter professor of ancient religions takes this to mean God wants to have sex with her. But amidst all the hokum and horsefeathers of her Hebrew anthropomorphism, she does get one thing right. She begins the book with God's "Feet and Legs."

    When it comes to divine physicality, she insists, Yahweh clearly is a walking God. God uses the Temple as a footstool and enjoys plodding the Earth in sandaled feet (leather flip-flops) while worshipers kept up and kept company in bare feet, as Moses learned from a divine scolding. Francesca Stavrakopoulou, *God: An Anatomy* (2022).

3. Although the precise origins of this song are cloudy, most hymnologists attribute it to African-American origins, and the first known recording was by the Selah Jubilee Singers in October, 1941.

4. Matthew 5:41

5. Graham B. Usher, *The Way Under Our Feet: A Spirituality of Walking* (2020) 58.

6. Amanda Rees and Charlotte Sleigh, *Human* (2020), 9–10.

NOTES

7. Ephrem the Syrian, "Commentary on Genesis 2.24," as found in *Commentary on Genesis, Vol. 1.* Translated by Edward G. Mathews Jr. and Joseph P. Amar (1994), 89.

8. John Chrysostom, "Homilies on Genesis 17.3.4," as found in *Homilies on Genesis, Homily XXXVIII.* Translated by Robert C. Hill (1981), 245–246.

9. Job 9:8 LEB

10. For the Jesus' Walk on the Sea, see Matthew 14:22–36; Mark 6:45–56; John 6:16–21.

11. Matthew 12:1–8

12. Luke 23:26–32

13. John 18:12

14. "Jesus knew that the Father had put all things under his power, and that he had come from God and was returning to God . . . After that, he poured water into a basin and began to wash his disciples' feet, drying them with the towel that was wrapped around him" John 13:3–5 NIV.

15. Acts 3:1–10

16. Welsh poet George Herbert (d. 1633) deemed and esteemed Isaiah 35 one of his favorites, so beautiful he simply couldn't stop reading it. He especially loved the passage about the holy highway Isaiah called "The Way of Holiness:"

    The wilderness and the solitary place shall be glad for them; and the desert shall rejoice, and blossom as the rose. It shall blossom abundantly, and rejoice even with joy and singing . . . and the parched ground shall become a pool and the thirsty land springs of water . . . and a highway shall be there . . . and it shall be called The Way of Holiness . . . the redeemed shall walk there: and the ransomed of the Lord shall return, and come to Zion with songs and everlasting joy upon their heads: they shall obtain joy and gladness, and sorrow and sighing shall flee away.

17. T. S. Eliot, "Little Gidding," 1942.

18. For more see Leonard Sweet, *I Am a Follower: The Way, Truth and Life of Following Jesus* (2012).

19. See Nicholas of Cusa's Epiphany sermon (Sermon 216) that he preached in 1456 as found in *Opera Omnia* [Complete Works], edited by Jasper Hopkins, *Volume 6: Nicholas of Cusa's Dialectical Mysticism: Text, Translation, and Interpretive Study of De Visione Dei* (1988), 335–339.

20. Philippians 2:12 ESV

21. 2 Corinthians 12:18 NIV
22. "John Muir in Conversation with Marion Randall Parsons," an August 1913 oral quote transcribed, published and sourced in Sally M. Miller's *John Muir: Life and Work* (1993), 198.
23. David Adam, *The Awesome Journey: Life's Pilgrimage* (2015), 1.
24. After being given his sight, blind Bartimaeus "followed him on the way" (Mark 10:52).
25. Henry David Thoreau, *Walden* (1854), "Conclusion." For a more recent edition, see Thoreau's Walden (2000 ed. Penguin Classics), 94.
26. Dov Peretz Elkins, Rabbi of the Jewish Center of Princeton, "Hasidic Wisdom for the Heart and Soul," *Sacred Journey*, 47 (October 1996), as quoted in *Sacred Journey*, 51 (February 2000), 62.
27. Matthew 11:28–30 NIV
28. John 5:8; Mark 2:9
29. E. Stanley Jones, *The Way* (1946), 9.
30. Omar Costilla-Reyes, Patricia Scully, Krikor B Ozanyan, "Temporal pattern recognition for gait analysis applications using an "intelligent carpet" system," *IEEE* (07 January 2016).
31. There is even an online presbytery on Facebook called "Silly Walks Presbytery of the Pines."
32. With thanks to Teri Hyrkas for helping me think these through.
33. 2 Corinthians 5:7 NIV
34. George Fox, Epistle X, Section 5, Letter to Ministers (1655) written down by Ann Dawney, *Journal of George Fox* (1694), 263. Paragraph begins "Plow up the fallow ground . . ."
35. From Simon Mawer's novel *Tightrope* (2016), 21, as quoted in Timothy Radcliffe, *Alive in God* (2019), 296.
36. Galatians 5:25 NIV
37. After discussing how the Torah scholar should act, and then talk, one of the most respected Jewish scholars of all time, Moses Maimonides (1135–1204), gave specific instructions on how the Torah scholar should walk: NOT with erect stature and head held high ("throat thrust out" Isaiah 3:16), but rather should walk in a posture of prayer, with eyes slightly downward with an even pace, not hurried but determined. See Chapter 5, Law 8—"Walking the Walk."

NOTES

38. For the Greeks in particular having a rap for being so caught up in conversation and business that they paid no attention to their surroundings while walking, with the humor that emanates from this, see Timothy O'Sullivan, *Walking in Roman Culture* (2012), 91.

39. Friedrich Nietzsche, *Thus Spoke Zarathustra* (1883), Chapter 2, "The Prologue," page 6 (Penguin Classics edition).

40. Stephan Joubert, "Embracing obscurity: The enigmatic walk of the Son of God in Mark." Unpublished manuscript.

41. With thanks to my colleague and friend Dr. Terry Rankin for this insight.

42. As quoted in Graham B. Usher, *The Way Under Our Feet: A Spirituality of Walking* (2020), 3–4.

43. *Talmud* of Jerusalem, Berakoth, ix; Sota, v. 7: *Talmud* of Babylon, Sota, 22b.

44. Matthew 21:44

45. Mark 8:18

46. See also the "Thorn in the Flesh" entry in *The Dictionary of Phrase and Fable* (11th edition; 2006), 673.

47. Matthew 19:16–22

48. Matthew 6:2

49. Matthew 15:14

50. Matthew 6:5

51. Flavius Josephus. *Antiquities of the Jews*. Translated by William Whiston. Revised by Ralph Marcus (1965), Volume 10, 18:1, 1–25.

52. Timothy M. O'Sullivan, *Walking in Roman Culture* (2012), 16.

53. Timothy O'Sullivan, *Walking in Roman Culture*, 14.

54. Timothy O'Sullivan, *Walking in Roman Culture*, 52.

55. Koheles, Ecclesiastes 10:3.

56. http://www.torah.org/learning/mlife/chapter5-8.html?print=1. Accessed 08 January 2024.

57. See Thomas Bernhard essay "Wittgenstein's Nephew" (1972), as found in *The Penguin Book of Thomas Bernhard* (1999), translated by David McLintock.

58. See Kosuke Koyama, *Three Mile an Hour God* (1979); Graham B. Usher, *The Way Under Our Feet: A Spirituality of Walking* (2020).

59. With thanks to Erin Healy for reminding me of this. See https://www.emdr.com/history-of-emdr/. Accessed 08 January 2024.
60. *Times Literary Supplement,* 15 November 2021.
61. Stephen Budiansky, *Journey to the Edge of Reason: The Life of Kurt Gödel* (2021).
62. See Sarah Baxter, *A History of the World in 500 Walks* (2016).
63. *The Midrash Rabbah* (Numbers 14:8): "A disciple of the sages is better than a high priest, and the dust of the feet of a disciple of the sages is better than the blood of a sacrifice."

    The blessing is often given to students of rabbis as a reminder of the importance of learning from and following the teachings of a mentor.
64. Margaret Guenther, *Walking Home: From Eden to Emmaus* (2011).
65. Acts 24:7 KJV
66. 2 Corinthians 10:3–5: "We are destroying speculations and every lofty thing raised up against the knowledge of God, and we are taking every thought captive to the obedience of Christ"
67. Gerard Manley Hopkins, "The Leaden Echo and the Golden Echo," *Poems and Prose of Gerard Manley Hopkins* (1970), 54.
68. Gary Hayden, *Walking with Plato: A Philosophical Hike Through the British Isles* (2016).
69. Colossians 1:9–12 KJV
70. Proverbs 23:7
71. Philippians 4:8 KJV
72. 1 John 2:6
73. Actually, Maimonides was the first to call for a walk that was prayer in motion.
74. Galatians 2:20
75. Matthew 10:20
76. Galatians 4:6
77. Romans 8:26–27
78. Genesis 5:22–24 KJV
79. Hebrews 11:5–6
80. Guy Hibbert, "Dordogne Travels: The Lure of Périgord," *France Today,* 21

September 2016. https://francetoday.com/activity/family-kids/dordogne-travels-the-lure-of-perigord/.d 09 January 2024.

81. Martin Luther King, Jr., "Letter from a Birmingham Jail" in *Autobiography of Martin Luther King, Jr.* (1998), 203.

82. Matthew 28:20 ESV

83. Rodgers and Hammerstein's musical *Carousel* was first published in 1945.

84. "Friedrich Nietzsche used to walk for up to eight hours a day, often rising well before dawn. 'I am always on the road two hours before the sun comes over the mountains,' he wrote from Switzerland in 1877, 'and especially in the long shadows of afternoon and evening.'" Gary Hayden, *Walking with Plato* (2016).

85. Virginia Woolf saw herself as an urban walker. See her essay "Street Haunting" (1930) originally published in *The Death of the Moth and Other Essays* (1942), 148–55.

86. For more on the notable events in fiction that occur simply through characters walking, see Duncan Minshull, ed., *The Burning Leg: Walking Scenes from Classic Fiction* (2010).

87. James Hillman, "Perambulate to Paradise," *Utne Reader*, March–April, 2000, 88.

88. James Hillman, "Perambulate to Paradise," *Utne Reader*, March–April, 2000, 89.

89. Robert Louis Stevenson, *Essays of Travel* (Chatto & Windus, 1904) page 170. This has become one of Stevenson's most famous quotes, and an internet meme, but I first found it quoted by Jerry Toth, "The Life and Death of the Rainforest," *Parabola*, Spring 2011, 45.

90. For more on "The Most Beautiful Feet Ever," see LenTalk #175, YouTube, 13 August 2023, https://www.youtube.com/watch?v=LnncopPGE3A. Accessed 09 January 2024.

CHAPTER 2

1. See Oprah's foreword to the David J. Linden book *Touch: The Science of Hand, Heart, and Mind* (2016), ix.

2. Matthew 10:8 NIV

3. For more see chapter 4, "The Senses," in William James's *Principles of Psychology* (1890), Volume 1, 18–52.

4. John Wesley, "The Circumcision of the Heart," *The Works of the Rev. John Wesley in Ten Volumes: Volume 5* (1826), 167.

5. This was a key difference between John and Jesus besides fasting and feasting. John focused on sin; Jesus focused on suffering. John calls out sin; Jesus calls on the suffering. For John God was a Judge; for Jesus God was a Healer and Friend. John lived out an eschatology; Jesus lived out a teleology. For John's eschatological discipleship, the "end" was the eschaton: the end of times which were coming to judge and indict the present. For Jesus' teleological discipleship, the "end" was the telos, the ultimate end and purpose of life: to glorify God with one's service and enjoy God forever. For more see Leonard Sweet and Len Wilson, *Telos: The Hope of Heaven Today* (2022).

6. For more on this, see the "Sozo" entry in my *Jesus Human: Primer for a Common Humanity* (2023). Also see Leonard I. Sweet, *Health and Medicine in the Evangelical Tradition* (1994) and *The Jesus Prescription for a Healthy Life* (1996).

7. Mark 12:28–31 NIV

8. Bruce E. Wexler, *Brain and Culture: Neurobiology, Ideology and Social Change* (2007).

9. See Helen Macdonald's prize-winning *"H" is for Hawk* (2014), 167.

10. In *De Anima* (Book II, Chapter 11, 423b31–424a10), Aristotle writes: "Touch is the first sense, and it is co-extensive with life itself. For even plants seem to have a sense of touch, as is shown by their shunning what is harmful to them and turning towards what is beneficial. And in animals, touch is the most fundamental sense, since all animals have it, even those that have no other sense. And touch is the sense that is most closely connected with life, since it is the only sense that is present in all living things, even plants. Death is the opposite of life, and so touch is also the opposite of death. For when an animal dies, the first thing that it loses is its sense of touch. And when an animal is revived, the first sense that it regains is its sense of touch. So, touch is co-extensive with life itself and death. It is the first sense to appear in living things, and it is the last sense to disappear."

11. Aristotle, *De Anima*, Book III, Chapter 2, 425b–32.

12. See the essay by Jean-Louis Chrétien, "Body and Touch" in *The Call and The Response* (2004), 13. "Touch is the sense of life. It is the sense that allows us to feel the life force within us, and it is the sense that allows us

to feel the life force in others. Touch is the sense that connects us to the world of the living."

13. W. H. Auden, "Epistle to a Godson" poem (1972) in *Forewords and Afterwords* (1973), Part III, "Thanksgiving for a Habitat," 94.

14. James Hillman, "Perambulate to Paradise," *Utne Reader*, March–April, 2000, 87.

15. The last quote is from T. S. Eliot in his acclaimed 1922 poem "The Love Song of J. Alfred Prufrock." For James Hillman, see his "Perambulate to Paradise," *Utne Reader*, March–April, 2000, 86–87. James Hillman continues: "Automobiles do more than locomote us. Dutch psychologist Bernd Jager has observed the differences in facial expressions in the newer western and southern cities of the United States, which depend on cars, and the older northern and eastern cities, where there is still jostling in the streets, subways, buses, and pavements."

16. Naohiko Omata, *The Myth of Self-Reliance: Economic Lives Inside a Liberian Refugee Camp* (2017).

17. Rebecca Perry, *Beauty/Beauty* (2015). This debut volume was shortlisted for the T. S. Eliot Prize.

18. For more, see the study of Kaitlin Woolley (Cornell) and Ayelet Fishbach (University of Chicago), "Shared Plates, Shared Minds: Consuming From a Shared Plate Promotes Cooperation," *Psychological Science* 30 (March 2019), 381–393. https://journals.sagepub.com/doi/abs/10.1177/0956797619830633. Accessed 08 January 2024.

19. Written by Albert W. T. Orsborn (d. 1967), the first stanza goes this way:

    Let the beauty of Jesus be seen in me,
    All His wonderful passion and purity;
    O my Savior divine, All my being refine,
    Till the beauty of Jesus be seen in me.

    For more on growing up in the holiness tradition, see my *Mother Tongue: How Our Heritage Shapes Our Story* (2017).

20. This is the thesis of Leonard Sweet and Frank Viola, *Jesus Manifesto: Restoring the Supremacy and Sovereignty of Jesus Christ* (2016).

21. Ephem, *Hymni de Nativitate* xxiii.13. Translated by Sebastian Brock.

22. The word "entheogenic" can mean, most widely, anything that generates God within. Not a divine presence from the outside in, but from the inside out. *Jesus Living* is based on a concept of entheogenic discipleship,

and entheogenic evangelism is part of a larger framework of entheogenic ecclesiology.

23. Simone Weil, *Waiting on God* (1951), 69.
24. With thanks to Carmen Barber for giving me the idea for this paragraph.
25. https://www.youtube.com/watch?v=mwlYt9xNVtE. Accessed 08 January 2024.
26. 1 Kings 17:21; 2 Kings 4:54.
27. Matthew 8:15; Mark 1:31; Mark 5:41; Matthew 8:20; Luke 8:54; Matthew 8:20; Mark 5:29; Luke 8:44; Mark 7:31–37.
28. Myrick C. Shinall Jr., "The Social Condition of Lepers in the Gospels," *Journal of Biblical Literature* 4(2018), 915–934.
29. John Kinsella, "Interlude," in by Kwame Dawes & John Kinsella, *unHistory—being a poem cycle: Codicil to History, Coda to History, Footnotes to History, Index to History* (2022), 27.
30. John 12:32
31. Charles Darwin, *On the Origin of Species by Means of Natural Selection* (1859), Chapter 5, "Laws of Variation," 66.
32. Fernando Pessoa, *The Book of Disquiet* (Serpent's Tail edition, translated by Richard Zenith) 27 August 1922 entry, page 122.
33. Sherry Turkle, *Reclaiming Conversation: The Power of Talk in a Digital Age* (2015), 200.
34. William James' *The Principles of Psychology* (1890), Chapter 10, "The Perception of Space," 274.
35. William James, *The Principles of Psychology* (1890), 274.
36. Caroline Walker Bynum, *Christian Materiality* (2012). Bynum wrote the intro to the catalog *Treasures of Heaven: Saints, Relics, and Devotion in Medieval Europe* (2010).
37. Some artistic masters of this art form include Ed Elliott (I love his angel images), Heather Chontos, and Elliot Adams. The blackened wood called "yakisugi" is still to this day used to make fire-proof chests and facades in hopes of making homes safe from forest fires.
38. As quoted in Judith Flanders, *Christmas: A Biography* (2017), 121. The original source is a letter from Kate Perugini to Bernard Shaw dated 04 March 1897, housed in the British Library.
39. Pew Research Center, "32% of Americans Have a Tattoo, Including

22% Who Have More Than One" (August 15, 2023). https://www.pewresearch.org/short-reads/2023/08/15/32-of-americans-have-a-tattoo-including-22-who-have-more-than-one/. Accessed 08 January 2024.

40. Brian J. Willoughby, Michael D. Park, Joseph P. Uhlmann, "Tattoos and Religion: A Social Cognitive Perspective," *Social Psychological and Personality Science*, 10 (June 2019), 731–40. This study found that religious people are more likely to have tattoos than non-religious people, and that this is especially true for Christians.

CHAPTER 3

1. Ludwig Wittgenstein, *Culture and Value* (Rev. edition, 1998), 23.
2. Colossians 3:1 ESV
3. Allen C. Guelzo's *Abraham Lincoln: Redeemer President* (1999) notes Lincoln's lifelong affinity for physiognomy and the reading of faces on pages 52–53 and 120–121.
4. See T. J. Clark, "Rembrandt: The Late Works," *The Art Newspaper*, 10 January 2014, 2.
5. Milan Kundera, *The Unbearable Lightness of Being* (1984), 26.
6. Margaret Cavendish (1623–73), opening life of her poem "A Posset for Natures Breakfast"
7. The name "Veronica" comes from a Latin alteration of the Greek word for "true image."
8. Mark 5:25–34; Matthew 9:20–22; Luke 8:43–48.
9. John 18:22
10. Matthew 26:67
11. Mark 14:65
12. Matthew 27:39
13. Mark 3:5; 5:25–32
14. Mark 6:41 KJV
15. Mark 10:21
16. Luke 9:29 KJV
17. Matthew 17:2 NIV
18. Joan E. Taylor, *What Did Jesus Look Like* (2018), 104. Joan Taylor is

Professor of Christian Origins and Second Temple Judaism at King's College London.

19. J. Christian Wilson, *Jesus and the Pleasures* (2003), 20. "The final two images, that Judah's eyes are darker than wine and his teeth whiter than milk, are ancient metaphors intended to show Judah as a handsome man. His dark eyes convey a sense of mystery. White teeth, though commonplace in our age, were rare in all the ages before toothpaste and dentistry. Few people had white teeth—or all their teeth."

20. Psalm 45:2–3 KJV

21. 1 Samuel 16:12

22. Frei Betto, "A Portrait of Jesus: What Did Jesus Look Like?" *Spirituality*, 8 (May–June 2002), 141–42.

23. Isaiah 52:13–53:12.

24. Tertullian, *Against Marcion*, Book III, Chapter 4. In Tertullian, Against Marcion, edited by Ernest Evans, translated by Ernest Evans. Oxford University Press, 1972, p. 313. The mention of Jesus having "no form nor comeliness" is found in Chapter 4 of Book III of Tertullian's Against Marcion. It appears on page 313 of the 1972 Oxford University Press edition edited and translated by Ernest Evans.

25. Isaiah 53:2–5

26. Irenaeus of Lyons, *Against Heresies*, Book IV, Chapter 6. In *The Apostolic Fathers*, ed. by Alexander Roberts, James Donaldson, and A. Cleveland Coxe, translated by Alexander Roberts and William Rambaut, vol. 1 (1885), 466.

27. *Contra Celsus* 1:33.

28. "The Lord will shave with a razor," Isaiah 7:20 warns; he'll "sweep away the beard." I have no idea what this prophesy means.

29. I disagree with Adam Clarke's Commentary on Lamentations 4:7, where he sees a messianic reference. "Her Nazarites were purer than snow, they were whiter than milk, they were more ruddy in body than rubies, their polishing was of sapphire: their visage is blacker than a coal; they are not known in the streets: their skin cleaveth to their bones; it is withered, it is become like a stick." Clarke writes: "This passage is supposed to have a typical reference to the Messiah, Jesus Christ. He was a Nazarite, or a consecrated one, in the highest sense of the term. He was perfectly pure and spotless, and his face was the image of the divine glory. But when he suffered on the cross, his face was disfigured by the thorns and the

spitting, and it became black as a coal. He was so disfigured that his own disciples could hardly recognize him." See *The Holy Bible, with Notes, Critical, Explanatory, and Practical: Designed for Families and Individuals* (1852), Lamentations 4:7. I see this passage as referring to the beauty of the Israelite people, both inside and outside.

30. Some people suspect that he was very short and base this theory on the fact that Zacchaeus, "a short man," when he heard that Jesus was entering Jericho, climbed up into a sycamore tree so as to be able to see him (Luke 19:1–4). Frankly, I don't see the connection.

    Preaching at Whitehall in the presence of Charles I on 01 April 1627, John Donne quoted Luke 2:52, 'Jesus grew in stature,' qualifying the words by saying 'But he grew not to his life's end', and then adding 'we know to how many feet he grew'. Oxford literary critic David Colclough, the learned editor of the third volume of the magnificent *Oxford Edition of the Sermons of John Donne*, provides the reader with a note that goes far to answer a question that has probably never bothered most people. He refers to the early fourteenth-century Greek historian Nicephorus Callistus Xanthopulus, who reported that Christ's "body's stature was altogether seven *palmos.*" If a palm is nine inches, then by this reckoning Jesus was five foot three inches tall. For scholars still curious about Christ's appearance, Publius Lentulus supplies a few more details (cited by Colclough). Lentulus says that he as '*Homo quidem statura procerus, mediocris et spectabilis*', or, as it was translated in a single-sheet broadside edition of the letter published at London a couple of years before Donne preached his sermon, a "man of stature somewhat tall and comely." Lentulus was said to have been Pontius Pilate's predecessor as Governor of Judaea and author of a letter to the Roman Senate containing this physical account of Jesus.

    His face is so venerable that anyone who looks upon it may fear him and love him at the same time. His hair is the colour of ripe hazel nuts, with a bluish sheen, smooth almost to his ears and them tumbling down on his shoulders. His skin is rosy and his nose and mouth perfect. He has a thick beard, the same colour as his hair, divided at the chin and not very long . . . He is the most beautiful of all the sons of men!

    However, as Colclough points out, Lentulus's letter is a forgery that "circulated widely in the early modern period." The question is, if Donne knew this description, did he also know that it was spurious? Donne was not the only one hoodwinked by forgeries.

31. Joan E. Taylor reveals that eight out of ten combs from men's hair in the

first century found in a Judean desert cave had lice. See *What did Jesus Look Like?* (2018), 167.

32. Joan E. Taylor, *What Did Jesus Look Like?* (2018), 155.

33. Matthew 26:48. Suggested by Edward Lucie-Smith, *The Face of Jesus* (2011), 14.

34. Luke 4:30. The Old Testament prophesied in Isaiah 53 that Jesus would not have any external features or beauty that would attract or draw people to Him. Isaiah adds that Jesus would grow up like a plant out of dry ground with no form of kingly majesty. In short, Jesus looked like an average person with no look-at-me distinguishing characteristics.

35. Joan Taylor makes an issue of the fact that there is no description of Jesus in the gospels, since one would have expected them. Their absence for her means that there must have been a reason why they didn't provide any physical characterization: "Was there something that may have been problematic in the appearance of Jesus?" (Joan E. Taylor, *What Did Jesus Look Like?* [2018], 12.) Maybe he wasn't good-looking enough?

But then if Jesus were "of no comeliness," that would have made a theological point. The fact that the gospel writers didn't feature his non-good-looks is as problematic as the first. Second century anti-Christian writers like Celsus portrayed Jesus as ugly and short, but the oft-quoted words of Justin Martyr who supposedly said Jesus was "with no beauty that we should desire him" never occur in Martyr's writing, including his "Dialogue with Trypho" where Martyr does reference Isaiah 53 and the idea that the Jews failed to recognize the Messiah because he appeared in humble ordinary form—"He had no beauty or majesty to attract us to him, nothing in his appearance that we should desire him . . . a man of sorrows, acquainted with grief." But never do the words describing Jesus as "with no beauty that we should desire him" appear in Justin Martyr's writings.

36. The quote is found in his *Treatise on the Lord's Prayer* (252), chapter 23.

37. John 14:1–31 NIV

38. Matthew 25:40

39. Psalm 4:66 ESV

40. Psalm 27:8–9 LEB

41. 2 Chronicles 7:14

42. Hans Urs von Balthasar, *The Glory of the Lord: A Theological Aesthetics* (1982), volume I, 137.

NOTES

43. Marilynne Robinson's novel *Gilead* (2004), 66.
44. For the interplay of religion and politics, see Lesley Chamberlain, *Arc of Utopia: The Beautiful Story of the Russian Revolution* (2019).
45. 1 Corinthians 13:10 KJV
46. Edgar Allen Poe, "Ligeia," 1838.
47. Nathaniel Hawthorne, "The Birthmark" (1843).
48. *The Collected Works of St. John of Avila*, translated by Kieran Kavanaugh and Otilio Rodriguez (1976), volume 3, pages 304–305. Letter 140 of *Letters and Instructions of Saint John of Avila*, translated into English and published as a collection in 1964. See p. 201.
49. Psalm 36:9 ESV
50. John 15:15 NLT
51. Matthew 26:50; Mark 14:45. In Luke 22:48, Jesus refers to Judas by name NIV.
52. Sister Helen Prejean, *Dead Man Walking: An Eyewitness Account of the Death Penalty in the US* (1996), 37.
53. For an opposite view that ends up at the same place, see John Rapley and Peter Heather's, *Why Empires Fall: Rome, America and the Future of the West* (2023), where they argue that imperial systems tend to fall apart at the moment of their maximum power and prosperity, and when they appear strongest.
54. See Mark 12:14ff.
55. For other biblical passages where God doesn't look on outward appearances, see 1 Samuel 16:7; John 7:24, 2 Corinthians 5:12.
56. See R. S. Riddick, Watercolor, "Smiling Jesus" (1988).
57. Colin Jones, *The Smile Revolution in Eighteenth-Century Paris* (2014). The modern toothbrush wasn't invented until the eighteenth century in Paris.
58. Walter Isaacson demonstrates how the "Mona Lisa" is a masterpiece of the union of brilliant science (anatomy, math, optics) and art in *Leonardo da Vinci* (2017), 340–343.
59. 2 Corinthians 1 KJV
60. Matthew 17:2 NIV
61. Numbers 6:24–26
62. Some examples of earlier blessings include: God blessing the living

creatures and mankind in Genesis 1 after creating them; Isaac blessing Jacob in Genesis 27; Jacob blessing Joseph in Genesis 48; Joseph blessing his brothers in Genesis 49.

63. Gabriel Barkay, "The Priestly Benediction on the Ketef Hinnom Plaques," *Cathedra*, No. 52 (1989), 37–76. G. Barkay, "The Silver Scrolls from Ketef Hinnom in Jerusalem," *Textus*, 22(2005), 35–57. Professor Barkay is the Israeli archaeologist and Professor Emeritus at Bar-Ilan University who led the excavations at Ketef Hinnom in 1979–1980 where the silver scrolls were uncovered.

64. Exodus 34:29–30

65. Ephesians 5:14

66. 2 Corinthians 4:6 NIV

67. Revelation 22:4–5 KJV

68. Matthew 6:22–23 NIV

69. John's gospel is known for Jesus' "I am" sayings. Just as God's revelation to Moses was an "I AM" (Exodus 3:14), so Jesus used the same words to describe who he is in seven "I Am" statements in John.

    "I am the bread of life" (John 6:35, 41, 48, 51)
    "I am the light of the world" (John 8:12)
    "I am the door of the sheep" (John 10:7, 9)
    "I am the resurrection and the life" (John 11:25)
    "I am the good shepherd" (John 10:11, 14)
    "I am the way, the truth, and the life" (John 14:6)
    "I am the true vine" (John 15:1, 5)

70. Isaiah 45:6–7

71. Gregory J. Gbur, *Invisibility: The History and Science of How Not to Be Seen* (2023).

72. For more on Mother Teresa's spiritual struggles that could lead to such utterances as "The darkness is so thick that I cannot feel the presence of God at all. I have no faith, no love, no zeal. The saving of souls means nothing, heaven means nothing," see Brian Kolodiejchuk, ed., *Mother Teresa: Come Be My Light: The Private Writings of the Saint of Calcutta* (2009), 206–207. This quote from Mother Teresa comes from a letter she wrote on 03 September 1961 to her spiritual advisor Father Joseph Neuner.

73. Daniel Heller-Roazen, *The Inner Touch: Archaeology of a Sensation* (2007).

74. Flannery O'Connor wrote whole books about what she called the "action of grace."

75. George MacDonald, "The Eloi," in Επεα *[Epea] Aptera: Unspoken Sermons*, by George MacDonald and Robert Browning (1997), 1:120.

76. With thanks to Hilary Horn of Bedford, UK, for this.

77. William James's essay "The Gospel of Relaxation" (1892), 21. James is arguing that we can change our emotions by changing our behavior. If we want to feel kindly to someone we have been inimical to, we can't just try to force ourselves to feel kindly. That will only make us focus on the bad feeling and make it worse. Instead, act as if we already feel kindly. This might involve smiling, making sympathetic enquiries, and saying genial things. By acting in this way, we can trick our brains into actually feeling kindly.

78. The full journal entry is as follows: "Immediately it struck into my mind, 'Leave off preaching. How can you preach to others, who have not faith yourself?' I asked Bohler whether he thought I should leave it off or not. He answered, 'By no means.' I asked, 'But what can I preach?' He said, 'Preach faith till you have it; and then, because you have it, you will preach faith.'" See the Journal entry for 04 March 1738 in N. Curnock, ed., *The journal of the Rev. John Wesley: enlarged from original mss., with notes from unpublished diaries, annotations, maps, and illustrations*. I (1875), 61–62.

79. Leviticus 2:11 reads: "Every grain offering you bring to the LORD must be made without yeast, for you are not to burn any yeast or honey in an offering made to the LORD by fire. You may bring them to the LORD as an offering of the firstfruits, but they are not to be offered on the altar as a pleasing aroma."

80. Louis Jacobs, *Jewish Preaching* (2004), 107.

81. The term "hardness of the forehead" is used in this sense in Jeremiah 3:3; "you have the forehead of a whore; you refuse to be ashamed" ESV. The Aramaic term *tokfa de-mitzcha*, "hardness of the forehead."

82. I have developed this theology of humbleconfidence in my writings and video publications. For some examples see my *11 Genetic Gateways to Spiritual Awakening* (1988) where I show how "Jesus exemplified this paradoxical combination of confident humility and humble confidence." See also my *Me and We: God's New Social Gospel* (2014).

83. See Paul Klee's 1920 lecture "Creative Confession" as found in J. J. Sweeney and A. C. Ritchie, eds., *Klee on Art and Design* (1964), 176–183.

84. See the Gene Weingarten interview with Maya Angelou's son, Guy Johnson, featured on the cover of *The Washington Post Magazine* titled "Remembering Maya Angelou" (08 June 2014), page 4 of the online article.
85. 2 Corinthians 4
86. Although widely attributed to Orwell, no one has yet found exactly where Orwell said this. I suspect the quote may have been inspired by a passage in Orwell's 1949 novel *Nineteen Eighty-Four*, in which the protagonist Winston Smith describes how the faces of people in Oceania change over time to reflect their inner thoughts and emotions.
87. Brian Kolodiejchuk, ed., *Mother Teresa. Come Be My Light: The Private Writings of the Saint of Calcutta* (2007), 169.
88. See Act 3 of Shaw's play *The Devil's Disciple* (1897).
89. See Newton's diary entry where he confesses, "My spirits are in a flutter, my frame disjoynted. Perplex'd about trifles . . . my harp is out of tune," as quoted in Bernard Martin, *An Ancient Mariner: A Biography of John Newton* (revised ed., 1960), 172. Newton also used musical benchmarks in his theological assessments. In a letter to Hannah More, he wrote "The talk of some reputed Calvinists is no more musical in my ear than the mewing of a cat" (quoted page 240).
90. Jean Renoir, *My Father* (2001; original French edition published in 1962), 195. Translated by Randolph and Dorothy Weaver.
91. Nicholas Wadley, *Renoir* (1991), 460. Wadley quotes Matisse recalling Renoir saying, "The pain passes, but the beauty remains."
92. Marcus Aurelius, *Meditations*. Translated by Gregory Hays (Penguin Classics, 2002), 11.16.8.

CHAPTER 4

1. Numbers 12:6–8 NIV
2. Matthew 4:4 PHILLIPS
3. Matthew 13:34–35 ESV
4. Exodus 25:22; 33:11
5. Exodus 33:11
6. 1 Kings 17:2–4, 9, 10
7. Genesis 35:1 KJV

NOTES

8. Exodus 31:1–11
9. The quote is not from Pythagoras but a description of his correlation of music and mathematics, as found in Steven Harrison, *The Essence of Spirituality* (1995), 87.
10. Frederic Raphael, *Antiquity Matters* (2017), 151.
11. Over two decades I have developed this "Perfect Pitch" metaphor of attunement in various books, including *SoulTsunami: Sink or Swim in New Millennium Culture* (1999); *Out of the Question . . . Into the Mystery* (2004); *Nudge* (2010); *The Greatest Story Never Told: Revive Us Again* (2012); and *From Tablet to Table* (2014).
12. Waldo Williams, "In the Days of Caesar" (1938), as translated from the Welsh by Rowan Williams and found in his editing of *The Collected Poems of Waldo Williams* (1990), 144–45. Easier to find is *Anthology of Welsh Verse* (1984), 521, edited by Gwyn Jones and Thomas Jones, translated by Gwyn Jones.
13. For my reframing as a Great Cloud of Withnesses see my *11: Indispensable Relationship You Can't Be Without* (2012).
14. Oscar Wilde, *De Profundis* (1905) wrote that "it is always a source of pleasure and awe to me to remember that the ultimate survival of the Greek chorus, lost elsewhere to art, is to be found in the servitor answering the priest at Mass" (55).
15. From "Great Is Thy Faithfulness" written by Thomas Obediah Chisholm (d. 1960).
16. Abraham Joshua Heschel, *Who is Man?* (1965), 116. Heschel liked to talk about the closing of the "distance between," as part of "the adjustment of the details to the whole." Heschel, *The Earth is the Lord's* (1950), 166.
17. See Mark 2, where it says Jesus went "home" or "to his house" in Capernaum. You also get a sense of the chaotic from the crowd gathering in and around his house as he preached.
18. Andrew Underhile, *Comfort in Chaos: A Study of Nahum* (2014).
19. See the work of urban historian Jinnai Hidenobu, *Tokyo: A Spatial Anthropology* (1985).
20. Hilaire Belloc, "A Meditation on Cheese" as found in *First and Last* (1911), 209–14. The section is called "This, That, and the Other."
21. Exodus 20:5
22. The Bible does not explicitly state how many languages the voice of God

was heard in at Mount Sinai. The Talmud, however, records a tradition that the voice of God was heard in seventy languages, with the number seventy the symbol of completeness or totality.

23. Exodus 20:4–6

24. Rabbi Levi's commentary on Exodus 20:2, as found in Midrash Rabbah-Shemot (Exodus), Parshat Yitro, 20:4.

25. Ibid. The full context of the quote is as follows: "It is for this reason that Scripture says: 'I am the Eternal, your God.' Why is the word 'your' in the singular number? To teach you that even though 600,000 people stood before God, He said this to each and every one according to his capacity to understand, and they all heard it as individuals. The text does not say: 'Ani Adonai Elohaychem,' 'I am the Eternal your God,' with the plural form of the word 'your.' Rather, when it says 'Ani Adonai Elohecha, 'your God,' the text intentionally uses the singular form."

Rabbi Levi shows how the "your God" is singular in Exodus 20:2, as if the revelation were directed to each Israelite, even though the whole nation stood together at Sinai.

26. John Muir, "A Bread Famine," as found in *My First Summer in the Sierra* (1911), 110.

27. Mark 16:15 NKJV

28. John 20:21 RSV

29. John Crowe Ransom, "An Approach to the Criticism of Modern Poetry" in *The World's Body* (1930), 155.

30. Quoted by P. N. Furbank, "Misreading Gulliver," *Times Literary Supplement*: 12 November 2019, 16.

31. The quote comes from a newspaper interview with Naim Attallah, "Arthur Koestler at 70: Still Scorching the Midnight Sun," *Sunday Times*, 25 January 1976. Also quoted by Michael Scammell, "Koestler the Dangerous Intellectual," *Times Literary Supplement*: 21 July 2010, 5.

32. Mark 7:32

33. John 12:20–22

34. Luke 23:8

35. Matthew 21:14

36. Luke 8:41–42

37. Luke 10:25

38. Luke 10:40–41
39. John 3:1–2; John 19:39–40
40. Matthew 8:5, 10
41. Mark 2:1–12.
42. Mark 5:24–34
43. John 4:7–42
44. Luke 8:26–27
45. Luke 17:12
46. John 18:13–14; John 18:33–34
47. Luke 21:1–3
48. Mark 7:24–30; Matthew 15:21–28
49. Mark 1:29–31
50. Matthew 19:22
51. Luke 19:9
52. Matthew 12:46–50
53. 1 Peter 2:9 KJV
54. Isaiah 40:15
55. Vaclav Havel, "The Power of the Powerless" in *Living in Truth* (1986), 23.
56. Pierre Teilhard de Chardin, *Letters to Two Friends, 1926–1952* (1968), 146.
57. J. C., "N. B.," *TLS: Times Literary Supplement*, 18 July 2003, 16.
58. See the Gandhi article "The Jews" in his newspaper *Harijan*, 26 November 1938, and quoted in Simone Panter-Brick, *Gandhi and the Middle East* (2008), 28.
59. John 11:45–57
60. Karl Barth, "The Doctrine of Reconciliation," in *Church Dogmatics*, Volume 4, Part 2.
61. See Oscar Wilde, *The Picture of Dorian Gray*, chapter 11.
62. Augustine, *On Christian Teaching*, trans. R. P. H. Green (1997), I.29.29.
63. Susan Rogers in *This is What It Sounds Like: What the Music You love Says About You* (2022) adds three more to the classic quadrivium to make it seven: novelty—do you embrace the unexpected; authenticity—does the

genuine emotion come through; realism—do you feel that you are sitting in front of the band?

64. As quoted by George Steiner, *Led into Mystery: Faith Seeking Answers in Life and Death* (1982), 131. Steiner goes on to say in his own words, "A Bach fugue, a Mozart clarinet quintet lead us into the same awesome puzzles, into the same graced dark, as do the shaping of selfhood or the life of the mind in history." In *The Savage Mind* (1962), Lévi-Strauss writes extensively about the importance of music in human culture.

65. Matthew 18:21–22

66. Psalm 19:14 NIV

67. Hebrews 12:26

68. Matthew 15:23; Mark 14:61; Mark 15:5; Luke 23:9; Matthew 26:63–64

69. *The Seven Epistles of St. Ignatius of Antioch*, Ch. XV

70. As quoted in Angela Leighton, *Hearing Things: The Work of Sound in Literature* (2018), 107.

71. Niccolò Machiavelli in *The Prince* (1513) in Chapter 19.

72. Isaiah 43:19 NIV

73. For example, St. Irenaeus's statement that Jesus brought with him a "total newness" can be found in his work "Against Heresies," specifically in Book 2, Chapter 22.

74. The phrase "*Omnen novitatem attulit semetipsum afferens*" is Latin for "He brought with him all newness, offering himself." It is attributed to the early Church Father St. Ambrose (d. 397), who used it in his sermons and commentaries. See also his "*De Fide*" (On Faith), where Ambrose wrote: "*Christus enim, qui omnia innovavit, et ipsum hominem renovavit*" (Christ, who renewed all things, also renewed man himself).

75. Revelation 21:5 NLT

76. 2 Corinthians 7:5

77. 1 John 4:18

78. Ephesians 4:15

79. In Plato's writings, Logos meant four things: 1) mental thought without words, as conveyed in images and metaphors; 2) discourse of the mind expressed by voice; 3) explanation of the elements of the universe, the voice of reason; 4) ratio of proportion, which was the highest meaning for Plato, the voice of harmony. In the Timaeus, Plato describes the creation

of the universe by the Demiurge, who uses logos to create order and harmony from chaos. In this passage, logos can be interpreted as the ratio of proportion, which is the highest meaning of logos for Plato. In the Phaedrus, Plato argues that logos is the most powerful tool of persuasion, and that it can be used to lead people to the truth. In this passage, logos can be interpreted as the discourse of the mind expressed by voice. In the Republic, Plato argues that logos is the only way to achieve true knowledge, and that logos can be interpreted as mental thought without words, as conveyed in images and metaphors. Finally, in the Sophist, Plato portrays logos as the voice of reason and the sophist as a dangerous figure who can undermine the foundations of society.

80. Dan Wakefield, ed., *Kurt Vonnegut: Letters* (Vintage, 2013).
81. William Law, *A Serious Call to a Devout and Holy Life* (2nd ed. 1730), 109.
82. William Law, *A Serious Call to a Devout and Holy Life* (1729) as found in *The Works of the Reverend William Law*, vol. 3, (1893), 109.
83. John Wesley, "The Law Established through Faith, II" Sermon 35. *The Works of John Wesley*, vol. 2, Sermons II: 34–70, ed. Albert C. Outler (1985), 36–46.
84. *Mother Teresa: In My Own Words* (1997), "The Distressing Disguise," pages 67–71.
85. See Booker T. Washington's autobiography *Up from Slavery* (1901), 161.
86. "Where Charity and Love Prevail" by Omer Westendorf.
87. See 1 Thessalonians 2:13 for a description of this mode of the church's voice.
88. We cannot read the England translation of the Greek New Testament without understanding the Hebrew text that was the base of the Greek version. We think of Hebrew First Testament and Greek Second Testament, but the Greek was a translation from the Hebrew, and many of those who translated the Bible from the Greek into English (like the NEB) were classical scholars who knew Greek but didn't know the Hebrew behind the Greek. David Flusser reminds us that the New Testament is a Jewish text, full of Jewish idioms and allusions, and that it should be interpreted in light of its Jewish context by scholars who know Hebrew. See his *Jesus: As Seen by His Jewish Contemporaries* (1985); *The New Testament and Rabbinic Literature* (1988); *Judaism and the Origins of Christianity* (1988); and *The Dead Sea Scrolls and the New Testament* (1995).

89. Acts 2:42

90. A. J. Swoboda, *Subversive Sabbath: The Surprising Power of Rest in a Nonstop World* (2018), 12.

91. The junglefowl, a.k.a. domestic chicken, is the most numerous species of bird on the planet, and the most abused.

92. As Michael Dobbs documents in *The Unwanted: America, Auschwitz, and a Village Caught In Between* (2020), around 150,000 Jews successfully immigrated to the United States during Hitler's regime—exceeding even British Palestine in admitted refugees. Yet USAmerica's bureaucracies erected hurdles swifter than many could clear, dooming them to the disposal of even more efficient German bureaucracies. Like Max and Fanny Valfer, their names now litter *Stolpersteine*—those "stumbling stone" memorials embedded in German streets to haunt passersby with memories those denied haven. While some 150,000 names escaped such memorial fate thanks to USAmerican refuge, for countless thousands more, US bureaucratic obstacles aggravated rather than alleviated their fate in the Holocaust's wake. America erected her own bureaucratic barriers alongside the walls of Auschwitz, and voices cry from beneath both ruins.

93. As computed by Clifford Longley in *The Tablet*, 21 July 2007, 7.

94. Patrick Lindsay Bowles, "Suffering and the Children," TLS, 16 April 2010, 29. See Christa Brown's story in *This Little Light* of her abuse by a SBC pastor and on her website, https://www.stopbabptistpredators.org and blog, https://stopbaptistpredators.blogspot.com/. Accessed 08 January 2024.

95. In the eighteenth and nineteenth centuries, no complaint against Anglican clergy was more common that they abused choirboys.

96. As quoted and translated by Frank Wilczek in *A Beautiful Question: Finding Nature's Deep Design* (2016), 299. The original Italian is as follows: "L'acqua percossa dall'acqua fa cerchi intorno al punto d'intoppo. La voce nell'aria fa lo stesso per maggior distanza; e nel fuoco ancor più larghi; e la mente nell'universo fa cerchi ancor più lunghi; ma, essendo la mente finita, l'impeto non si estende all'infinito."

97. See Waterman Sweet, *Views of Anatomy And Practice of Natural Bonesetting* (1843).

98. In addition to its healing meaning, καταρτίζω can also be used to describe the preparation of something for use: "And as shoes for your feet put on the readiness given by the gospel of peace" (Ephesians 6:15). Here,

NOTES

καταρτίζω is used to describe the preparation of the gospel for use as a weapon of spiritual warfare.

99. See also Matthew 4:21; Mark 1:20; Luke 6:10; Acts 21:16.
100. See Simon Jackson, *George Herbert and Early Modern Musical Culture* (2023).
101. George Herbert poem "The Reprisal" (Second Stanza) in *The Temple* (1633).
102. In the eighteenth and nineteenth centuries, no complaint against Anglican clergy was more common that they abused choirboys.
103. George Herbert, "The Collar" in *The Temple: Sacred Poems and Private Ejaculations* (1633).
104. Charles Darwin, *The Descent of Man* (1871), Chapter XIX.
105. The quote "Music is auditory cheesecake" is on page 534 of Steven Pinker's *How the Mind Works* (1997).
106. *Tomorrow's Child: Imagination, Creativity, and the Renewal of the Church* (1972), 8.
107. Roger Scruton, *Modern Philosophy: An Introduction and Survey* (1996).

CHAPTER 5

1. Drew Doss & N. K. Carlson, *The Smelly Gospel: Making Scents of the Good News* (2020).
2. Psalm 141
3. Genesis 8:21 NIV
4. For the association of smells and idols, see Deuteronomy 4:28 and Psalm 115:5–6.
5. Nard or spikenard was derived from the roots of the Nardostachys jatamansi plant, which grows in the Himalayas.
6. Genesis 2:7 NIV
7. Job 27:3 ESV
8. Susan Ashbrook Harvey, *Scenting Salvation: Ancient Christianity and the Olfactory Imagination* (2006), 30. This is not take into account, of course, anosmia (loss of smell), which was often induced by COVID-19 but restored after the departure of the disease.
9. 2 Corinthians 2:15 DRA

10. Philippians 4:18 DRA
11. Ephesians 5:2 DRA
12. Song of Songs 1:3 KJV
13. Song of Solomon 1:3; 4:11
14. This was especially true for Dorothy Day, currently a candidate for canonization. See Timothy Radcliffe, *Alive in God* (2019), 300.
15. From a 13 January 2015 blog post "Worship Leaves an Aroma" with the full quote as follows: "Praise leaves a sound, worship leaves an aroma. Praise requires effort and volume, but worship is easy and almost effortless. Praise takes gravity and collisions to make noise. Worship rides quietly on the wind. Praise is felt through our senses. Worship is smelled and lingers in the air around us." See https://www.brookeligertwood.com/. Accessed 08 January 2024.
16. Exodus mentions the ingredients used in sacred anointing oil in Exodus 30:22–25, and incense for worship practices in Exodus 30:34–38. The holy anointing oil described in Exodus 30:22–25 was created from:

    Pure myrrh (mar deror) 500 shekels (about 6 kg)
    Sweet cinnamon (kinnemon besem) 250 shekels (about 3 kg)
    Kaneh bosem (kaneh bosm) 250 shekels (about 3 kg)
    Cassia (kiddah) 500 shekels (about 6 kg)
    Olive oil (shemen zayit) one hin (about 5.35 kg)

17. See her article, with which I mostly disagree, "In the Beginning God created the heavens and the earth: So Begins the Bible. But is this the Correct Translation?" *The Guardian*, 21 March 2011.
18. Francesca Stavrakopoulou, *God: An Anatomy* (2021), 26. Theologian Stavrakopoulou writes that God's nose "is a symbol of his presence, his power, and his love."
19. For more on this see my chapter on "smell" in *Nudge: Awakening Each Other to the God Who's Already There* (2010), chapter 8 "Promise: Use Your Nose," 249–274.
20. Drew Doss & N. K. Carlson, *The Smelly Gospel: Making Scents of the Good News* (2023).
21. More patched on than woven into its fabric, fabrics used to be symbolic of the sacred and sublime: "A Widow might donate her finest robes to the church to be adapted for use as vestments, or bequeath her best tablecloth of Perugian linen to serve as an altar cloth." Paul Hillis, *Veiled Presence: Body and Drapery from Giotto to Titian* (2018).

NOTES

22. One fossores catacomb art is of a woman buried there in three stages of her life, the largest one (most probably) in her resurrected state wearing a purple garment and lifting up her arms in prayer. The spacious cubicula (mortuary room also used for Christian worship) suggests that the spread of Christianity in the first few centuries included all economic sectors, from the very rich to the very poor. In fact, Priscilla was a wealthy Roman woman who donated the land under which 40,000 Christians would be buried three stories underground between the second century and the end of the fourth century. For a virtual tour of the Priscilla catacombs, see https://www.youtube.com/watch?v=z_5AAk1jABI&vl=en-US. Accessed 08 January 2024.

23. Howard Rheingold, "The Smell of Things to Come," in *Excursions to the Far Side of the Mind: A Book of Memes* (1988), 59.

24. Exodus 30:7–8; 2 Chronicles 13:11. Cf. Luke 1:10; Acts 3:1.

25. Luke 1:10 LEB

26. Luke 1:10 LEB

27. Genesis 8:21 NIV

28. For "reiah nihoah" see Numbers 15:7, 10, 14, and Leviticus 2.

29. Exodus 30:34; Song of Solomon 3:6.

30. Mark 15:23

31. John 11:39 NLT

32. "Seventy-five percent of the emotions we generate on a daily basis are affected by smell," says Martin Lindstrom in *Brand Sense: Build Powerful Brands through Touch, Taste, Smell, Sight and Sound* (2005), 23. Lindstrom does not provide a source for his statistic.

33. Christopher Bamford, "Smell," *Parabola*, 31 (Spring 2006), 59, 59–65.

34. John 18:18 ESV

35. John 21:7–14. John 18 and 21 are the only two references to a charcoal "*anthrakian*" fire in the New Testament.

36. Robert A. Heinlein's novel *Job: A Comedy of Justice* (1984). In the multi-volume *A Cultural History of the Senses* (2014), Jerry P. Toner, Constance Classen et al., eds., there is an article on religious sensibilities in each of the six volumes.

37. Susan Ashbrook Harvey, *Scenting Salvation: Ancient Christianity and the Olfactory Imagination* (2006).

38. Susan Ashbrook Harvey, *Scenting Salvation*, 30.
39. Susan Ashbrook Harvey, *Song and Memory: Biblical Women in Syriac Tradition* (2010), 24, 22–23.
40. As quoted by Donald Nicholl, *Triumphs of the Spirit in Russia* (1997), 211.
41. There is a rabbinical midrash of this passage that says that the Messiah will be able to sniff out both reverence and wickedness, and will judge not by outward appearances (v. 4) but by the smell.
42. Breath is more than 99% water, but roughly 3000 other compounds have been detected in human breath. An average sample contains at least 200, with bits of DNA, proteins and fats floating in the mist.
43. Karen Armstrong, in *The Great Transformation: The Beginning of Our Religious Traditions* (2007), defines "religion" as "ethical alchemy" or a mix of these same three ingredients: concern (sympathy), compassion (empathy), and justice (which must always be mixed with mercy).
44. Quoted by Toby Crockford in "The Brisbane Nun who Defied Sir John's Government to Help AIDS Sufferers," *Brisbane Times*, 02 December 2017.
45. Graham Greene, *Brighton Rock* (1938; Vintage Classics 2006 edition), 292.
46. Taste has five sensory buds. Nose has 400 sensory buds.
47. If beauty is in the eye of the beholder, odor is even more in the nose of the smeller.

    Marshall McLuhan, in conjunction with his nephew chemist Ross Hall, announced in 1971 the patent of a formula for the removal of urine odor from undergarments. Registered under the trademark Prohtex, McLuhan's compound removed the one odor without obliterating other smells—that of perspiration, for instance. In the aural and tactile environment of preliterate man, McLuhan explained, body odor (BO) had been a prime method of communication. He predicted that in the global village created by electronic technology, tribal odors would make a comeback as well. See "The Tactile and the Visual" in Marshall McLuhan's *Understanding Media: The Extensions of Man* (1964), 39–49.

48. "The odors a person emits are the product of that person's metabolism—their body chemistry. If it is possible to speculate about people's metabolism by analyzing their odors, it is also possible to make some predictions about their moods." Howard Rheingold, "The Smell of

NOTES

Things to Come," in *Excursions to the Far Side of the Mind: A Book of Memes* (1988), 57, 49–60.

49. For more on this, see my whole book called *Nudge: Awakening Each Other to the God Who's Already There* (2010).
50. Ephesians 5:2b TLB
51. John 11:39 KJV
52. Shepherds had a social standing in Jewish society just above the "unclean." They were barely clean. The Talmud ("Sanhedrin" 26b) listed shepherds, along with other less than reputable professionals, as being debarred from giving independent evidence in court, whatever their age.
53. 2 Corinthians 2:15
54. George Offor, ed., *The Works of John Bunyan: Volume 1* (1859), "Memoir of John Bunyan: Third Period," xxiv.
55. Luke 1:10
56. *The Divine Liturgy of St. Gregory the Illuminator* (1973) translated by Abp. Tiran Nersoyan. This is a bilingual edition, with the Armenian text on one side and the English translation on the other. Parts of this liturgy date from the fifth century.
57. Edward M. Bounds, *Purpose in Prayer* (1920), 77.
58. www.derbyshire-peakdistrict.co.uk. Accessed 08 January 2024. https://welldressing.com/. Accessed 08 January 2024.
59. Mark C O'Flaherty, "Heavenly Scents: The Latest Perfumes Smell Divine," *Financial Times*, 04 December 2015.
60. Augustine, *Confessions* (397–400), Book X, Chapter 6.

CHAPTER 6

1. Prayer the church's banquet, angel's age,
   God's breath in man returning to his birth,
   The soul in paraphrase, heart in pilgrimage,
   The Christian plummet sounding heav'n and earth
   Engine against th' Almighty, sinner's tow'r,
   Reversed thunder, Christ-side-piercing spear,
   The six-days world transposing in an hour,
   A kind of tune, which all things hear and fear;
   Softness, and peace, and joy, and love, and bliss,
   Exalted manna, gladness of the best,

Heaven in ordinary, man well drest,
The milky way, the bird of Paradise,
Church-bells beyond the stars heard, the soul's blood,
The land of spices; something understood.

2. Matthew 22:1–14

3. Cyril of Alexandria, *Commentary on the Gospel of Saint Luke*, Sermon 33. Translated by R. Payne Smith (1983), 159.

4. Luke 12:22, 23, 27, 28

5. See my *From Tablet to Table: Where Community is Found and Identity is Formed* (2019).

6. I thank Deron Spoo for this insight in his *The Bible in 10 Words* (2020), 16.

7. Joan Taylor makes the opposite case about Jesus' grooming. In her view, Jesus looked shamefully scruffy.

8. In this I also disagree with Joan E. Taylor, who says "I doubt his hair was particularly long as depicted in most artwork, given male norms of the time, but it was surely not well-tended." *What Did Jesus Look Like?* (2018), 140.

9. Matthew 6:17

10. Matthew 6:16–18 NIV

11. Genesis 2:25

12. Merle Johnson, comp., *More Maxims of Mark* (1927), 6.

13. 1 Corinthians 9:22 NIV

14. Chong-hun Kim, *The Significance of Clothing Imagery in the Pauline Corpus* (2004), 12–13. Some sample chapters are as follows: Part 1. Clothing imagery in its history-of-religions background; Clothing imagery in the Old Testament; Clothing imagery in other Jewish literature; Clothing imagery in Joseph and Aseneth; Clothing imagery in The Hymn of the Pearl; Clothing imagery in mystery religions. Chapter 6. Roman apparel: Toga Virilis; Baptismal practices in the Early Church. Part 2. Clothing imagery in the Pauline corpus: Clothing with a person (I): 'Christ'; Clothing with a person (II): 'The new man'; Clothing with the resurrection body."

15. Gerard Manley Hopkins, *Poems and Prose* (1953), 51.

16. Galatians 3:27 CSB

17. Galatians 3:27; Romans 13:14
18. Colossians 3:9–10; Ephesians 4:22–24
19. 1 Cor 15:49, 50–54; 2 Cor 5:1–4
20. Galatians 3:27–28. Isaiah 64:6 NLT says that "Before God our righteous actions are but rags," or in other words, we are all dressed the same and in need of new clothing, clothing that can only come from God. Or as Paul put it "We groan, longing to be clothed with our heavenly dwelling" (2 Corinthians 5:2 NRSVA).
21. Several early Christian writers mention nude baptism, including Tertullian, Hippolytus, and Cyril of Jerusalem. They indicated it was practiced in places like Syria, Jerusalem, and Greece. However, the practice was controversial even in early centuries. Many criticized it as immodest and it was condemned at the Council of Laodicea around the year 360. By the Middle Ages, nude baptism had declined significantly and became very rare, replaced by robe-wearing or pouring/sprinkling water over clothed individuals.
22. See Galatians 3:26–29; Romans 13:12; Colossians 3:9–10; Ephesians 4:22–24.
23. The evidence is overwhelming that some catechumens entered the font in a state of nakedness. See particularly St. Cyril of Jerusalem, *Mystagogical Catecheses*, ii, *ad initium*; St. Ambrose, Sermon 20 in *Opera Omnia (Complete Works)* (1642), 153; and St. Ambrose's commentary on Psalm 61, verse 32, as found in *Biblia Sacra Vulgata (The Holy Bible According to the Vulgate Version)* (1969), 966; John Chrysostom, "Catecheses ad Illuminandos 1" in *Opera omnia*, edited by Jacques-Paul Migne, Volume 49 of *Patrologia Graeca*, cols. 223–40 (1857–1866), 268. Possibly a cincture of some kind may have been worn, as indicated in some medieval works of art.

For one example, this is from fourth century St. Cyril of Jerusalem's *Catechetical Lecture* 20, "On the Mysteries. II," specifically sections 2–3:

> Therefore, I shall necessarily lay before you the sequel of yesterday's Lecture, that ye may learn of what those things, which were done by you in the inner chamber, were symbolical. 2. As soon, then, as ye entered, ye put off your tunic; and this was an image of putting off the old man with his deeds. Having stripped yourselves, ye were naked; in this also imitating Christ, who was stripped naked on the Cross, and by His nakedness put off from Himself the

principalities and powers, and openly triumphed over them on the tree. For since the adverse powers made their lair in your members, ye may no longer wear that old garment; I do not at all mean this visible one, but the old man, which waxeth corrupt in the lusts of deceit. May the soul which has once put him off, never again put him on, but say with the Spouse of Christ in the Song of Songs, I have put off my garment, how shall I put it on? O wondrous thing! ye were naked in the sight of all, and were not ashamed; for truly ye bore the likeness of the first-formed Adam, who was naked in the garden, and was not ashamed. 3. Then, when ye were stripped, ye were anointed with exorcised oil, from the very hairs of your head to your feet, and were made partakers of the good olive-tree, Jesus Christ. For ye were cut off from the wild olive-tree, and grafted into the good one, and were made to share the fatness of the true olive-tree.

For modesty, women were baptised in darkness. I don't think the practice of naked baptism lasted very long, since by the time of the Didache which is the turn of the first century it was not mentioned. Here is chapter 7 from this early Christian document:

Chapter 7. Concerning Baptism. And concerning baptism, baptize this way: Having first said all these things, baptize into the name of the Father, and of the Son, and of the Holy Spirit, in living water. But if you have no living water, baptize into other water; and if you cannot do so in cold water, do so in warm. But if you have neither, pour out water three times upon the head into the name of Father and Son and Holy Spirit. But before the baptism let the baptizer fast, and the baptized, and whoever else can; but you shall order the baptized to fast one or two days before.

The Didache details instructions regarding baptism that were common practice regarding baptism in Christian communities in the late first century. It speaks about what kind of water to use, what the priest is to say during the ceremony, the person should fast etc. But no naked baptisms were mentioned, which makes one wonder if this custom was of short duration, or so common that they were assumed by the author(s) of the Didache.

24. The concept of "Putting off the old and putting on the new man"

NOTES

(Colossians 3:9–10 and Ephesians 4:22–24; also Romans 13:14 and Galatians 3:27) is drawn from early baptismal practice of undressing and redressing, taking off and putting on new clothes.

25. Ephesians 4:23 and Colossians 3:9
26. 2 Corinthians 5:3
27. Romans 13:14 ESV
28. Isaiah 61:3 NIV
29. Isaiah 64:6 KJV
30. See Ephesians 1:18: "I pray that the eyes of your heart may be enlightened in order that you may know the hope to which he has called you, the riches of his glorious inheritance in his holy people."
31. Galatians 3:27–28 NIV
32. Genesis 9:23
33. Isaiah 58:7
34. Ezekiel 16:8
35. Isaiah 61:3–4
36. Mark 10:49–50 CEV. The naming occurs only in Mark. Another "only" is the feeding of the 5000+—the only miracle reported by all the gospels.
37. The full reading of this passage from Isaiah 61:10 is:

    For he has clothed me with garments of salvation
    and arrayed me in a robe of his righteousness,
    as a bridegroom adorns his head like a priest,
    and as a bride adorns herself with her jewels.

38. Luke 10:30
39. Luke 23:11 NIV
40. Robert L. Brawley, *Text to Text Pours Forth Speech: Voices of Scripture in Luke–Acts* (1995), 42–60.
41. Luke 9:29 ESV
42. Gildas Hamel, *Poverty and Charity in Roman Palestine, First Three Centuries* (1990), 81.
43. James L. Resseguie, *Spiritual Landscape: Images of the Spiritual Life in the Gospel of Luke* (2004), Chapter 5 "Clothing: A Map of the Spiritual Life," 89–100.

44. Matthew 28:3
45. Lauren Winner, *Wearing God*, (2015), 40.
46. Ephesians 6:12 NRSVA
47. Ephesians 4:17–21; 6:10–20 NRSVA
48. Ephesians 2:14; Hebrews 4:12
49. See Andrew Pettegree's book *The Book in the Renaissance* (2010), 291, as well as Bernal's memoir *Sage: A Life of J. D. Berna* (1982).
50. Luke 15:22 YLT
51. Joan Taylor, *What Did Jesus Look Like?* (2018), 141–42.
52. Luke 15:22, 24
53. Luke 24:49 NIV
54. Luke 9:3
55. Luke 10:4 NLT
56. Luke 22:35 NIV; Luke 10:4; Matthew 10:5–15
57. Matthew 5:39–40. See Hans Dieter Betz's *Sermon on the Mount: A Commentary on The Sermon on the Mount* (1995), 97.
58. In Jesus' parable about the wedding feast, all the guests must be appropriately attired to have access to the feast. That clothing was a passport to the feast because it showed your heart and where your loyalty lies.
59. Acts 1:8, Luke 24:49 ESV
60. With thanks to Lori Wagner for inspiring some of these ideas in this paragraph in her sermon "You Are What You Wear," https://PreachTheStory.com, 02 June 2019.
61. This story appears in Noel Jones, *Treasury of Celebration* (1995), "Of Birdsong and Beethoven," 68–69. Jones attributes the story to someone sharing memories at Hoy's memorial service.
62. Carol Zaleski and Philip Zaleski, *Prayer: A History* (2006), 246.
63. Hippolytus, "Apostolic Traditions" of Hippolytus, 21:1–11. Translated by Kevin P. Edgecomb, derived from Bernard Botte (*La Tradition Apostolique. Sources Chretiennes*, (1984) and of Gregory Dix, *The Treatise on the Apostolic Tradition of St. Hippolytus of Rome, Bishop and Martyr* (1992).
64. See Alexandra Shulman, *Clothes . . . And Other Things That Matter* (2021).

65. Like macaroni, which swells to several times its size when cooked, macaroni men were people of swollen pride. The metaphor was made immortal in the song "Yankee Doodle" (1767), a patriotic verse referring to the troops in the Seven Years War (much of it fought in North America):

    Yankee Doodle came to town
    Riding on a pony,
    Stuck a feather in his cap
    And called it Macaroni!

66. See the six-volume *The Cultural History of Hair: Volumes 1–6*, Geraldine Biddle-Perry, general editor (2019).

67. Joan E. Taylor, *What Did Jesus Look Like?* (2018), 51.

68. https://static.trinityroad.com/sites/gf/2016/08/Untitled-design-3.png. Accessed 08 January 2024.

CHAPTER 7

1. Meister Eckhardt, *Book of Secrets*, eds. Mark S. Burrows and Jon M. Sweeney (2019).

2. Doris Donnelly, "Divine Folly: Being Religious and the Exercise of Humor," *Theology Today*, XLVIII (January 1992), 388.

3. Matthew 10:5–8 : "Jesus sent his twelve harvest hands out with this charge: "Don't begin by traveling to some far-off place to convert unbelievers. And don't try to be dramatic by tackling some public enemy. Go to the lost, confused people right here in the neighborhood. Tell them that the kingdom is here. Bring health to the sick. Raise the dead. Touch the untouchables. Kick out the demons. You have been treated generously, so live generously" MSG.

4. Matthew 23:12 BSB

5. The "Sursum Corda" was first found in The Anaphora of the Apostolic Tradition, a third century document containing the earliest known ritual of ordination attributed to Hippolytus of Rome (d. 236), a second to third-century theologian and priest.

6. For more on this see Marianne Sawicki, *Seeing the Lord: Resurrection and Early Christian Practices* (1994), 239.

7. See also Ezekiel 11:19: "I will give them an undivided heart and put a new spirit in them; I will remove from them their heart of stone and give them a heart of flesh" NIV.

8. Jeremiah 31:31–33 NIV

9. For more see Leonard Sweet and Len Wilson, *Telos: The Hope of Heaven Today* (2022).

10. "Clevinger is a very bright guy, a Harvard man, who knows everything about literature except how to enjoy it" is found in Chapter 8 of Joseph Heller's *Catch-22* (1961), page 69 of the Penguin Classics edition.

11. The German version ("*Wer nicht liebt Wein, Weib und Gesang, der bleibt ein Narr sein Leben lang*") appears by the 1600s, but no one has been able to find the quote in Luther's writings.

12. See William North and Laura L. Gathagan, eds., *Haskins Society Journal. 24: Studies in Medieval History* (2014).

13. Georges A. Barrois, "Calvin and the Genevans," *Theology Today*, XXI (January 1965), 458.

14. Georges A. Barrois, 459–60.

15. John Wesley wrote to his brother Charles on 25 February 1741 expressing his concern that Whitefield's emotional style of preaching was leading people to a false sense of assurance of salvation: "I am afraid, dear brother, that some of our dear friends are carried away with the pomp and show of religion, with the amorous style of praying, and the luscious style of preaching. They are in danger of making religion a mere taste, a mere feeling, instead of a principle of the soul." The manuscript letter is held by the John Rylands Library in Manchester, England.

16. See the preface to the 1761 hymnal collection "*Select Hymns with Tunes Annext*" compiled by John Wesley, where Wesley wrote guidelines for hymn singing, including: ""Sing lustily and with good courage. Beware of singing as if you were half dead, or half asleep; but lift up your voice with strength.""

17. Jean Vanier, *Community and Growth* (1998), 16.

18. Colossians 1:19

19. Philippians 4:19

20. Romans 5:17 ESV

21. Ephesians 3:8 NIV

22. Colossians 2:3 KJV

23. From Bernard Manzo, "Our Patron Saint," *TLS: Times Literary Supplement*, 10 June 2011, 3.

NOTES

24. Heather Hood (Facebook friend).

25. From G. K. Chesterton's story "The Three Horsemen of the Apocalypse" as found in *The Paradoxes of Mr. Pond* (1937), 147.

26. "Humor and Faith," in *Discerning the Signs of the Times* (1946), 111.

27. For the problems of "good Christianity," see my *Bad Habits of Jesus: Doing Right in a World Gone Wrong* (2016).

28. John 2:1–11

29. Zephaniah 3:17–18 TJB

30. 1 Samuel 19:24

31. This is in reference to Psalm 48:13–14. Midrash Shir 7, 1.

32. For a look at what it's like to grow up as a PK (preacher's kid) when the preacher is your mother, see my *Mother Tongue: How Our Heritage Shapes Our Story* (2017).

33. Genesis 9:21 NASB

34. 1 Corinthians 11:20–21

35. Luke 22:20 NIV

36. Genesis 49:12

37. The full quatrain 51 in the *Rubaiyat of Omar Khayyam* reads: "A book of verses underneath the bough,/A jug of wine, a loaf of bread—and thou/Beside me singing in the wilderness–/Oh, wilderness were paradise enow!" Edward FitzGerald, *The Rubaiyat of Omar Khayyam*, 5th edition (1889), quatrain 51.

38. Genesis 2:16

39. Genesis 2:9 NLT

40. Psalm 104: 14–15

41. John 15:12–15

42. Romans 12:21 NIV

43. Matthew 7:7

44. "There is a river whose streams make glad the city of God, the holy habitation of the Most High" (Psalm 46:4 NRSV); "He makes springs gush forth in the valleys; they flow between the hills" (Psalm 65:9 NIV); "And the streams will flow on every high place" (Isaiah 33:21 NIV); "The streams will teem with fish, and the sea will be full of shoals; for the

mouth of the Lord has spoken" (Joel 3:18); "Let justice roll down like waters, and righteousness like an ever-flowing stream" (Amos 5:24 ESV).

45. Historically, there are three types of relics, according to Charles Freeman. Primary relics like the physical remains of saints. Secondary relics like objects that came in contact with Christ and the saints (the cloak of the Virgin Mary was very popular, as was Holy Cross). The third kind of relics were the places made holy by Christ or the presence of saints: for example, the church of the Holy Sepulchre in Jerusalem. For more see Charles Freeman, *Holy Bones, Holy Dust: How Relics Shaped the History of Medieval Europe* (2012).

46. See the church of Santa Maria del Popolo, located in Piazza del Popolo, one of the most famous squares in Rome, Italy. This Renaissance Basilica was built in the fifteenth and sixteenth and features the artwork of Raphael, Caravaggio, Gian Lorenzo Bernini, and the navel relic supposedly brought to Rome in the thirteenth by a monk named Saint Bonaventure.

47. The concept of "aura" in relation to works of art was introduced by Walter Benjamin in his influential 1936 essay "The Work of Art in the Age of Mechanical Reproduction" as found in Walter Benjamin, *Illuminations: Essays and Reflections* (1968), edited by Hannah Arendt, 217–251. Benjamin argues that mechanical reproduction like photography and film destroy the aura of an artwork by severing it from ritual tradition and its connection to a time and place.

48. Luke 6:29

49. See Walter Wink, *Engaging the Powers: Discernment and Resistance in a World of Domination* (1992), Chapter 13, "Jesus' Third Way," 175–182. See also 105–106.

50. Matthew 5:38–41

51. See Walter Wink, *Engaging the Powers: Discernment and Resistance in a World of Domination* (1992), 106–108.

52. The litany appeared first on Klein's blog, https://lauriekleinscribe.com/ (accessed 08 January 2024). Later, Klein sent a revised version to the Godspace blog.

53. Terry Eagleton, "Lunging, Flailing, Mispunching," *London Review of Books*, 19 October 2006, 33.

54. Andrew Farley *God Without Religion: Can It Really Be This Simple?* (2011), 93.

NOTES

55. Alan Kreider, *The Patient Ferment of the Early Church: The Improbable Rise of Christianity in the Roman Empire* (2016), 10.

56. John 16:21

CHAPTER 8

1. From a letter to H. G. Wells dated 10 July 1915, as found in Leon Edel, *Henry James and H. G. Wells: A Record of their Friendship, Their Criticism and their Work* (1975), 770. Also quoted in Sergio Perosa, *Art Making Life: Studies in Henry James* (2016), 103.

2. Herbert A. Simon, *The Sciences of the Artificial* (1969), xi.

3. Friedrich Nietzsche, *The Birth of Tragedy* (1872), 52.

4. The principle "form follows function" coined by architect Louis Sullivan late in the nineteenth century is widely misunderstood as a reductive maxim. Sullivan was inspired by sculptor Horatio Greenough (d. 1852) who circulated the belief that purpose predestined style as an expression of inherent content and an embodiment of aesthetic delight.

5. Virginia Postrel, *The Substance of Style: How the Rise of Aesthetic Value Is Remaking Commerce, Culture, and Consciousness* (2004).

6. 1 Corinthians 13:5 (LIS version of the KJV)

7. Matthew 15:21–28

8. Matthew 15:23 NRSV

9. Also attributed to Robert Walser (d. 1956), said to be the "missing link" between Kleist and Kafka.

10. For an extended essay on sprezzatura, see Chapter 3 of my book *The Three Hardest Words in the World to Get Right* (2006), where grace and artistry in ministry and preaching are celebrated.

11. See Baldassare Castiglione's influential *The Book of the Courtier* (1528), Part I, Section 26, where sprezzatura is portrayed as the ideal quality and conduct of a Renaissance person: "A certain nonchalance, so as to conceal all art and make whatever one does or says appear to be without effort and almost without any thought about it."

12. Matthew 15:28 NRSVA

13. Genesis 3:8 KJV

14. Shakespeare, *Hamlet* (1603), Act 1, Scene 3.

15. See my book *Carpe Mañana* (2001).

16. For more on this see the "Zeitgeist" section of my *Jesus Human: Primer for a Common Humanity* (2023).
17. *Confessions*, Book X, Chapter 36 (section 59)
18. John 4:23 (LIS Translation of NIV)
19. One of my favorite stores in North America is "Tender Buttons" in New York City. http://tenderbuttons-nyc.com/. Accessed 08 January 2024.
20. Revelation 3:16 NIV
21. Zillow reported that painting the walls of your house gray added an immediate $2512 to the value of your house in their 2023 Paint Color Trends: https://www.bhg.com/top-paint-colors-to-sell-house-zillow-2023-7547007 (Accessed 08 January 2024). The report is based on a survey of 4,700 recent and prospective home buyers across the country.
22. Paul Valery, "Odds and Ends," in his *Analects*, trans. Stuart Gilbert (1970), 8.
23. Ezekiel 18:23

CHAPTER 9

1. 1 Corinthians 6:19 NIV
2. Galatians 5:13–18
3. Jeremy Dauber, *Jewish Comedy: A Serious History* (2018), 172.
4. According to a 2019 NUS (National Union of Students) survey of 2500 respondents, as reported by Alice Wadsworth, "Sex and Sensibility," *Times Literary Supplement*, 23 & 30 August 2019, 27.
5. Alan Watts apparently once asked Joseph Campbell what his favored spiritual practice was. To which Campbell replied: 'I underline books.'" As told by Leigh Eric Schmidt, "The Aspiring Side of Religion: Nineteenth Century Religious Liberalism and the Birth of Contemporary American Spirituality," *Spiritus*, 7 (Spring 2007), 89.
6. Ephesians 1:22, 5:23; Colossians 1:18.
7. See David Halberstam's story of how we got into the Vietnam War in *The Best and the Brightest* (1972).
8. Mark Lilla in his study of *The Reckless Mind: Intellectuals in Politics* (2017) coins the term "philotyranny" for the philosophical support of tyrants by some of our greatest intellectuals.
9. Martin Luther, "On the Jews and Their Lies" in *Luther's Works*, ed.

Franklin Sherman (1971), 47:257, 265. Nazis were fond of quoting Luther's words: "We are even at fault in not avenging all this innocent blood of our Lord. . . . We are at fault in not slaying them. Rather we allow them to live freely in our midst despite all their murdering, cursing, blaspheming, lying, defaming" (267).

10. Pierre Teilhard de Chardin, *Letters to Two Friends, 1926–1952* (1968), 146.

11. Philippians 2:5–8; Romans 8:5–8

12. John 8:31–32 reads "If you abide in my word, you are truly my disciples, and you will know the truth, and the truth will set you free" ESV.

13. Here is the full journal entry from which the paraphrase is gleaned. It is from Kierkegaard's journal entry on May 16, 1839:

> What I really lack is to be clear in my mind what I am to do, not what I am to know, except in so far as a certain understanding must precede every action. The thing is to understand myself, to see what God really wishes me to do; the thing is to find a truth which is true for me, to find the idea for which I can live and die. And the reason why I cannot discover it by myself is that I need a revelation, and hence the prayer; Lord Jesus Christ, have mercy upon me. If I were to describe him I would be lying, because if I understood him I would be God; but the truth is that he is the only one who can keep up the dialectical tension in me, holding my heart so that it does not run away from him.
>
> Søren Kierkegaard, *Kierkegaard's Journals and Notebooks, Volume 1: Journals AA–DD*. Edited by Niels Jørgen Cappelørn, et al., (2007), 346.

14. John 21:25

15. Matthew 19:11

16. John 21:25

17. W. H. Vanstone, *The Stature of Waiting* (1982).

18. S. N. Behrman, *Duveen: The Story of the Most Spectacular Art Dealer of All Time* (2014).

19. Only Henry Ford resisted Duveen's charms.

20. 1 Corinthians 14:40

21. As found in the 1793 essay "Grace and Dignity" (original German title "*Anmut und Würde*") by Friedrich Schiller was first published in the

journal *Neue Thalia*. For the English translated version, see Schiller, Friedrich. "Grace and Dignity." Translated by Jane V. Curran, The Schiller Institute, 1991.

22. Brian Doyle, "Grace Notes" in *Leaping: Revelations and Epiphanies* (2003), 132. The full quote is too beautiful not to share: "Maybe we're stuffed with the stuff that makes stars and galaxies and God, so that it has to ooze out somehow. Maybe we're full of patience and kindness the way some people are full of anxiety or bitterness. Maybe there's no limit to the amount of gentleness a person can absorb. Maybe this is the secret to existence—just keep taking it all in, being replenished every day by the sheer force of grace."

23. Martin Luther, "Table Talk," *Works*, 54, No. 461, 76.

24. Martin Luther, "Precationes pro morte ferenda", Prayers for facing death, 1532. Published in *Sammtliche Schriften*, edited by Johann Georg Walch, vol. 10, (1910), 1937.

25. The letter may be lost, but this quotation is preserved in Emser's Auff des Stieres su Wittenberg wiettende replica (LUTHER TO JOHN TETZEL AT LEIPSIC. De Wette-Seidemann, vi. 18 (shortly before 02 August 1519).

26. G. K. Chesterton, *Irish Impressions* (1919), 108.

27. Philippians 1:27 NIV

28. Geoffrey Miller, *Spent: Sex, Evolution and the Secrets of Consumerism* (2009), 123–125, 130–132, 140–142, 150–152, 160–162, 170–172.

29. Philippians 4:13

30. G. K. Chesterton, *Orthodoxy* (1908), chapter 3 ("The Paradoxes of Christianity"), 85.

31. Philippians 4:13

32. Acts 4:13 NIV

33. Colossians 2:9

34. While not verbatim, this Letter #45 contains the same ideas as the quote about heaven being where "the good here unfinished is completed" and "the stories unwritten" are continued: "We have come from God, and inevitably the myths woven by us, though they contain error, will also reflect a splintered fragment of the true light, the eternal truth that is with God. Indeed only by myth-making, only by becoming 'sub-creator' and inventing stories, can Man aspire to the state of perfection that he knew

NOTES

before the Fall. Our myths may be misguided, but they steer however shakily towards the true harbour, while materialistic 'progress' leads only to a yawning abyss and the Iron Crown of the power of evil." *The Letters of J. R. R. Tolkien: Letter #45 to Michael Tolkien.* Edited by Humphrey Carpenter and Christopher Tolkien (2000), 53. Thanks to Teri Hyrkas for the paraphrased quote.

35. Ecclesiastes 4:9 KJV

36. 2 Kings 6:16 ESV

37. 1 John 4:4 NRSVA

38. Conferences on the Apostle's Creed, in *A Year with the Saints*, ed. Paul Thigpen (2013). For a theology of left-overs, see my *Bad Habits of Jesus* (2017).

39. For more on Mabel Boggs Sweet, who died on 26 July 1993, see my book *Mother Tongue: How Our Heritage Shapes Our Story* (2017).

40. Numbers 12:6–8; Exodus 33:11

41. Numbers 12:3

42. See *Times Literary Supplement*, 26 April 1985, 469.

43. The exact Augustine quote is "It was pride that changed angels into devils; humility that makes men as angels. Therefore, let us hold fast to humility, so that we may be lifted up by Him who lifts up the lowly." Augustine of Hippo. Sermon 198, in *The Works of Saint Augustine: A Translation for the 21st Century, Volume III/5, Sermons 151–183*, edited by John E. Rotelle, transl. by Edmund Hill (1992), 300.

44. Philippians 2:7–8

45. As quoted in Frederic Raphael, *Against the Stream: Personal Terms 7* (2018), 174.

46. Georges Bernanos, "*Lettre aux Anglais*" (1936), *The Diary of a Country Priest.* Translated by Pamela Morris (2002), 182. The full quote from chapter 8 is "God does not choose the same people to keep his word as to fulfil it. He entrusts his word to people whose part is simply to transmit it, once they have understood it. No more than that. But those who are to fulfil it must first take it to heart, plunge into it with all their being, becoming incarnate: they must become the word."

47. Joel 2:12–13

48. Saint Bonaventure, Sermo VI in Festo S. Francisci. In *Opera Omnia S. Bonaventurae*, vol. 9, Collegii S. Bonaventurae, 1882, 629.

49. "Five Facts About Saint David," as found in https://www.visitwales.com/info/history-heritage-and-traditions/st-david-five-facts. Accessed 08 January 2024.

50. 1 John 4:19

51. From the speech Mother Teresa gave at the United Nations in 1979, as found on the Nobel Peace Center website: https://www.nobelprize.org/prizes/peace/1979/teresa/lecture/. Accessed 08 January 2024.

52. Jim Giles, "Internet Encyclopedias Go Head to Head," *Nature*, 438 (15 December 2005), 900–901.

53. See James 3:13ff.

54. James 3:13ff

55. For more on this see Stanley Grenz, *The Social God and the Relational Self: A Trinitarian Theology of the Imago Dei* (2007), 135.

56. This famous quote is a paraphrase of a statement he made in 1957 in response to a question from an Algerian nationalist at a press conference. It was reported in the press as "Je crois à la Justice, mais je défendrai ma mère avant la Justice" ("I believe in justice, but I will defend my mother before justice"). Jeffrey C. Isaac, "Camus On Trial," *Dissent Magazine*, 63 (Winter 2016), 81–86.

57. Jeremiah 33:3 NIV

58. 1 Corinthians 2:9 KJV

59. The lyrics of the song mention various rides and attractions at the Palisades Amusement Park in New Jersey, including the Ferris wheel.

60. Hugo of St. Victor, "De tribus diebus," 4. *Patrologia Latina* 176:184.

61. Juli Berwald, Spineless: The Science of Jellyfish and the Art of Growing a Backbone (2018).

62. John 11:44

63. See Matthew 18:18 NIV: "Truly I tell you, whatever you bind on earth will be bound in heaven, and whatever you loose on earth will be loosed in heaven."

64. Deuteronomy 31:6–8; John 16:16–33.

65. Wallace Stevens, *The Necessary Angel* (1942), 81.

66. Matthew 16:18

67. Matthew 16:18

NOTES

68. The prayer first appeared in print in a 1944 book called *Prayers and Meditations of the Saints*, edited by John Henry Newman. The book attributed the prayer to Sir Thomas More.

69. John Chrysostom, "Homily XV on the Epistle to the Hebrews," in *The Nicene and Post-Nicene Fathers of the Christian Church, First Series, Vol. 14*, ed. Philip Schaff (1956), 434.

70. "But laughter also fell and can be demonic. In dealing with 'idols,' however, laughter is salutary, since it allows us to see them in perspective." See Russian Orthodox theologian Alexander Schmemann (d. 1983), *The Journals of Father Alexander Schmemann 1973–1983* (2000), Friday, 14 December 1973.

71. Reinhold Niebuhr, *The Irony of American History* (1952), Chapter One, 6.

72. Umberto Eco, *The Name of the Rose*, translated by William Weaver (1983), 486.

73. Umberto Eco, *The Name of the Rose*, 492.

74. Steve Case, *Great Moments in Biblical Flatulence* (2019), riffing off the passage from Isaiah 16:11 KJV: "Wherefore my bowels shall sound like an harp for Moab, and mine inward parts for Kirharesh."

75. As referenced by Timothy Radcliffe, *Why Go to Church: The Drama of the Eucharist* (2009), 1. Lennon's comment came out of an interview given in 1969, broadcast on BBC's Sunday, 13 July 2008.

76. William Blake, Letter to Thomas Butts, 23 September 1800. In *Letters from William Blake to Thomas Butts, 1800–1803*, edited by Geoffrey Keynes (1926), 36.

77. See Genesis 1:1.

78. See her Chapter 30 in Timothy Larsen, ed., *The Oxford Handbook of Christmas* (2020), 389.

79. This is the theme of the companion volume to this one, *Jesus Human: Primer for a Common Humanity* (2023).

80. For the "overlap," see J. R. Briggs, *The Sacred Overlap: Learning to Live Faithfully in the Space Between* (2020), and my section on the Mandorla in *Jesus Human: Primer for a Common Humanity* (2023).

81. Ian McEwan, "Dear Bookseller." *Times Literary Supplement*, 22 October 2010, 3.

82. With thanks to Facebook friend John Haberlin for helping me formulate this.

83. Henri de Lubac, *Paradoxes of Faith* (originally published in French in 1945). Translated by Ernest Bevilacqua (1987), 236.
84. 2 Corinthians 4:18 NIV
85. R. S. Thomas, "Pilgrimages," *Counterpoint* (1968), 44.
86. 2 Samuel 6:14–16
87. See Erik Varden's 2018 lecture at the Notre Dame Center for Ethics and Culture titled "Tradition in the Public Square", as published in the journal *VoegelinView* (04 March 2019), 11: "We think of tradition as that which has been handed down to us, not that which is handing things down. But the Latin word traditio means handing down, not that which has been handed down. And the word praesul, which is most often translated as protector, literally means someone who leaps or dances in front, like David did before the Ark."
88. See Francis Bacon's essay "Of Building" in his collection *Essayes or Counsels, Civill and Morall* (1625).
89. Frederic Raphael, *Antiquity Matters* (2017), 303.
90. See Jeff Bezos' 11 April 2018 letter titled "2018 Letter to Shareholders", which was published on the Amazon investor relations website. See Jeff Bezos, "2018 Letter to Shareholders." *Amazon*, 11 Apr. 2018, https://www.aboutamazon.com/news/company-news/2018-letter-to-shareholders. Accessed 18 November 2023.

CHAPTER 10

1. Philippians 2:5 ESV
2. Matthew 27:37–40, Mark 12:28–34, Luke 10:25–37. Jesus was not the first to do this, however, as the Septuagint included the word δι νοια (mind) in its rehash of the Shema in Joshua 22:5.
3. Romans 1:16
4. For the phrase "the mind of Christ," see Philippians 2:5 and 1 Corinthians 2:16: "For who has understood the mind of the Lord so as to instruct him? But we have the mind of Christ" ESV.
5. Michael Stillman, "A Collector Left a 70,000 Book Collection with No Instructions on How to Proceed," *Rare Book Monthly* (March 2023).

   See the story of Bruno Schroder, a mining engineer in the small German town of Mettingen. He spent most of his life underground, but when he was above ground, he spent it surrounded by books in a small

NOTES

inconspicuous house where he stuffed books in the attic, the ceiling, in every room of the house, and even built bookshelves into the ceilings of the attic. Here is his story:

It is not the largest book collection ever amassed by a private owner. It does not equal the 100,000 book and manuscript collection of nineteenth century obsessive Thomas Phillipps. Nor, obviously, does it match the 300,000 books amassed by the late fashion designer Karl Lagerfeld. There is no need to compare it with those of the two individuals who have claimed the largest collections, John Q. Benham of Avoca, Indiana, and Anke Gowda of India. They both estimate (at this level you can only estimate) collections of 1.5 million books. Bruno Schroder's collection of 70,000 books may not be the largest, but there haven't been too many larger private ones either.

Bruno Schroder was a mining engineer in the small German town of Mettingen. He spent much of his working life underground. Above ground, it was spent with books. His wife's legally appointed caretaker described him as a very reserved man. Few people in his hometown knew anything about his book collection. Schroder's home is an inconspicuous one, perhaps even somewhat worn-looking from outside. Inside, it is a wonderland of books, amassed over his long lifetime, Schroder died last year at the age of 88.

One notable feature about Schroder is that he was no Phillipps, with books strewn in piles all over the house. Nor did he have the money of a Lagerfeld to have storage professionally built. Schroder was a handy man and built the bookshelves with his own hands. Virtually every room was filled with books. Add the cellar and the attic to that . . . he even built shelves into the attic's sloped ceiling to house his books. His home was neat, despite all the books. You could describe it as a library, except no one but the librarian ever went there and he could not possibly have read more than a small fraction of the books.

Schroder bought most of his books from the local bookstore. The proprietor described him as his best customer. No surprise there. He might buy 10–20 books a week. The subjects were varied and they might be hard or soft cover. The only place he drew a line was with romance novels. He didn't like them. What motivated his collecting interests is unknown. He did not explain himself, not even to his bookseller. Whatever it was, it enabled him to build a very attractive library but not a valuable one. That clearly did not matter to him. He must have simply loved the look of his books.

When the time came for his wife to move to a retirement home, her doctor and caregiver tried to convince Schroder to join her. He declined. He wanted to stay with his books. That was where they found him one morning. A care team checking up on him found Schroder on the floor in the hallway of his house, his books watching over him.

6. Umberto Eco, "De Bibliotheca," speech given at the twenty-fifth anniversary of the Sormani Library in Milan. Essay first published in Italian in 1981. See *The Complete Works of Umberto Eco* (2018), Volume 9, 245–262.

7. See his book *The Philosophy of Physics* (1936), Lecture VI, "Causality and Free Will," page 113 of 1949 Frank Gaynor translation. Here is the full quote: "The first act, whereby the mind seizes hold of itself and makes itself its own object, remains even then a mystery. But of one thing I am convinced: just as the material world around us is immediately and indubitably given to our consciousness, and just in the fact that it is given, so too is the higher spiritual world given by the intuitive power of mind. We accept mind as the matrix of all matter in the world."

8. Luke 24:19 NIV

9. This is the title of Madeline L'Engle's defense of children's literature, delivered at Wheaton College as part of the Chancellor's Lecture Series in 1983. The lecture's title "Do I Dare Disturb the Universe?'" was inspired by a line from the T. S. Eliot poem "The Love Song of J. Alfred Prufrock." The full text of L'Engle's lecture was later published as a book titled *Do I Dare Disturb the Universe?* (1989).

10. Judith Shklar, Ordinary Vices (1984), ix. The full quote is: "This is a book meant to raise questions and promote disagreement, a ton of perplexities, not a guide for the perplexed. It is an essay in intellectual history, an attempt to trace the careers and changes in moral concepts for the sake of political theory."

11. Pseudo-Dionysius the Areopagite's theological treatise "On the Celestial Hierarchy," written around the late fifth to early sixth century, states in Chapter VII: "The mode of praising Him is not adequate which merely employs speech or silence, but that which reaches the above the heavens and brings down the sweetness of melody." In other words, music is the best means to offer praises and thanks to God, more so than spoken or silent prayer alone.

12. Technically, "mindfulness" is a psychological technique derived from Buddhism that puts you in a state of present awareness without

any judgment or oughtiness. In fact, in "mindfulness" oughtiness is naughtiness.

13. See Leonard Sweet, *From Tablet to Table: Where Community is Formed and Identity is Found* (2019).

14. Madeleine L'Engle, *The Rock That Is Higher: Story as Truth* (2018), 38.

15. Robert Nozick's concept of the "narrative self" can be found in *The Examined Life: Philosophical Meditations* (1990).

16. Erich Auerbach, *Mimesis: The Representation of Reality in Western Literature*, translated by Willard R. Trask (1946), chapter 2, "Odysseus' Scar," 29.

17. Clyde S. Kilby, *The Arts and the Christian Imagination: Essays on Art, Literature and Aesthetics* (2017), 15.

18. John Updike's memorable phrase "the mundane its beautiful due" is found in the last line of his poem "Olympic" as found in *Endpoint and Other Poems* (2009), 39–40.

19. "Reflections: Madeleine L'Engle on Family, Friendship, Aging, and the Hereafter," *Kenyon Review*, 20 (Fall 1998), 237. See the section titled "Keep the Mundanes in Mind."

20. Paul Ricoeur, "The Parables," *Criterion* (Spring 1974), 19.

21. Romans 8:6 ESV

22. Elena Ferrante uses this word to describe her life as a writer in *Frantumaglia: A Writer's Journey* (2016).

23. Seamus Sweeney, "No Off-Switch," *Times Literary Supplement*, 18 July 2014, 13.

24. James 1:8 NIV

25. Romans 8:6

26. Matthew 10:39 ESV. See also Matthew 16:25 where Jesus states: "For whoever wants to save their life will lose it, but whoever loses their life for me will find it" NIV

27. See Howard Pollack, *Arthur Rubinstein: A Life* (1998), 528.

28. Colossians 3:1–3

29. Matthew 13:51–52 NSRVA

30. Matthew 6:28 KJV

31. 1 Corinthians 1:30

32. Colossians 3:10

33. Colossians 3:11 NRSVA

34. For a whole new way of thinking about trust, see Joseph R. Myers, *Trust Me: Discovering Trust in a Culture of Distrust* (2023).

35. For the role of digital culture in building this culture of distrust, see Shoshana Zuboff's *The Age of Surveillance Capitalism: The Fight to Be Human in the Algorithmic Age* (2019).

36. Matthew 27:43 NIV

37. Matthew 1:1–17

38. George Orwell, "Why I Write," *Gangrel*, Summer 1946, 14–18.

39. Tertullian, "On the Flesh of Christ" (*De Carne Christi*) (203–206). He believed that the idea of God becoming human and dying on the cross was so absurd that it could only be true. He wrote: "The Son of God died . . . it is credible because it is absurd. And He was buried and rose again . . . it is certain because it is impossible."

40. A. N. Wilson, *Jesus: A Life* (1992), 127–28.

41. John 16:12–13 ESV

42. 1 Corinthians 13:7

43. This is the first Hippocratic aphorism in his collection of medical writings known as the *Aphorisms* (450–350 BC). Paul Potter, ed., *Hippocrates, Volume VI* (1988), 91.

44. John 14:12

45. Italo Calvino first defined a classic as "a book that has never finished saying what it has to say" in his seminal literary essay "Why Read the Classics?" as found in his collection of essays *Why Read the Classics* (1981). There are now three definitions of a "classic" if one has a sense of humor. First, it is "a book that has never finished saying what it has to say" (Calvino). Second, it is "something that everybody wants to have read and nobody wants to read" (Mark Twain) and often thinks they have read themselves. Third, "a book that is given to a child as a present by a well-meaning parent or grandparent" (Jonathan Gibbs in his blog Tiny Camels entitled "Penguin mini-books: pocketing the canon," 22 February 2018.

46. 2 Corinthians 12:2–4

47. Paul Bloom, Yale psychologist, argues in *Against Empathy: A Case for Rational Compassion* (2018) that empathy is a sentiment that is making the world worse. Empathy is "a sugary soda," tempting and delicious

NOTES

and bad for us. Instead we need diet of reason, compassion and self-control or what Bloom calls cognitive empathy, not emotional empathy. The full quote is "Empathy is like a sugary soda. It tastes great going down, but it's not ultimately healthy or nourishing. Indeed, the sugary rush of sympathetic compassion makes it harder to engage in more morally respectable, emotionally difficult responses like restraint or moral criticism. Empathy is a way to enjoy the sugar high of moral righteousness" (19).

48. Intellectual victory over a political opponent or rival group may matter more to us than the truth, and so "we are motivated to regulate our information diet." Canadian-American cognitive psychologist, psycholinguist Steven Pinker calls this "the myside bias" in chapter 15 of his book *Enlightenment Now: The Case for Reason, Science, Humanism, and Progress* (2018), 358–59. He titles the section "Reason as an Antidote to Rationalization."

49. The ancient Hebrews had a more holistic perspective on the seat of emotions compared to the ancient Greeks. They located the source of feelings not just in the intestines but in all the body's internal organs. In the Hebrew Bible, the term "*me'eh*" refers to the internal organs, viscera or bowels in general, and was described metaphorically as the seat of deep emotions like grief, anguish, joy and affection. For example, the Hebrews described feeling compassion as the "*rachamim*"—literally meaning the "womb," representing mercy. The Song of Songs metaphorically describes love and desire arising from the *me'eh*. However, the Hebrews did not completely separate emotion from the heart. The term "*leb*" for heart could also represent the inner self, mind, will and feelings. But the *me'eh* suggests Hebrews saw emotions as originating from the inner vital organs overall—including the heart.

50. Francis Schaeffer, *Art and the Bible* (1970), 33. As quoted in Cindy West, *Saying Yes: Accepting God's Amazing Invitation to Artists and The Church* (2018), 114.

51. Luke 2:52 KJV

52. See James Baldwin's two-page essay "White Man's Guilt," *Ebony* magazine, 20 (August 1965), 47–48 of this issue, 722–724 of entire magazine pagination. This issue featured Muhammad Ali on the cover.

53. The story is told in the *Autobiography of Alice B. Toklas* (1933), which was written by Gertrude Stein in the form of an autobiography by Toklas, but it is actually a fictionalized account of Stein's life. So whether this story if fact of fiction is widely contested.

54. In his commentaries Sir John Harington attached to his translation of Aeneid VI, he professes to follow "no authority but" Scripture and St. Augustine, who "is preferred before all the other fathers in all Disputes and questions." See Gerard Kilroy's review of Brian Cummings, *Mortal Thoughts: Religion, Secularity and Identity in Shakespeare and Early Modern Culture* [2015]), in *Times Literary Supplement*, 24 July 2015, 10.

55. See paragraph 621 of Part I of Ludwig Wittgenstein's seminal *Philosophical Investigations* (1953), 150.

56. Leonard Sweet and Mark Chironna, *Rings of Fire: Walking in Faith Through a Volcanic Future*, (2019), 75–76, Kindle.

57. Samuel Taylor Coleridge, *Aids to Reflection* (1825), 148, fn.1.

58. Hannah Arendt, *The Life of the Mind (1978)*, from the chapter "Thinking Without a Banister."

59. K. M. Cherwien, "Pneumaplasticity: Rewiring the Human Soul," *Journal of Pastoral Care Counseling, 70* (June 2016), 143–7.

60. See Acts 10:9–33

61. Acts 10:44–49

62. Matthew 3:15

CHAPTER 11

1. Taken from Peter Seewald's biography *Benedict XVI: A Life. Volume One: Youth in Nazi Germany to the Second Vatican Council (1927–1965)*. Translated by Damian Costello and Rupert Shortt (2020), 32.

2. The ancient Egyptians also taught that the heart was "the seat of the soul," and associated it with love. See Marilyn Yalom, *The Amorous Heart: An Unconventional History of Love* (2018). Thomas Hobbes, who didn't like metaphors and embraced a materialistic, mechanistic view of human beings, argued that the heart was nothing "but a spring" in his *De Corpore* (On the Body), Part IV, chapter 25. The full quote is: "The heart, it is well known, is but a spring; and the nerves, strings; and the joints, but wheels, giving motion to the whole body, such as was intended by the Artificer." The view of humans as nothing but machines has a long history.

3. You go to a therapist to understand your emotions, your feelings. Once you get the idea of what is going and can name it you can now move on, lay it to the side, find healing.

NOTES

4. Mark 7:21 NRSV
5. See the companion volume to this one, *Jesus Human: Primer for a Common Humanity* (2023).
6. Matthew 15:17–20
7. Augustine and classical scholars like James J. O'Donnell view the quote as unverified at best, apocryphal most likely. See his *Augustine: Christianity and Roman Society* (2004), 125. Besides not being able to find the quotation in Augustine's writing, O'Donnell notes that it does not match Augustine's typical writing style or manner of speaking.
8. John 2:24–25 NRSV
9. John 4:29 ESV
10. John 1:48 NRSVCE
11. Augustine, *Confessions* (397–400), Book IV, Chapter 1.
12. Romans 2:15 ESV
13. Ruth E. Rosenberg, "Perfect Pitch: 432 Hz Music and the Promise of Frequency," *Journal of Popular Music Studies* (2021) 33 (1): 137–54. https://doi.org/10.1525/jpms.2021.33.1.137. Accessed 09 January 2024.
14. 1 Samuel 13:14
15. Acts 13:22
16. Romans 5:18 NIV
17. Mark 12:28–31 KJV
18. See the final line of the play in Act II, Scene 32.
19. *The Wall Street Journal*, 14 September 2010, A19.
20. He goes on to say: "But let's be honest. Islam has a problem today. The places that have trouble accommodating themselves to the modern world are disproportionately Muslim. . . . There is a cancer of extremism within Islam today. A small minority of Muslims celebrates violence and intolerance and harbors deeply reactionary attitudes toward women and minorities. While some confront these extremists, not enough do so, and the protests are not loud enough."
21. 21 November 2015, *The Tablet*, 2.
22. 1 Corinthians 16:15 KJV. The Greek verb "*tasso*" which the KJV translates as "addicted" is most often translated "devoted" or "appointed," but is best translated as the KJV does: "addicted."

23. Martin Luther King, Jr., "Letter from a Birmingham Jail." 16 April 1963. African Studies Center—University of Pennsylvania, https://www.africa.upenn.edu/Articles_Gen/Letter_Birmingham.html. Accessed 24 October 2023.

24. Quoted by Frances Wilson in *TLS: Times Literary Supplement*, 06 December 2013, 20.

25. Thanks to Derek White for teaching his teacher this.

26. Matthew 6:21 NIV

27. Luke 2:19 NIV

28. Luke 2:51 BLB

29. With thanks to Jean Fleming for this entry into the text.

30. Colossians 2:3

31. Proverbs 14:10 NIV

32. Quoted in Godfrey Lienhardt, "The Observers Observed," *TLS: Times Literary Supplement*, 26 August–1 September, 1988, 925.

33. From the beginning of Canto III of Dante Alighieri's epic poem *Inferno* (1308–14).

34. Psalm 51:17

35. Ephesians 4:1–2. See also Romans 16:4, where Paul pays tribute to those "who for my life their own neck laid down".

36. Mark 4:38 RSV

37. 1 Peter 5:7. With thanks to Dr. Tim Valentino for first connecting these dots for me.

38. This is a quote from the main protagonist Julian Messia in Gore Vidal's novel *Messiah* (1954), 149. Whether they reflect Vidal's actual sentiments is a matter of dispute. Here is the quote in full: "I have no friends to succeed! Each time a friend succeeds a part of me dies. I am not sure why. Perhaps it is because I am afraid of being compared to them. Perhaps it is because I am afraid of being forgotten. Or perhaps it is simply because I am envious of their success. Whatever the reason, I know that I am not alone in feeling this way. Many people have the same fear. We are all afraid of being left behind."

39. Rabbi Arthur Green, *The Art of Heartfulness: The Timeless Wisdom of the Hasidic Masters* (2020), chapter 7, "The Hidden Heart," 149.

40. Matthew 14:27

NOTES

41. Andy Johnson, "Gospel Themes as 'Glue' for Pauline Ecclesiological Images," in *Listening Again to the Text: New Testament Studies in Honor of George Lyons*, ed., Richard P. Thompson, ed. (Claremont Press, 2020), 93.

ANTIPHON

1. Frederick Buechner, *Whistling in the Dark: A Doubter's Dictionary* (1993), 104.
2. Quoted in Lauren Winner's essay "The Art Patron" in *For the Beauty of the Church*, ed. W. David O. Taylor (2010), 75.
3. Lauren Winner, "The Art Patron," in *For the Beauty of the Church*, ed. W. David O. Taylor (2010), 69–82.
4. Deuteronomy 21:23; Galatians 3:13
5. Gerard Manley Hopkins, *Poems and Prose* (1953), 51.
6. As quoted in Louis Nohl, *Life of Beethoven* (1910), 139.
7. Quoted in Jon M. Sweeney, *The Lure of Saints: A Protestant Experience of Catholic Tradition* (2004), 130.
8. 1 John 4:17 NKJV

PERSONAL NOTES

www.ingramcontent.com/pod-product-compliance
Lightning Source LLC
Chambersburg PA
CBHW072141070526
44585CB00015B/981